久保帯人

I judge any new anime by its opening sequence. The one for *Bleach* was better than I expected. I was so happy, I'burned a DVD of it so I can watch it over and over. Actually, I watch it every night before I go to bed. For those of you out there who love *Bleach* and think you're its biggest fan—sorry, but that's probably me!!!
–Tite Kubo

BLEACH is author Tite Kubo's second title. Kubo made his debut with *ZOMBIE POWDER*, a four-volume series for *WEEKLY SHONEN JUMP*. To date, *BLEACH* has been translated into numerous languages and has also inspired an animated TV series that began airing in Japan in 2004. Beginning its serialization in 2001, *BLEACH* is still a mainstay in the pages of *WEEKLY SHONEN JUMP*. In 2005, *BLEACH* was awarded the prestigious Shogakukan Manga Award in the *shonen* (boys) category.

BLEACH
Vol. 15: BEGINNING OF THE DEATH OF TOMORROW
SHONEN JUMP Manga Edition

STORY AND ART BY
TITE KUBO

English Adaptation/Lance Caselman
Translation/Joe Yamazaki
Touch-Up Art & Lettering/Andy Ristaino
Design/Sean Lee
Editor/Yuki Takagaki

Printed in the U.S.A.

Published by VIZ Media, LLC
P.O. Box 77010
San Francisco, CA 94107

10 9 8
First printing, October 2006
Eighth printing, September 2014

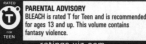

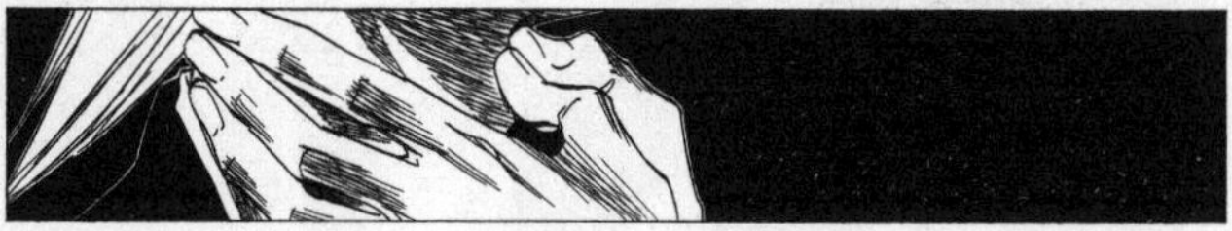

I just keep practicing
Saying goodbye to you

BLEACH15 BEGINING OF THE DEATH OF TOMORROW

Shonen Jump Manga

STARS AND

Zangetsu

Uryû Ishida

Ichigo Kurosaki

plot

Ichigo infiltrates the stronghold of the Soul Reapers and fights his way to the Senzaikyû, where Rukia is being held prisoner. Lying in wait for him is the merciless Byakuya Kuchiki! But Yoruichi pulls Ichigo out of the battle to give him three days of special training to make him stronger. Meanwhile, Uryû faces the Soul Reaper who killed his grandfather. Will Uryû have his long-awaited revenge or be added to the body count himself?

BLEACH ALL

涅ネム
Nemu Kurotsuchi

夜一
Yoruichi

Mayuri
Kurotsuchi
涅マユリ

STORIES

BLEACH15

BEGINNING OF THE DEATH OF TOMORROW

Contents

124. Crying Little People

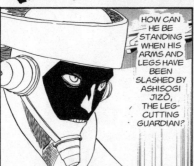

HOW CAN HE BE STANDING WHEN HIS ARMS AND LEGS HAVE BEEN SLASHED BY ASHISOGI JIZÔ, THE LEG-CUTTING GUARDIAN?

I KNOW...

SKRUSH

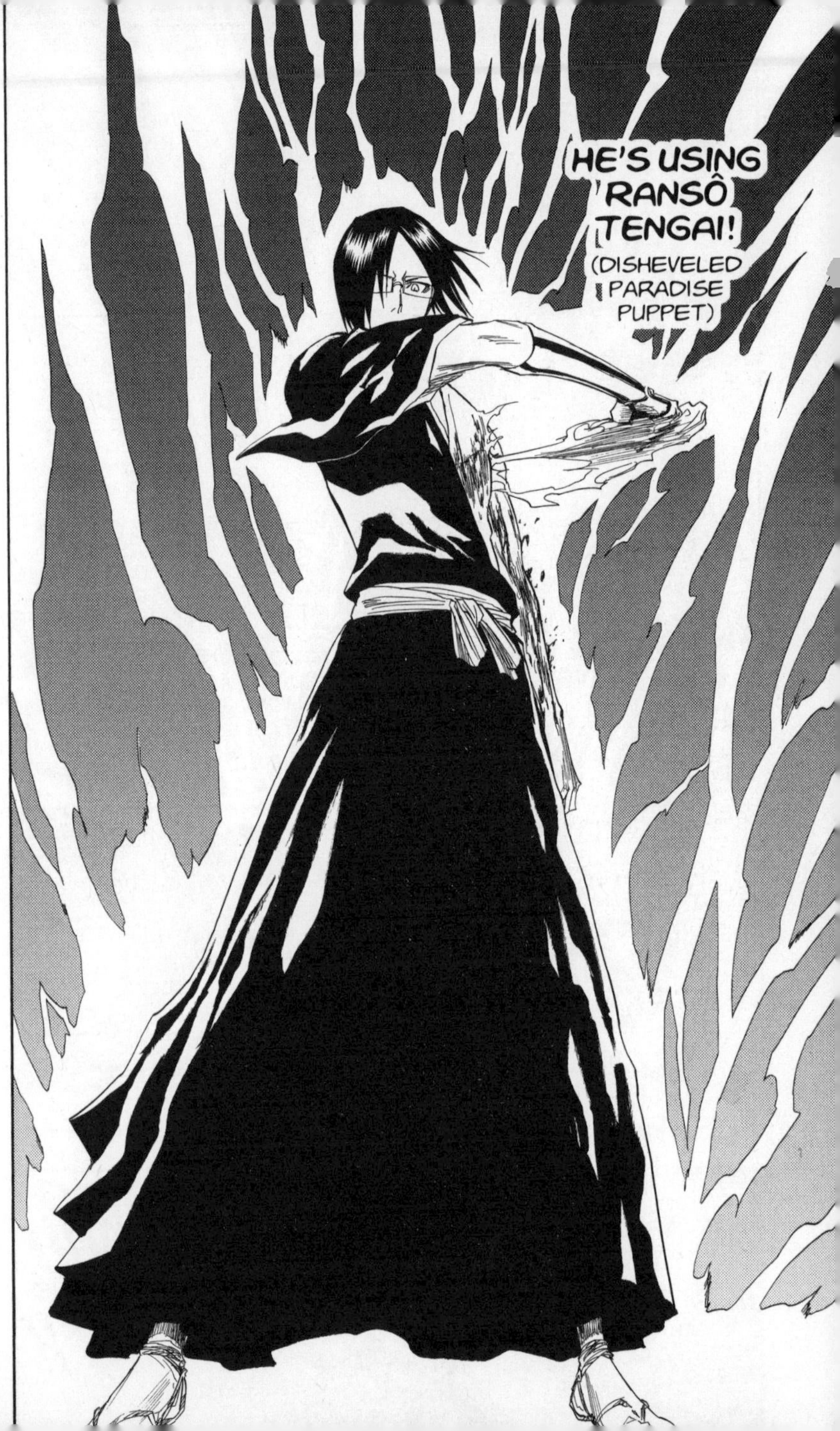
HE'S USING RANSÔ TENGAI!
(DISHEVELED PARADISE PUPPET)

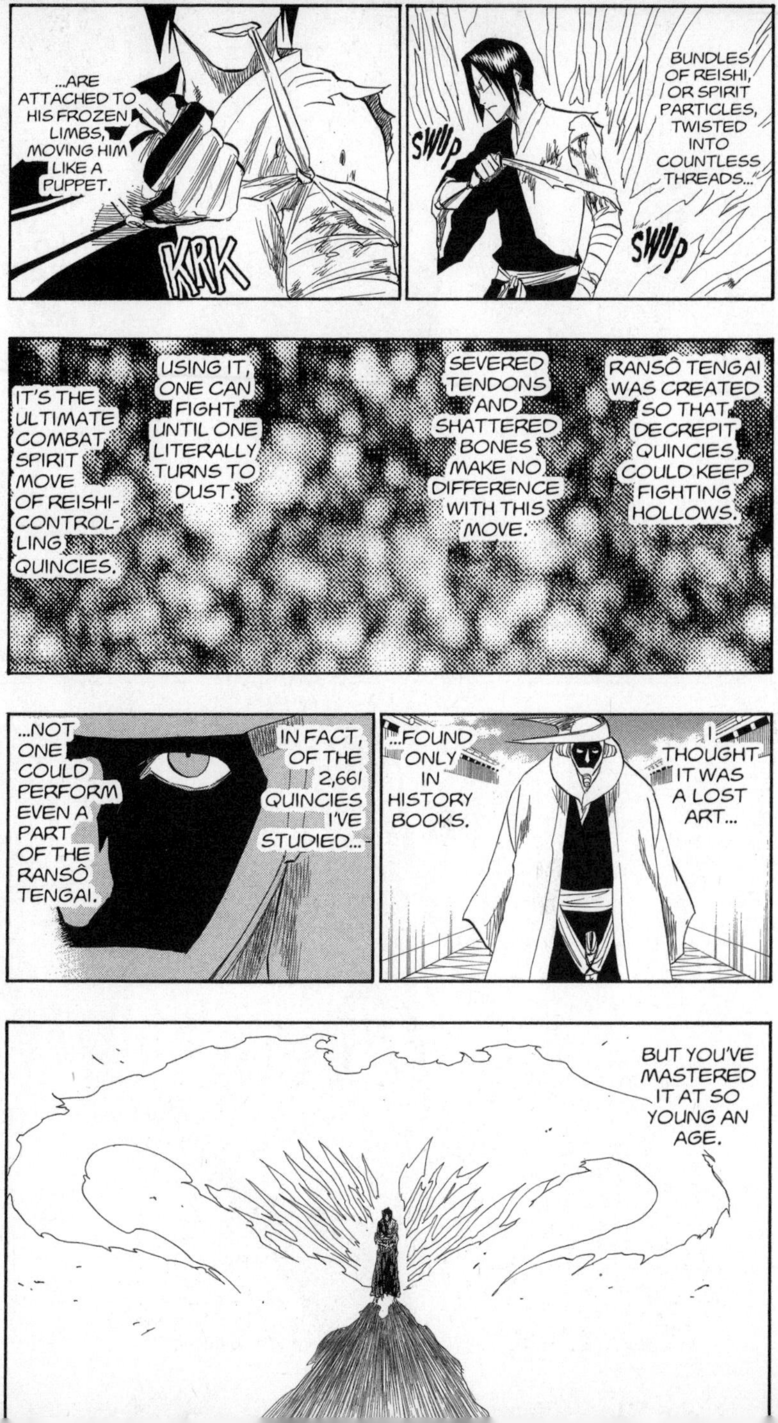
BUNDLES OF REISHI, OR SPIRIT PARTICLES, TWISTED INTO COUNTLESS THREADS...
SWUP
SWUP
...ARE ATTACHED TO HIS FROZEN LIMBS, MOVING HIM LIKE A PUPPET.
KRK
RANSÔ TENGAI WAS CREATED SO THAT DECREPIT QUINCIES COULD KEEP FIGHTING HOLLOWS.
SEVERED TENDONS AND SHATTERED BONES MAKE NO DIFFERENCE WITH THIS MOVE.
USING IT, ONE CAN FIGHT UNTIL ONE LITERALLY TURNS TO DUST.
IT'S THE ULTIMATE COMBAT SPIRIT MOVE OF REISHI-CONTROL-LING QUINCIES.
I THOUGHT IT WAS A LOST ART...
...FOUND ONLY IN HISTORY BOOKS.
IN FACT, OF THE 2,661 QUINCIES I'VE STUDIED...
...NOT ONE COULD PERFORM EVEN A PART OF THE RANSÔ TENGAI.
BUT YOU'VE MASTERED IT AT SO YOUNG AN AGE.

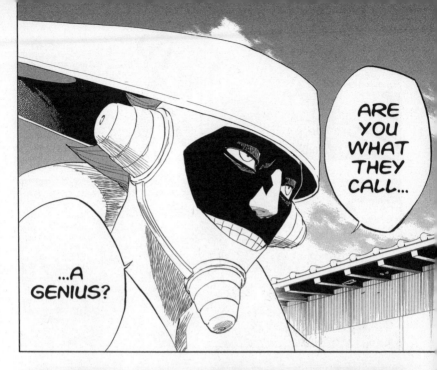

ARE YOU WHAT THEY CALL...

...A GENIUS?

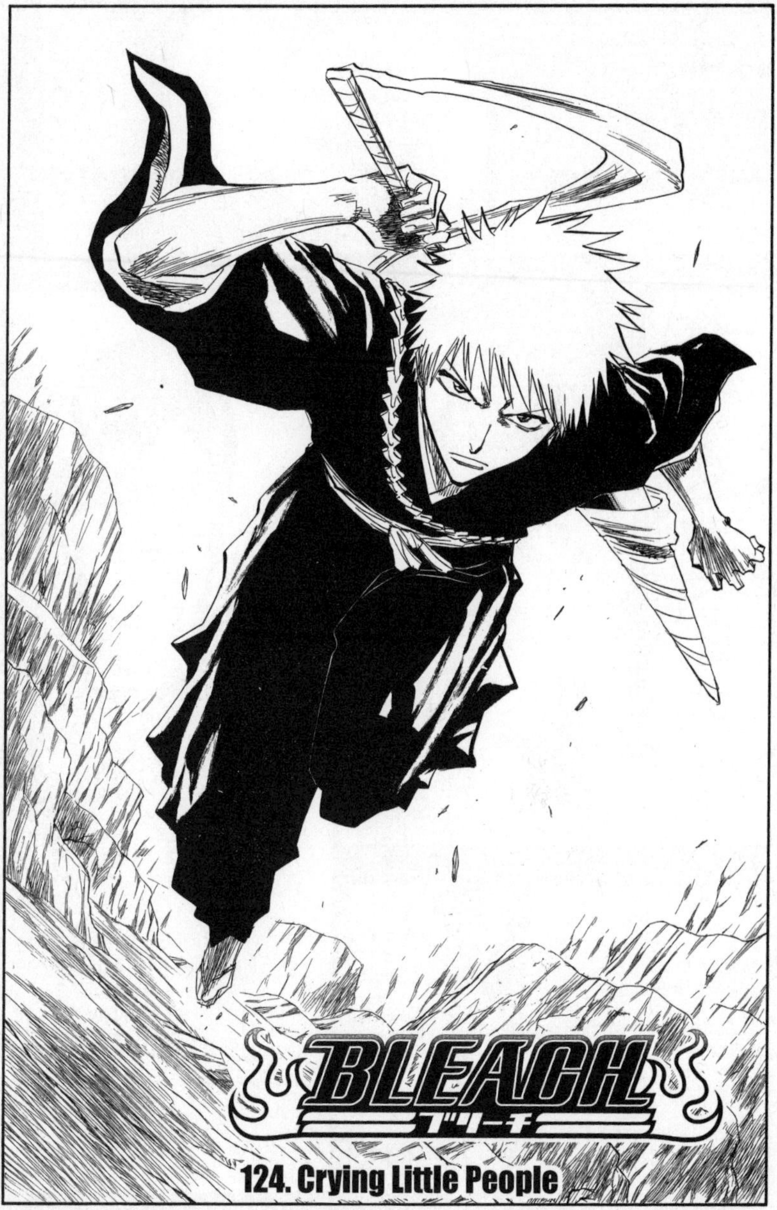
BLEACH
ブリーチ
124. Crying Little People

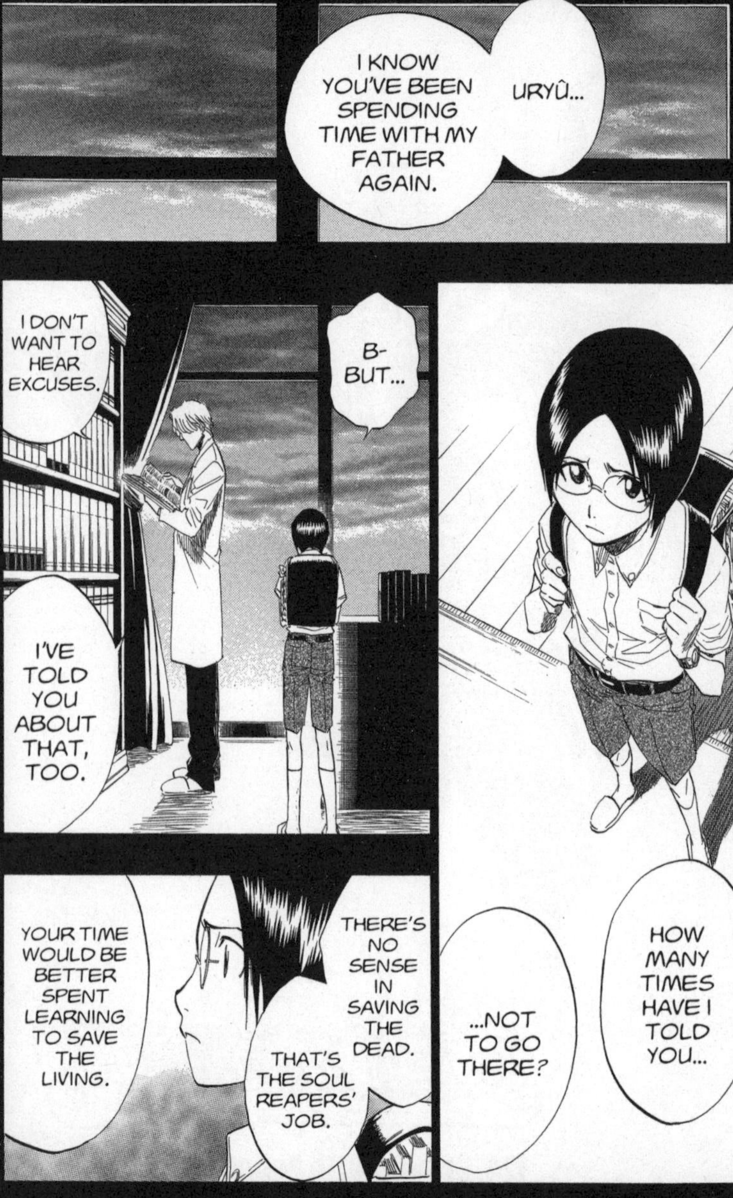
URYÛ...
I KNOW YOU'VE BEEN SPENDING TIME WITH MY FATHER AGAIN.
HOW MANY TIMES HAVE I TOLD YOU...
...NOT TO GO THERE?
B-BUT...
I DON'T WANT TO HEAR EXCUSES.
I'VE TOLD YOU ABOUT THAT, TOO.
THERE'S NO SENSE IN SAVING THE DEAD.
THAT'S THE SOUL REAPERS' JOB.
YOUR TIME WOULD BE BETTER SPENT LEARNING TO SAVE THE LIVING.

READ THIS WAY

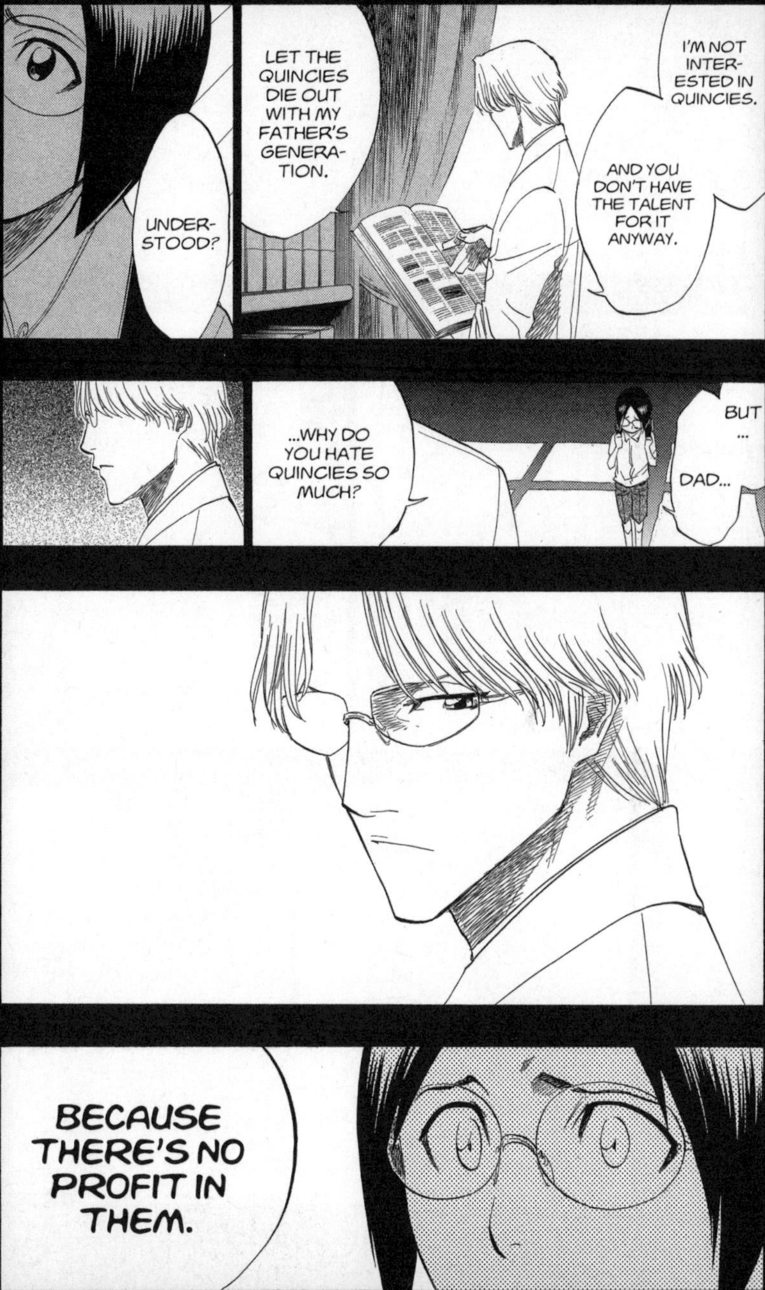

I'M NOT INTER-ESTED IN QUINCIES.
AND YOU DON'T HAVE THE TALENT FOR IT ANYWAY.
LET THE QUINCIES DIE OUT WITH MY FATHER'S GENERA-TION.
UNDER-STOOD?
BUT ... DAD...
...WHY DO YOU HATE QUINCIES SO MUCH?
BECAUSE THERE'S NO PROFIT IN THEM.

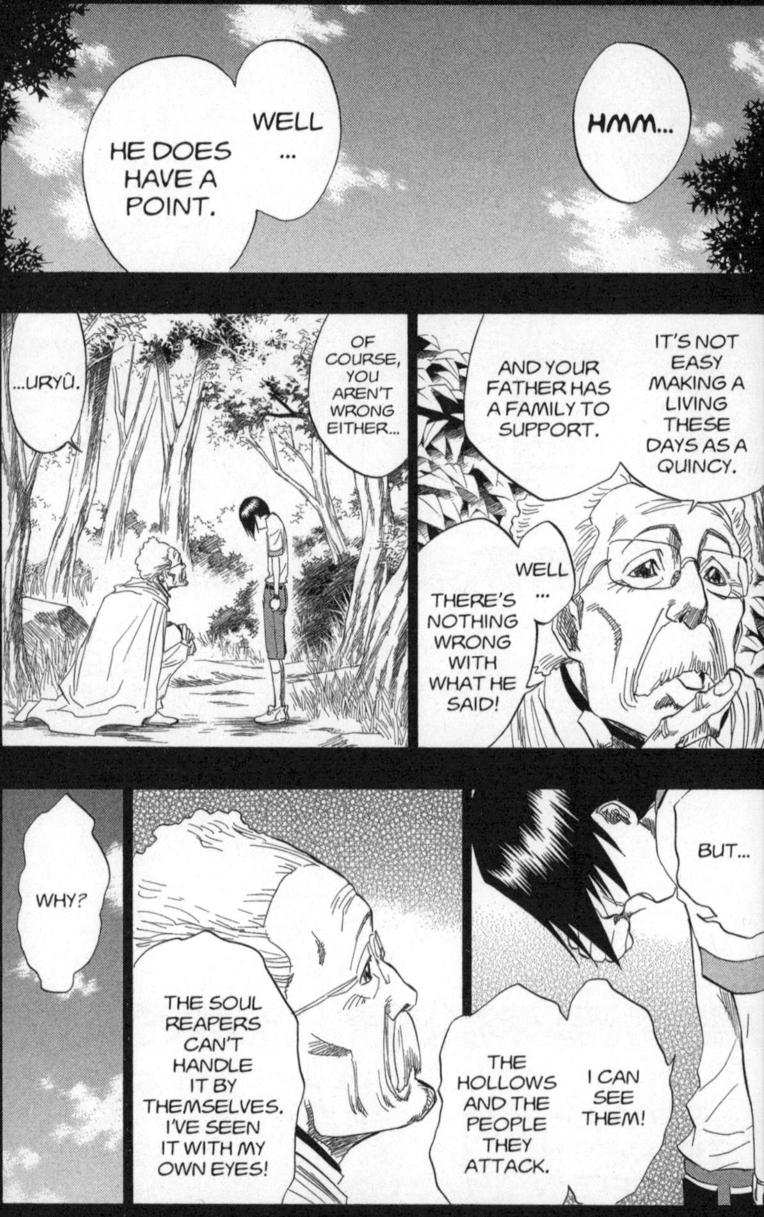
HMM...
WELL... HE DOES HAVE A POINT.
IT'S NOT EASY MAKING A LIVING THESE DAYS AS A QUINCY.
AND YOUR FATHER HAS A FAMILY TO SUPPORT.
WELL... THERE'S NOTHING WRONG WITH WHAT HE SAID!
OF COURSE, YOU AREN'T WRONG EITHER...
...URYÛ.
BUT...
I CAN SEE THEM!
THE HOLLOWS AND THE PEOPLE THEY ATTACK.
THE SOUL REAPERS CAN'T HANDLE IT BY THEMSELVES. I'VE SEEN IT WITH MY OWN EYES!
WHY?

READ THIS WAY

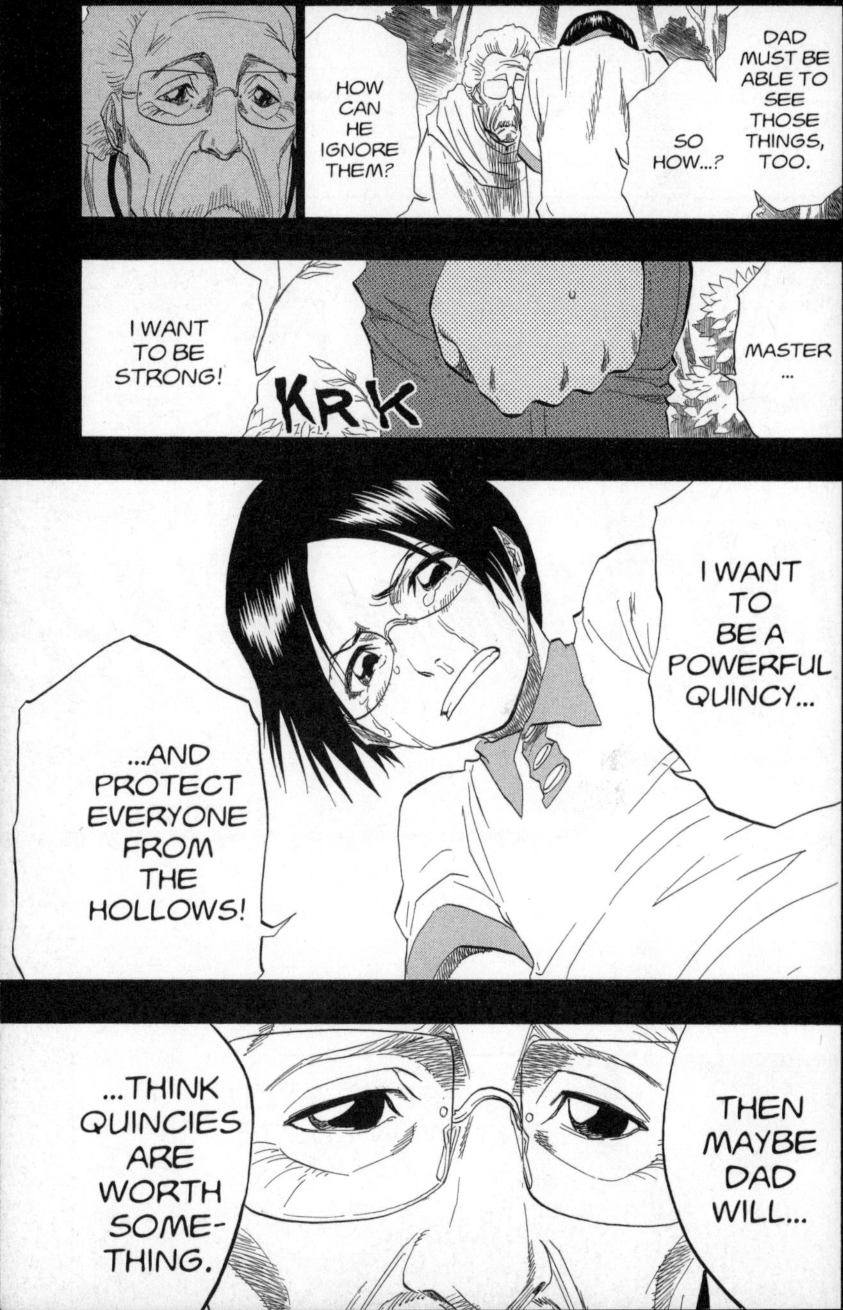

DAD MUST BE ABLE TO SEE THOSE THINGS, TOO.
SO HOW...?
HOW CAN HE IGNORE THEM?
MASTER ...
KRK
I WANT TO BE STRONG!
I WANT TO BE A POWERFUL QUINCY...
...AND PROTECT EVERYONE FROM THE HOLLOWS!
THEN MAYBE DAD WILL...
...THINK QUINCIES ARE WORTH SOMETHING.

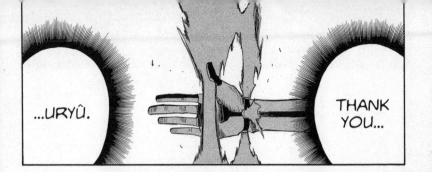

...URYÛ.

THANK YOU...

FWOOSH

RRRMMMMMMMBE

I BELIEVE YOU WON'T BORE ME AFTER ALL.

EXCELLENT.

SHLUK

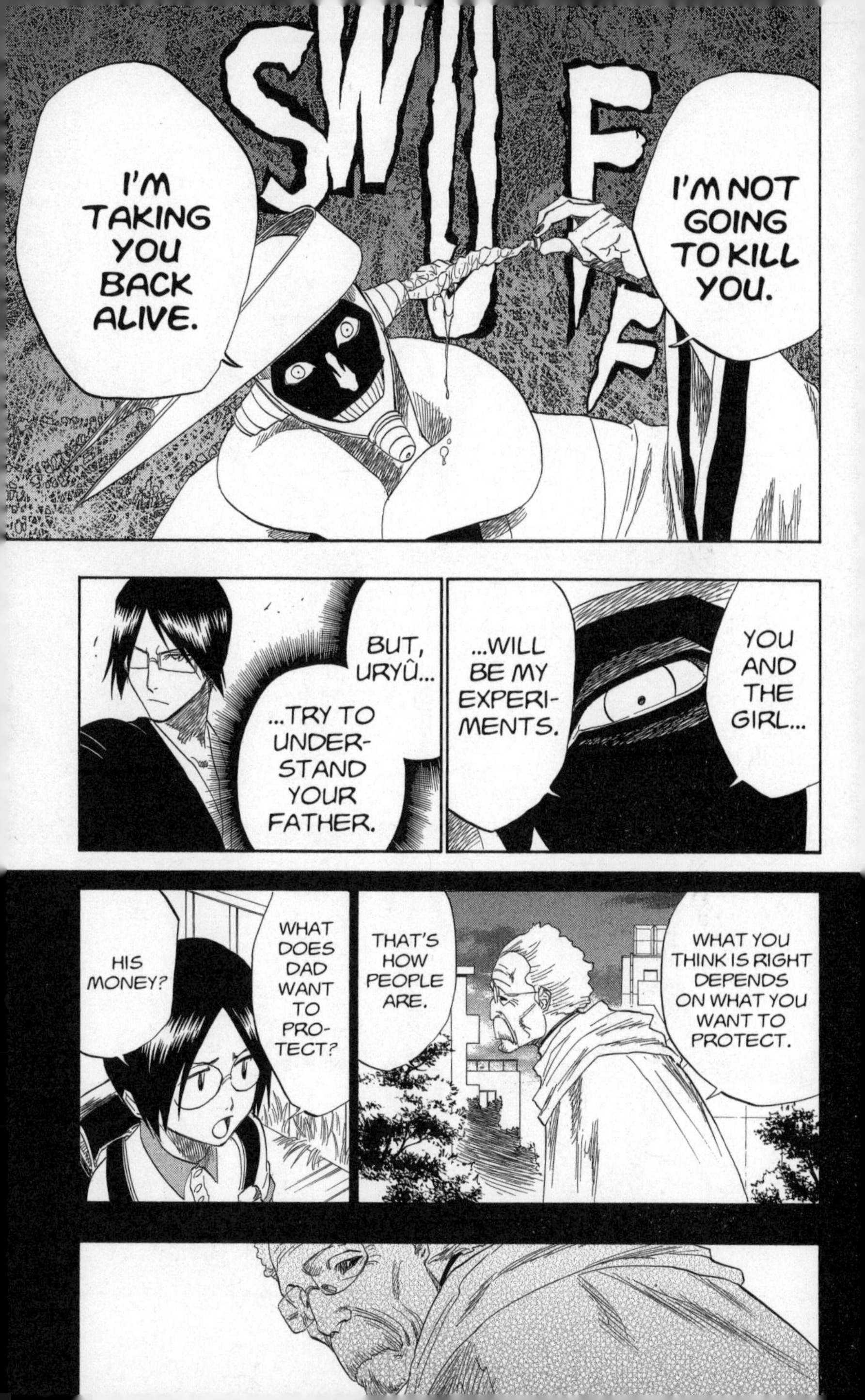
SWIFF
I'M NOT GOING TO KILL YOU.
I'M TAKING YOU BACK ALIVE.
YOU AND THE GIRL...
...WILL BE MY EXPERIMENTS.
BUT, URYÛ...
...TRY TO UNDERSTAND YOUR FATHER.
WHAT YOU THINK IS RIGHT DEPENDS ON WHAT YOU WANT TO PROTECT.
THAT'S HOW PEOPLE ARE.
WHAT DOES DAD WANT TO PROTECT?
HIS MONEY?

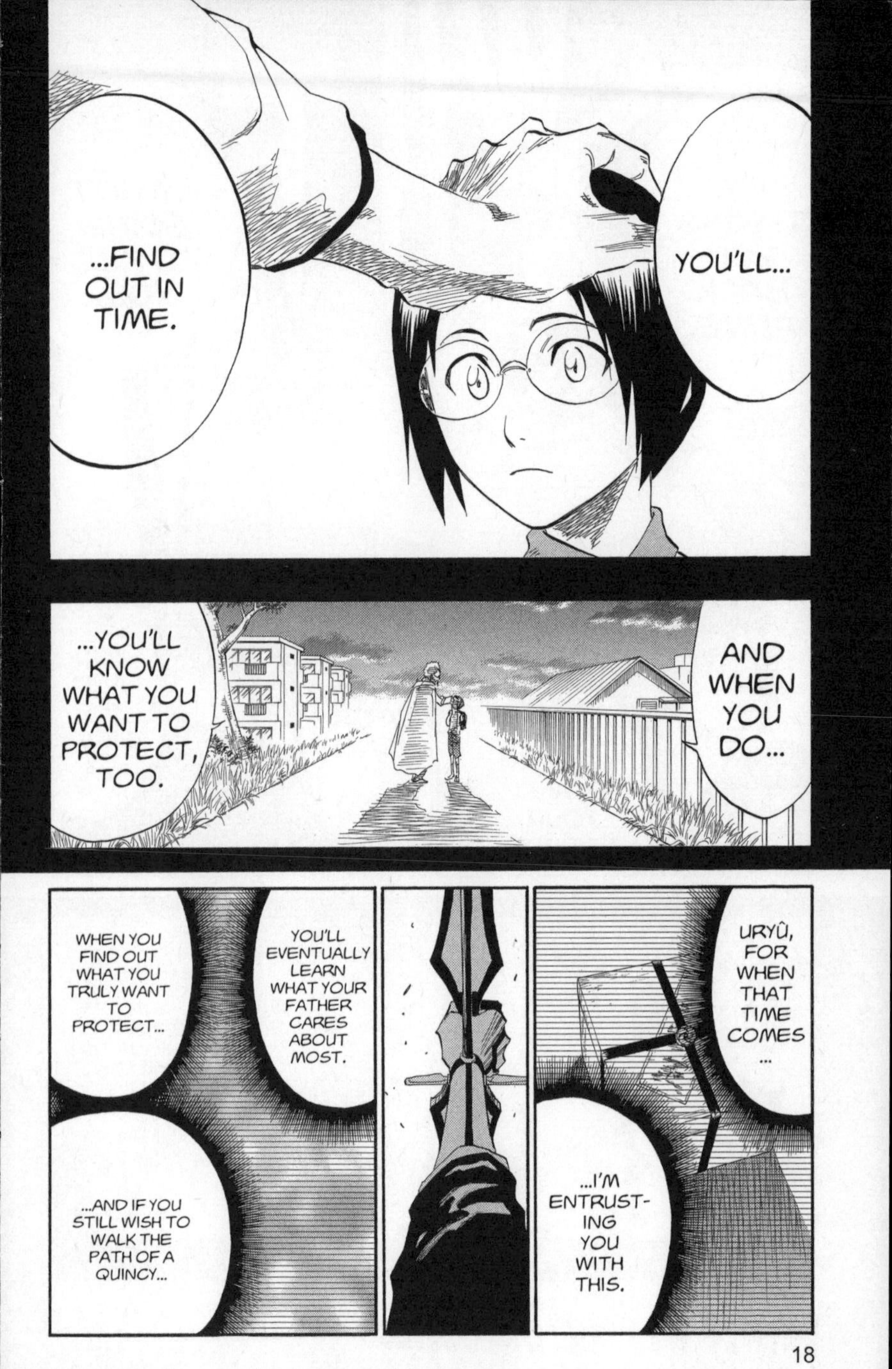
YOU'LL...
...FIND OUT IN TIME.
AND WHEN YOU DO...
...YOU'LL KNOW WHAT YOU WANT TO PROTECT, TOO.
URYÛ, FOR WHEN THAT TIME COMES ...
...I'M ENTRUST-ING YOU WITH THIS.
YOU'LL EVENTUALLY LEARN WHAT YOUR FATHER CARES ABOUT MOST.
WHEN YOU FIND OUT WHAT YOU TRULY WANT TO PROTECT...
...AND IF YOU STILL WISH TO WALK THE PATH OF A QUINCY...

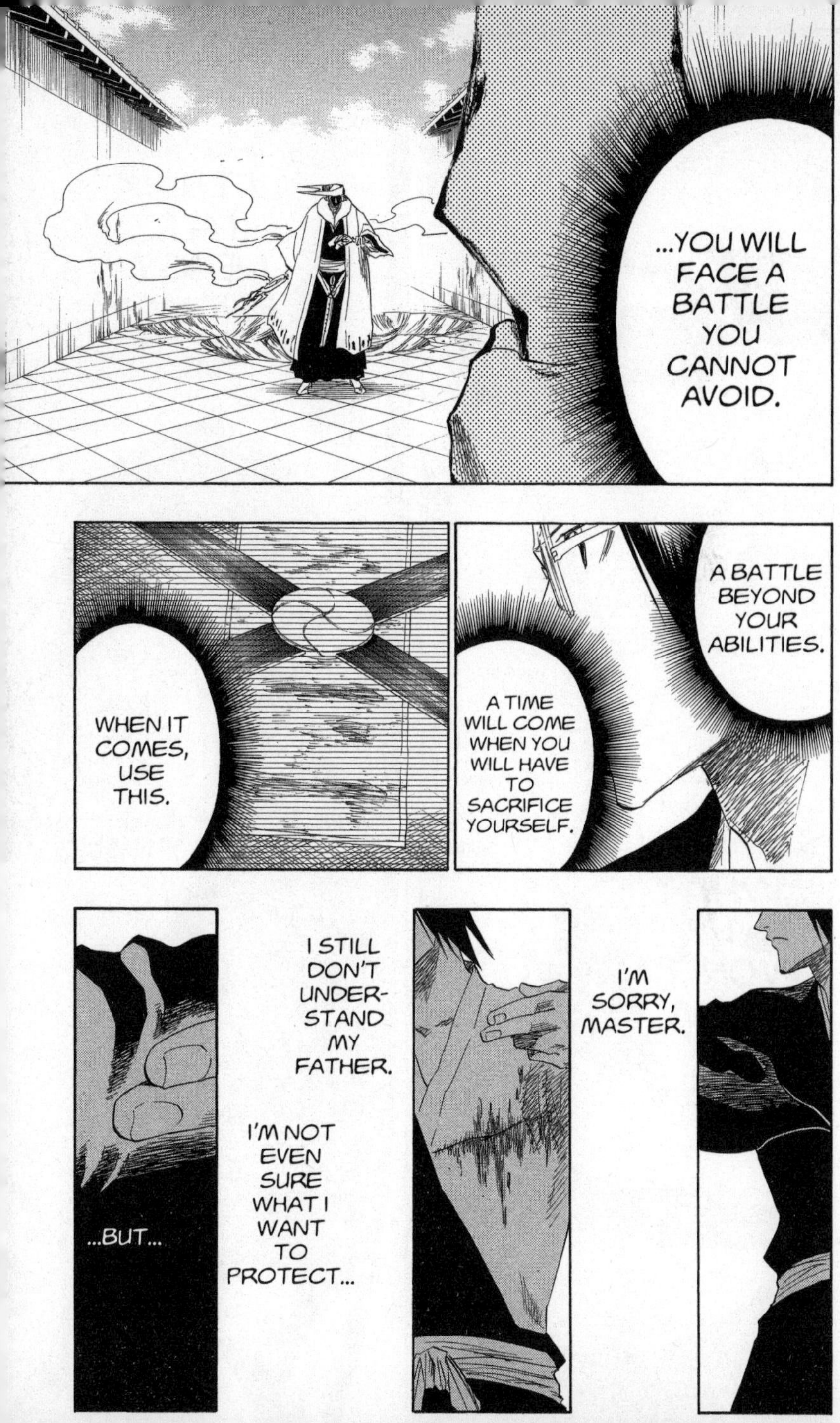
...YOU WILL FACE A BATTLE YOU CANNOT AVOID.
A BATTLE BEYOND YOUR ABILITIES.
A TIME WILL COME WHEN YOU WILL HAVE TO SACRIFICE YOURSELF.
WHEN IT COMES, USE THIS.
I'M SORRY, MASTER.
I STILL DON'T UNDER-STAND MY FATHER.
I'M NOT EVEN SURE WHAT I WANT TO PROTECT...
...BUT...

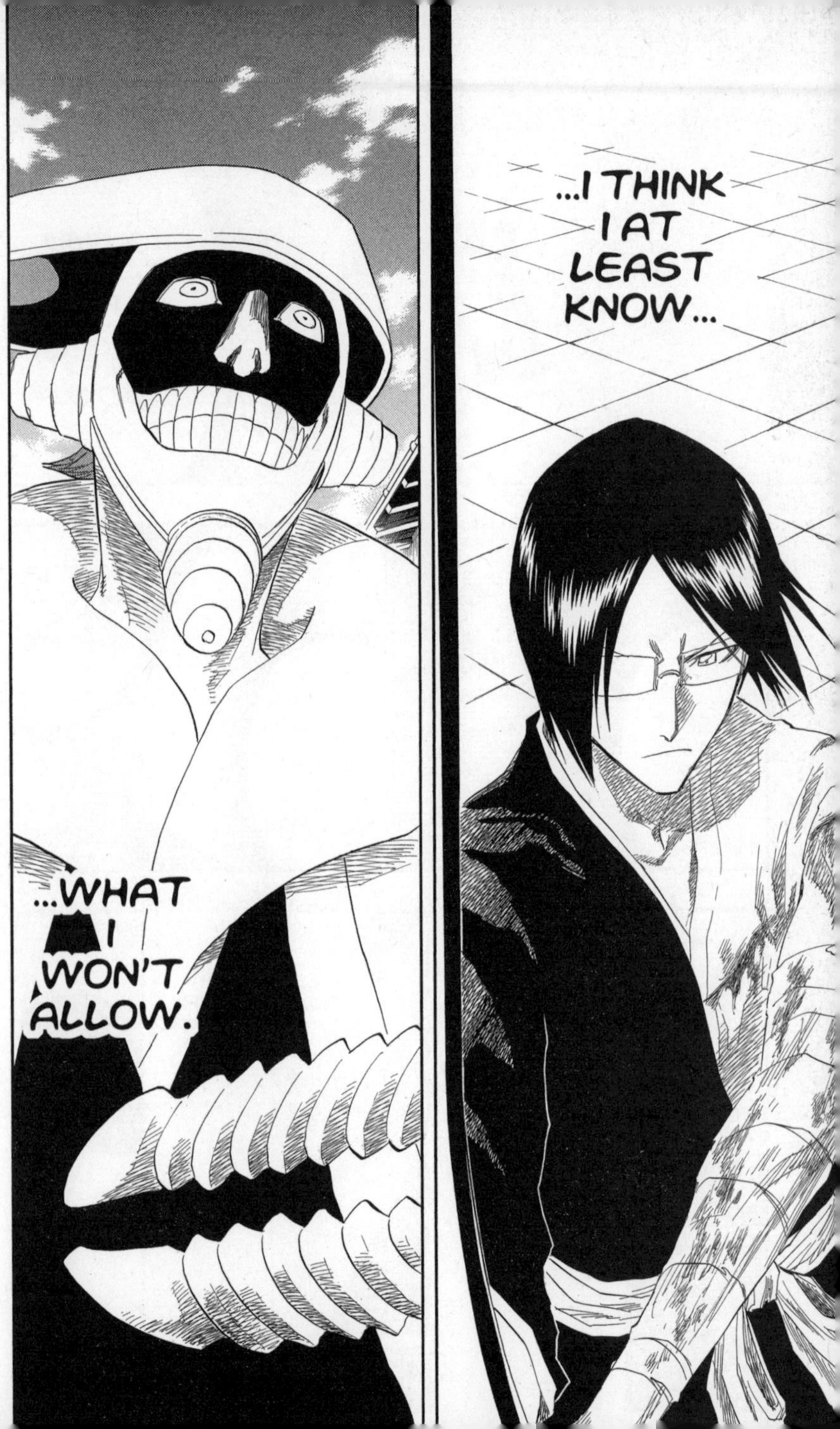
...I THINK I AT LEAST KNOW...
...WHAT I WON'T ALLOW.

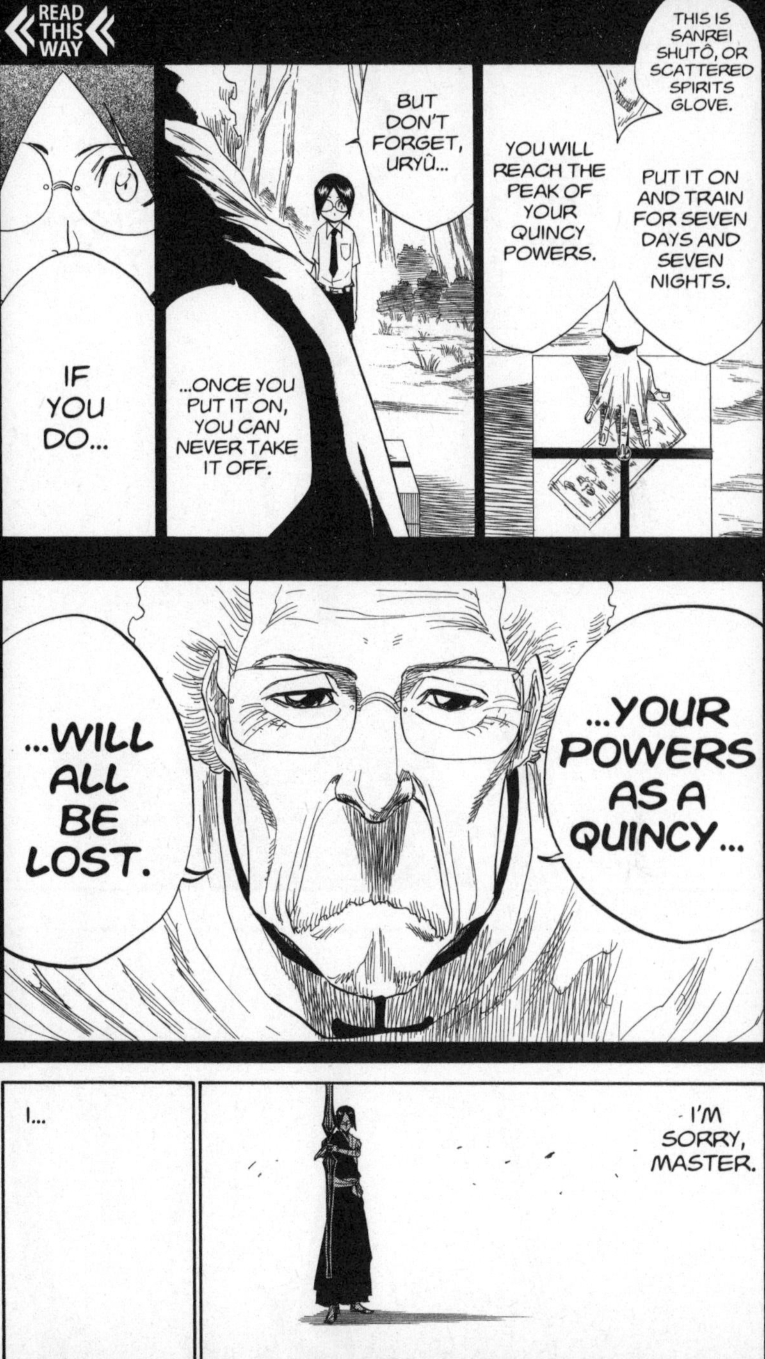
READ THIS WAY
THIS IS SANREI SHUTÔ, OR SCATTERED SPIRITS GLOVE.
PUT IT ON AND TRAIN FOR SEVEN DAYS AND SEVEN NIGHTS.
YOU WILL REACH THE PEAK OF YOUR QUINCY POWERS.
BUT DON'T FORGET, URYÛ...
...ONCE YOU PUT IT ON, YOU CAN NEVER TAKE IT OFF.
IF YOU DO...
...YOUR POWERS AS A QUINCY...
...WILL ALL BE LOST.
I'M SORRY, MASTER.
I...

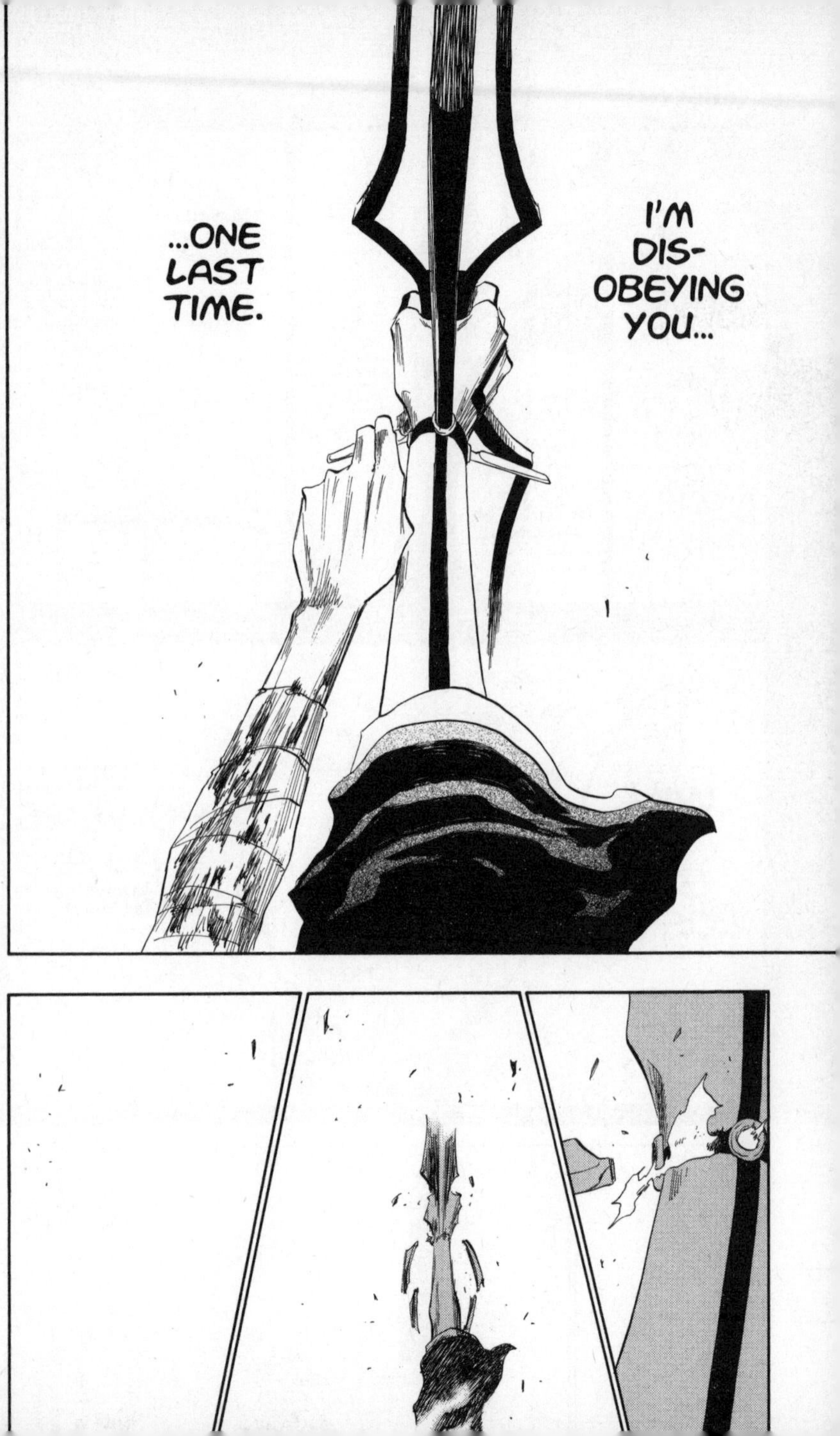
I'M DIS-OBEYING YOU...
...ONE LAST TIME.

READ THIS WAY

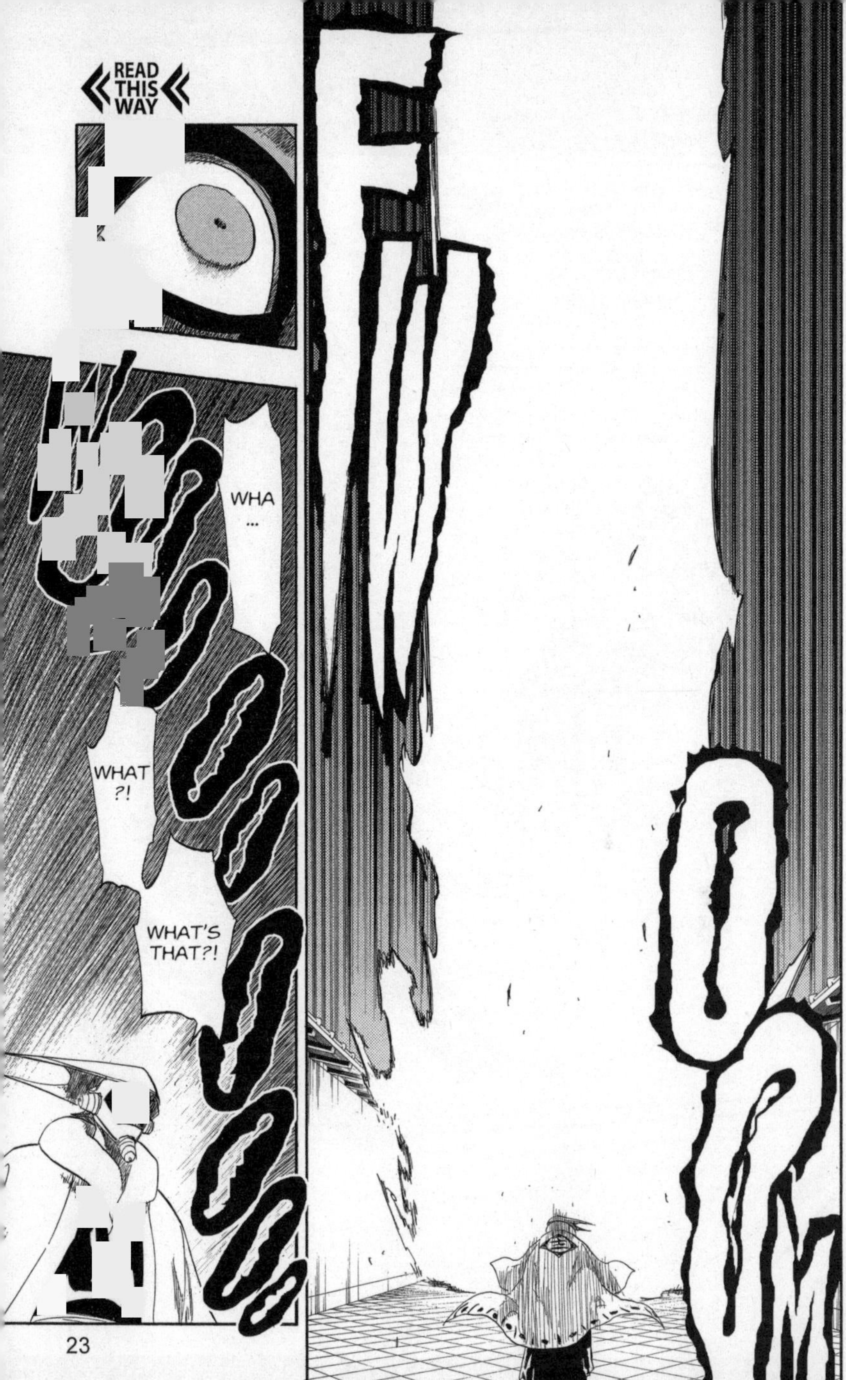
WHA...
WHAT?!
WHAT'S THAT?!

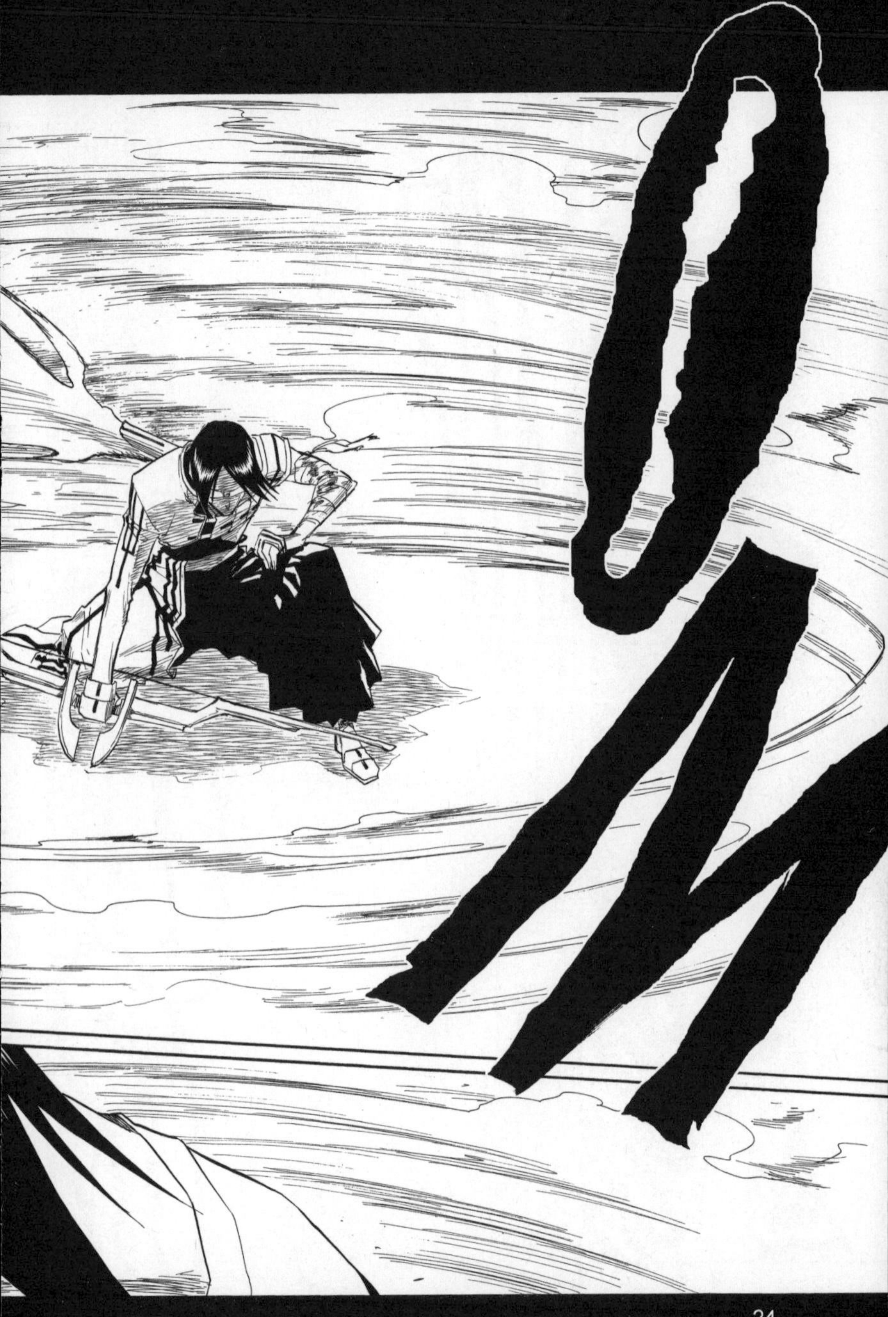
OM

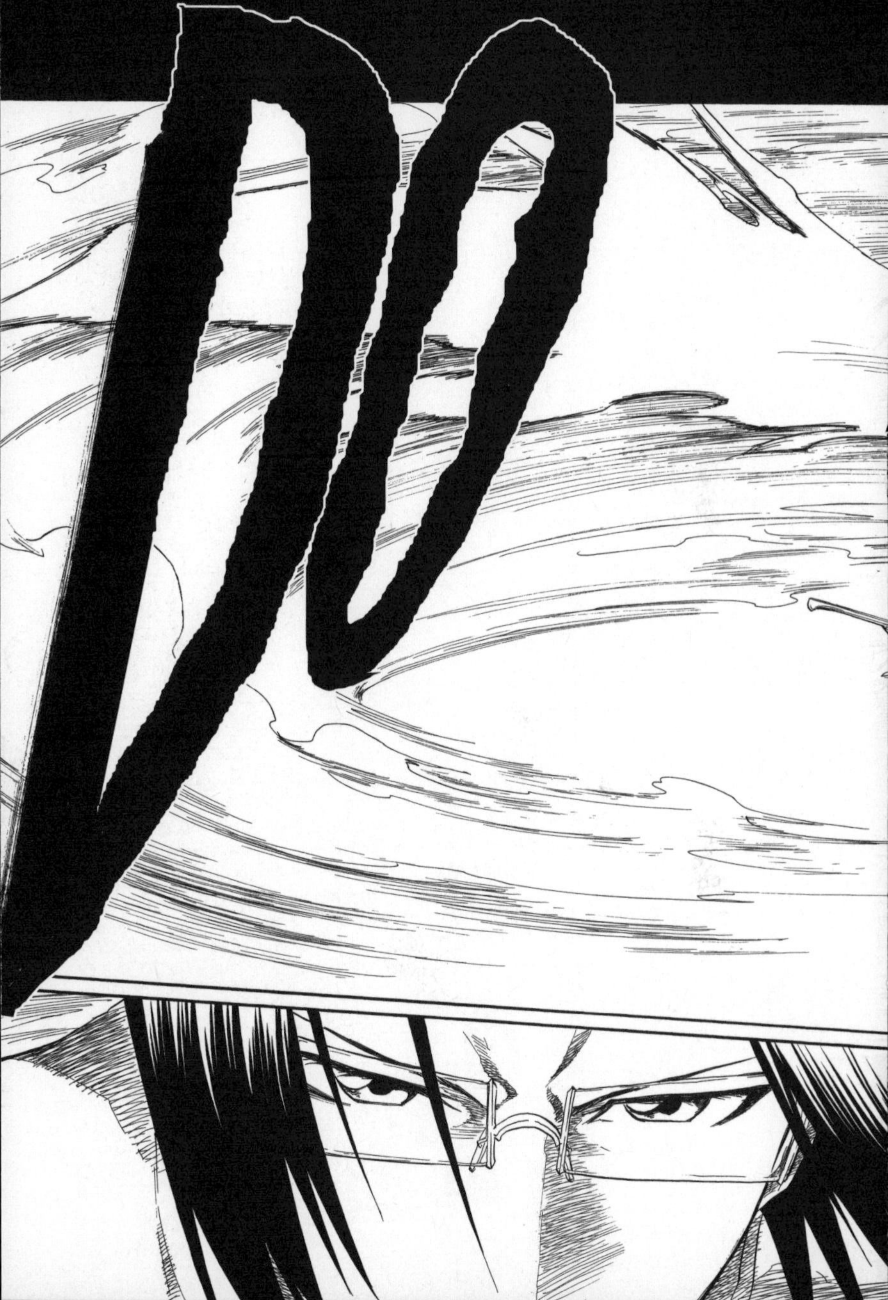
DO

MEANWHILE IN THE WORLD
OF THE LIVING, SERIES 3

GORGEOUS & SEXY & ROCK'N'ROLL & ME

Mr. KON'S
ME-ME DIARY

AUGUST 8, CLOUDY.
I TOOK ICHIGO'S PLACE WHEN
HE WENT TO THE SOUL SOCIETY.
I THOUGHT HIS FAMILY WOULD
BE OVERJOYED
TO SEE HIM.

SISTER A:
HAD A
GUILTY
LOOK
ON
HER
FACE.

SISTER B:
SEEMED
TOTALLY
UNINTER-
ESTED.

FATHER A:
WAS
OBVIOUSLY
ANNOYED.

WHAT
THE
HECK IS
THIS?

ARE
THEY
UPSET
ABOUT
SPLITTING
THE
WATERMELON
FOUR
WAYS?

SUMMER
OF
FOOD

125. Insanity & Genius

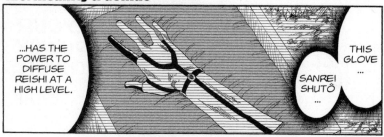

THIS GLOVE ...
SANREI SHUTÔ ...
...HAS THE POWER TO DIFFUSE REISHI AT A HIGH LEVEL.
IT HOLDS SO MUCH POWER THAT MOST QUINCIES COULDN'T EVEN PRODUCE THE BOW.
BUT IF YOU CAN PRODUCE THE BOW...
...AND MAINTAIN IT FOR SEVEN DAYS AND SEVEN NIGHTS...
...YOU'LL REACH THE PEAK OF YOUR QUINCY POWERS.
BUT ONCE YOU DO THAT, URYÛ...
...YOU CAN NEVER TAKE THE GLOVE OFF AGAIN...
...BECAUSE YOUR REISHI-COLLECTING POWER WILL BE BEYOND WHAT A QUINCY CAN CONTROL.
THE FLAME IT PRODUCES WOULD AFFECT YOU AS WELL.
IF YOU TAKE OFF THE GLOVE, YOU'LL MOMENTARILY GAIN IMMENSE POWER, BUT...

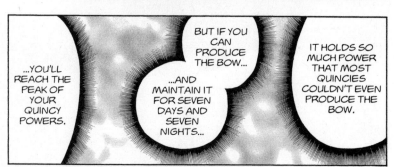

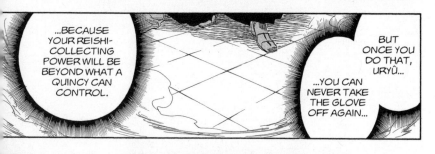

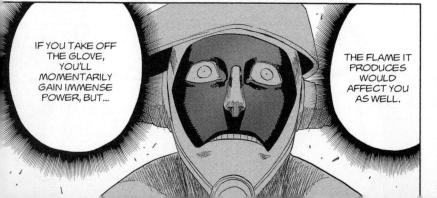

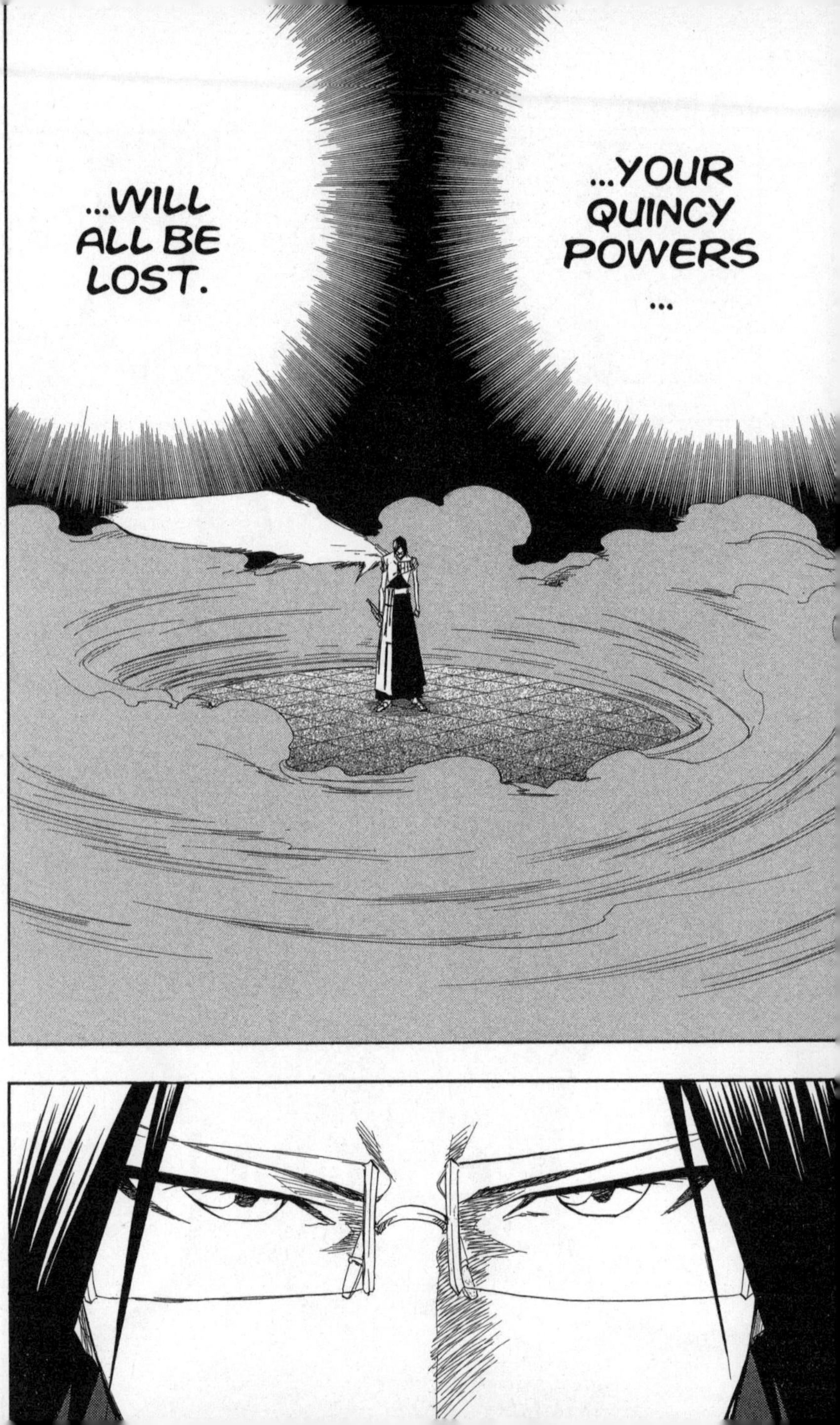
...YOUR QUINCY POWERS ...
...WILL ALL BE LOST.

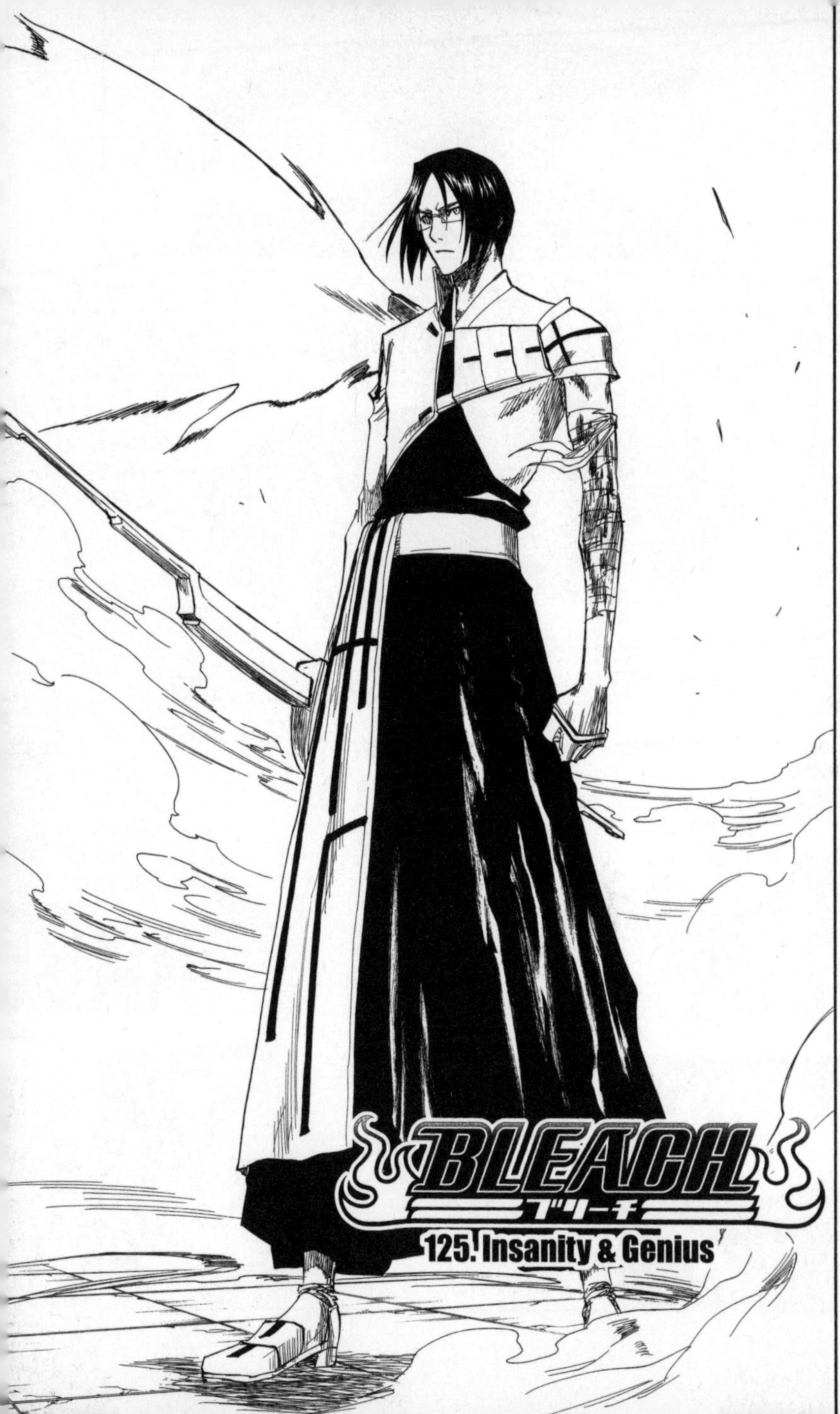
BLEACH
ブリーチ
125. Insanity & Genius

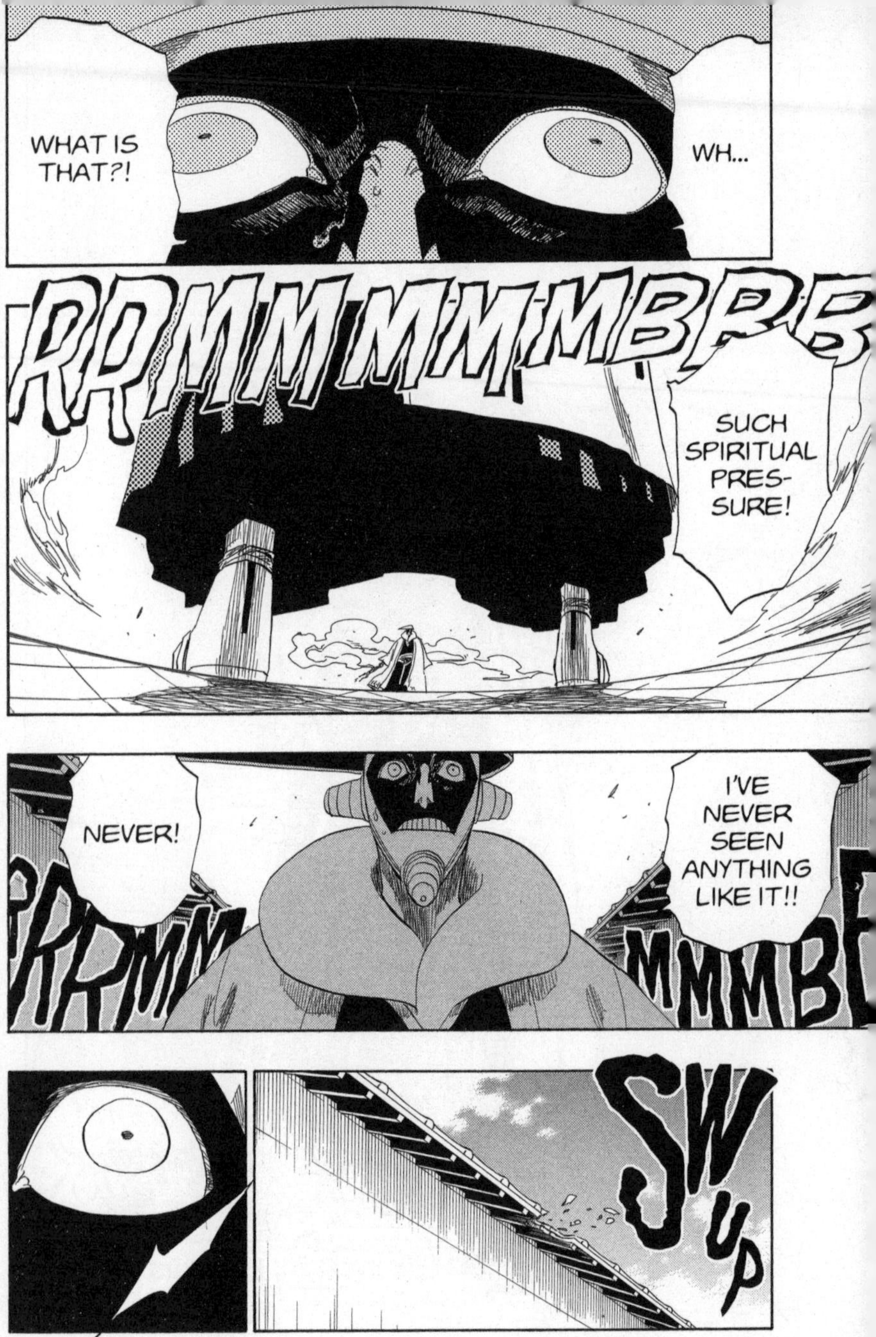
WH...
WHAT IS THAT?!
RRMMMMMMMBBB
SUCH SPIRITUAL PRES-SURE!
I'VE NEVER SEEN ANYTHING LIKE IT!!
NEVER!
RRMM
MMMBE
SWUP

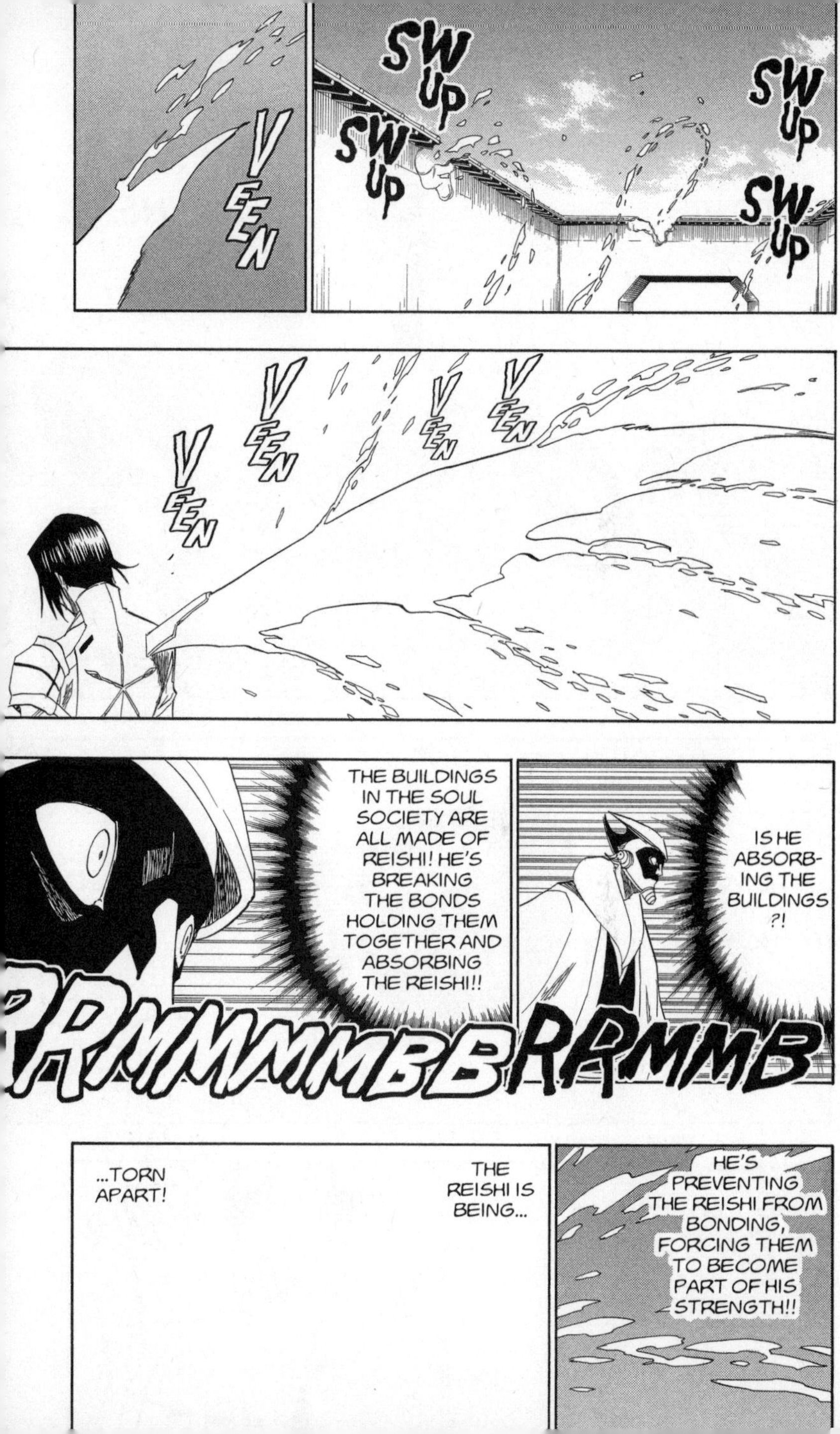
SWUP
SWUP
SWUP
SWUP
VEEN
VEEN
VEEN
VEEN
VEEN
IS HE ABSORBING THE BUILDINGS?!
BRRMMB
THE BUILDINGS IN THE SOUL SOCIETY ARE ALL MADE OF REISHI! HE'S BREAKING THE BONDS HOLDING THEM TOGETHER AND ABSORBING THE REISHI!!
RMMMMBB
HE'S PREVENTING THE REISHI FROM BONDING, FORCING THEM TO BECOME PART OF HIS STRENGTH!!
THE REISHI IS BEING...
...TORN APART!

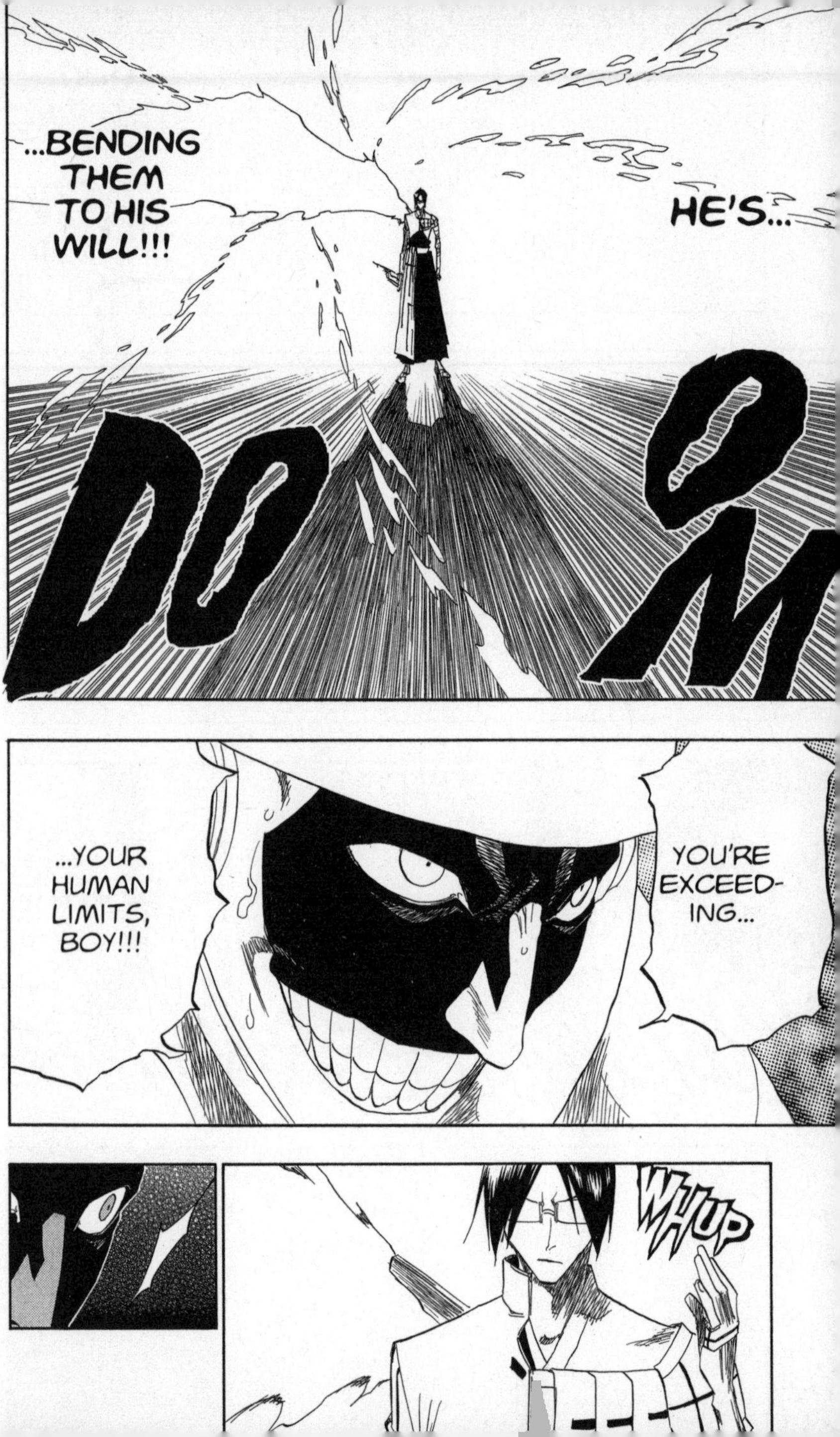
HE'S...
...BENDING THEM TO HIS WILL!!!
DOOM
YOU'RE EXCEED-ING...
...YOUR HUMAN LIMITS, BOY!!!
WHUP

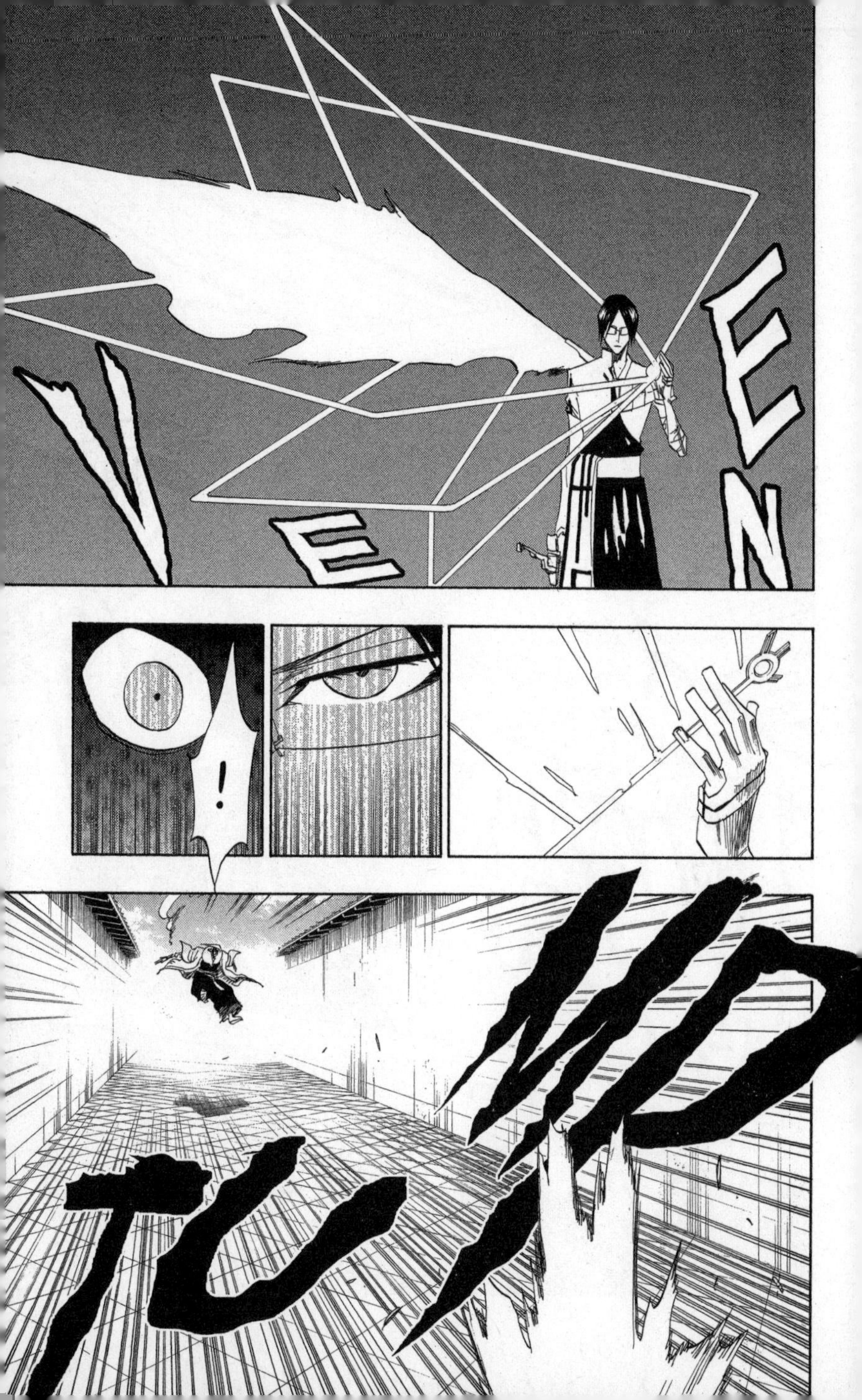
VEEN
!
TUMD

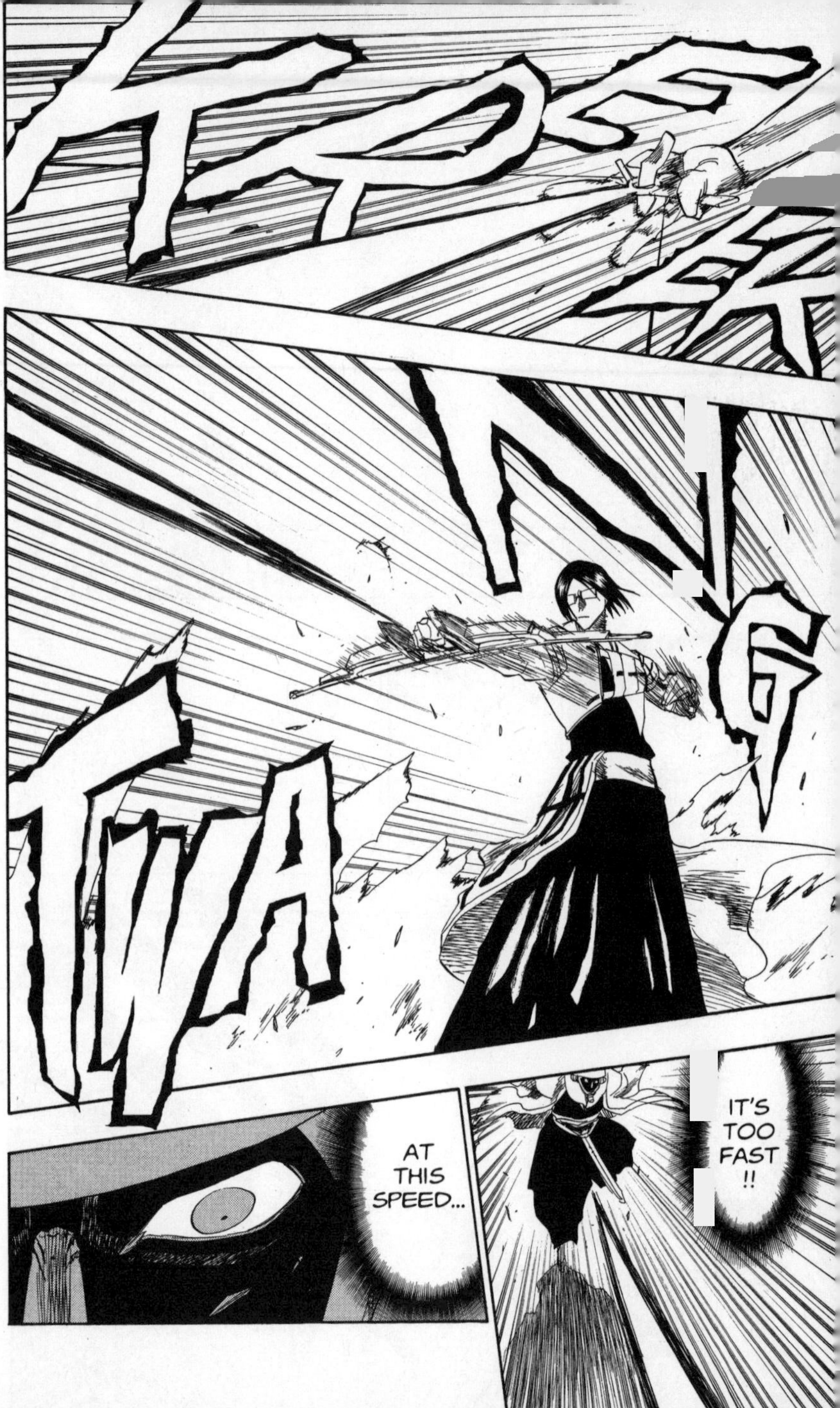
TWANG
IT'S TOO FAST!!
AT THIS SPEED...

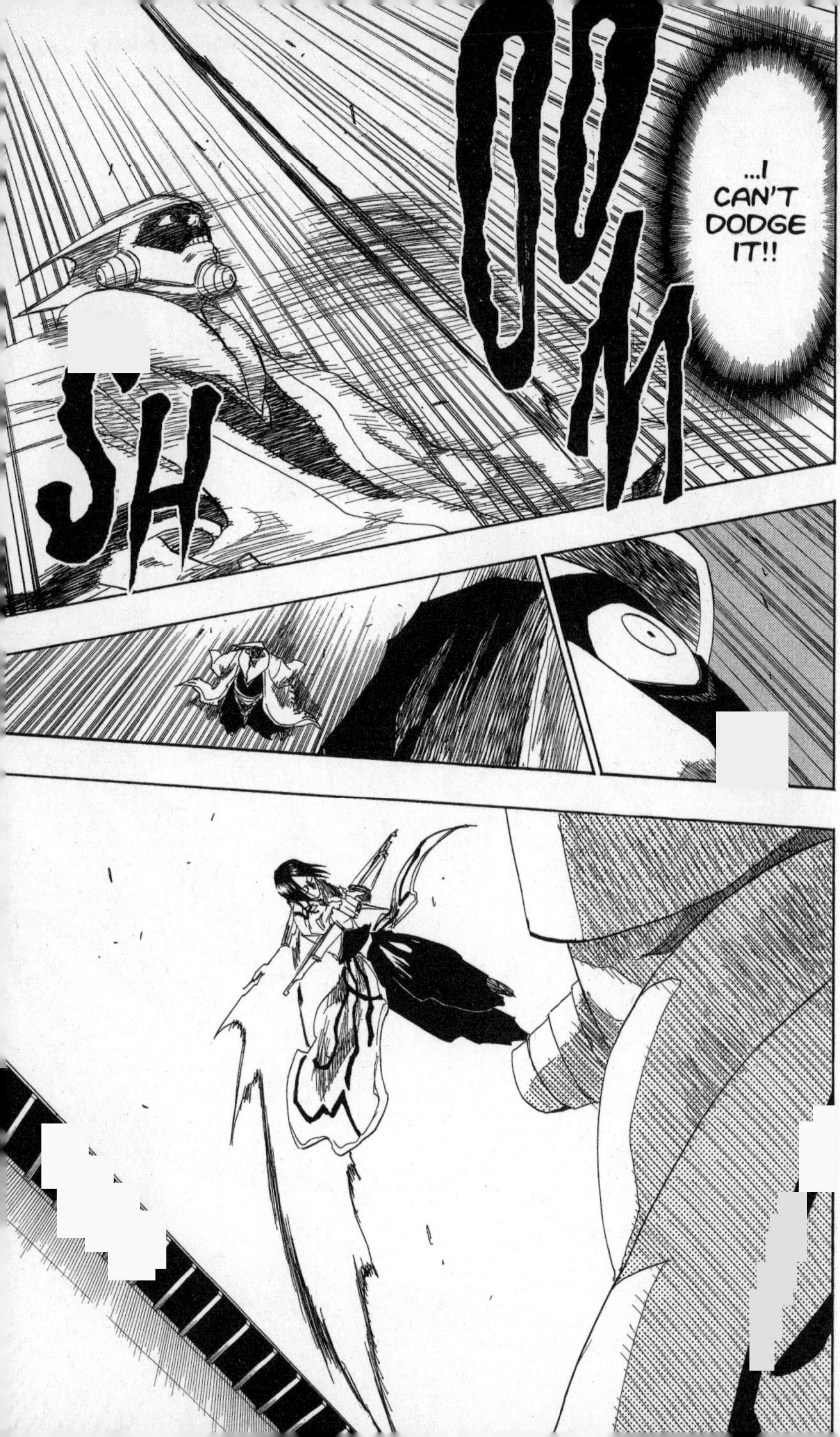
...I CAN'T DODGE IT!!

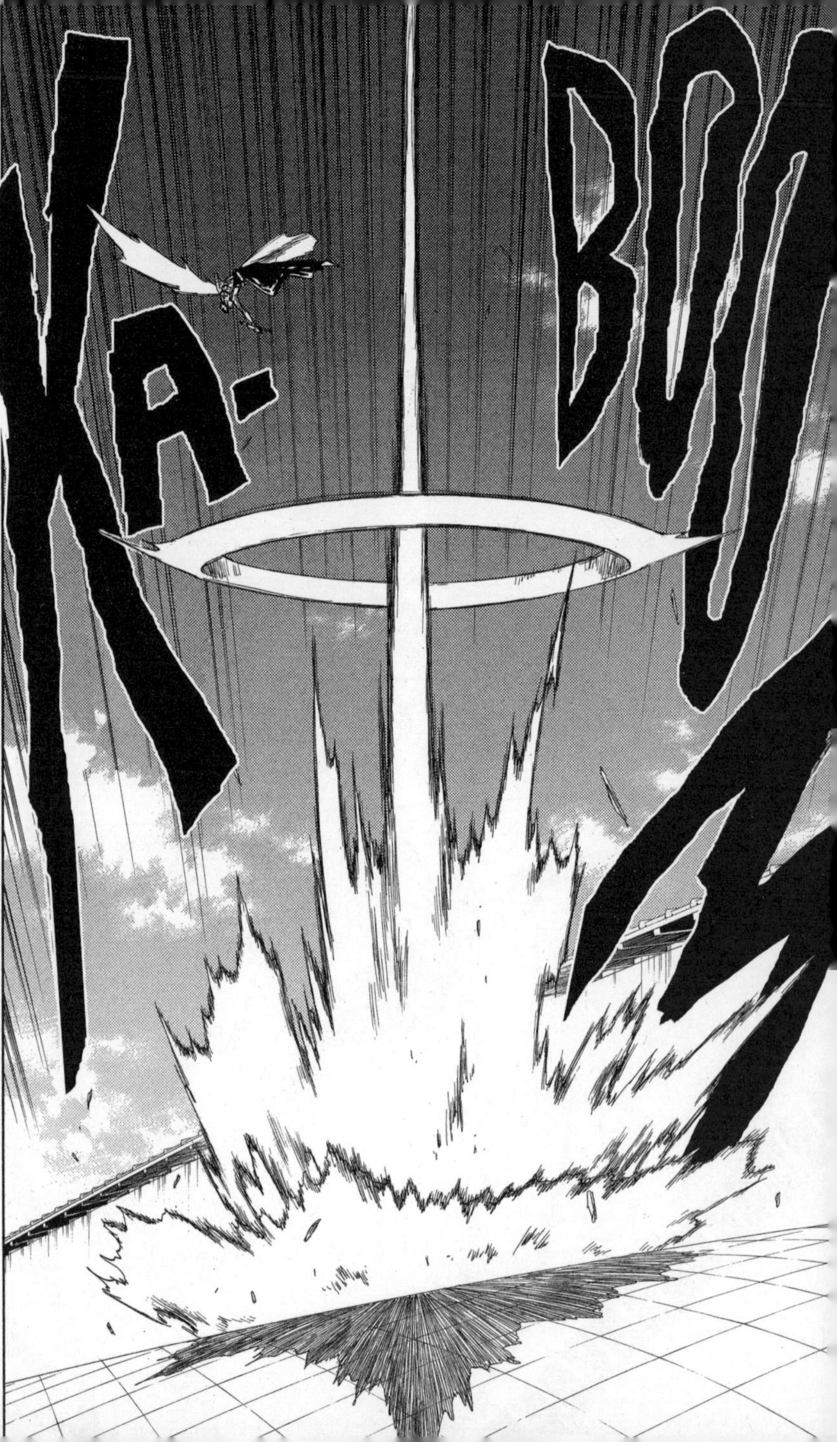
KA-BOOM

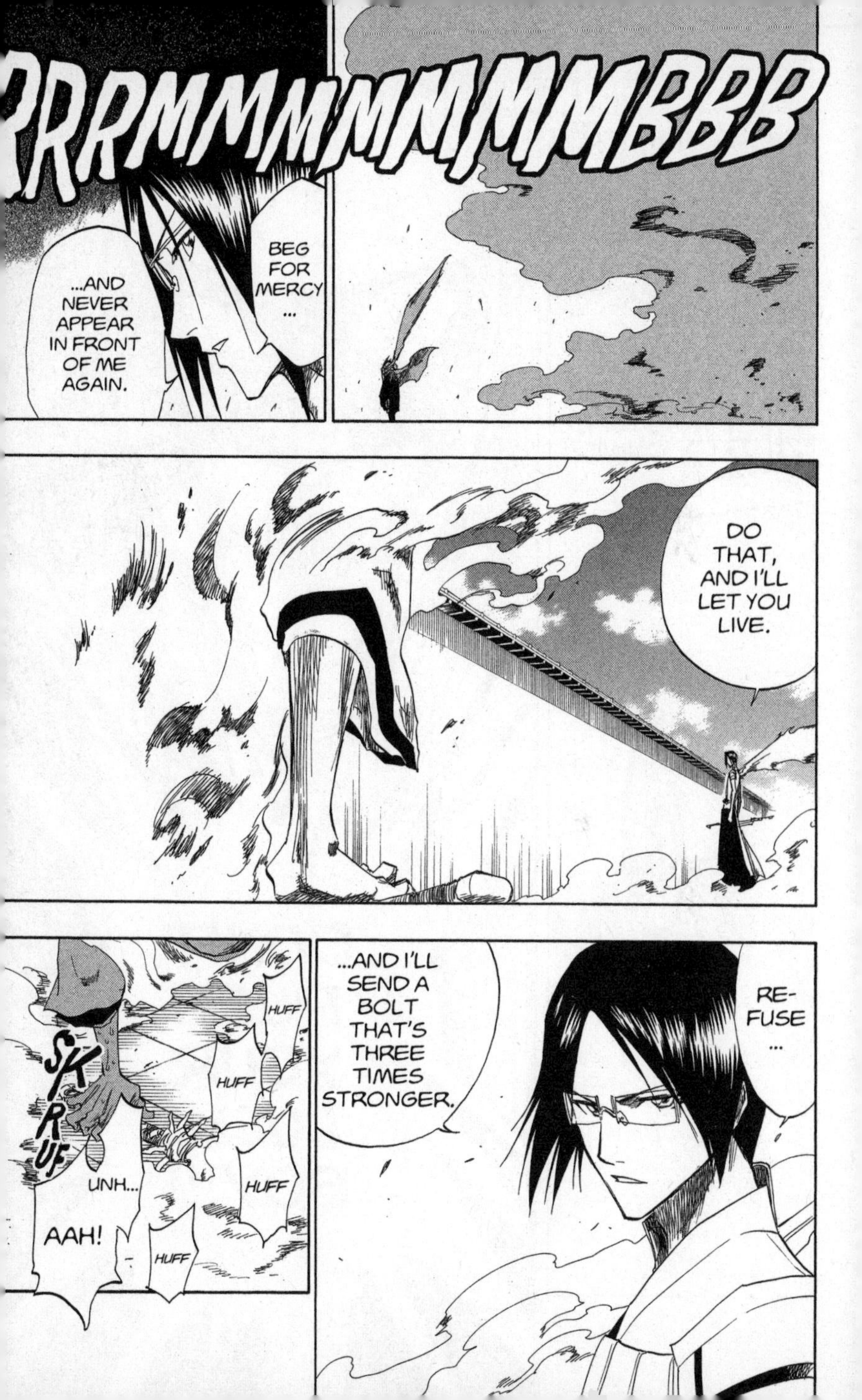
RRRMMMMMMMMMBBB
BEG FOR MERCY...
...AND NEVER APPEAR IN FRONT OF ME AGAIN.
DO THAT, AND I'LL LET YOU LIVE.
RE-FUSE...
...AND I'LL SEND A BOLT THAT'S THREE TIMES STRONGER.
HUFF
HUFF
SKRUF
UNH...
AAH!
HUFF
HUFF

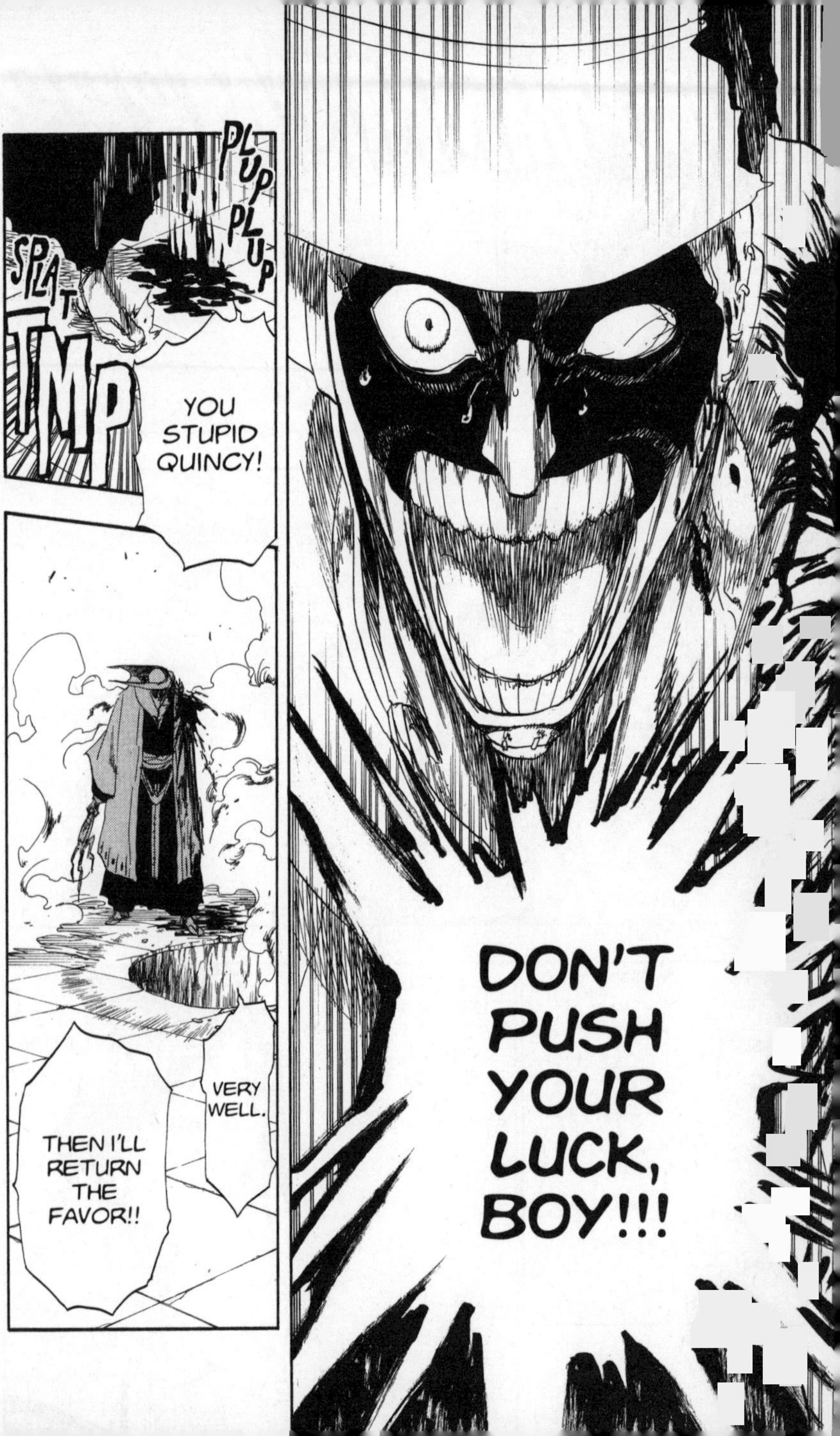
DON'T PUSH YOUR LUCK, BOY!!!
PLUP PLUP PLUP
SPLAT
TMP
YOU STUPID QUINCY!
VERY WELL.
THEN I'LL RETURN THE FAVOR!!

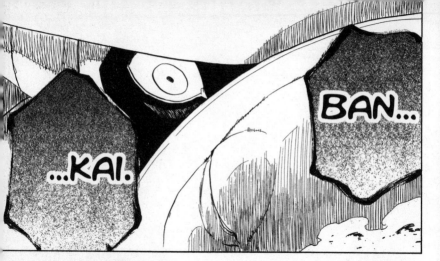

...KAI.

BAN...

BURBLE

BAN...?

? WHAT?

BOOM

KA-BOOM

BLU MP

BL UP

BLUP
BLUP
BLUP
BLUP

WHAT ?!

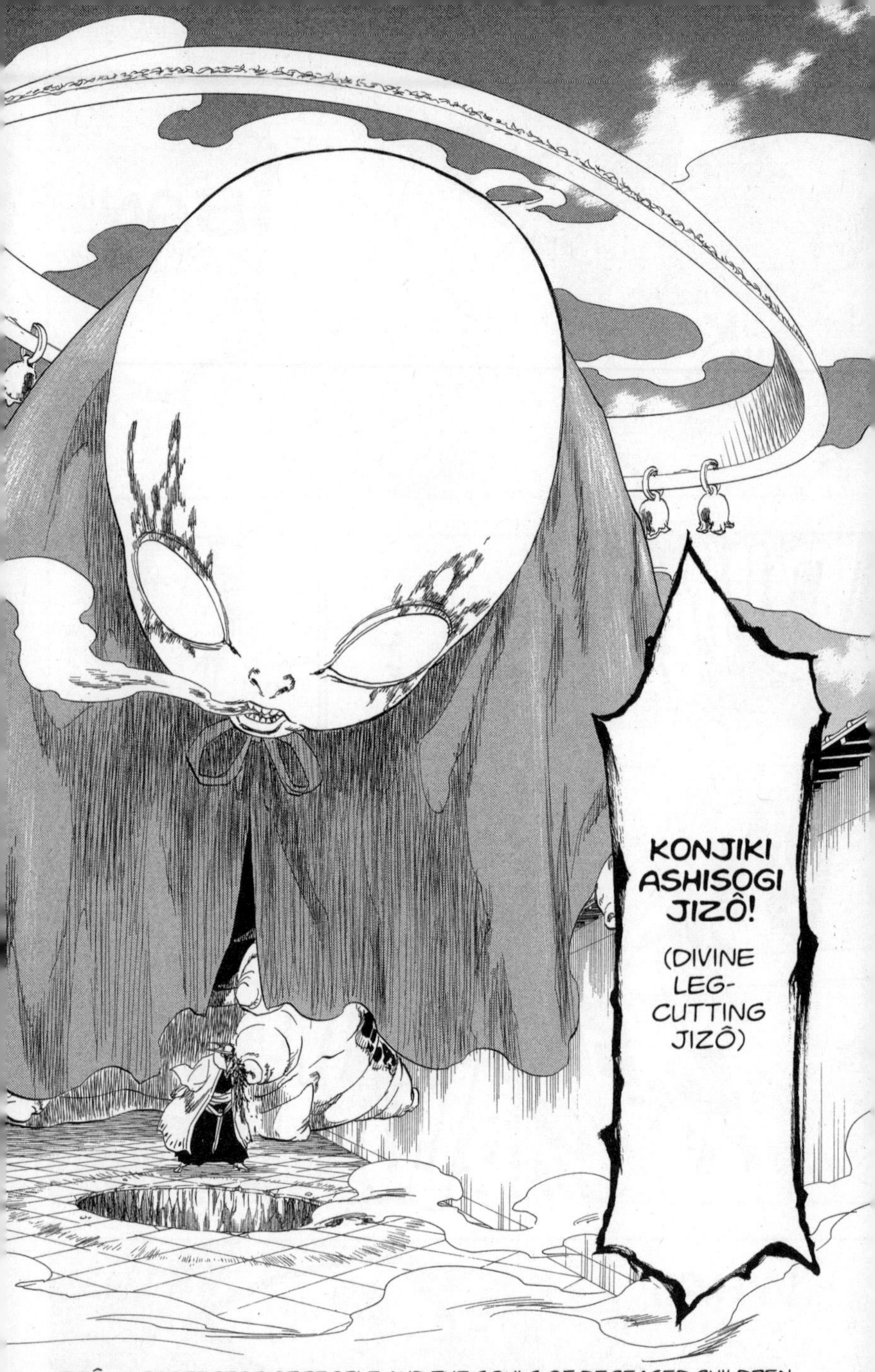
KONJIKI ASHISOGI JIZÔ!
(DIVINE LEG-CUTTING JIZÔ)

JIZÔ = A PROTECTOR OF PEOPLE AND THE SOULS OF DECEASED CHILDREN.

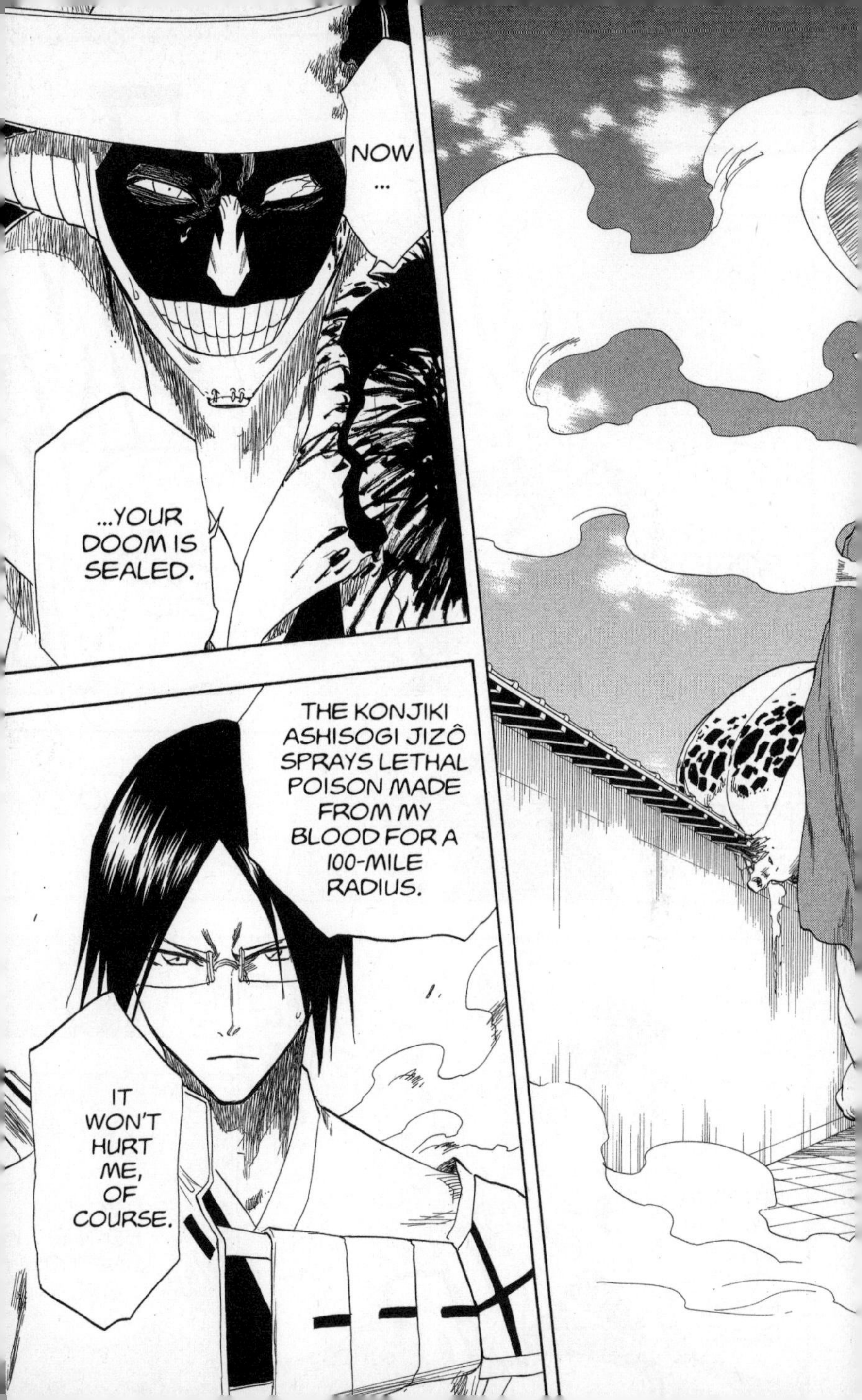
NOW ...
...YOUR DOOM IS SEALED.
THE KONJIKI ASHISOGI JIZÔ SPRAYS LETHAL POISON MADE FROM MY BLOOD FOR A 100-MILE RADIUS.
IT WON'T HURT ME, OF COURSE.

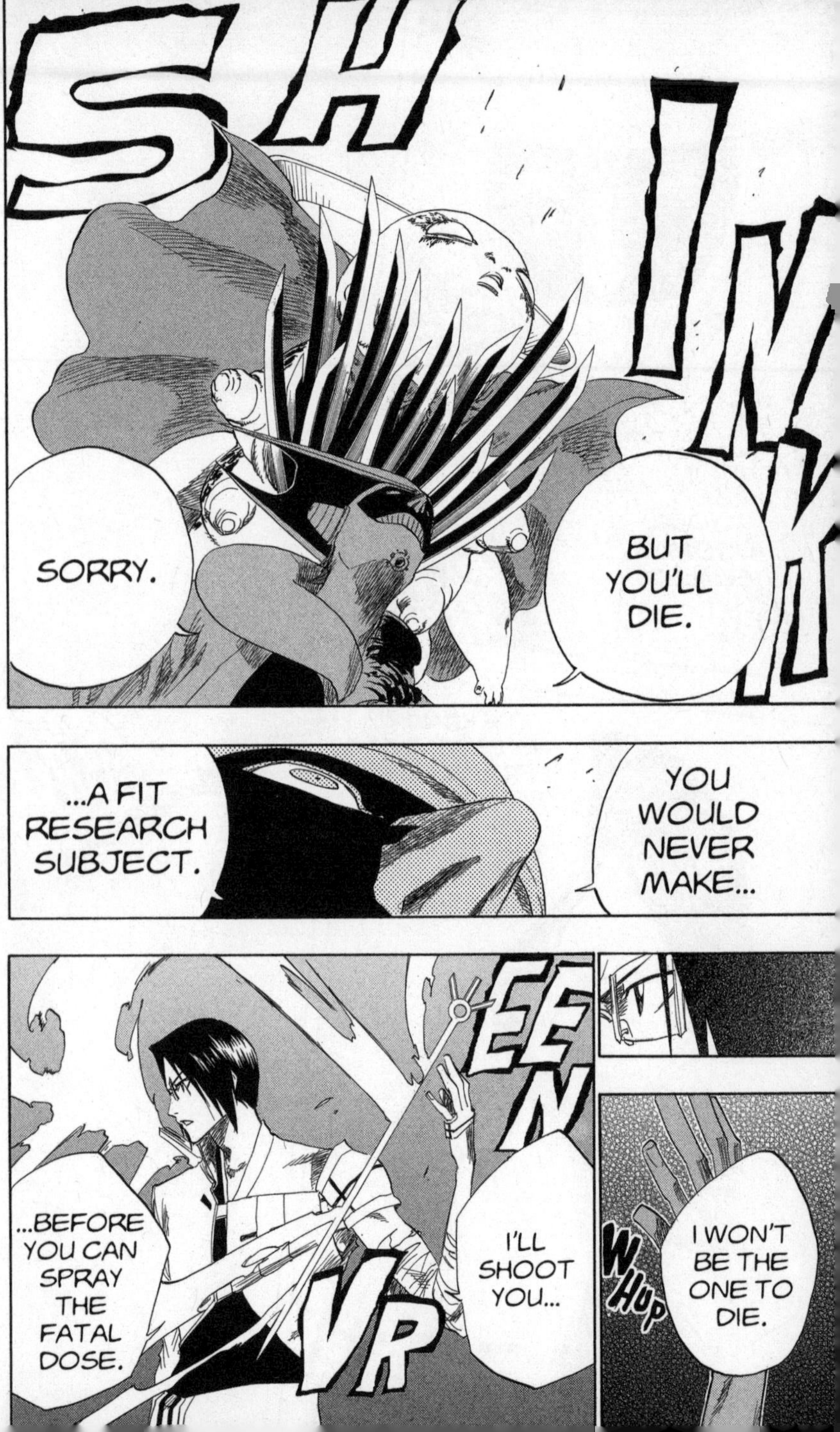
SHINK
BUT YOU'LL DIE.
SORRY.
YOU WOULD NEVER MAKE...
...A FIT RESEARCH SUBJECT.
WHUP
I WON'T BE THE ONE TO DIE.
EEN
I'LL SHOOT YOU...
...BEFORE YOU CAN SPRAY THE FATAL DOSE.
VR

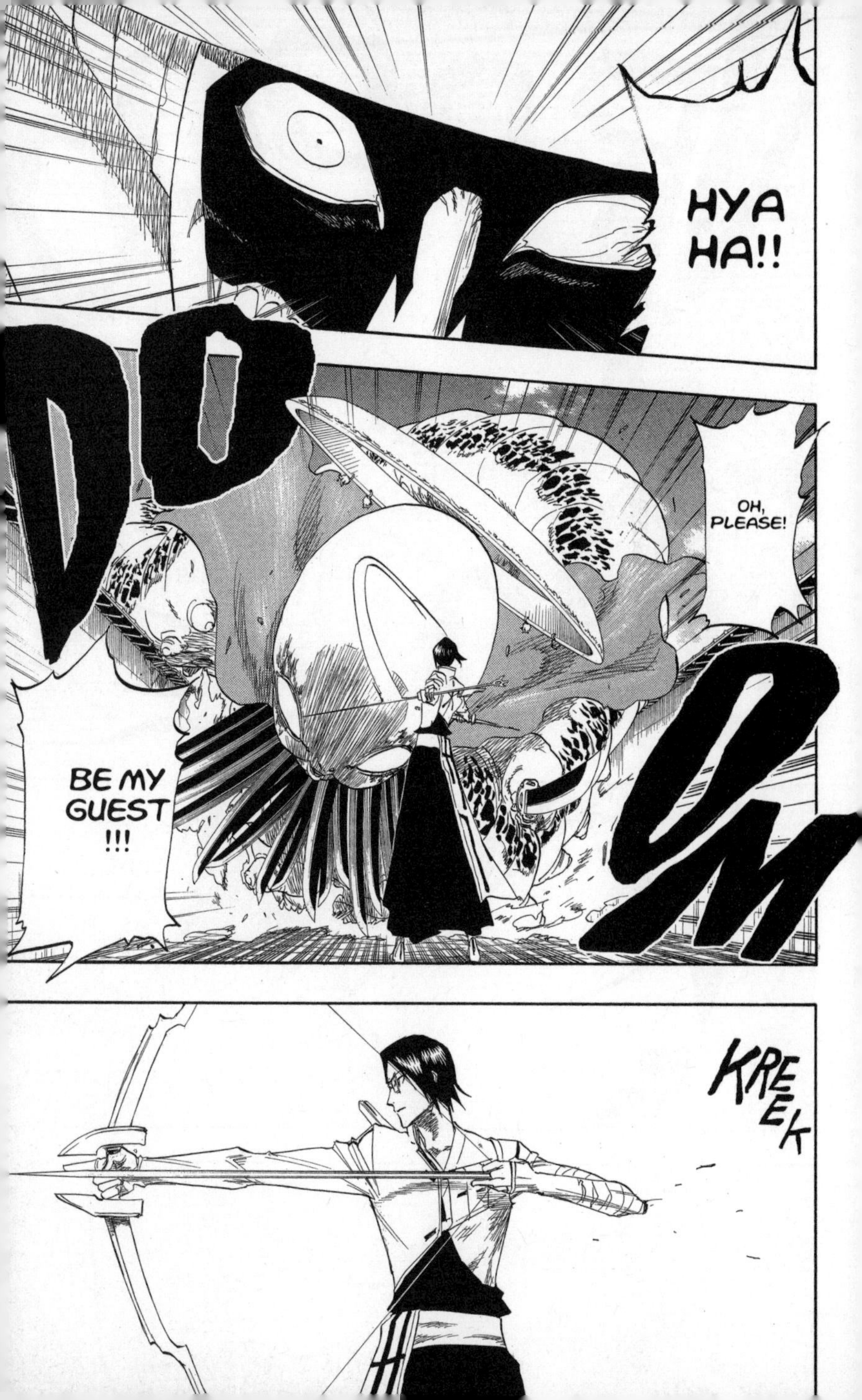
HYA HA!!
OH, PLEASE!
DOOM
BE MY GUEST!!!
KREEK

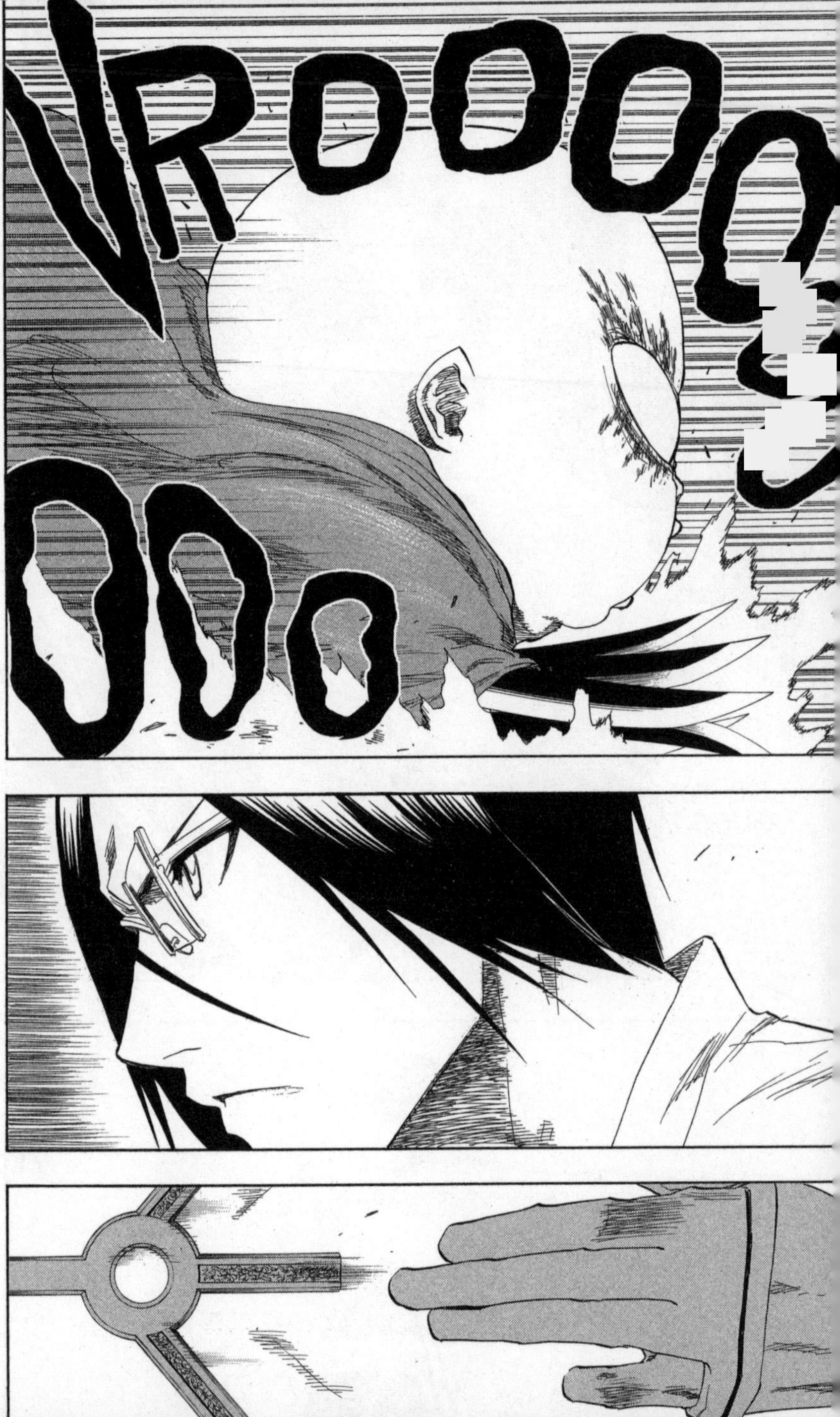
VROOOOOOOO

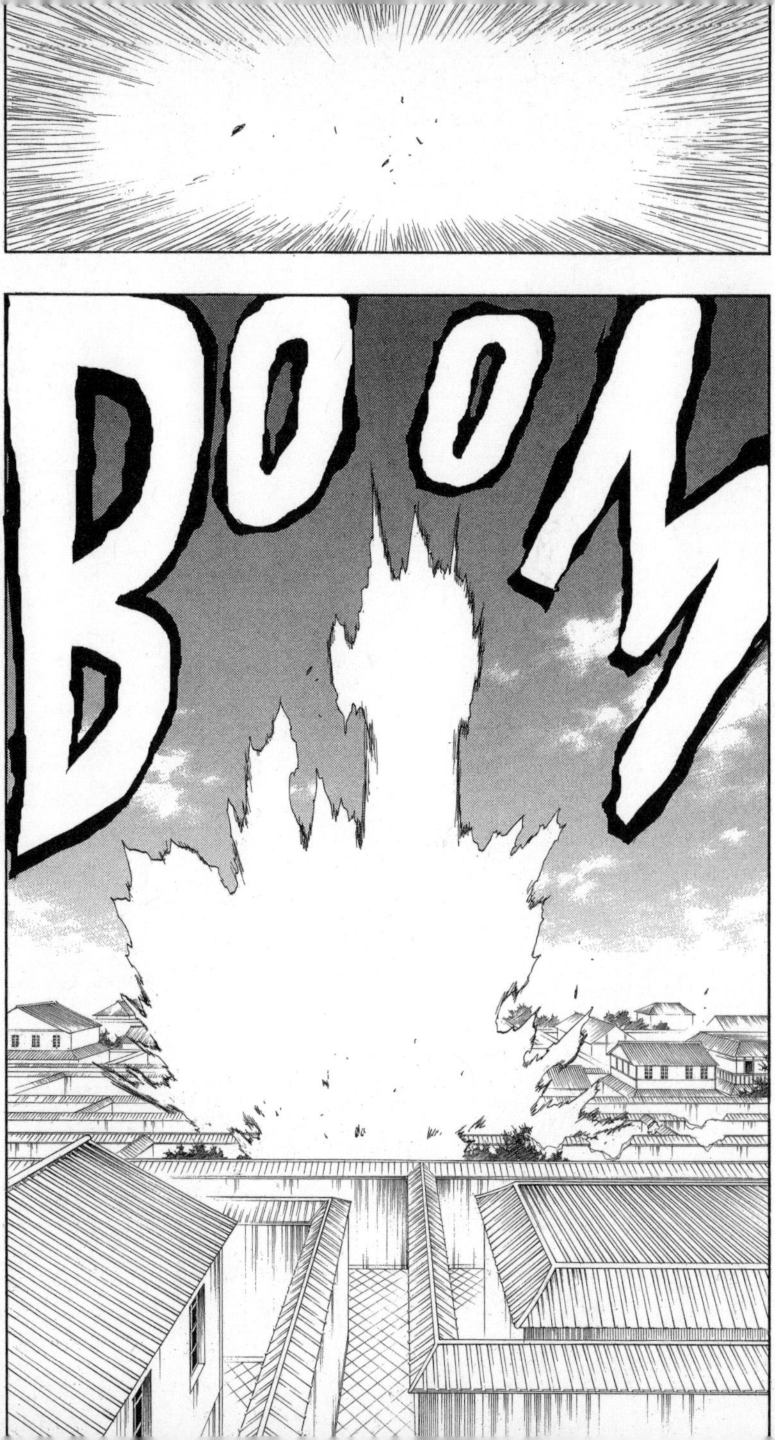
BOOM

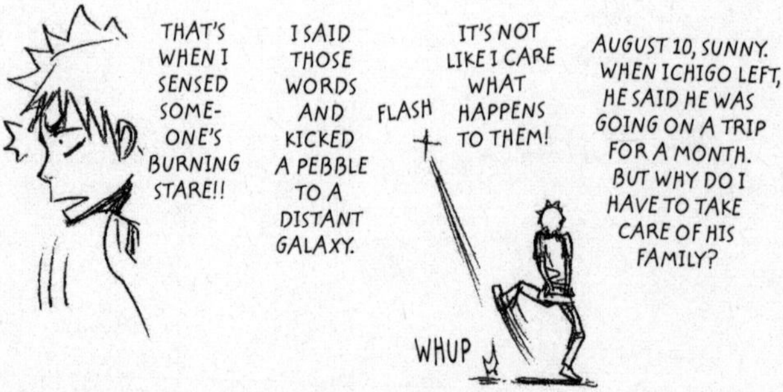

AUGUST 10, SUNNY. WHEN ICHIGO LEFT, HE SAID HE WAS GOING ON A TRIP FOR A MONTH. BUT WHY DO I HAVE TO TAKE CARE OF HIS FAMILY?
IT'S NOT LIKE I CARE WHAT HAPPENS TO THEM!
FLASH
WHUP
I SAID THOSE WORDS AND KICKED A PEBBLE TO A DISTANT GALAXY.
THAT'S WHEN I SENSED SOME-ONE'S BURNING STARE!!

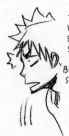

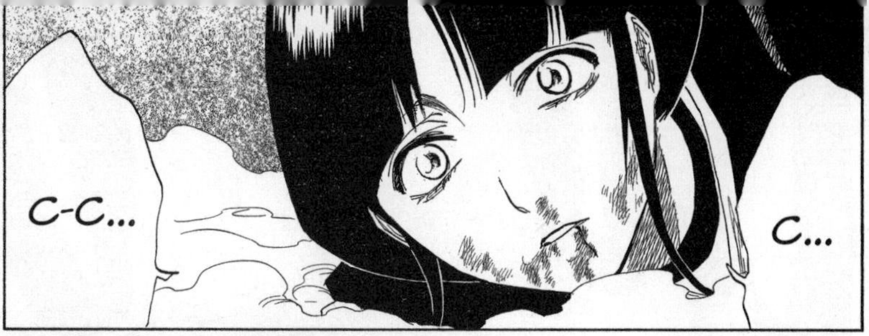
C...
C-C...

126. The Last of a Void War

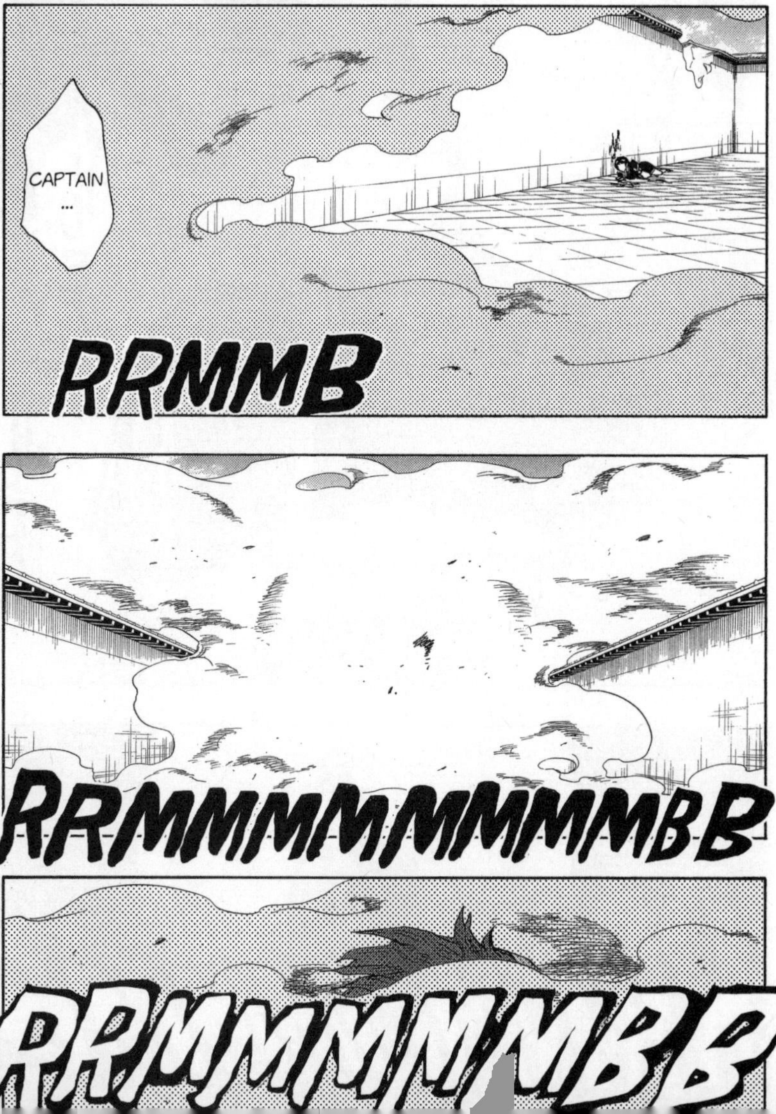
CAPTAIN ...
RRMMB
RRMMMMMMMMMBB
RRMMMMMMBB

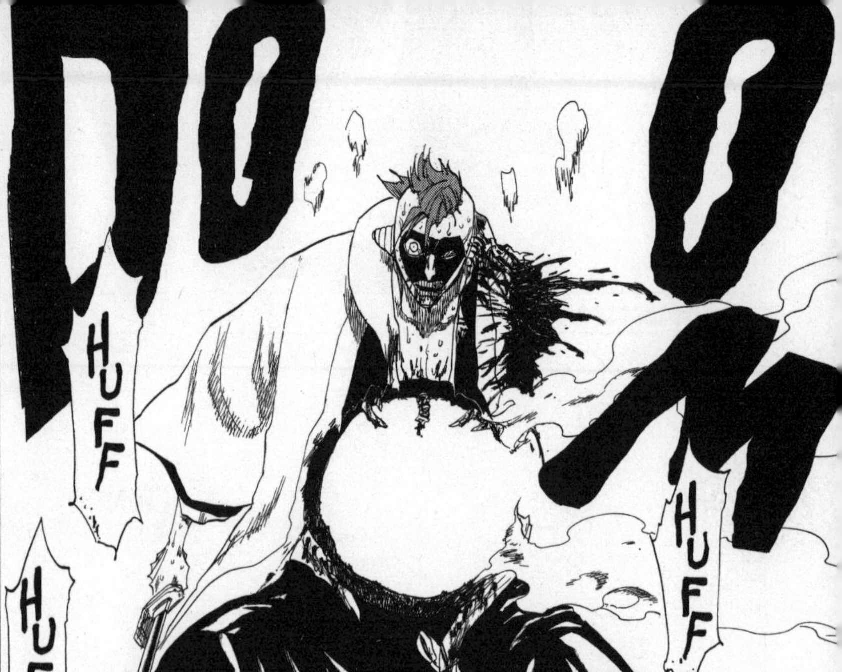
DOOM
HUFF
HUFF
HUFF
HUFF
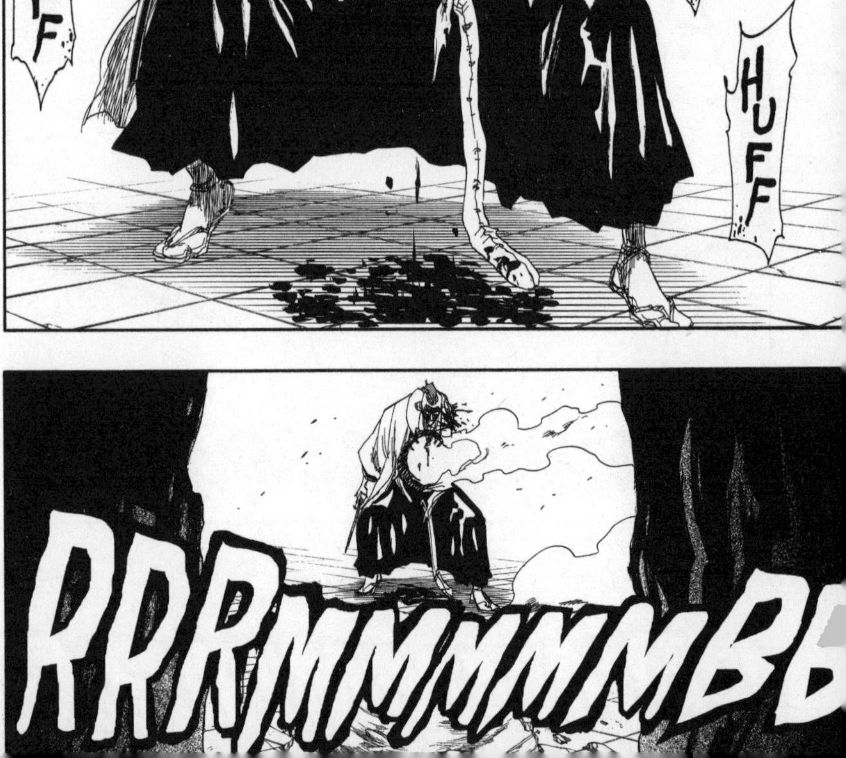
RRRMMMMMB

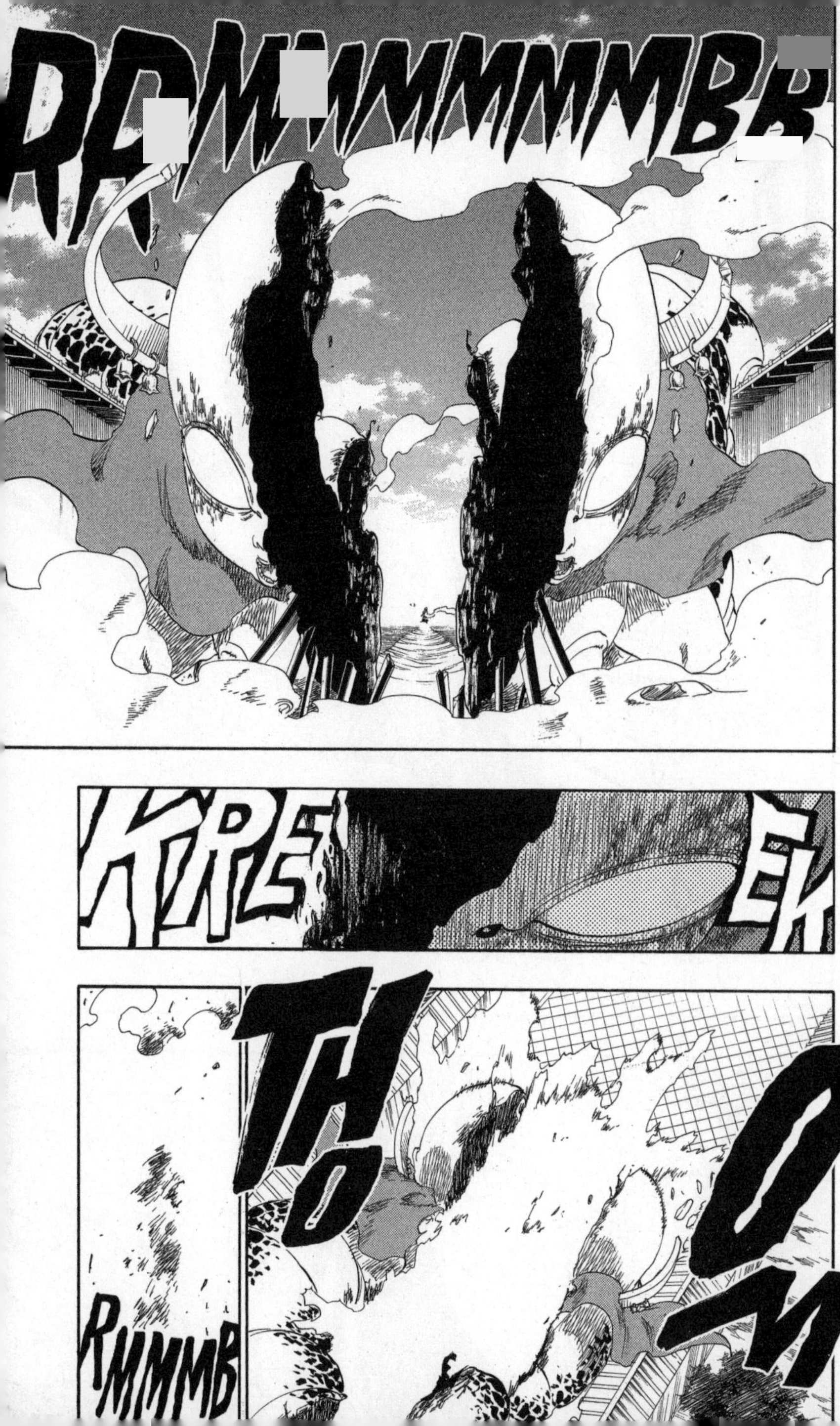
THOOM
RMMMB

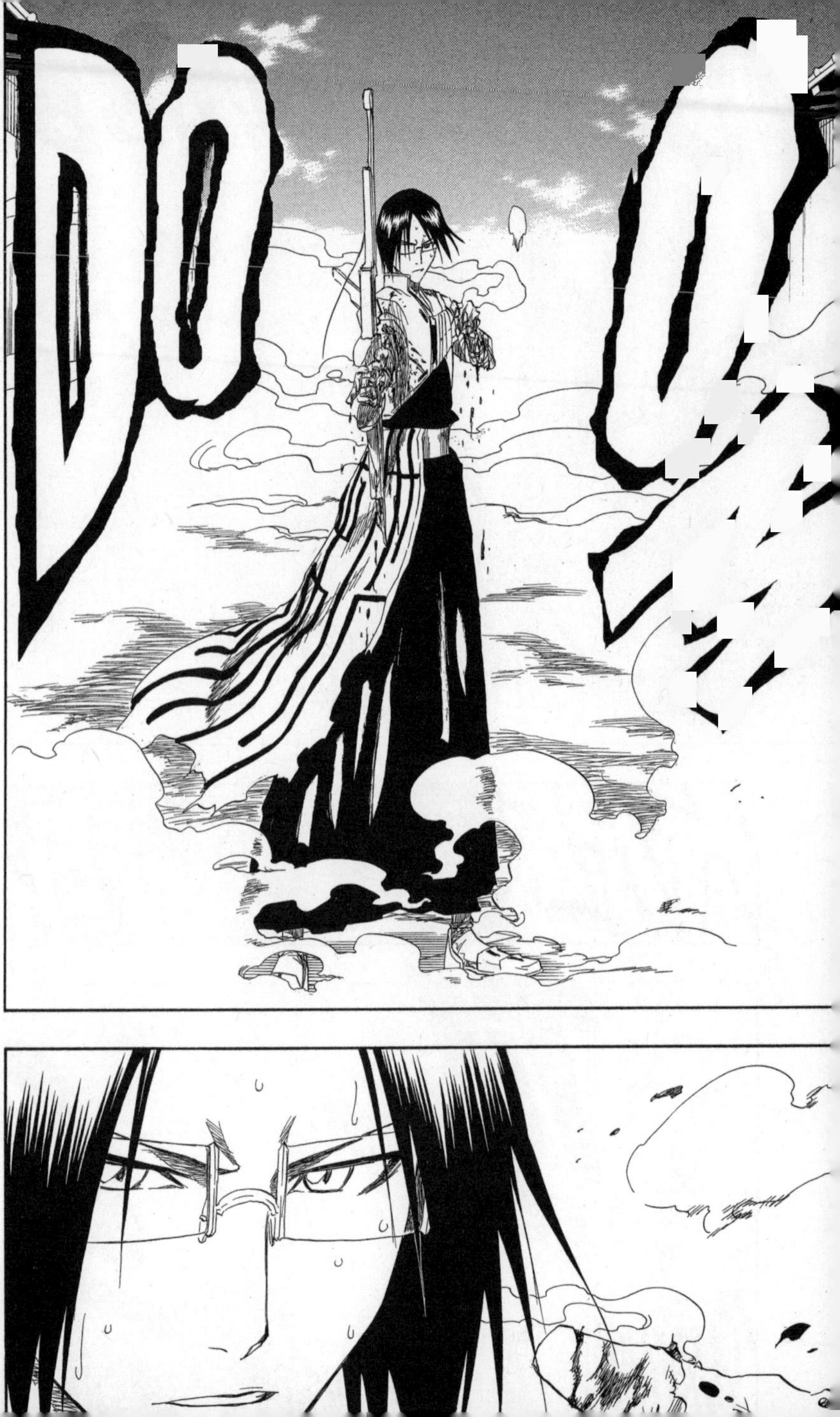
DO

READ THIS WAY

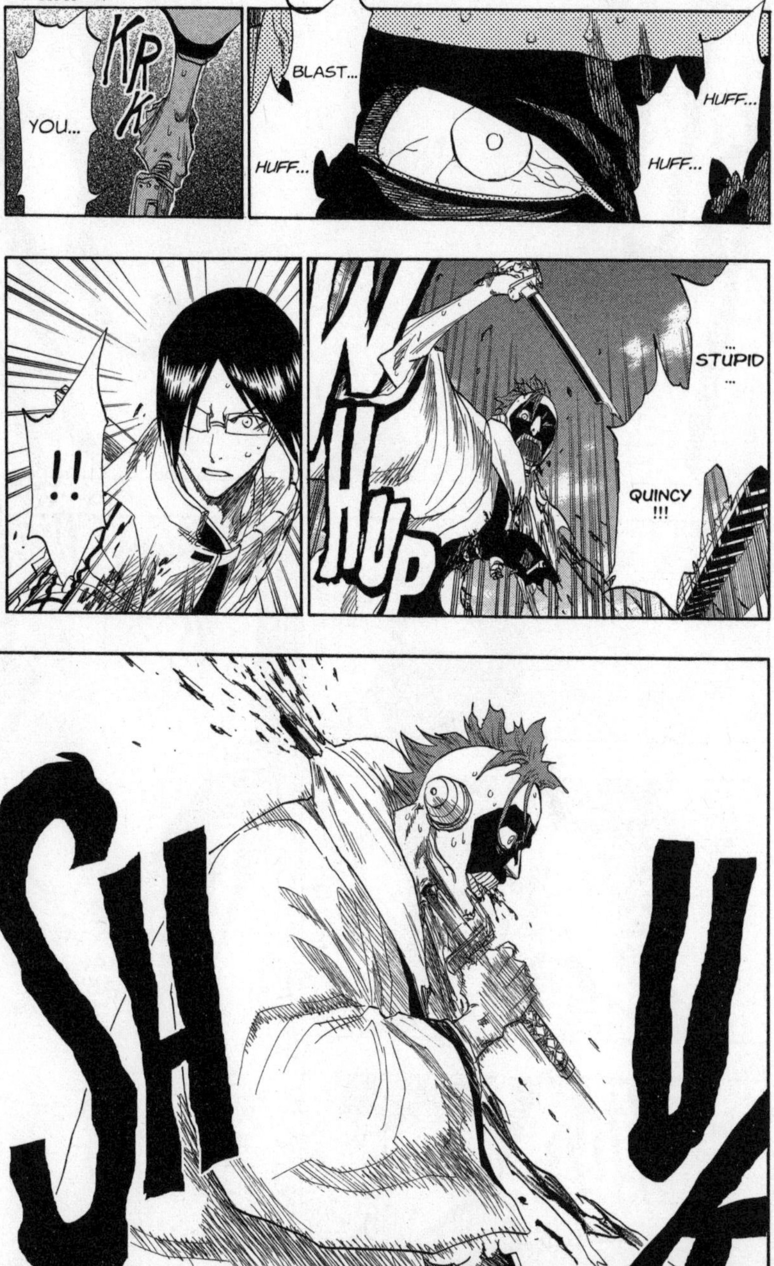
HUFF...
BLAST...
HUFF...
HUFF...
KRK
YOU...
...STUPID...
QUINCY!!!
WHUP
!!
SHUK

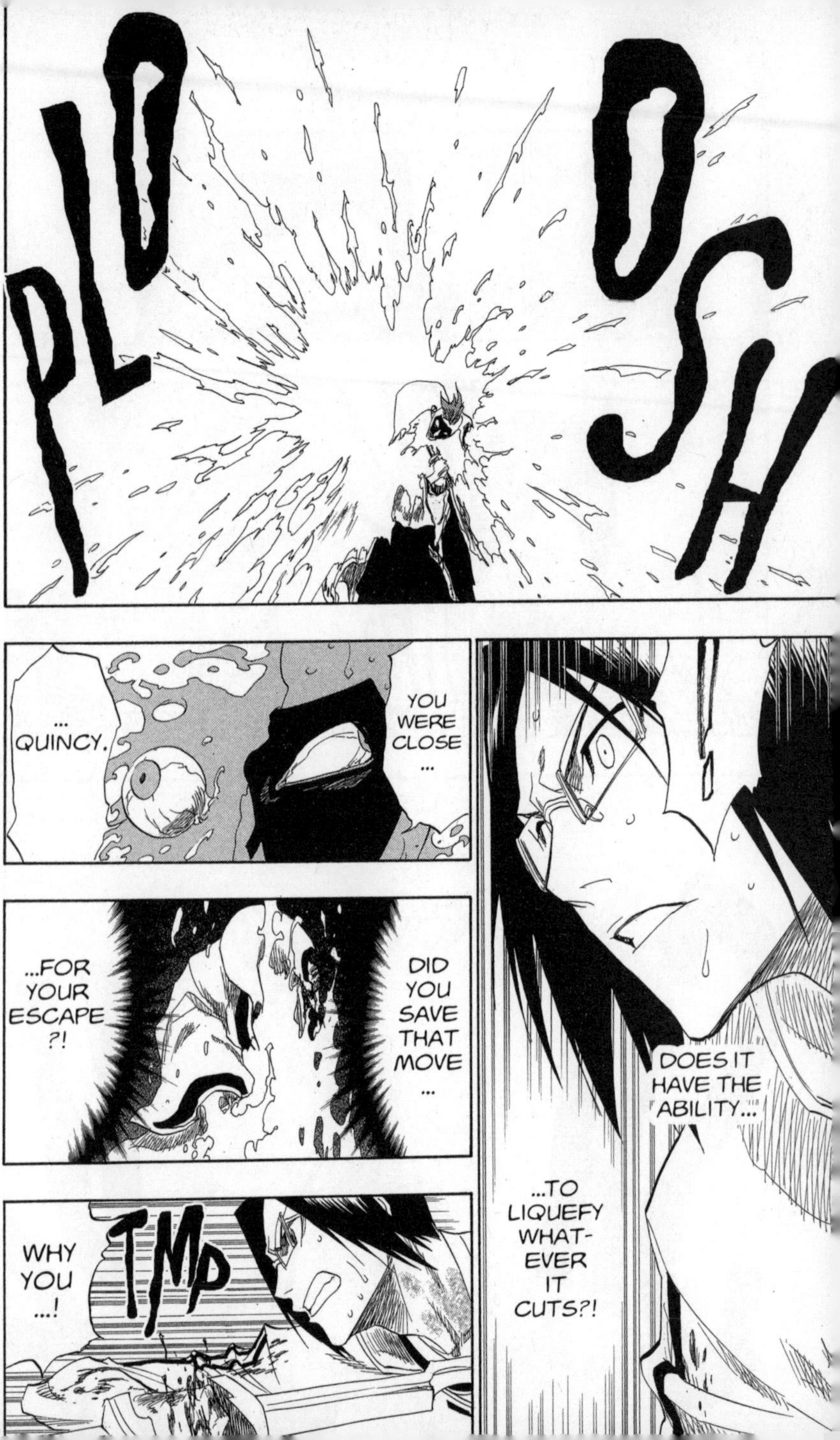
PLOOSH
DOES IT HAVE THE ABILITY...
...TO LIQUEFY WHAT-EVER IT CUTS?!
YOU WERE CLOSE ...
... QUINCY.
DID YOU SAVE THAT MOVE ...
...FOR YOUR ESCAPE ?!
TMP
WHY YOU ...!

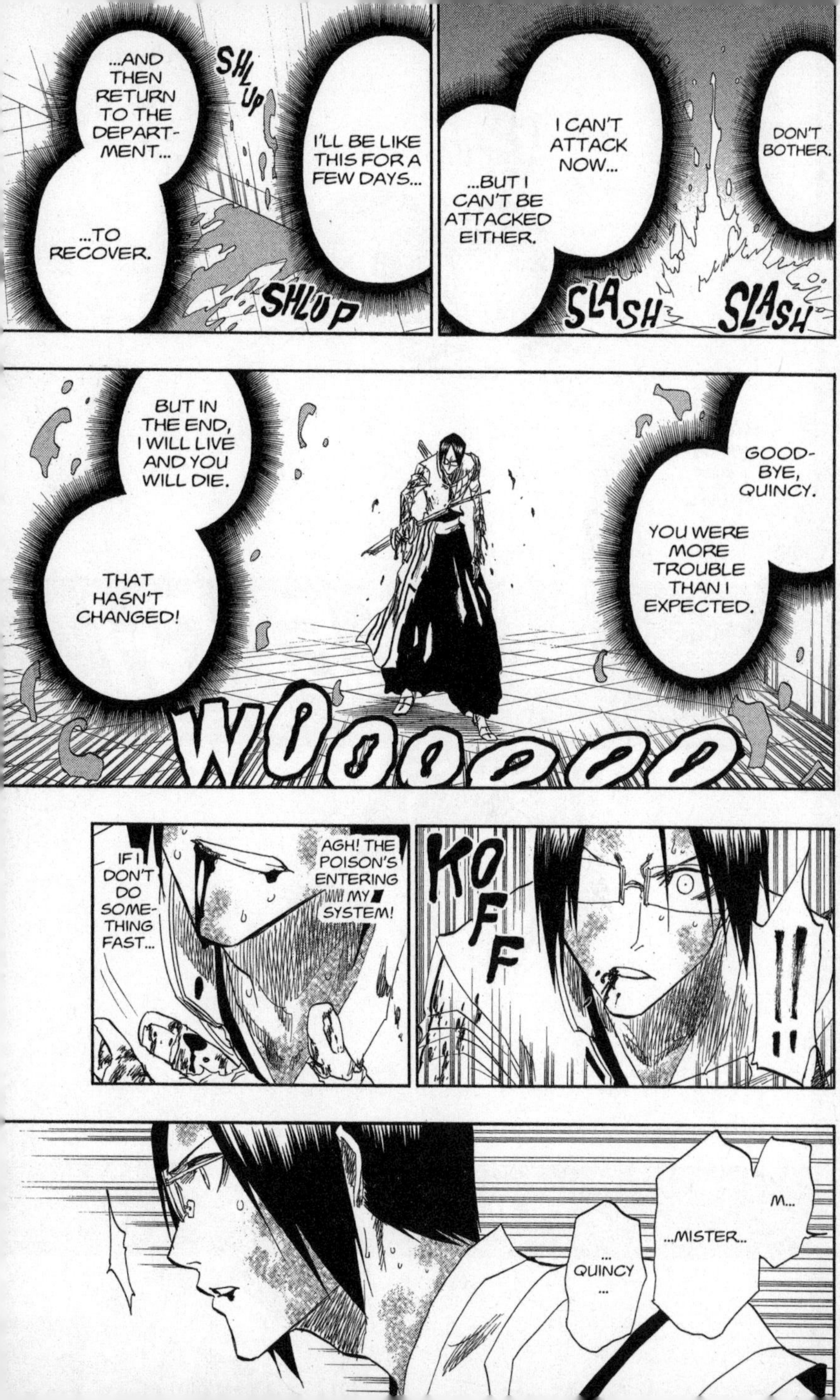
DON'T BOTHER.
I CAN'T ATTACK NOW...
...BUT I CAN'T BE ATTACKED EITHER.
SLASH
SLASH
I'LL BE LIKE THIS FOR A FEW DAYS...
SHLUP
...AND THEN RETURN TO THE DEPART-MENT...
...TO RECOVER.
SHLUP
GOOD-BYE, QUINCY.
YOU WERE MORE TROUBLE THAN I EXPECTED.
BUT IN THE END, I WILL LIVE AND YOU WILL DIE.
THAT HASN'T CHANGED!
WOOOOOOO
!!
KOFF
AGH! THE POISON'S ENTERING MY SYSTEM!
IF I DON'T DO SOME-THING FAST...
M...
...MISTER...
...QUINCY...

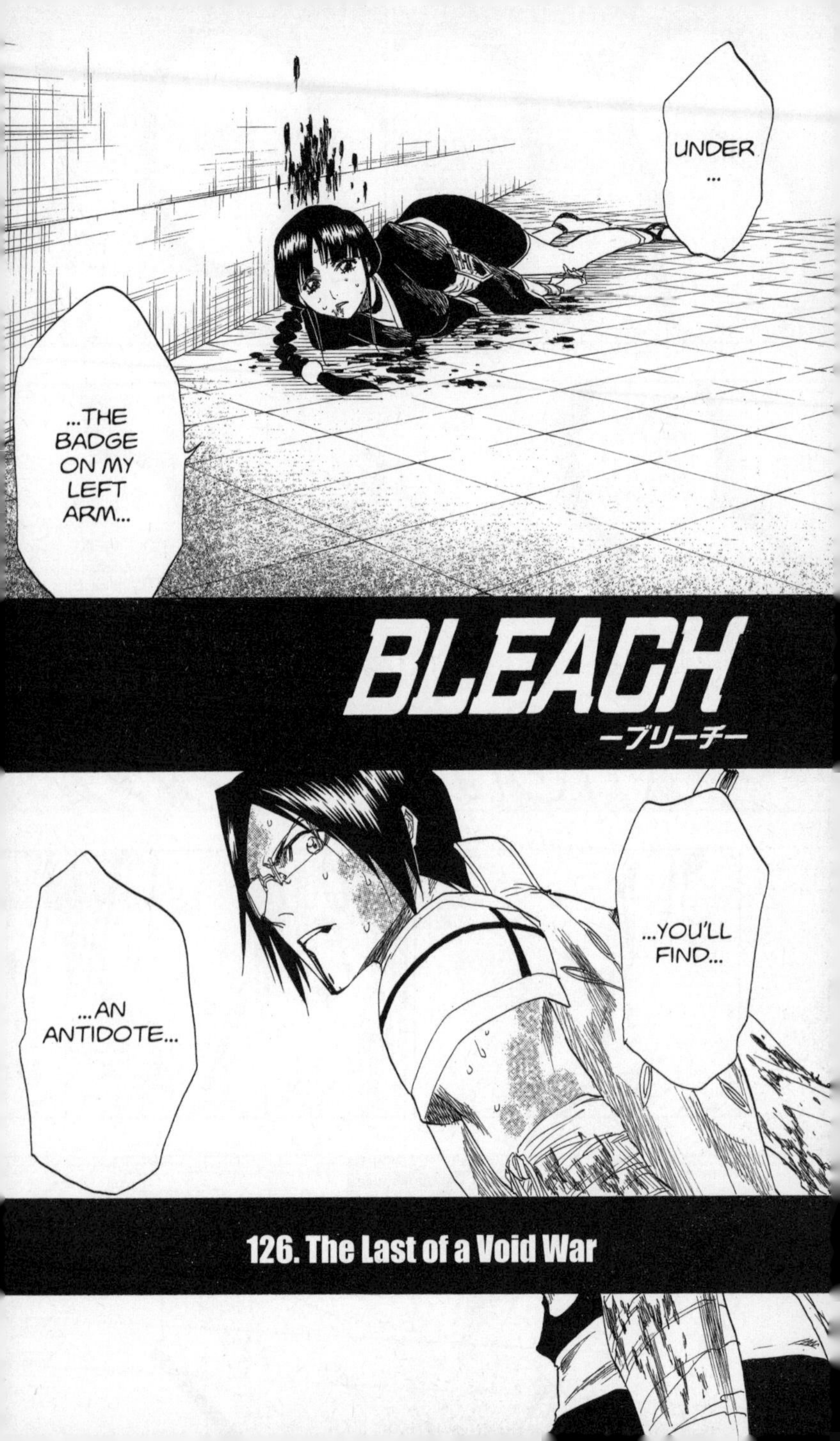
UNDER ...
...THE BADGE ON MY LEFT ARM...
BLEACH
ーブリーチー
...YOU'LL FIND...
...AN ANTIDOTE...
126. The Last of a Void War

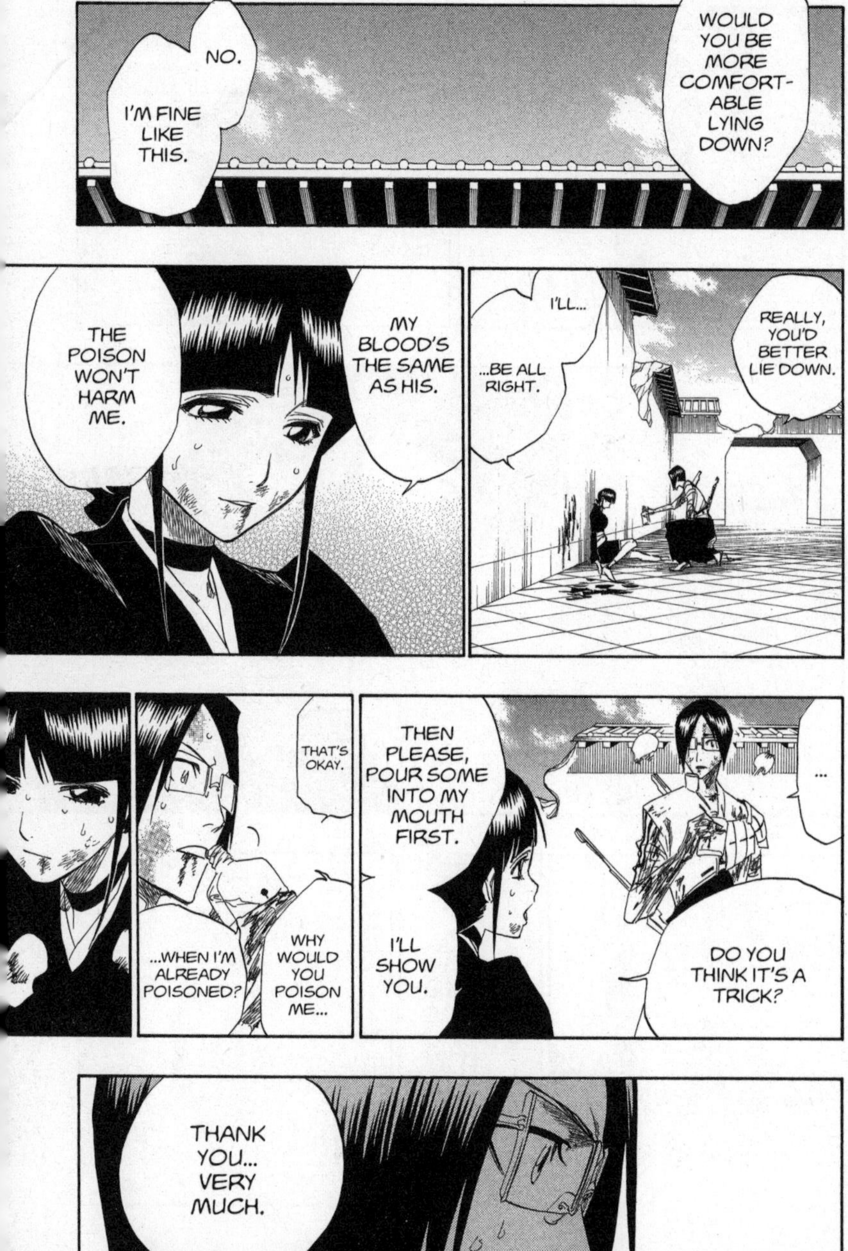
WOULD YOU BE MORE COMFORT-ABLE LYING DOWN?
NO.
I'M FINE LIKE THIS.
REALLY, YOU'D BETTER LIE DOWN.
I'LL...
...BE ALL RIGHT.
MY BLOOD'S THE SAME AS HIS.
THE POISON WON'T HARM ME.
...
DO YOU THINK IT'S A TRICK?
THEN PLEASE, POUR SOME INTO MY MOUTH FIRST.
I'LL SHOW YOU.
THAT'S OKAY.
WHY WOULD YOU POISON ME...
...WHEN I'M ALREADY POISONED?
THANK YOU... VERY MUCH.

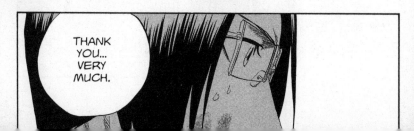

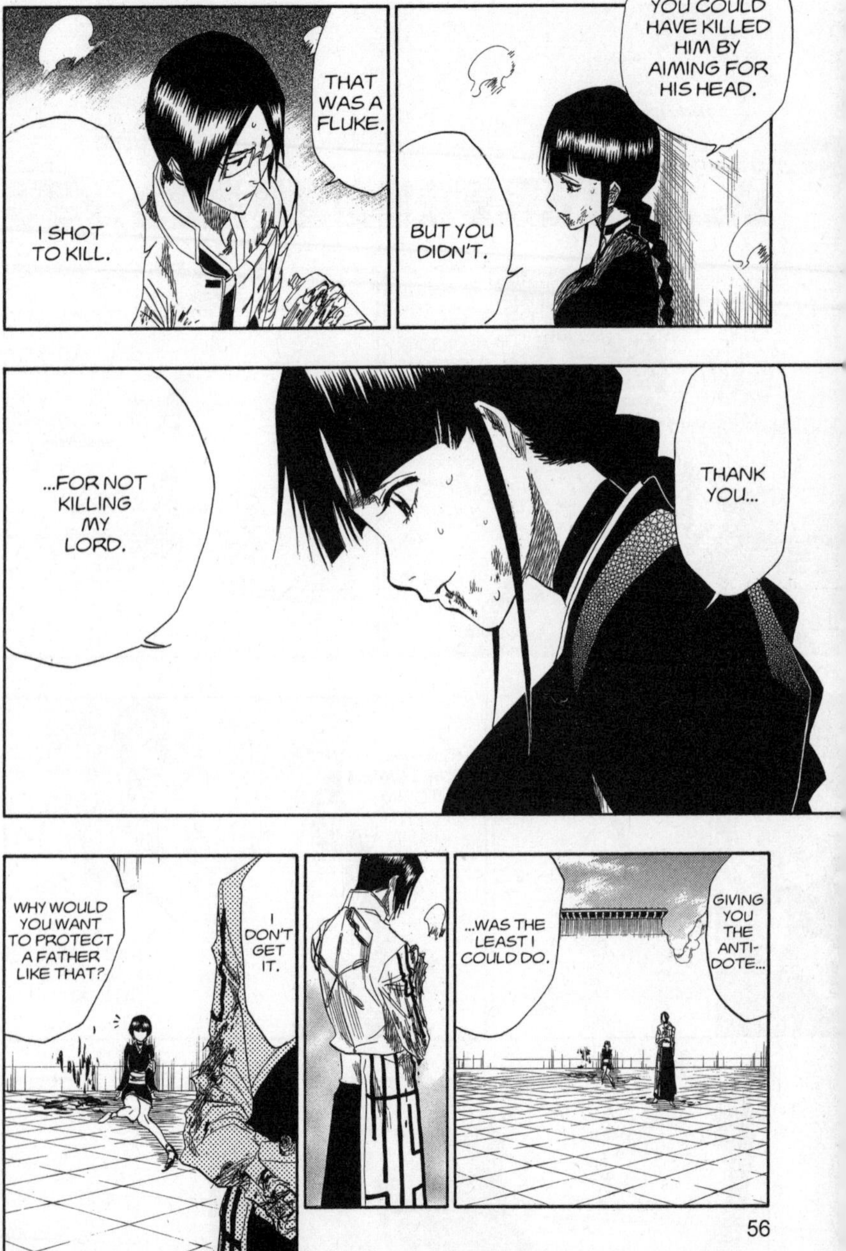
YOU COULD HAVE KILLED HIM BY AIMING FOR HIS HEAD.
BUT YOU DIDN'T.
THAT WAS A FLUKE.
I SHOT TO KILL.
THANK YOU...
...FOR NOT KILLING MY LORD.
GIVING YOU THE ANTI-DOTE...
...WAS THE LEAST I COULD DO.
I DON'T GET IT.
WHY WOULD YOU WANT TO PROTECT A FATHER LIKE THAT?

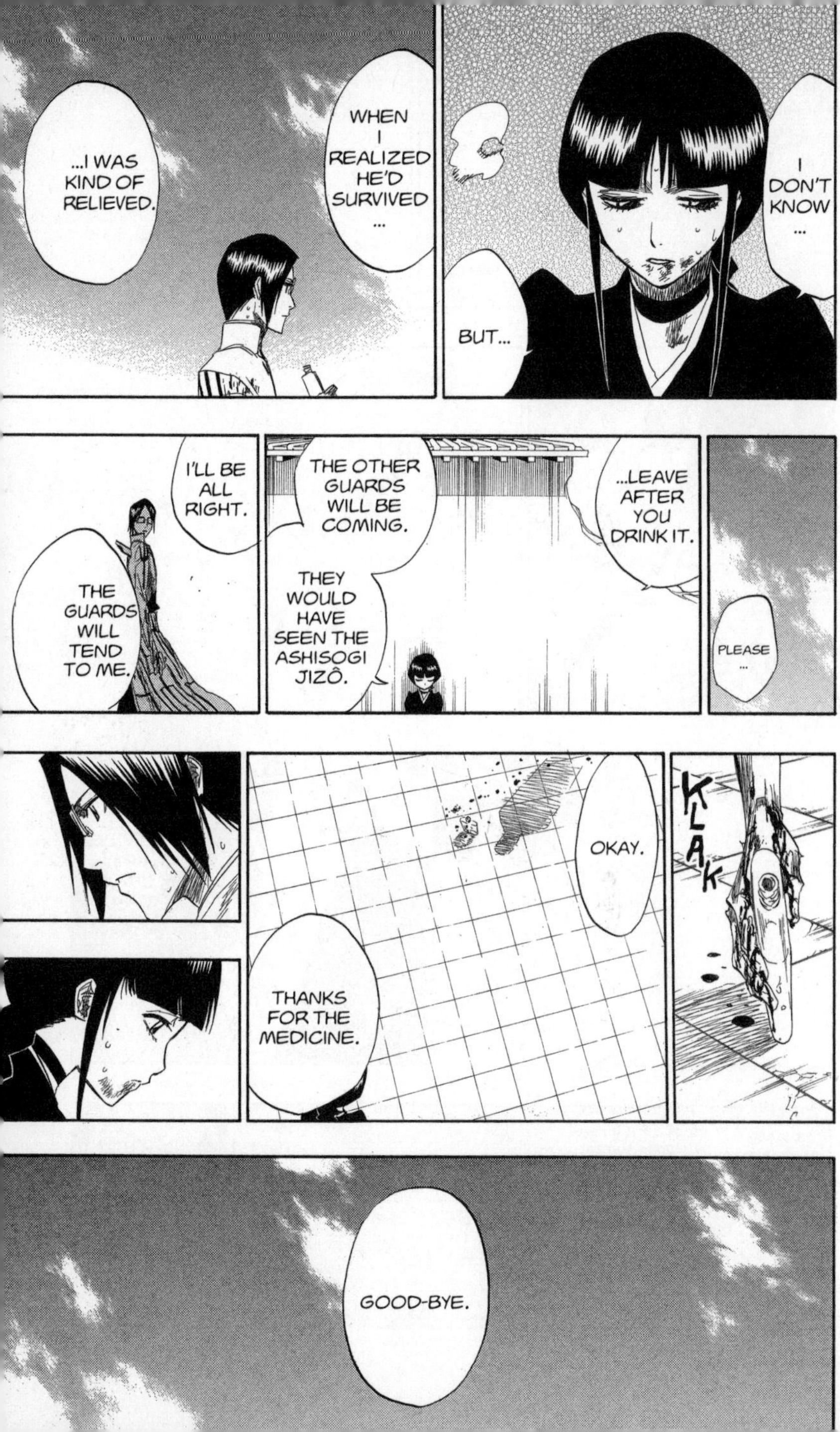
I DON'T KNOW ...
BUT...
WHEN I REALIZED HE'D SURVIVED ...
...I WAS KIND OF RELIEVED.
PLEASE ...
...LEAVE AFTER YOU DRINK IT.
THE OTHER GUARDS WILL BE COMING.
THEY WOULD HAVE SEEN THE ASHISOGI JIZÔ.
I'LL BE ALL RIGHT.
THE GUARDS WILL TEND TO ME.
KLAK
OKAY.
THANKS FOR THE MEDICINE.
GOOD-BYE.

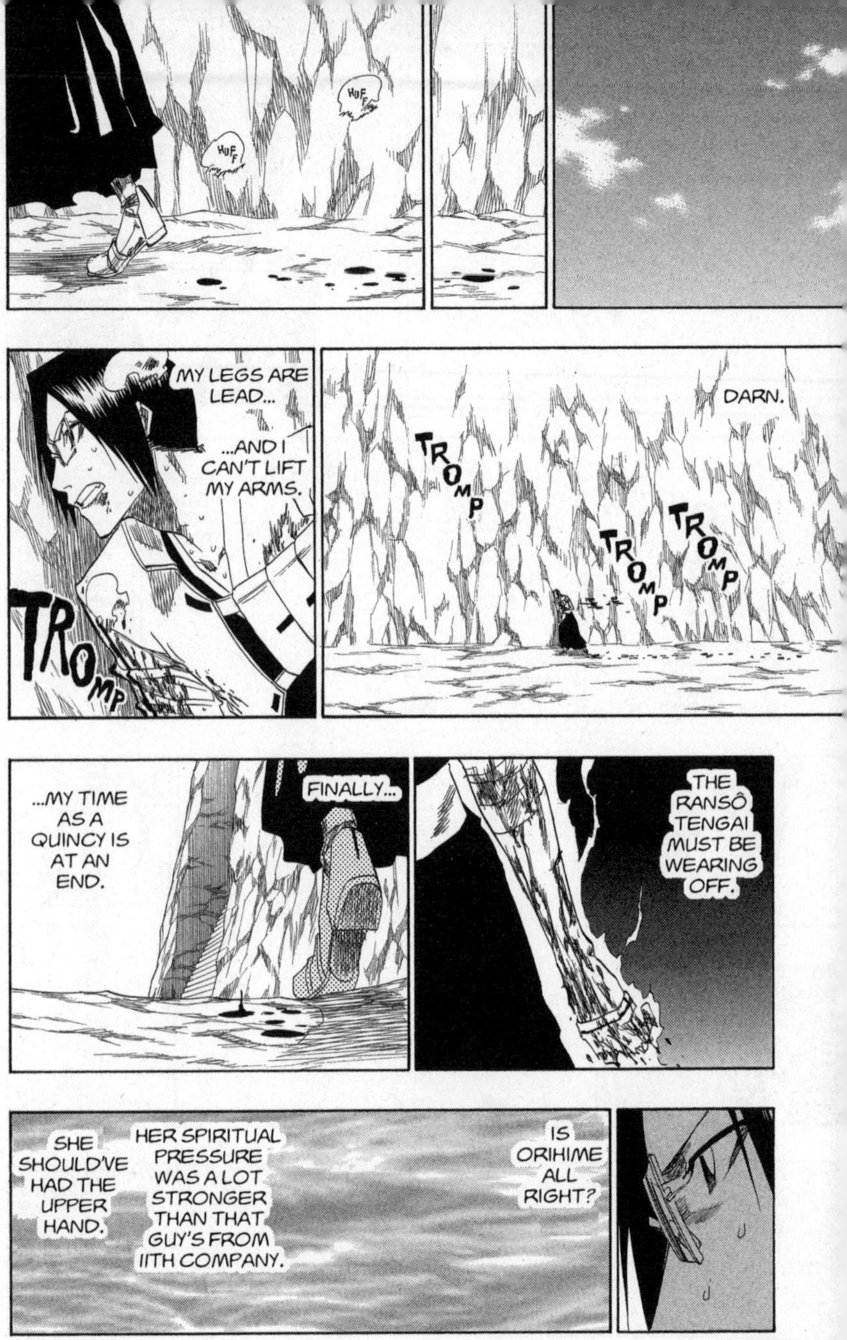
HUFF
HUFF
DARN.
TROMP
TROMP
TROMP
MY LEGS ARE LEAD...
...AND I CAN'T LIFT MY ARMS.
TROMP
THE RANSÔ TENGAI MUST BE WEARING OFF.
FINALLY...
...MY TIME AS A QUINCY IS AT AN END.
IS ORIHIME ALL RIGHT?
HER SPIRITUAL PRESSURE WAS A LOT STRONGER THAN THAT GUY'S FROM 11TH COMPANY.
SHE SHOULD'VE HAD THE UPPER HAND.

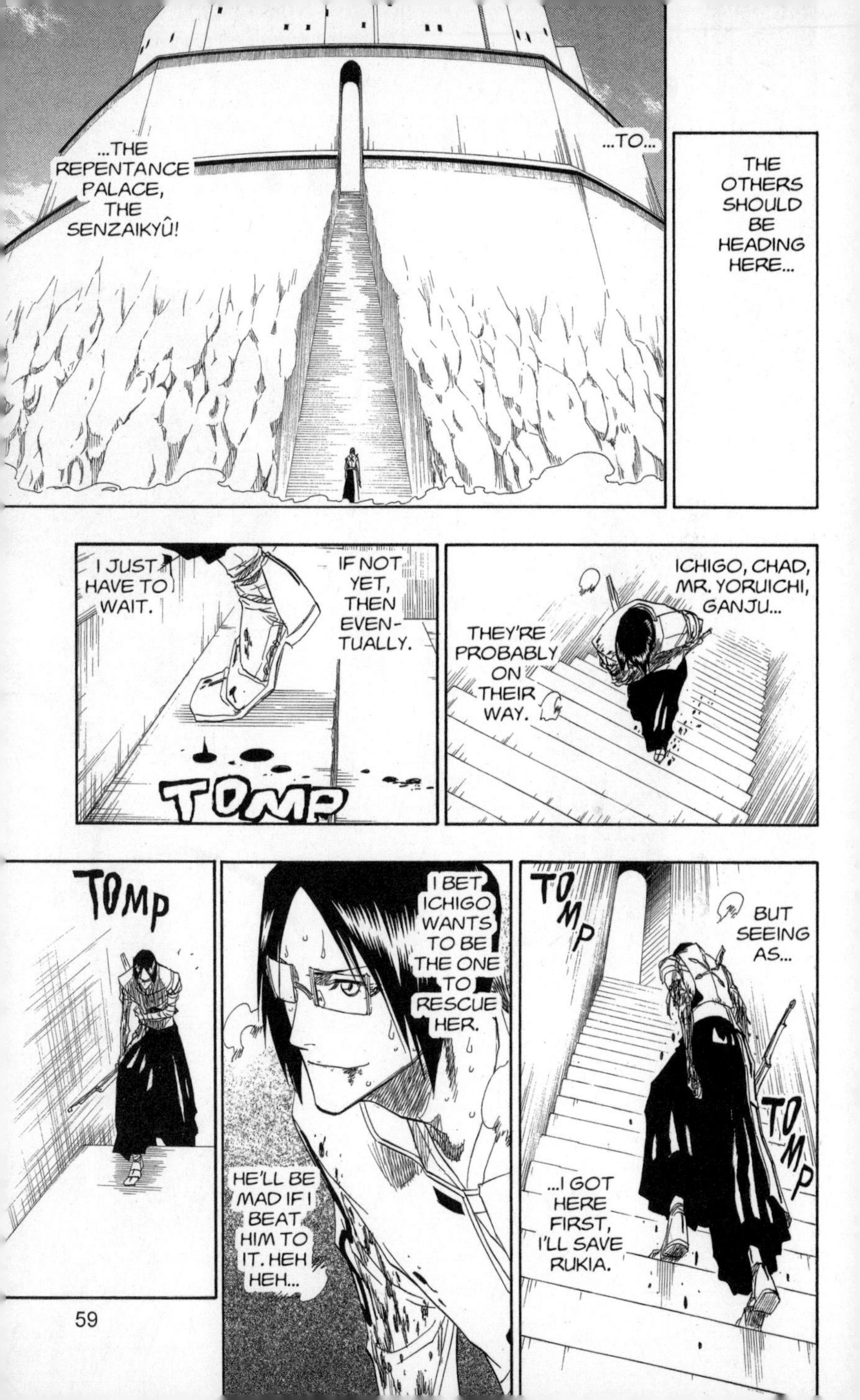
THE OTHERS SHOULD BE HEADING HERE...
...TO...
...THE REPENTANCE PALACE, THE SENZAIKYÛ!
ICHIGO, CHAD, MR. YORUICHI, GANJU...
THEY'RE PROBABLY ON THEIR WAY.
IF NOT YET, THEN EVENTUALLY.
I JUST HAVE TO WAIT.
TOMP
TOMP
BUT SEEING AS...
TOMP
...I GOT HERE FIRST, I'LL SAVE RUKIA.
I BET ICHIGO WANTS TO BE THE ONE TO RESCUE HER.
HE'LL BE MAD IF I BEAT HIM TO IT. HEH HEH...
TOMP

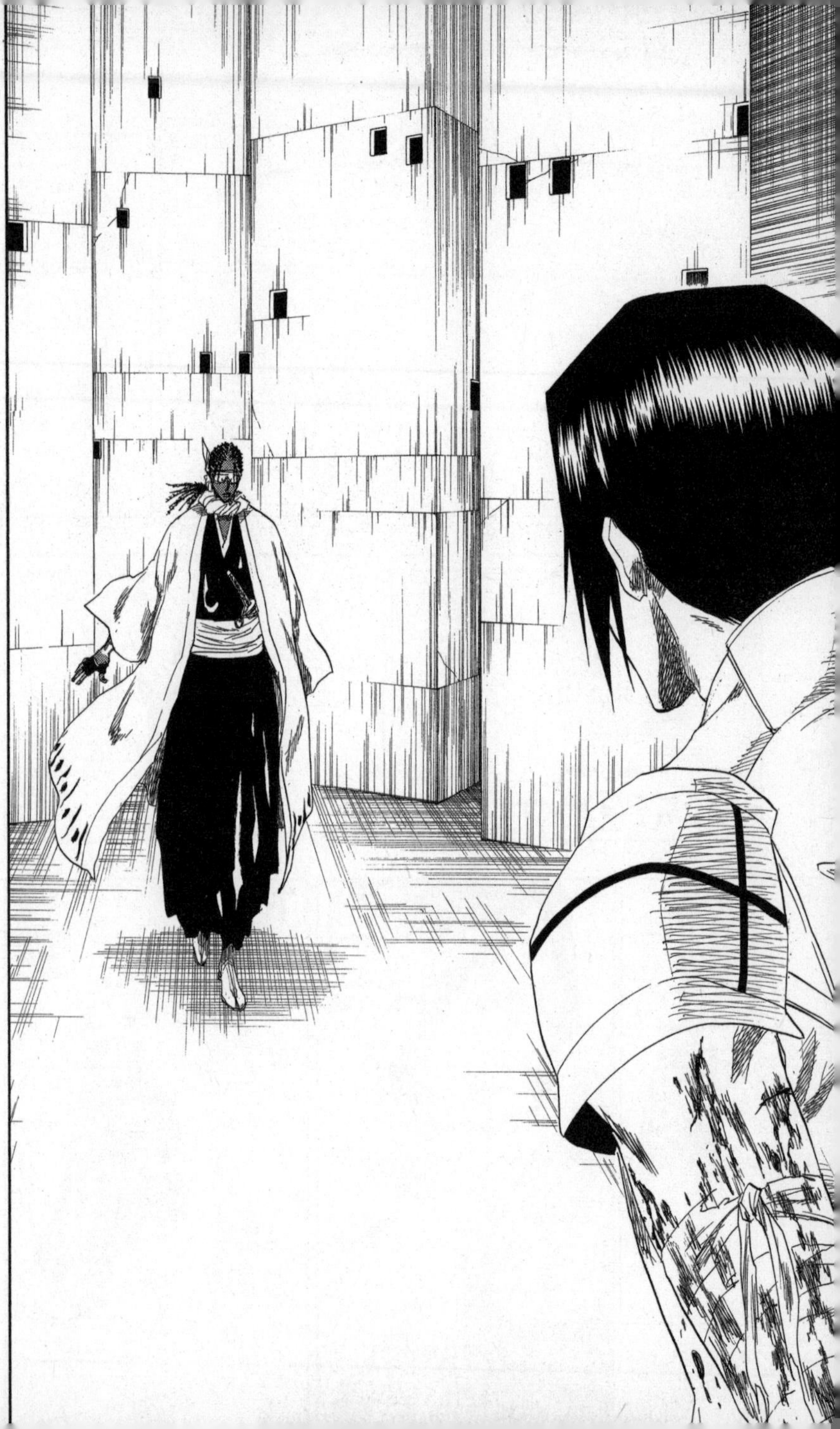

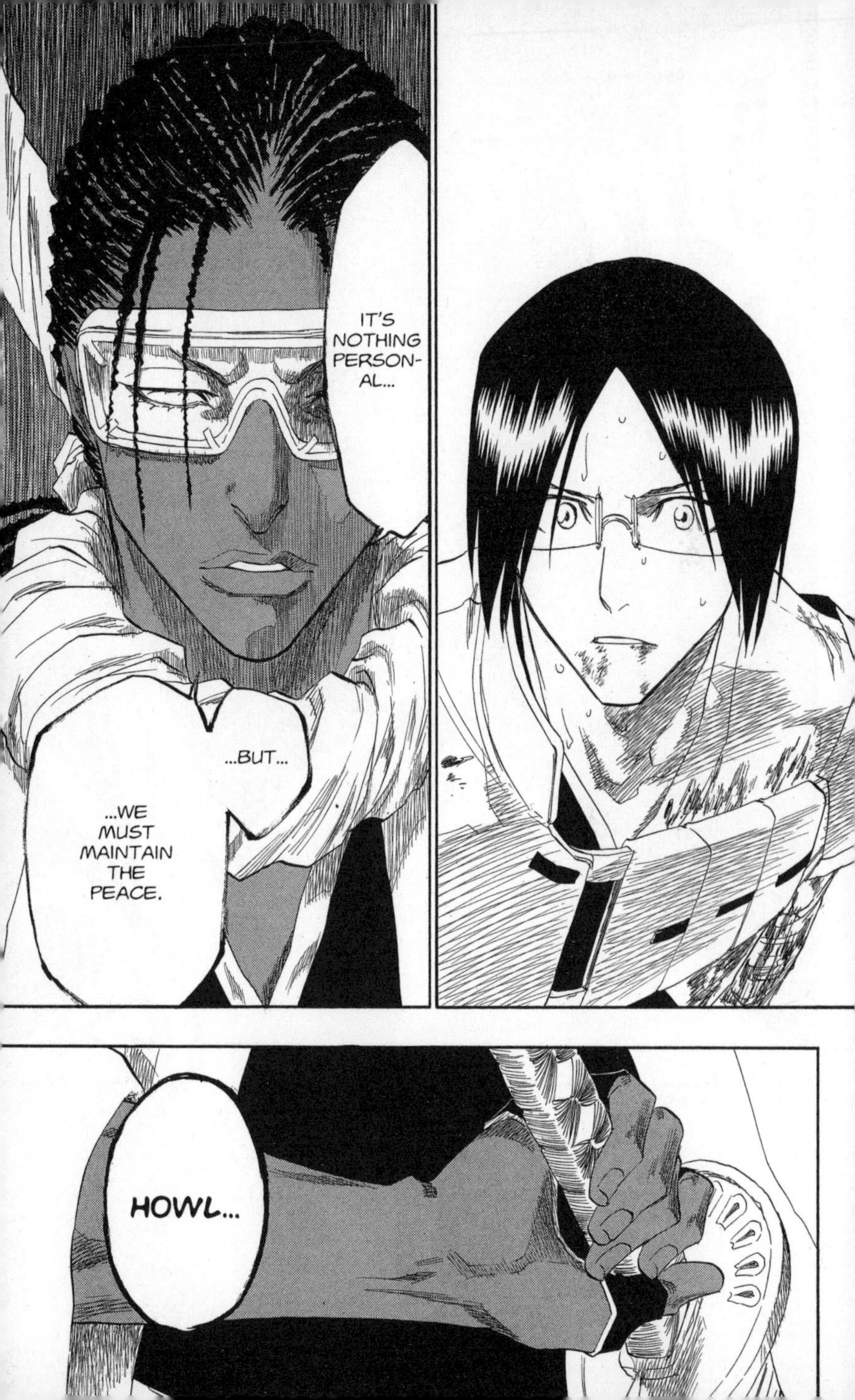
IT'S NOTHING PERSON-AL...
...BUT...
...WE MUST MAINTAIN THE PEACE.
HOWL...

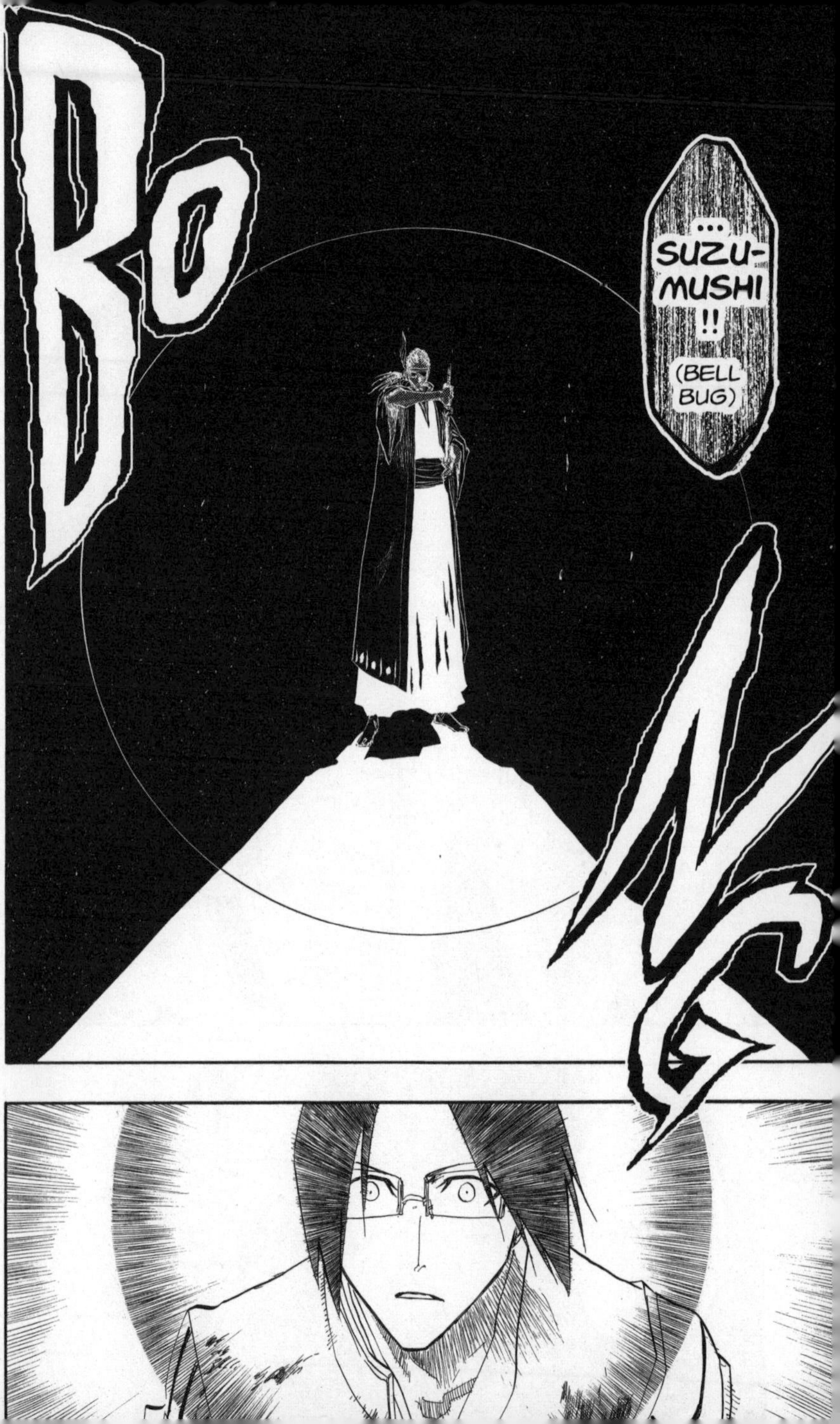
BOOO
...SUZU-MUSHI!!
(BELL BUG)
NG

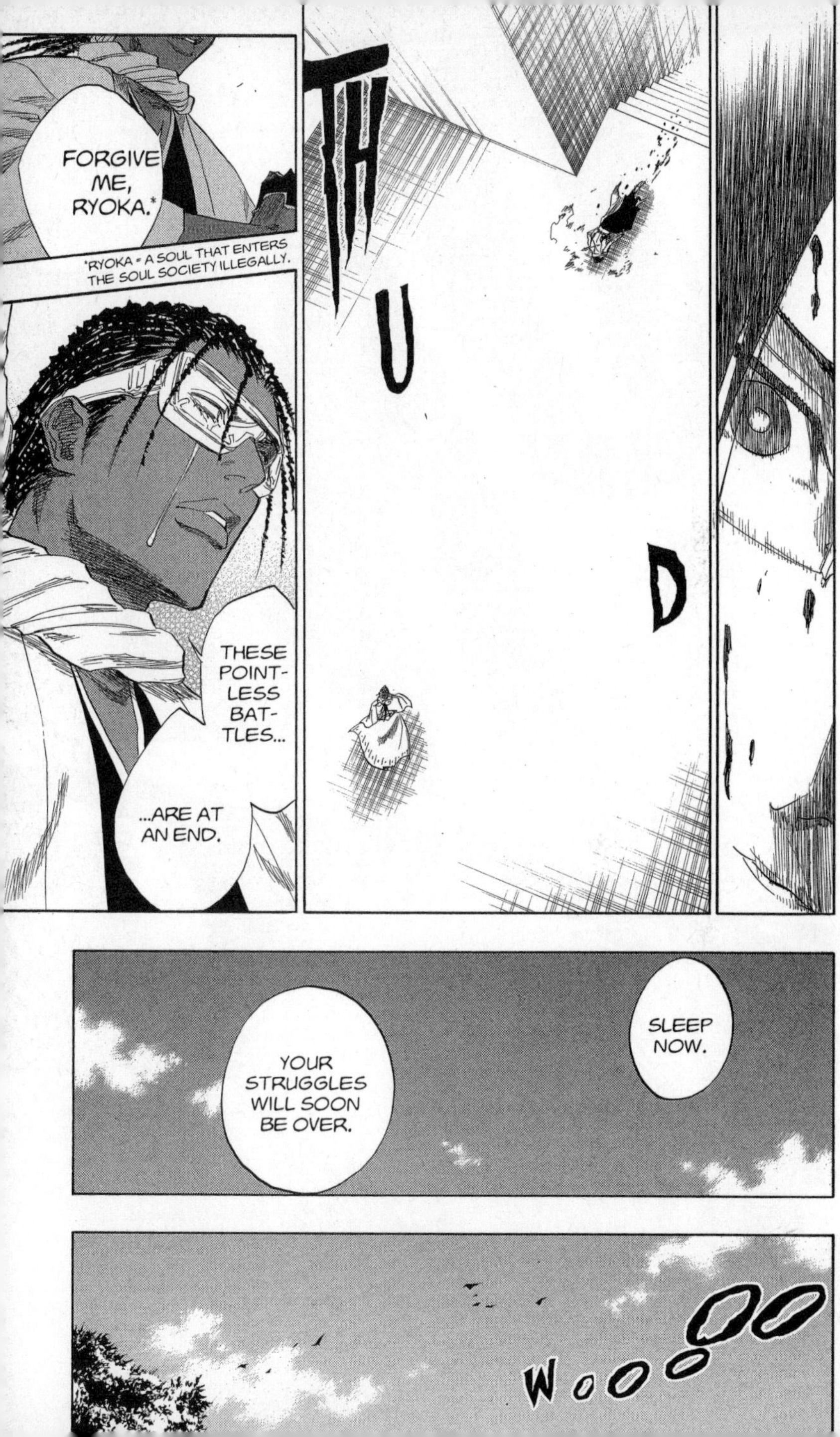
THUD
FORGIVE ME, RYOKA.*
*RYOKA = A SOUL THAT ENTERS THE SOUL SOCIETY ILLEGALLY.
THESE POINTLESS BATTLES...
...ARE AT AN END.
SLEEP NOW.
YOUR STRUGGLES WILL SOON BE OVER.
WOOOOO

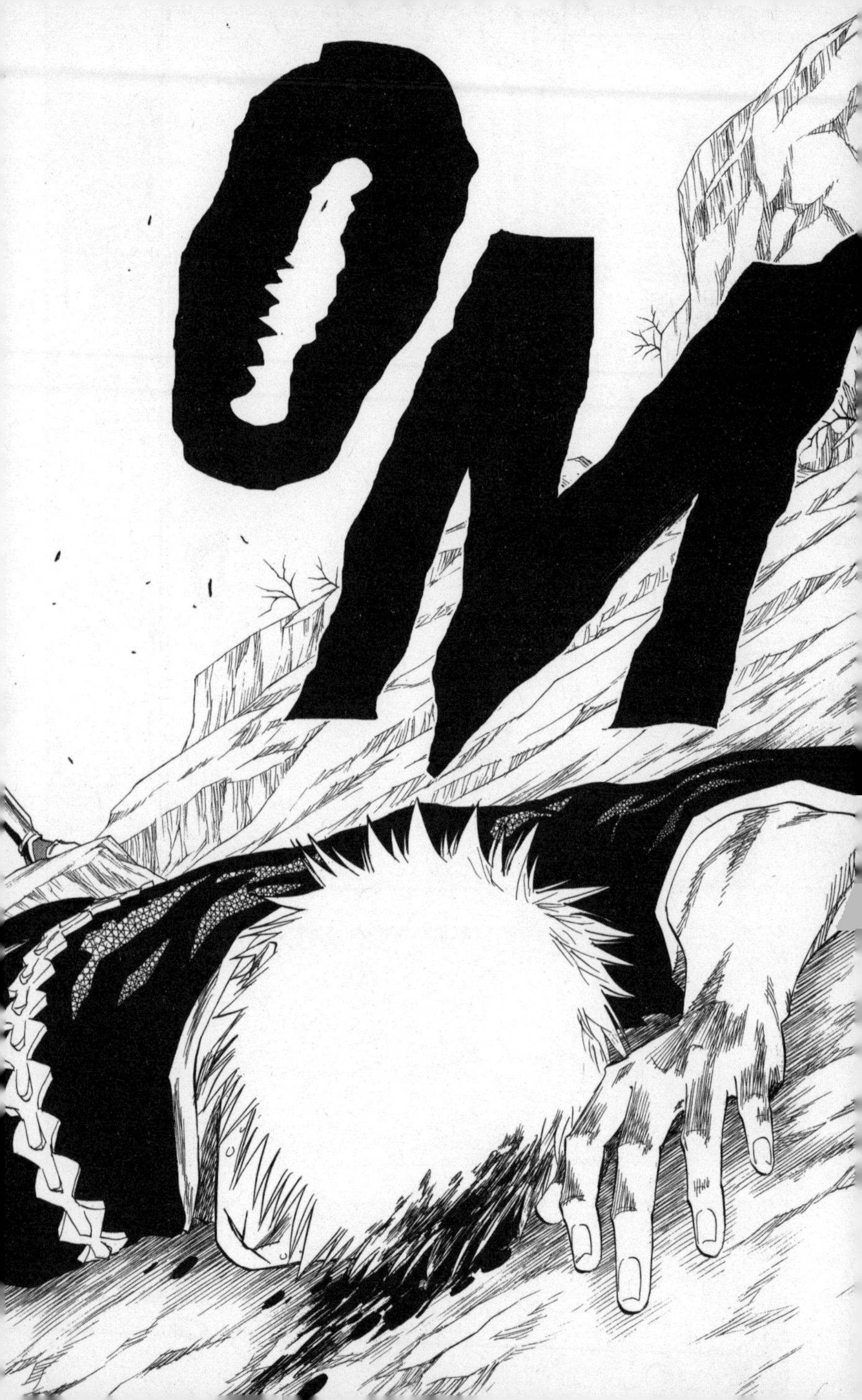
OM

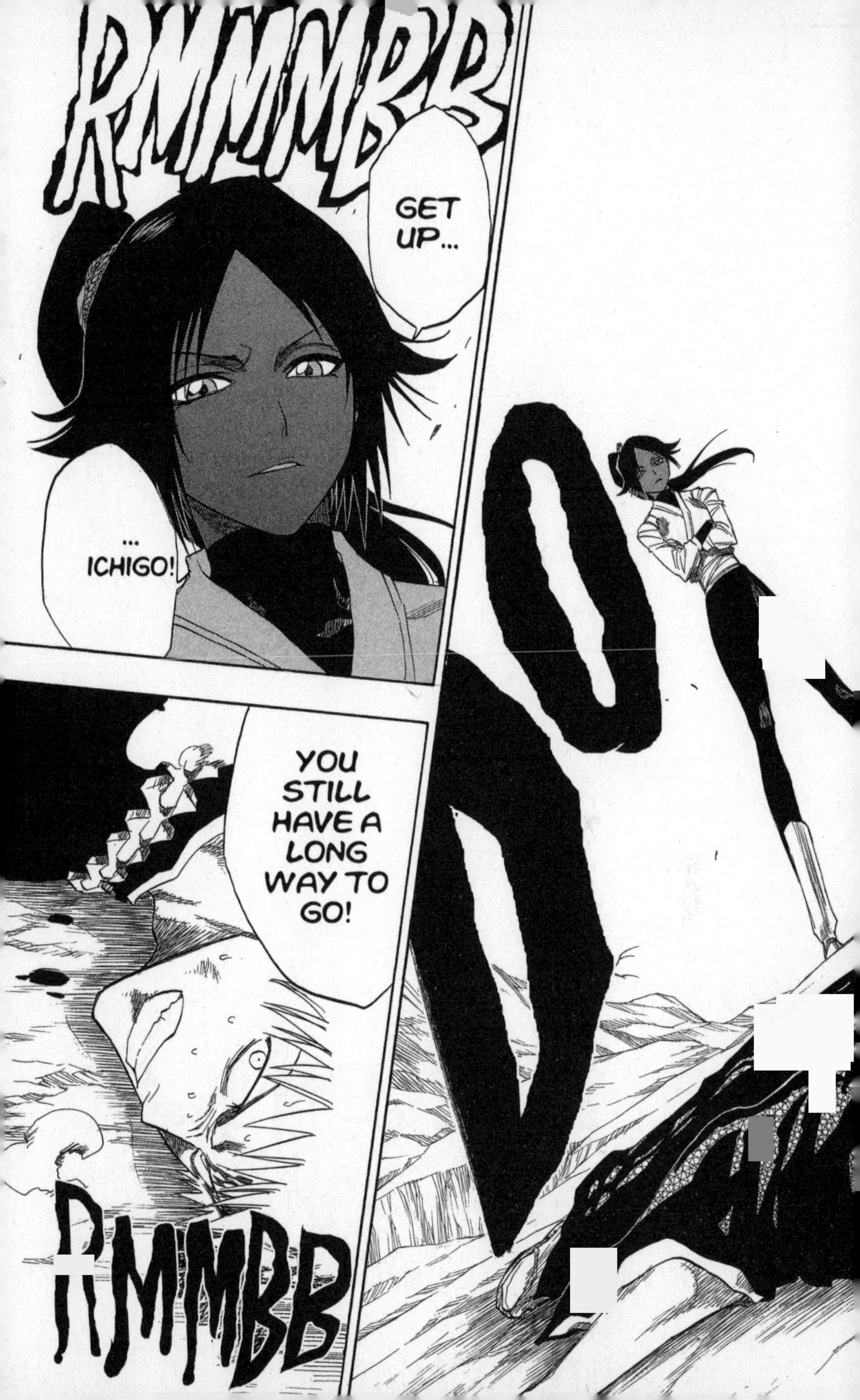
RMMMBB
GET UP...
... ICHIGO!
YOU STILL HAVE A LONG WAY TO GO!
RMMBB

IT TURNED OUT TO BE SOME WEIRD KIDS STARING AT ME.
THEY JUMPED ME BEFORE I EVEN HAD TIME TO THINK.
DANGER !!!

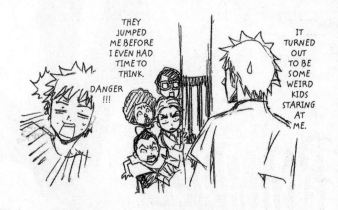

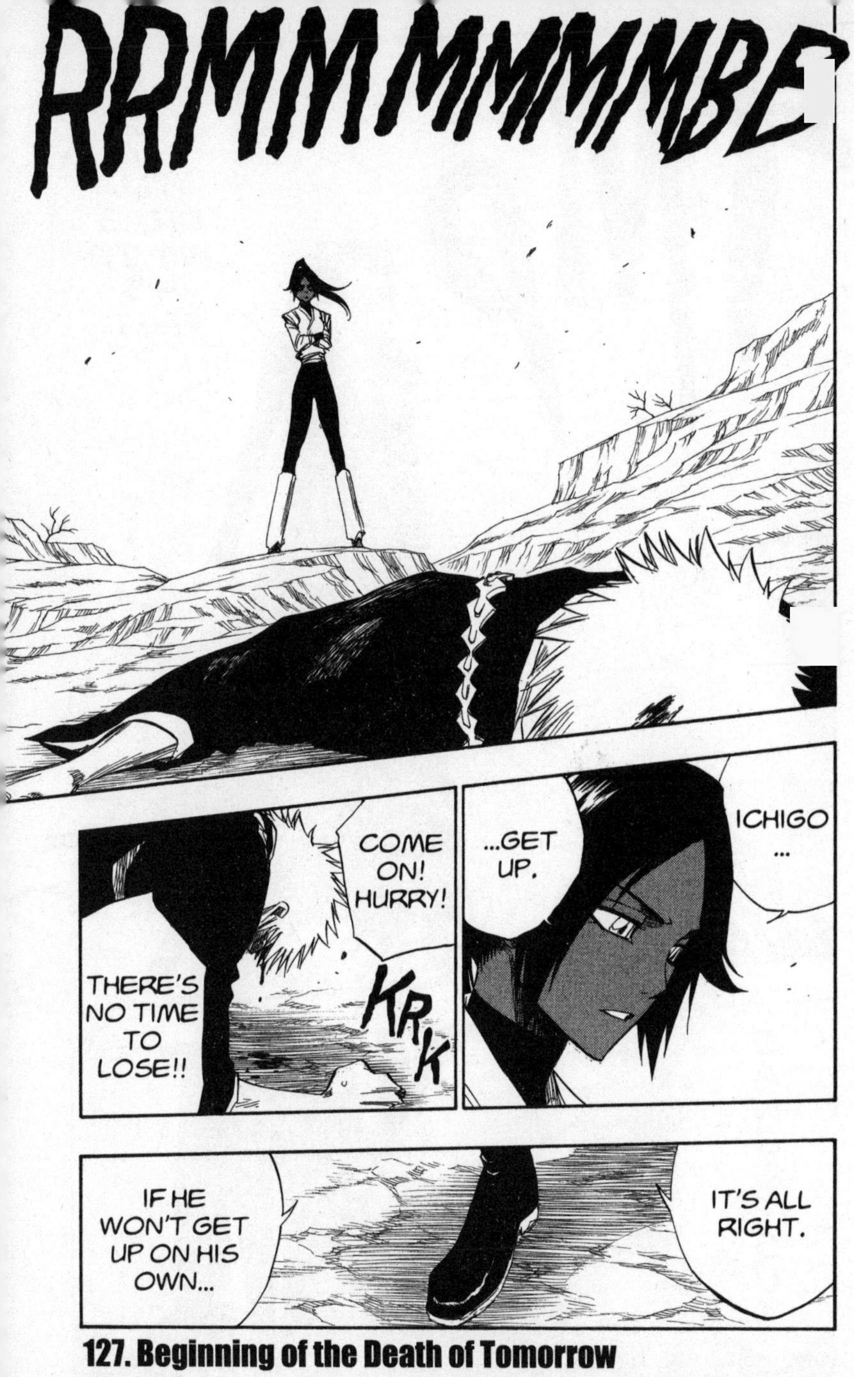
RRMMMMMMBE
ICHIGO ...
...GET UP.
COME ON! HURRY!
KRK
THERE'S NO TIME TO LOSE!!
IT'S ALL RIGHT.
IF HE WON'T GET UP ON HIS OWN...

127. Beginning of the Death of Tomorrow

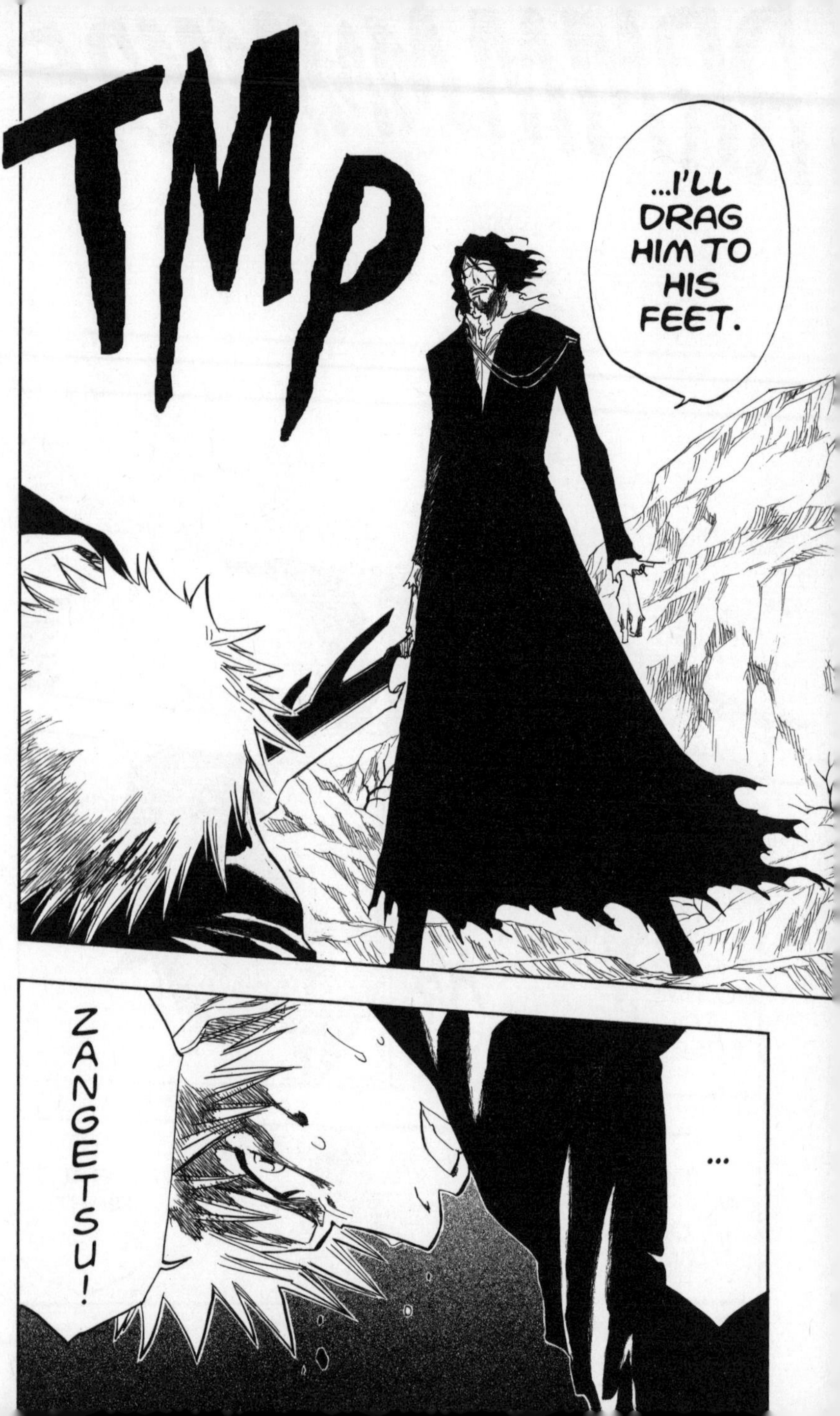
...I'LL DRAG HIM TO HIS FEET.
TMP
...
ZANGETSU!

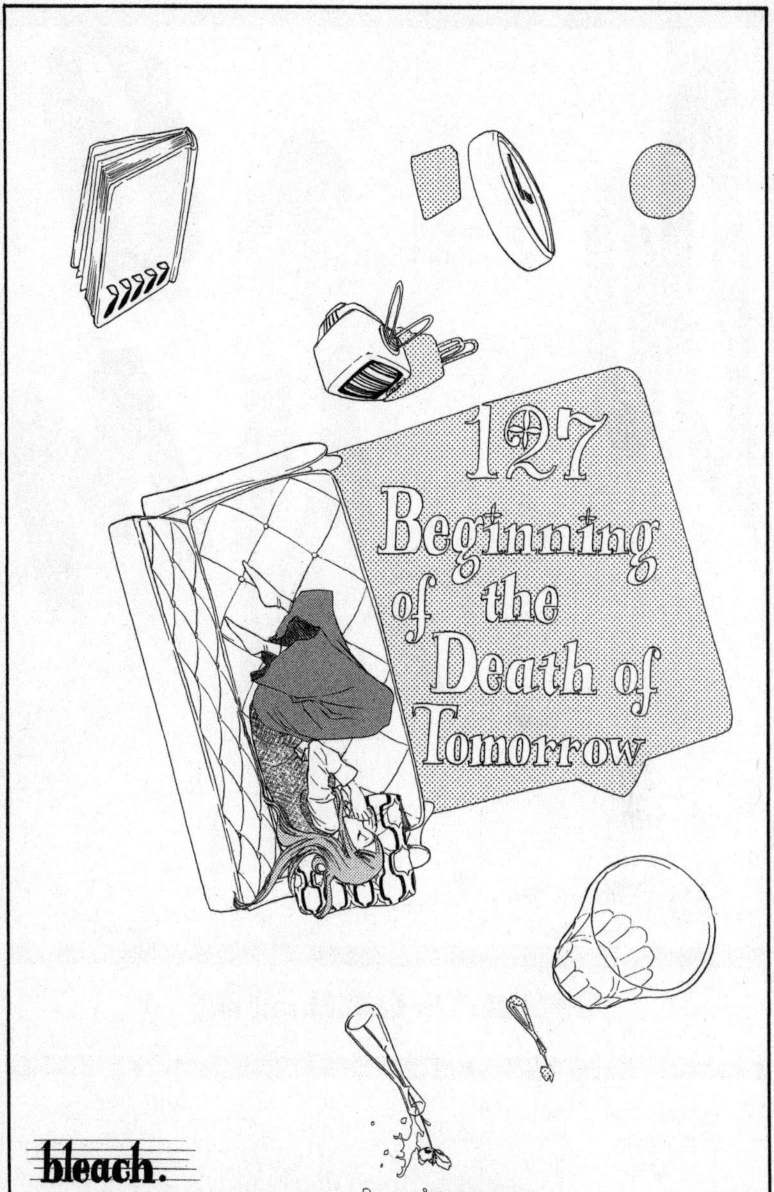
127
Beginning of the Death of Tomorrow
bleach.

127. Beginning of the Death of Tomorrow

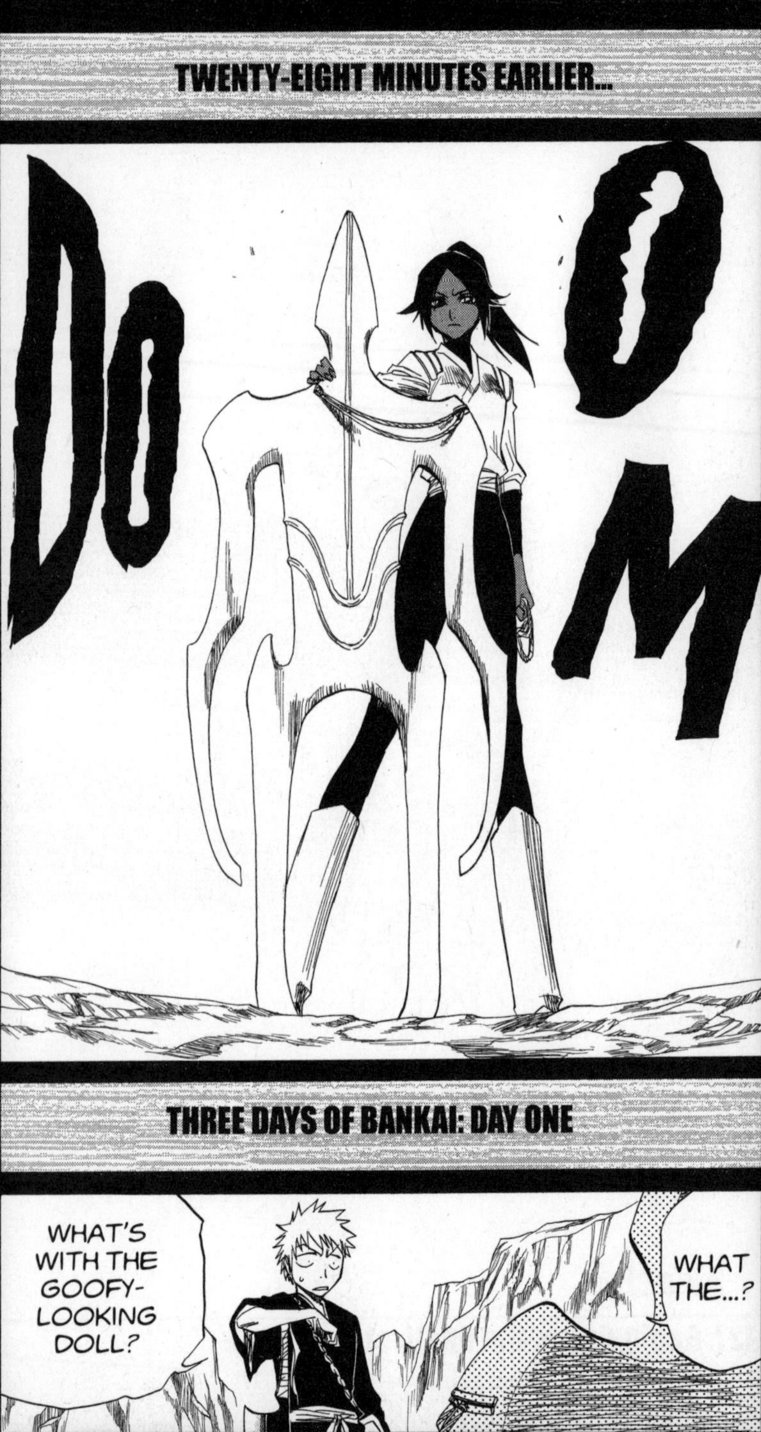
TWENTY-EIGHT MINUTES EARLIER...
DOOM
THREE DAYS OF BANKAI: DAY ONE
WHAT THE...?
WHAT'S WITH THE GOOFY-LOOKING DOLL?

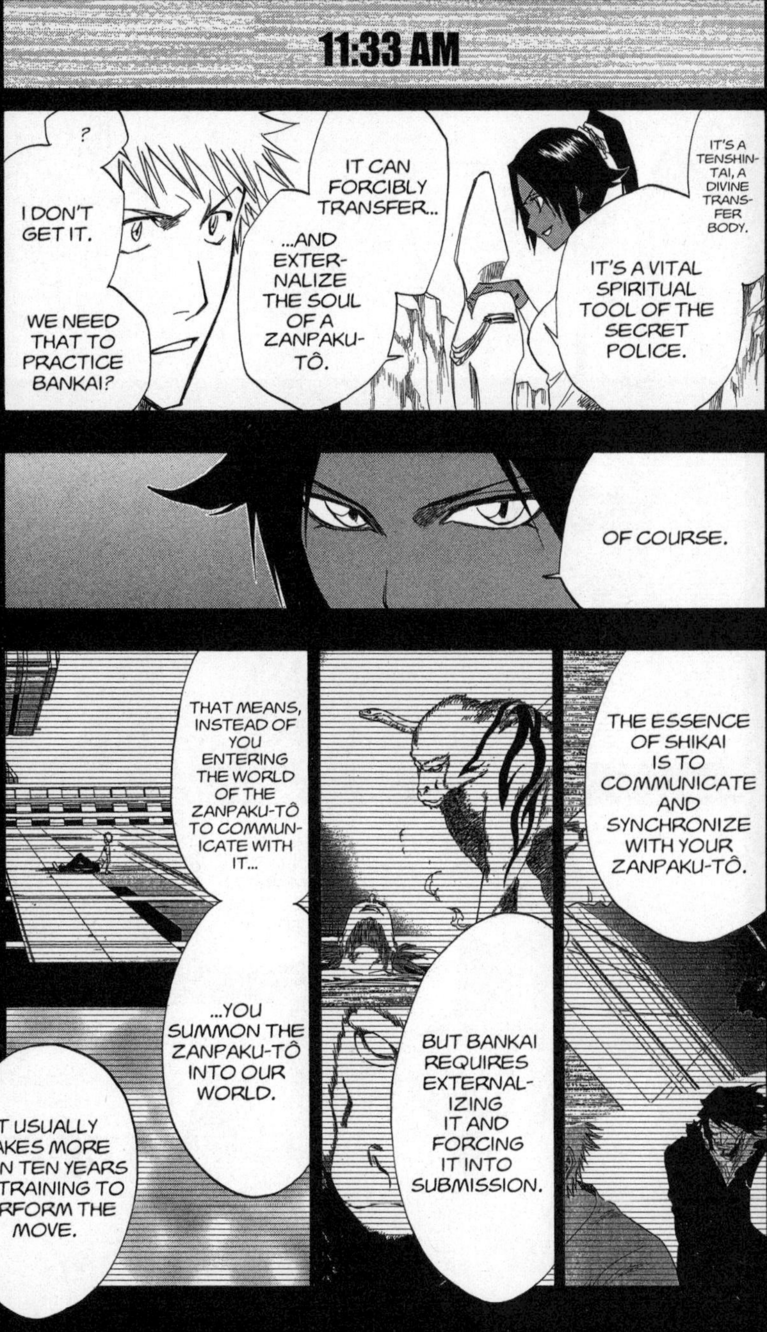
11:33 AM
IT'S A TENSHIN-TAI, A DIVINE TRANSFER BODY.
IT'S A VITAL SPIRITUAL TOOL OF THE SECRET POLICE.
IT CAN FORCIBLY TRANSFER...
...AND EXTERNALIZE THE SOUL OF A ZANPAKU-TÔ.
?
I DON'T GET IT.
WE NEED THAT TO PRACTICE BANKAI?
OF COURSE.
THE ESSENCE OF SHIKAI IS TO COMMUNICATE AND SYNCHRONIZE WITH YOUR ZANPAKU-TÔ.
BUT BANKAI REQUIRES EXTERNALIZING IT AND FORCING IT INTO SUBMISSION.
THAT MEANS, INSTEAD OF YOU ENTERING THE WORLD OF THE ZANPAKU-TÔ TO COMMUNICATE WITH IT...
...YOU SUMMON THE ZANPAKU-TÔ INTO OUR WORLD.
IT USUALLY TAKES MORE THAN TEN YEARS OF TRAINING TO PERFORM THE MOVE.

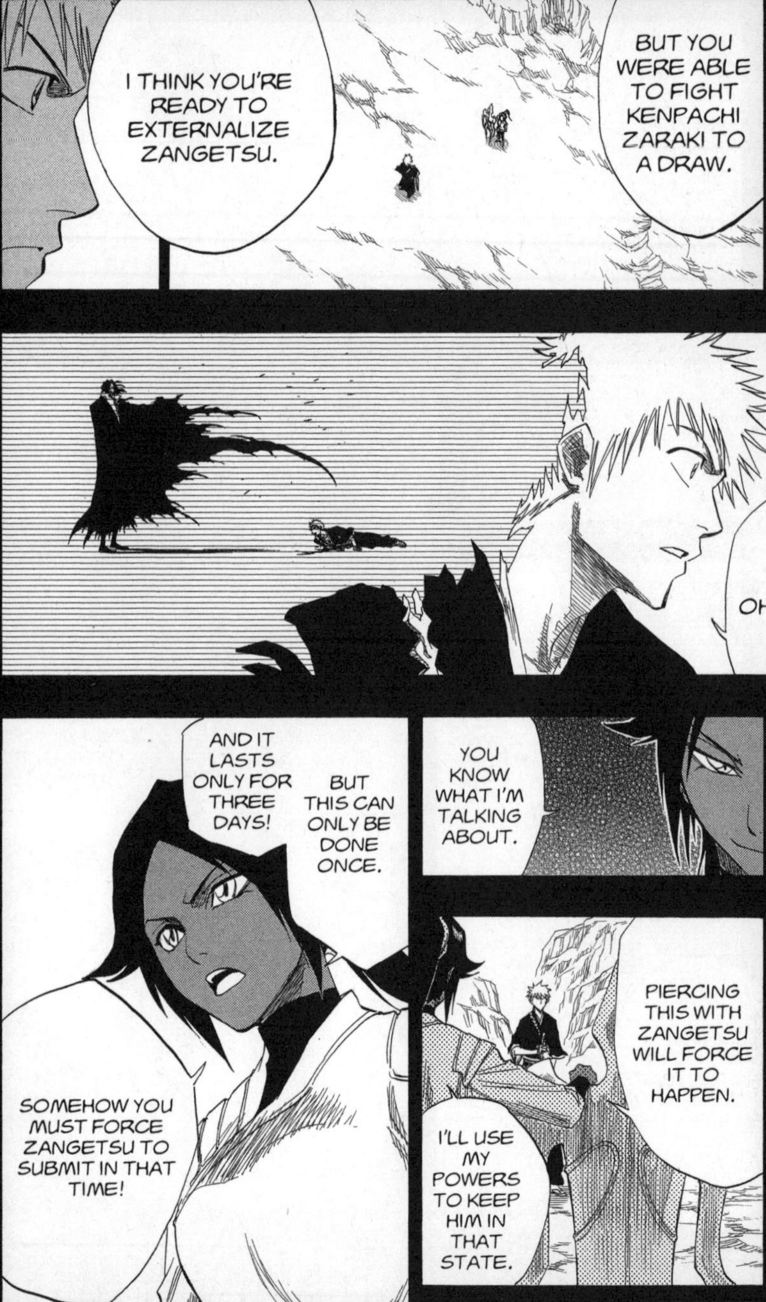
BUT YOU WERE ABLE TO FIGHT KENPACHI ZARAKI TO A DRAW.
I THINK YOU'RE READY TO EXTERNALIZE ZANGETSU.
OH.
YOU KNOW WHAT I'M TALKING ABOUT.
PIERCING THIS WITH ZANGETSU WILL FORCE IT TO HAPPEN.
I'LL USE MY POWERS TO KEEP HIM IN THAT STATE.
BUT THIS CAN ONLY BE DONE ONCE.
AND IT LASTS ONLY FOR THREE DAYS!
SOMEHOW YOU MUST FORCE ZANGETSU TO SUBMIT IN THAT TIME!

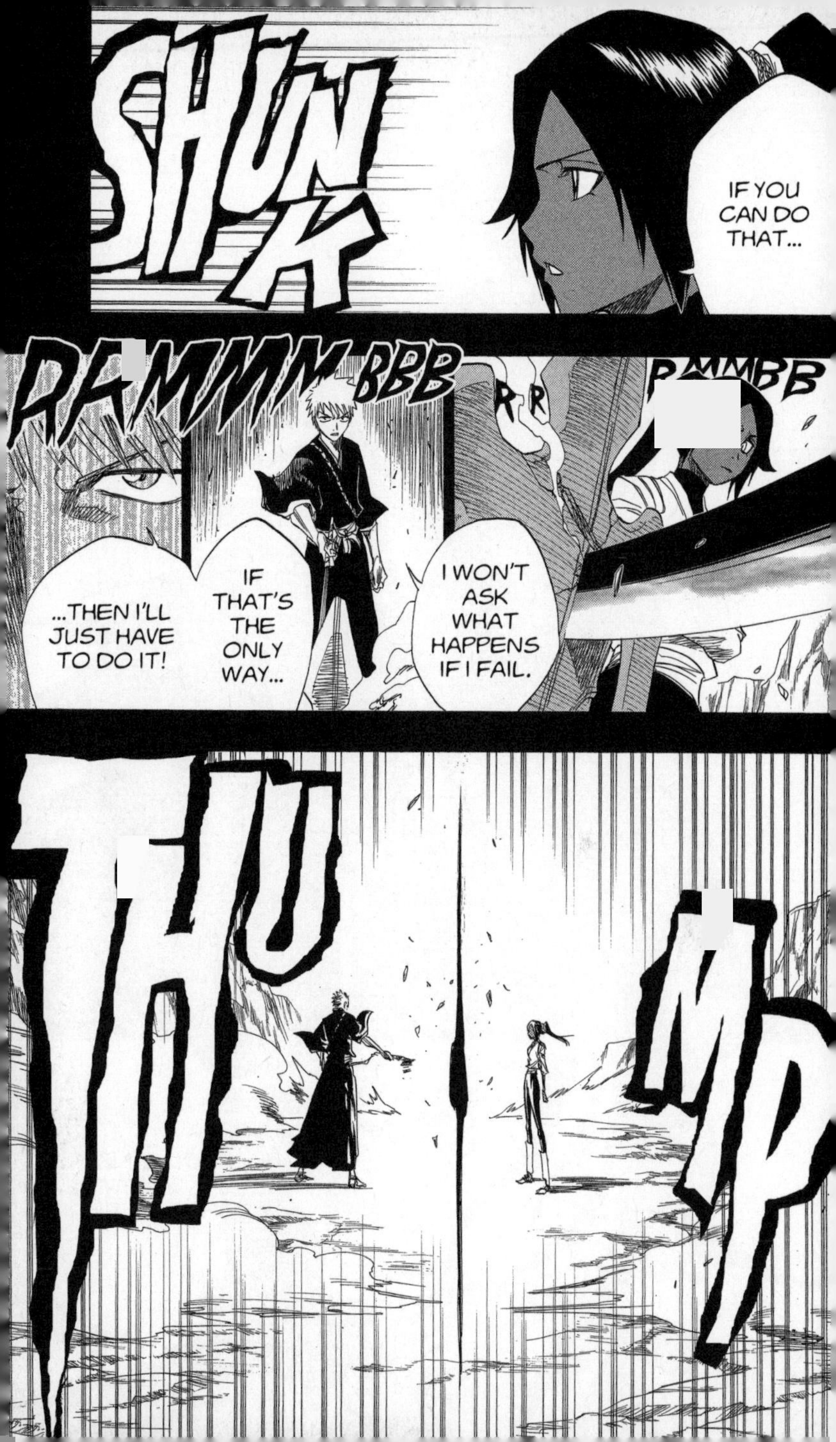
IF YOU CAN DO THAT...
SHUNK
RR
I WON'T ASK WHAT HAPPENS IF I FAIL.
IF THAT'S THE ONLY WAY...
...THEN I'LL JUST HAVE TO DO IT!
THUMP

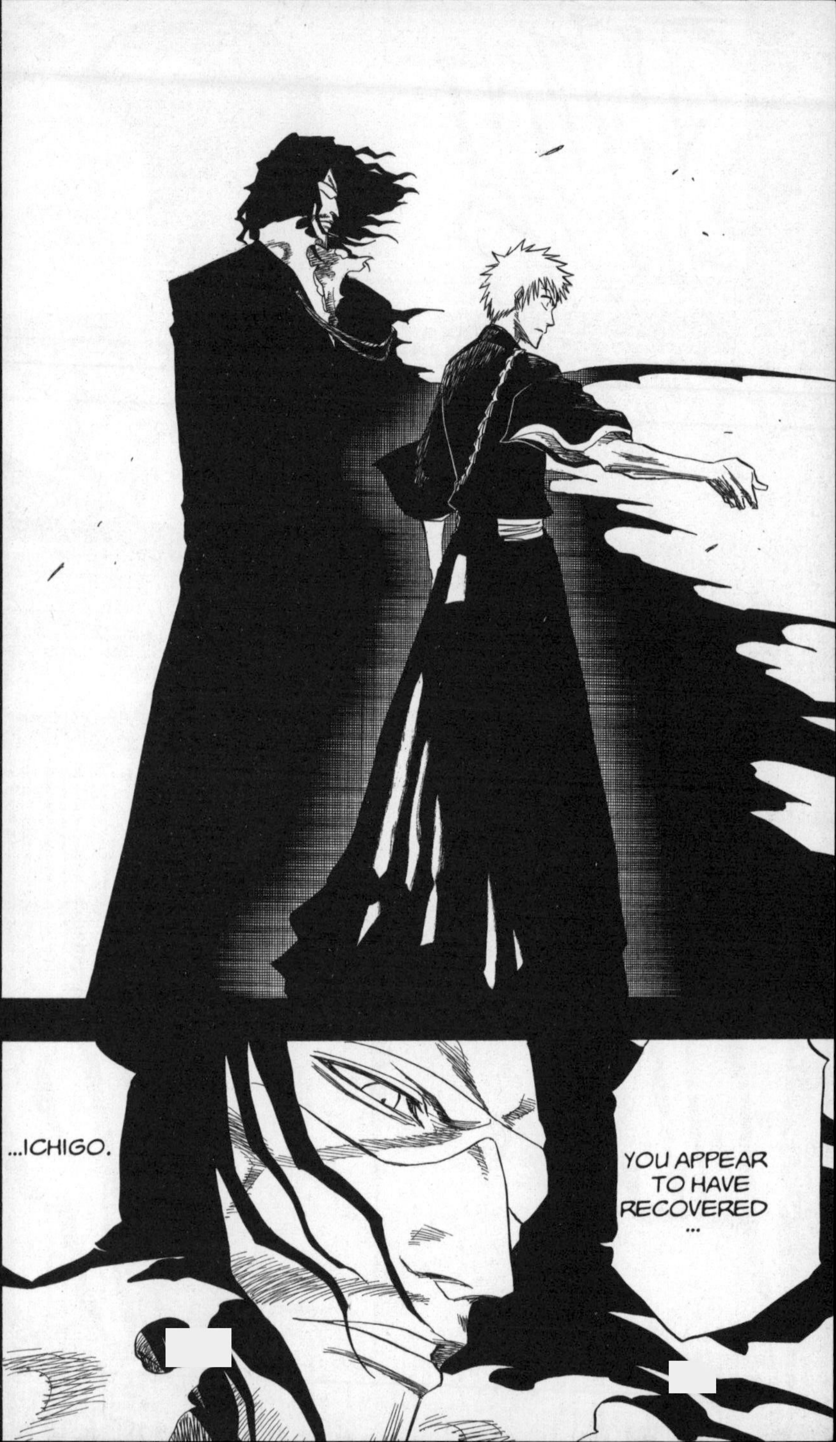
YOU APPEAR TO HAVE RECOVERED ...
...ICHIGO.

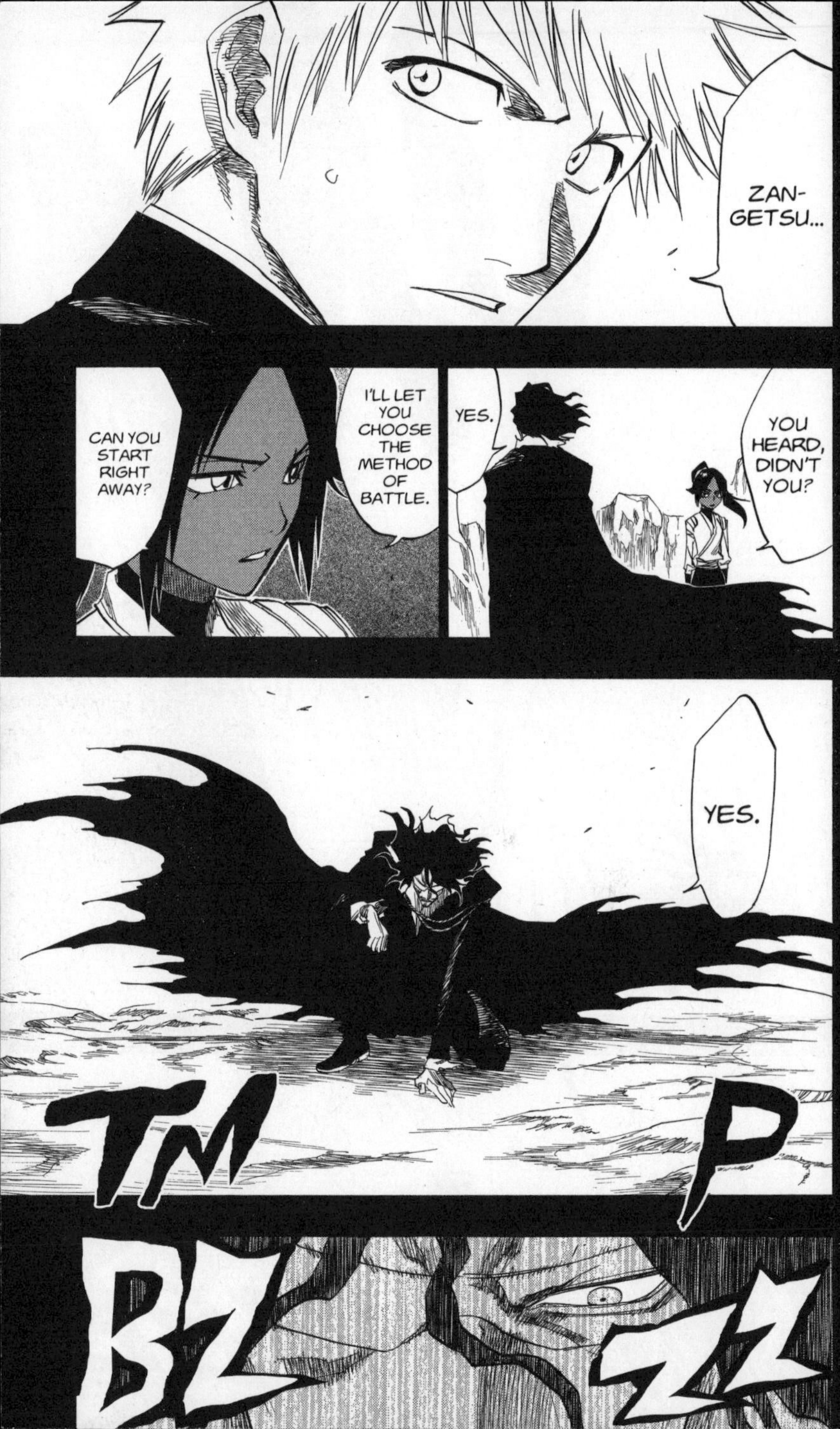
ZAN-GETSU...
YOU HEARD, DIDN'T YOU?
YES.
I'LL LET YOU CHOOSE THE METHOD OF BATTLE.
CAN YOU START RIGHT AWAY?
YES.
TMP
BZZZ

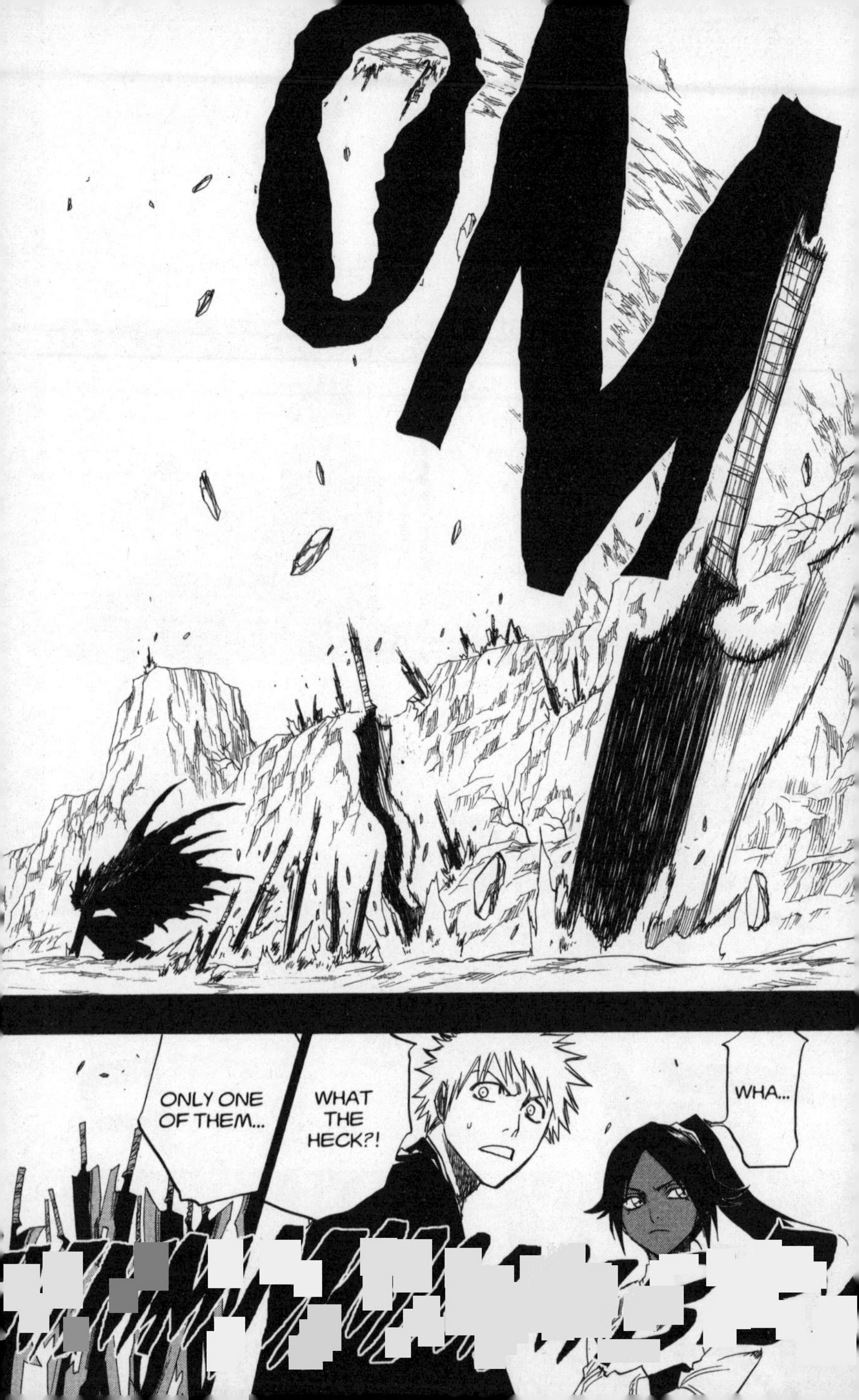
WHA...
WHAT THE HECK?!
ONLY ONE OF THEM...

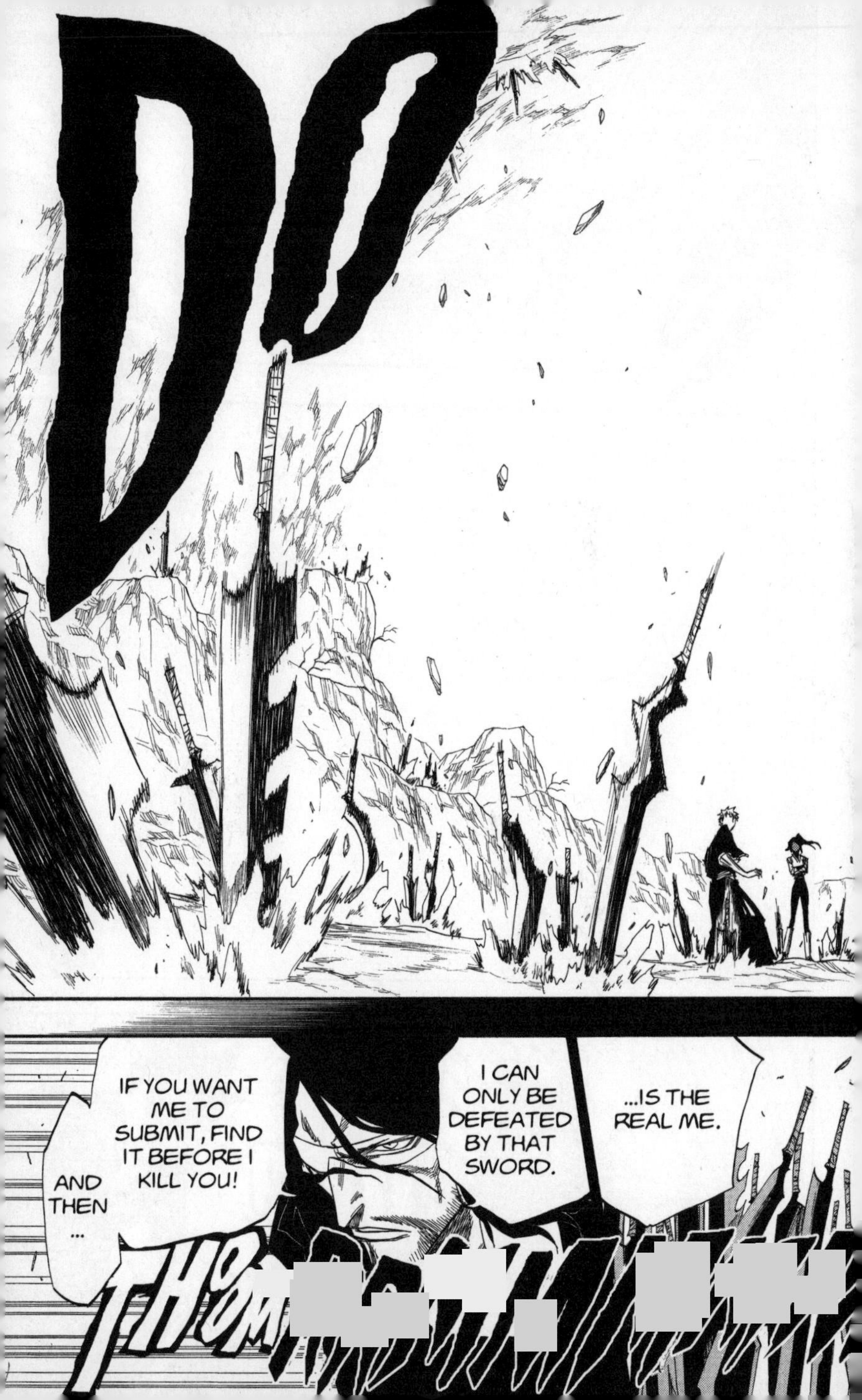
DO
...IS THE REAL ME.
I CAN ONLY BE DEFEATED BY THAT SWORD.
IF YOU WANT ME TO SUBMIT, FIND IT BEFORE I KILL YOU!
AND THEN ...

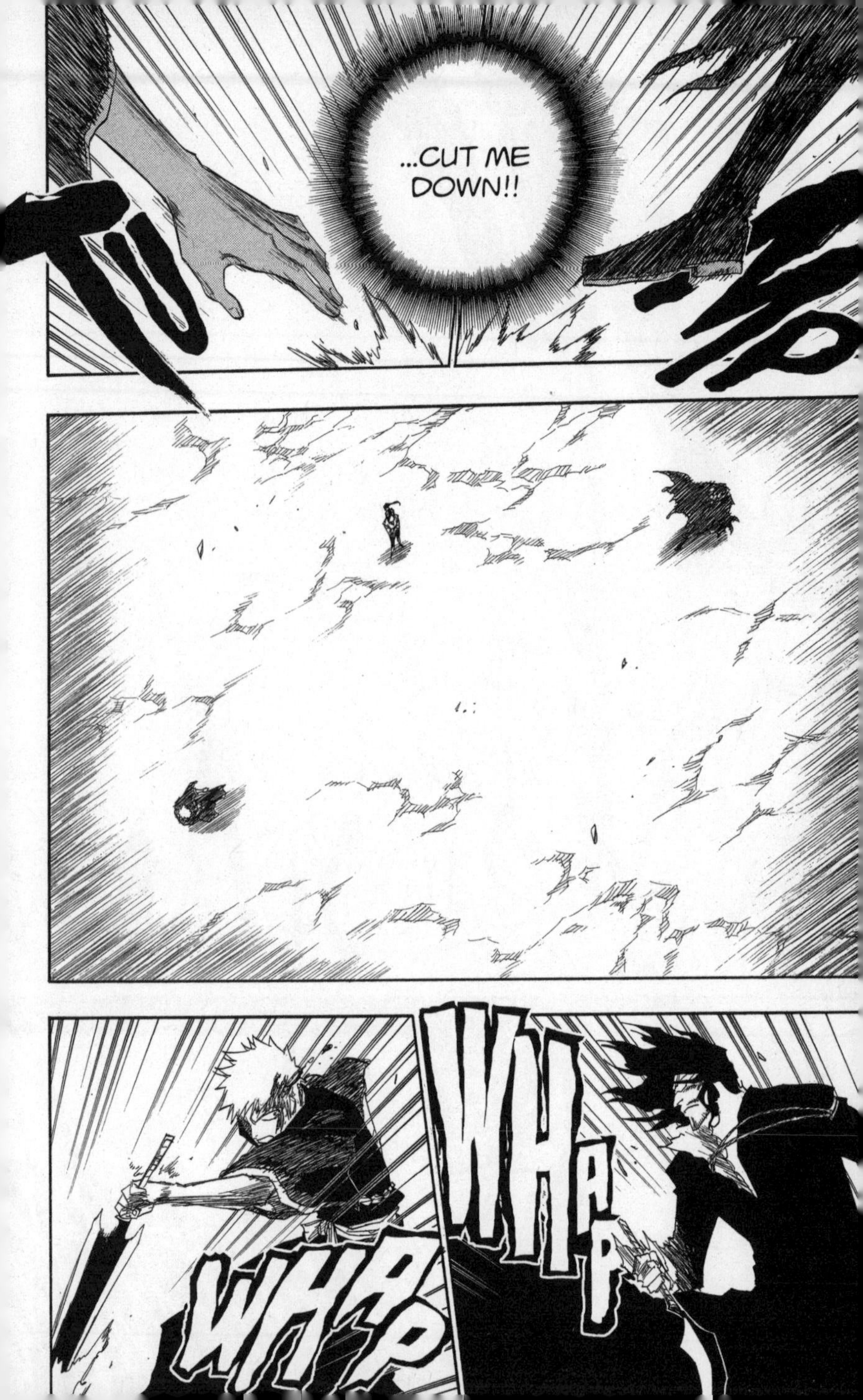
...CUT ME DOWN!!
WHAP
WHAP

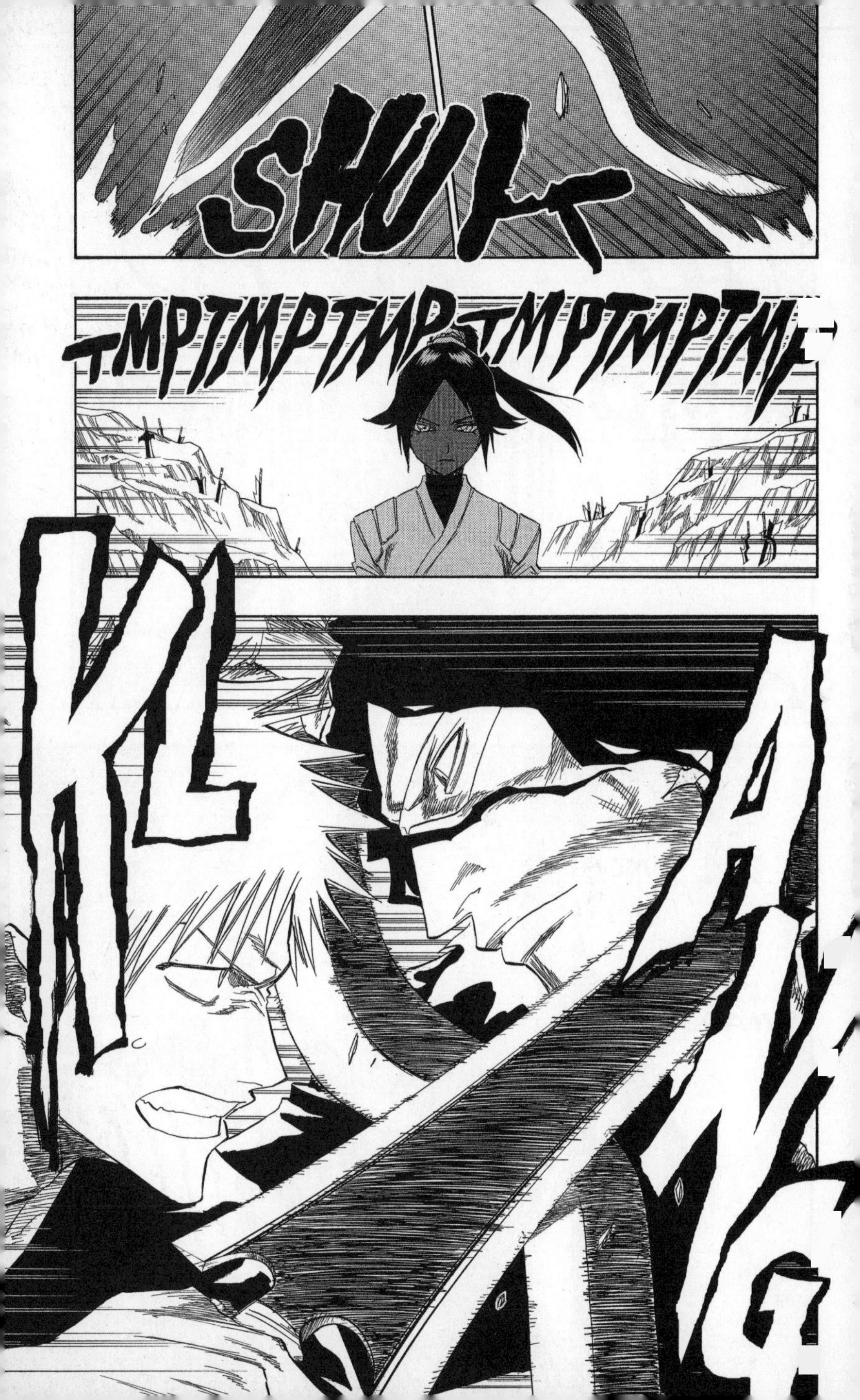
SHUK
TMPTMPTMPTMPTMPTMP
KLANG

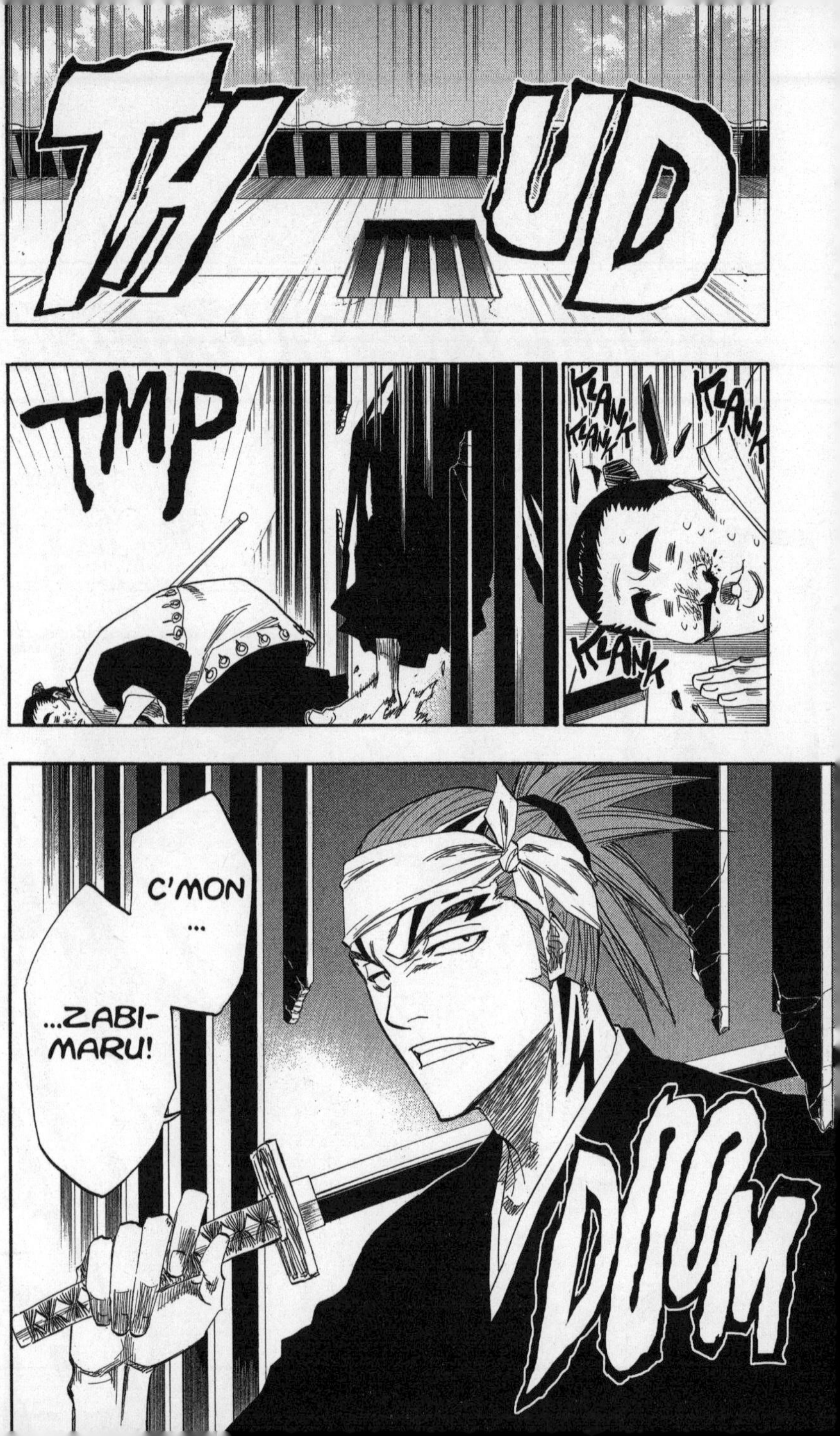
THUD
KLANK
KLANK KLANK
KLANK
TMP
C'MON ...
...ZABI-MARU!
DOOM

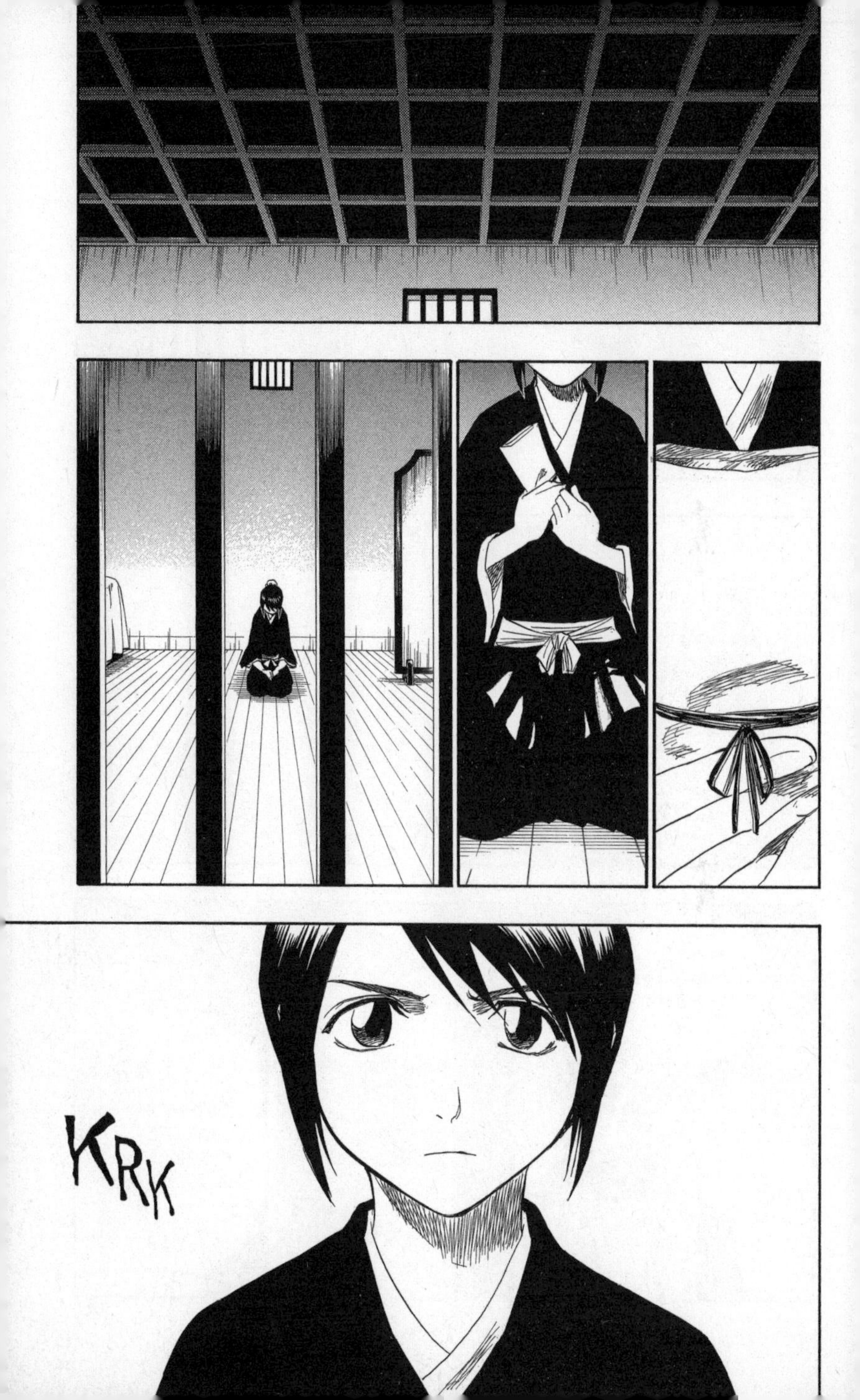
KRK

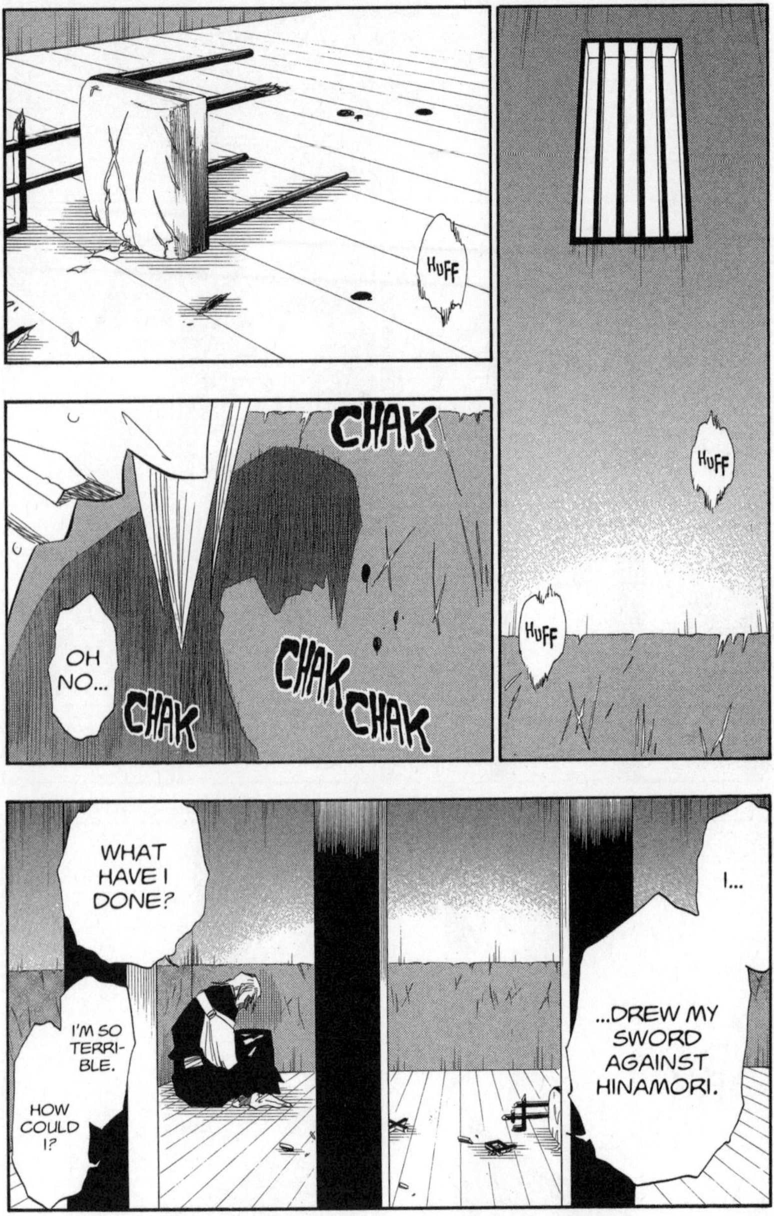
HUFF
HUFF
HUFF
CHAK
CHAK CHAK
OH NO...
CHAK
I...
...DREW MY SWORD AGAINST HINAMORI.
WHAT HAVE I DONE?
I'M SO TERRI-BLE.
HOW COULD I?

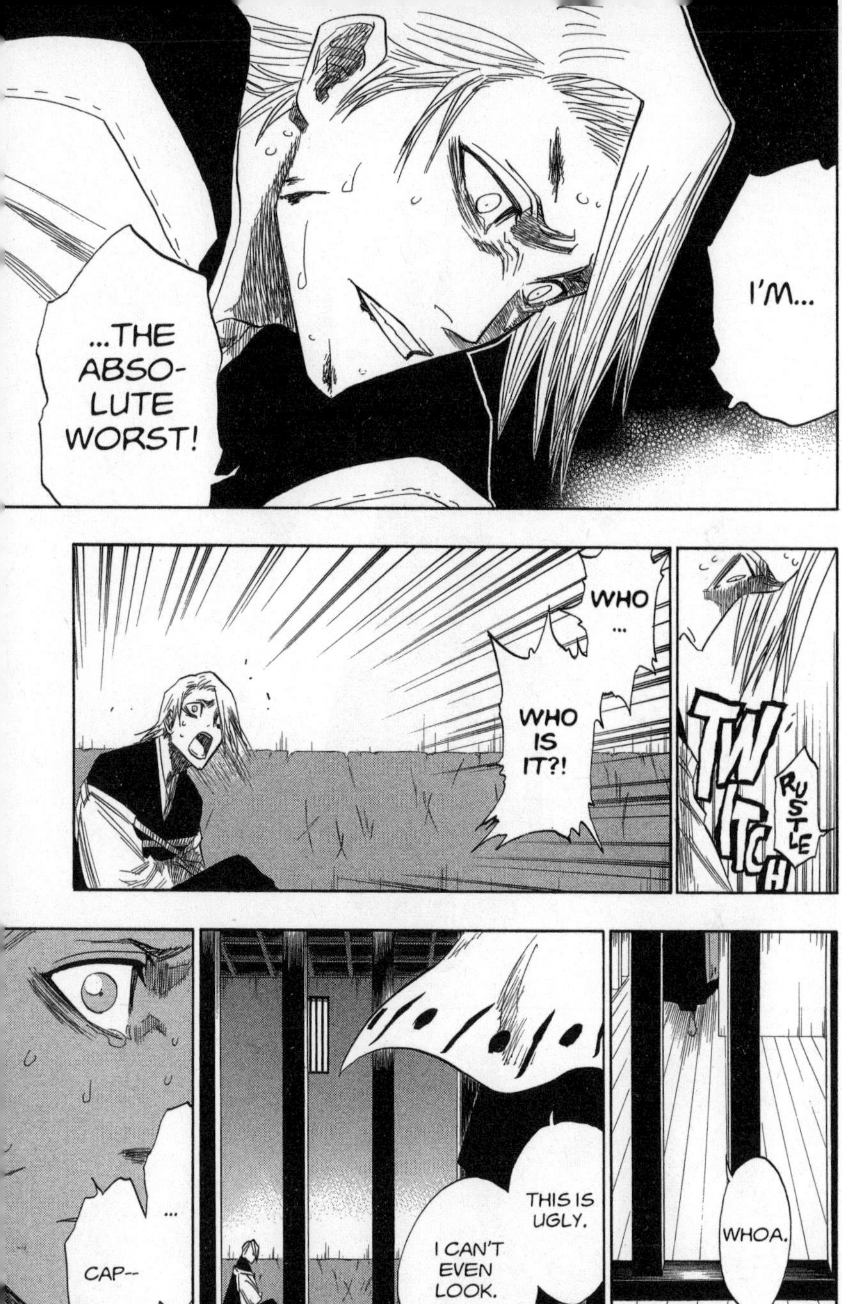
I'M...
...THE ABSO-LUTE WORST!
TWITCH
RUSTLE
WHO...
WHO IS IT?!
WHOA.
THIS IS UGLY.
I CAN'T EVEN LOOK.
...
CAP--

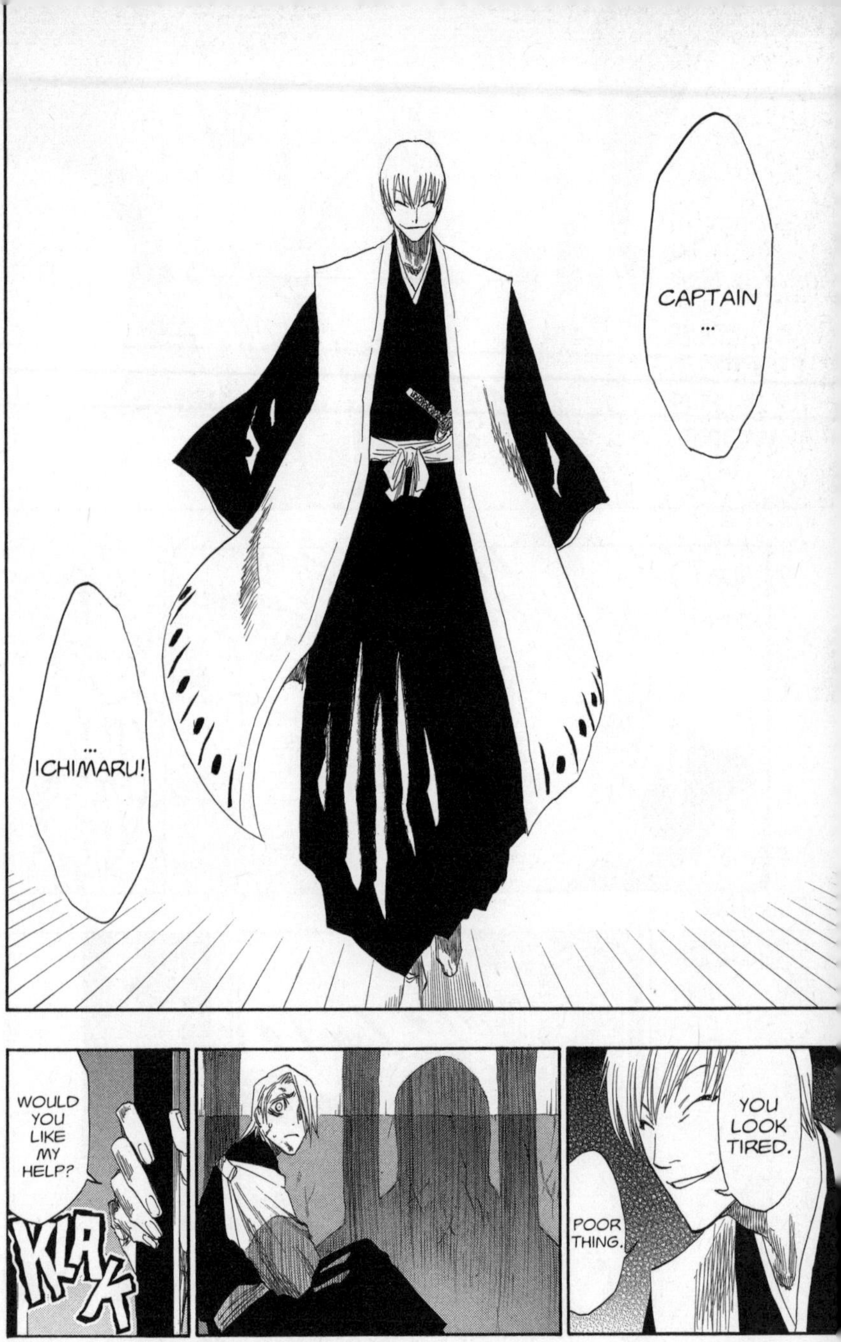
CAPTAIN ...
... ICHIMARU!
YOU LOOK TIRED.
POOR THING.
WOULD YOU LIKE MY HELP?
KLAK

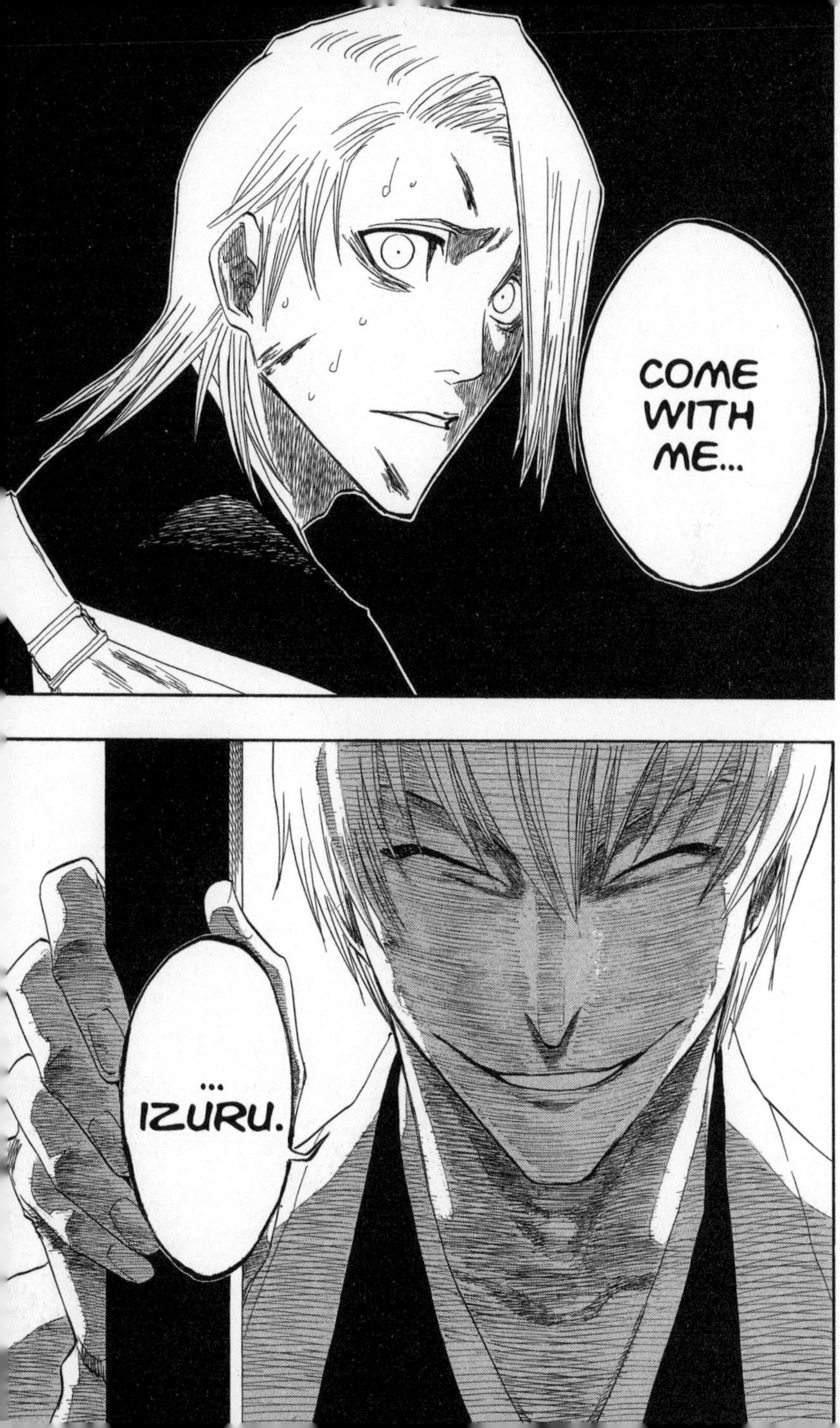
COME WITH ME...
... IZURU.

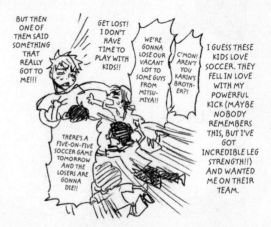

I GUESS THESE KIDS LOVE SOCCER. THEY FELL IN LOVE WITH MY POWERFUL KICK (MAYBE NOBODY REMEMBERS THIS, BUT I'VE GOT INCREDIBLE LEG STRENGTH!!) AND WANTED ME ON THEIR TEAM.
C'MON! AREN'T YOU KARIN'S BROTHER?!
WE'RE GONNA LOSE OUR VACANT LOT TO SOME GUYS FROM MITSU-MIYA!!
THERE'S A FIVE-ON-FIVE SOCCER GAME TOMORROW AND THE LOSERS ARE GONNA DIE!!
GET LOST! I DON'T HAVE TIME TO PLAY WITH KIDS!!
BUT THEN ONE OF THEM SAID SOMETHING THAT REALLY GOT TO ME!!!

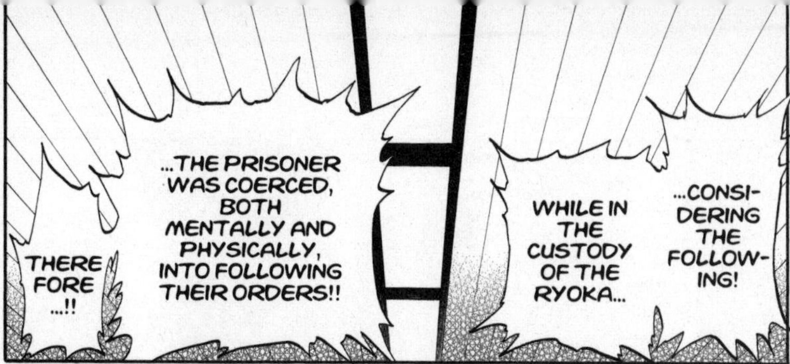
...CONSI-DERING THE FOLLOW-ING!
WHILE IN THE CUSTODY OF THE RYOKA...
...THE PRISONER WAS COERCED, BOTH MENTALLY AND PHYSICALLY, INTO FOLLOWING THEIR ORDERS!!
THERE FORE ...!!

128. The Great Joint-Struggle Union

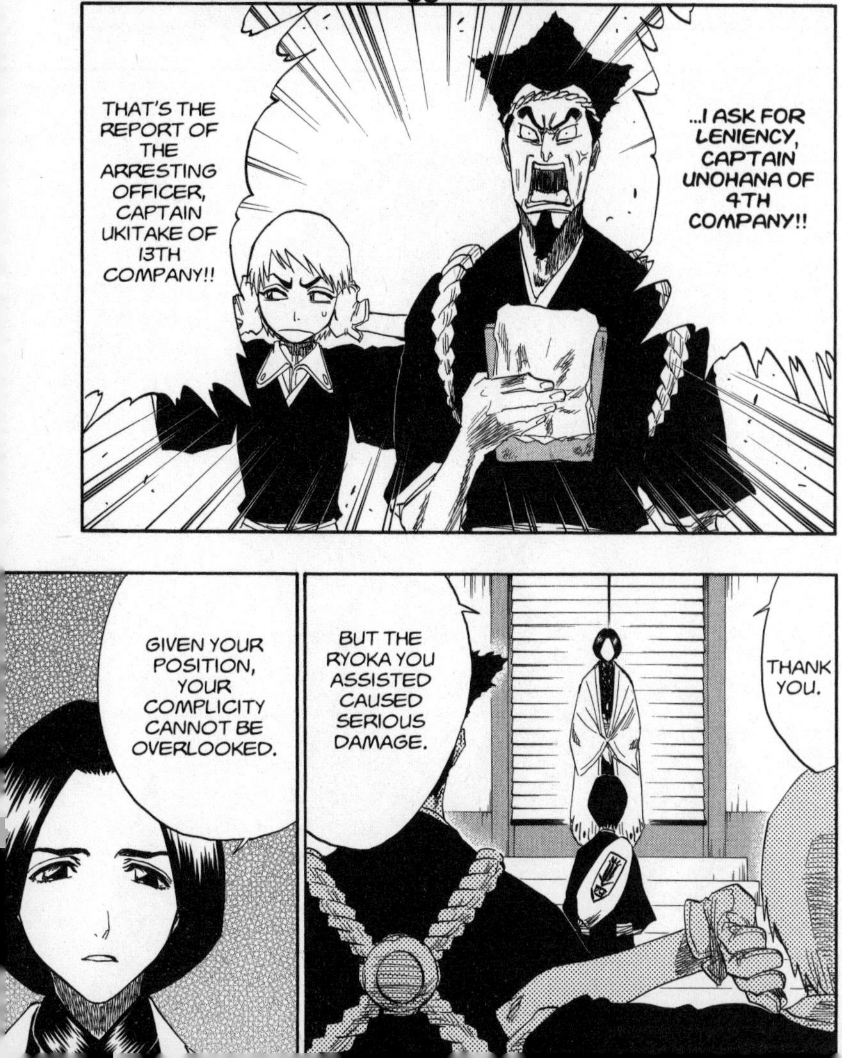
...I ASK FOR LENIENCY, CAPTAIN UNOHANA OF 4TH COMPANY!!
THAT'S THE REPORT OF THE ARRESTING OFFICER, CAPTAIN UKITAKE OF 13TH COMPANY!!
THANK YOU.
BUT THE RYOKA YOU ASSISTED CAUSED SERIOUS DAMAGE.
GIVEN YOUR POSITION, YOUR COMPLICITY CANNOT BE OVERLOOKED.

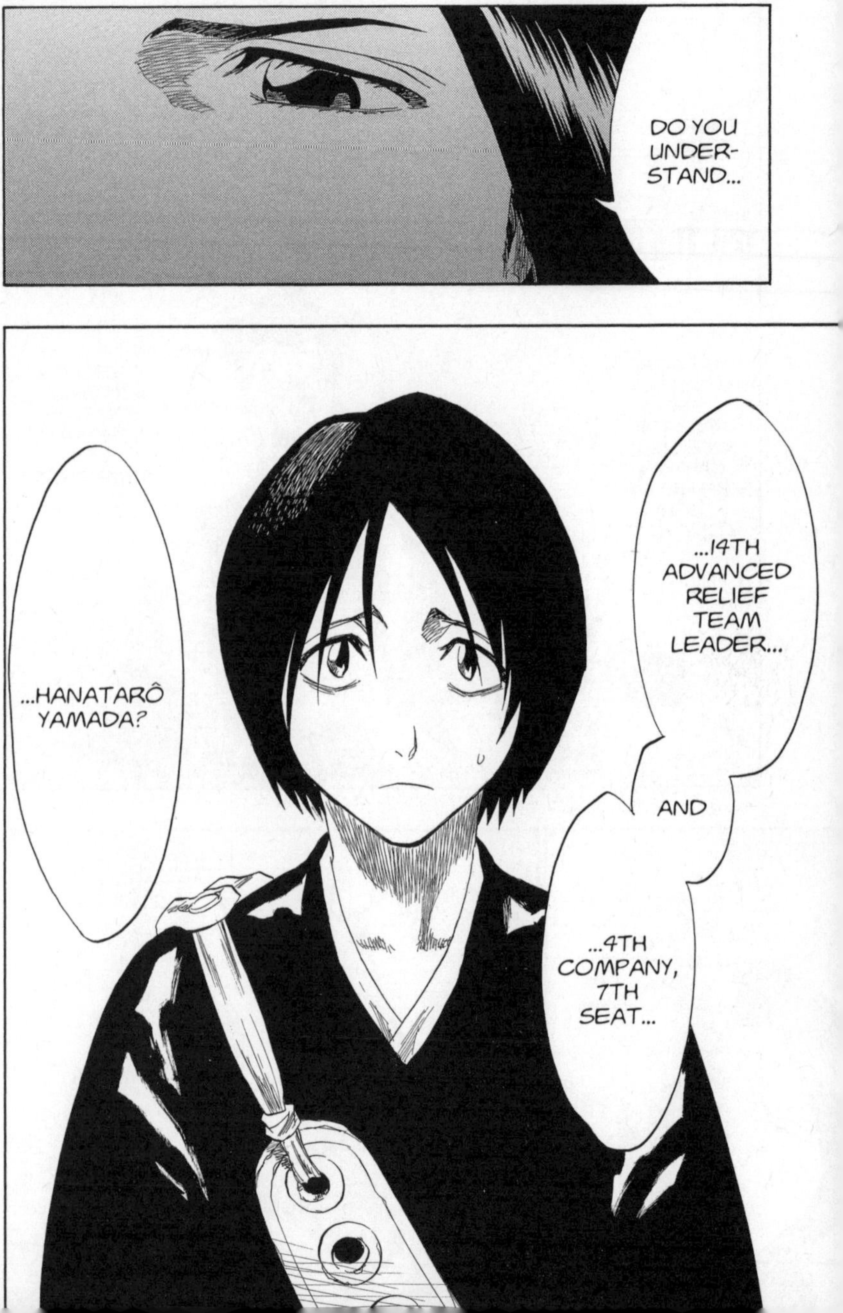
DO YOU UNDER-STAND...
...14TH ADVANCED RELIEF TEAM LEADER...
AND
...4TH COMPANY, 7TH SEAT...
...HANATARÔ YAMADA?

128. The Great Joint-Struggle Union

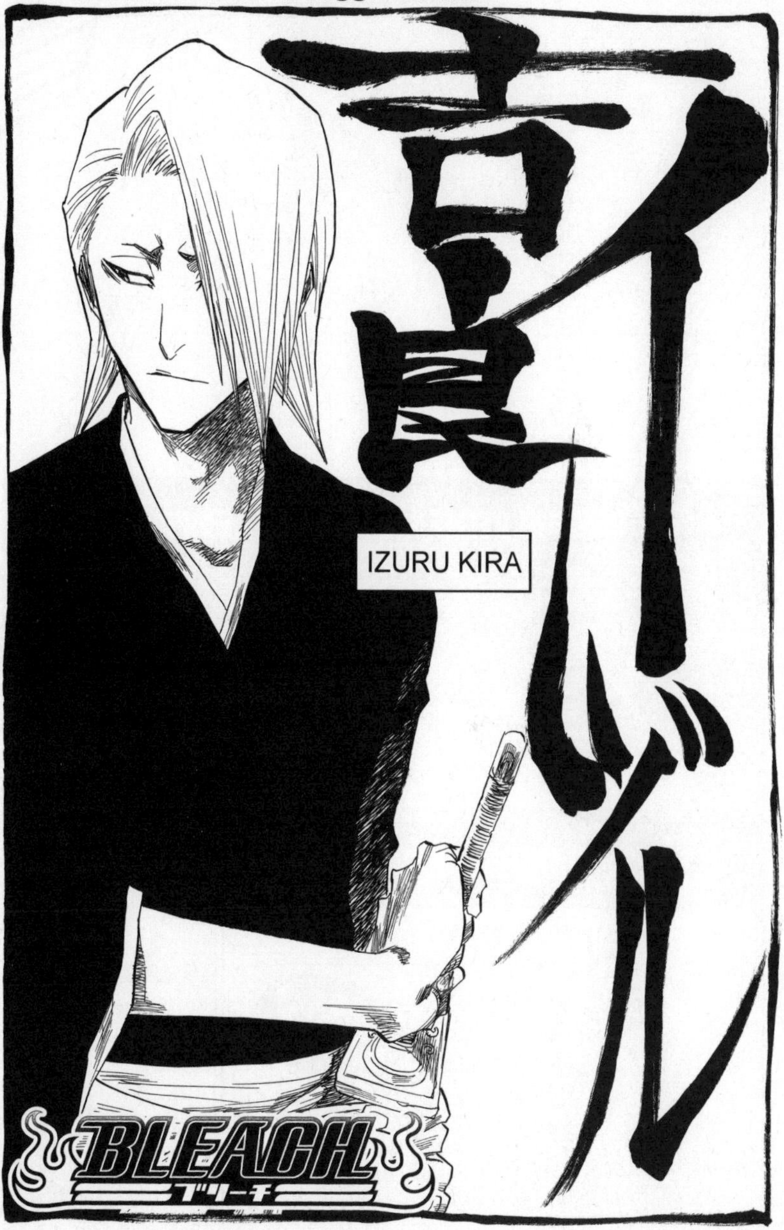
吉良イヅル
IZURU KIRA
BLEACH
ブリーチ

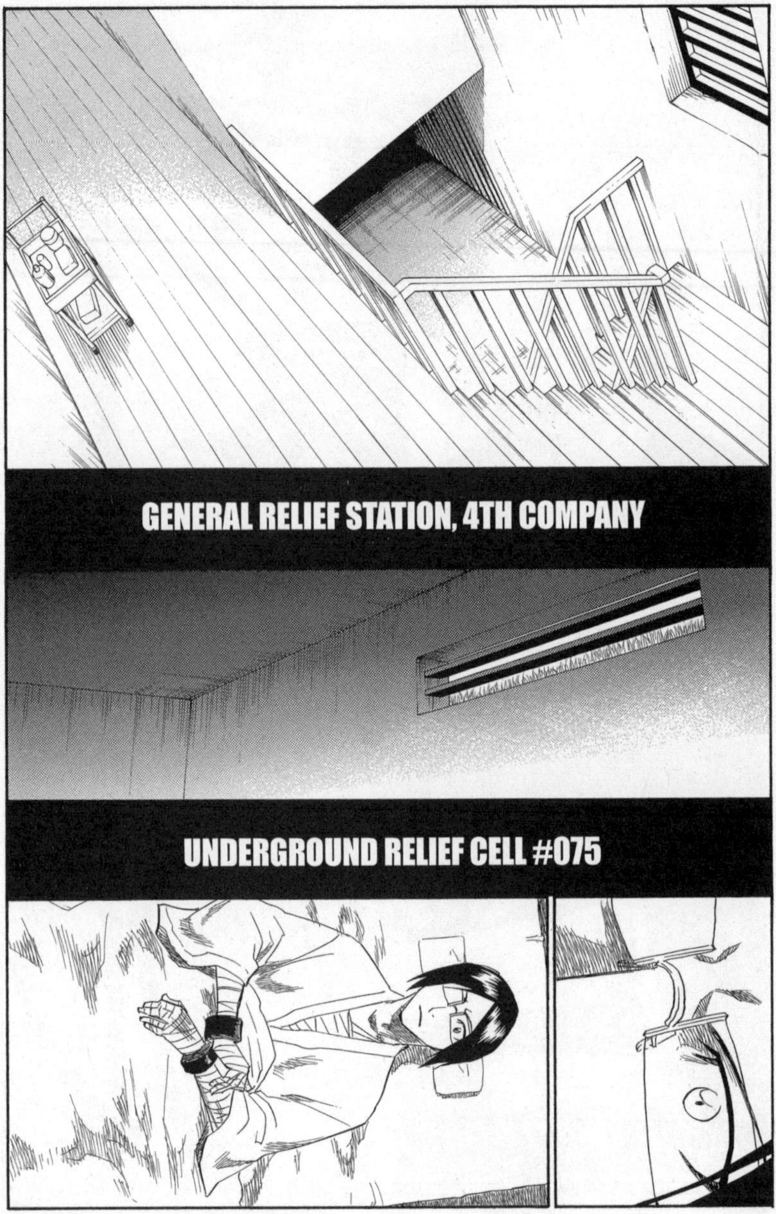
GENERAL RELIEF STATION, 4TH COMPANY
UNDERGROUND RELIEF CELL #075

READ THIS WAY

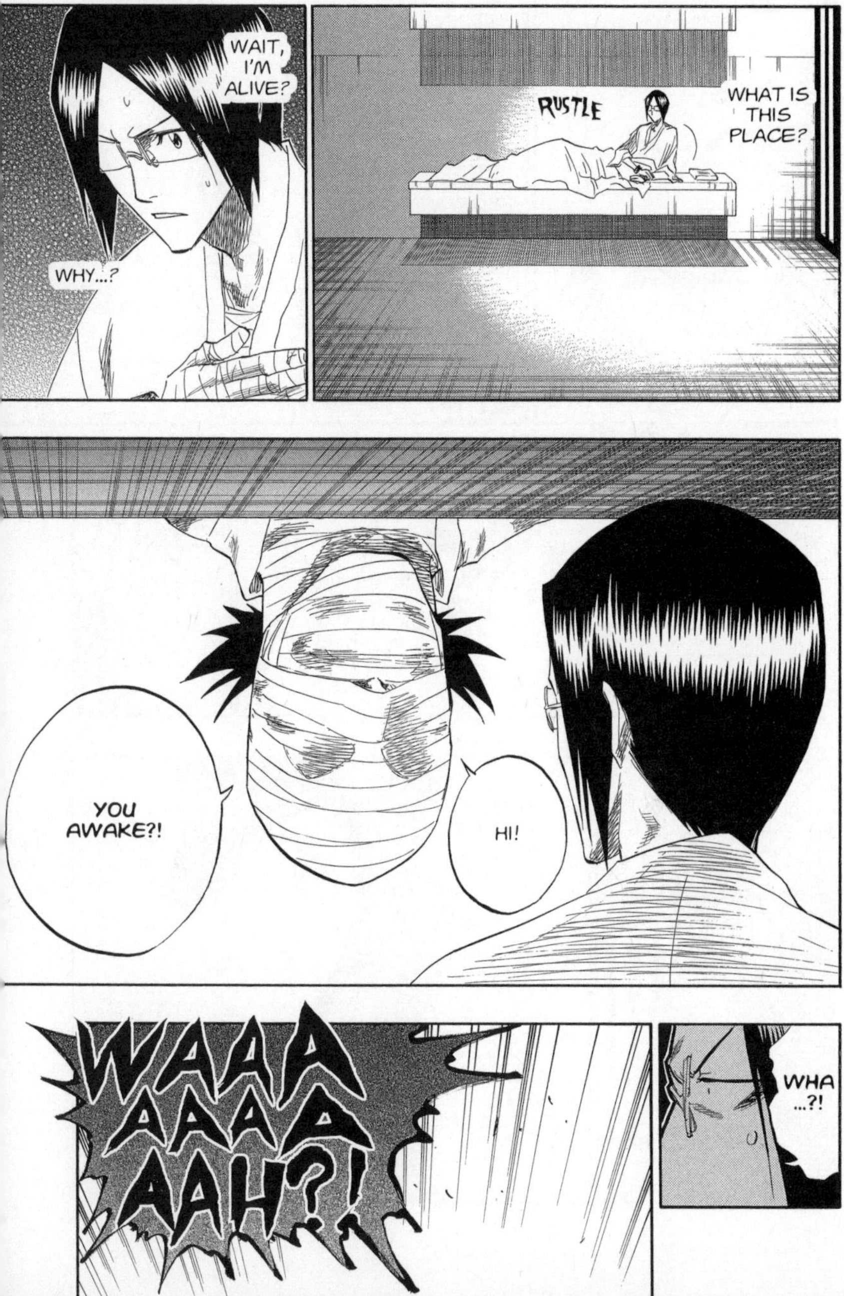
WHAT IS THIS PLACE?
RUSTLE
WAIT, I'M ALIVE?
WHY...?
HI!
YOU AWAKE?!
WHA ...?!
WAAA AAAA AAH?!

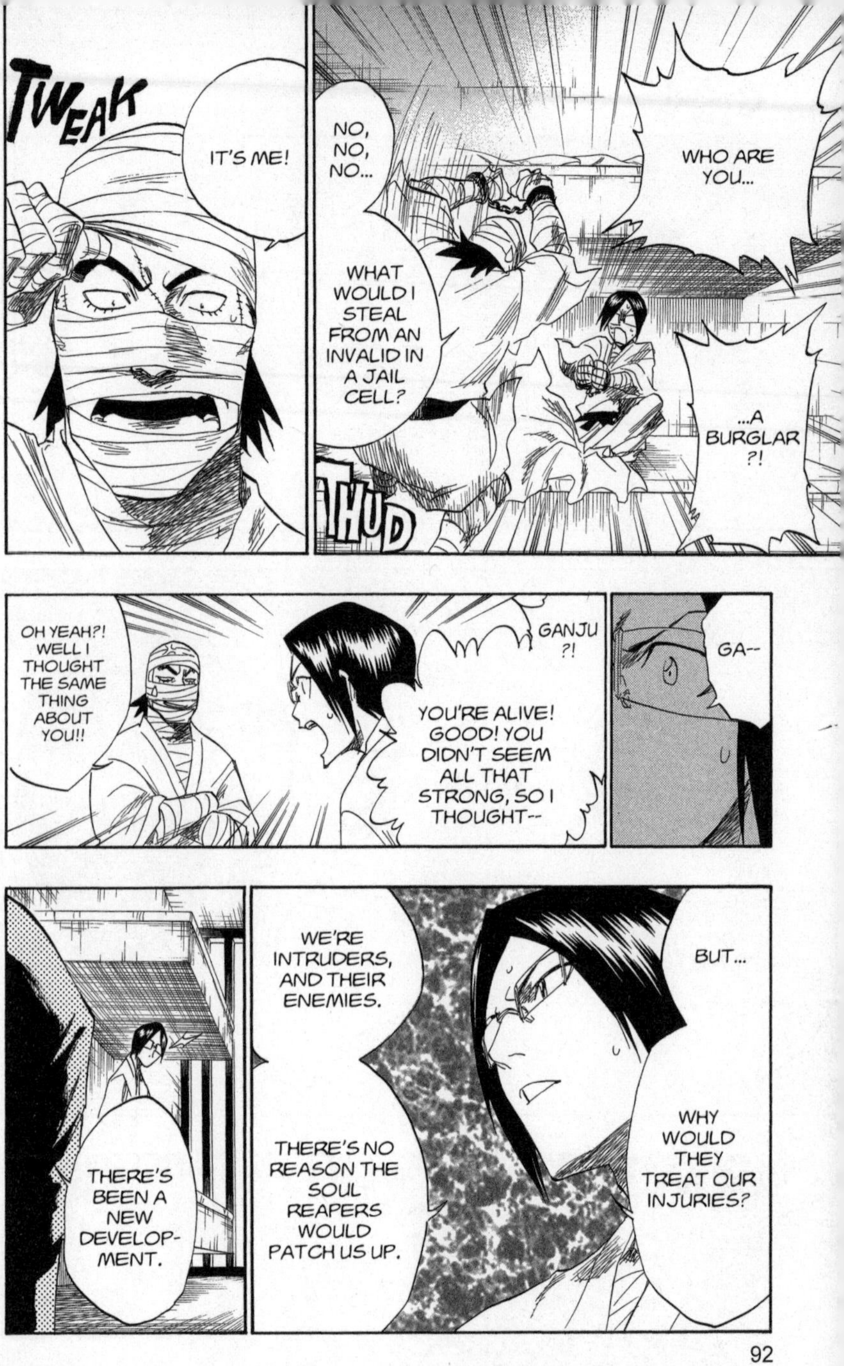
WHO ARE YOU...
...A BURGLAR?!
NO, NO, NO...
WHAT WOULD I STEAL FROM AN INVALID IN A JAIL CELL?
THUD
TWEAK
IT'S ME!
GA--
GANJU?!
YOU'RE ALIVE! GOOD! YOU DIDN'T SEEM ALL THAT STRONG, SO I THOUGHT--
OH YEAH?! WELL I THOUGHT THE SAME THING ABOUT YOU!!
BUT...
WHY WOULD THEY TREAT OUR INJURIES?
WE'RE INTRUDERS, AND THEIR ENEMIES.
THERE'S NO REASON THE SOUL REAPERS WOULD PATCH US UP.
THERE'S BEEN A NEW DEVELOPMENT.

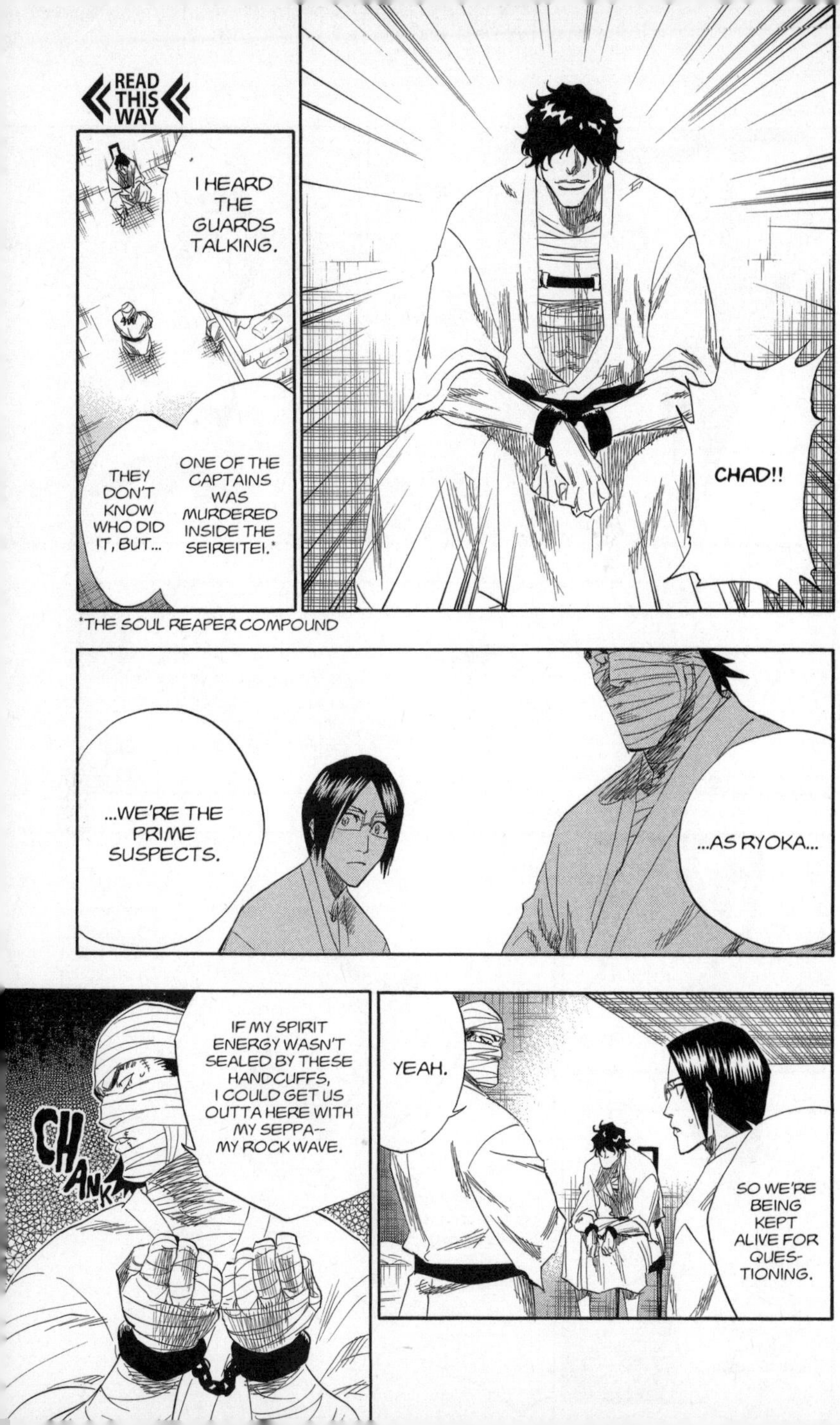
READ THIS WAY
CHAD!!
I HEARD THE GUARDS TALKING.
ONE OF THE CAPTAINS WAS MURDERED INSIDE THE SEIREITEI.*
THEY DON'T KNOW WHO DID IT, BUT...
...AS RYOKA...
...WE'RE THE PRIME SUSPECTS.
SO WE'RE BEING KEPT ALIVE FOR QUES-TIONING.
YEAH.
IF MY SPIRIT ENERGY WASN'T SEALED BY THESE HANDCUFFS, I COULD GET US OUTTA HERE WITH MY SEPPA-- MY ROCK WAVE.
CHANK

*THE SOUL REAPER COMPOUND

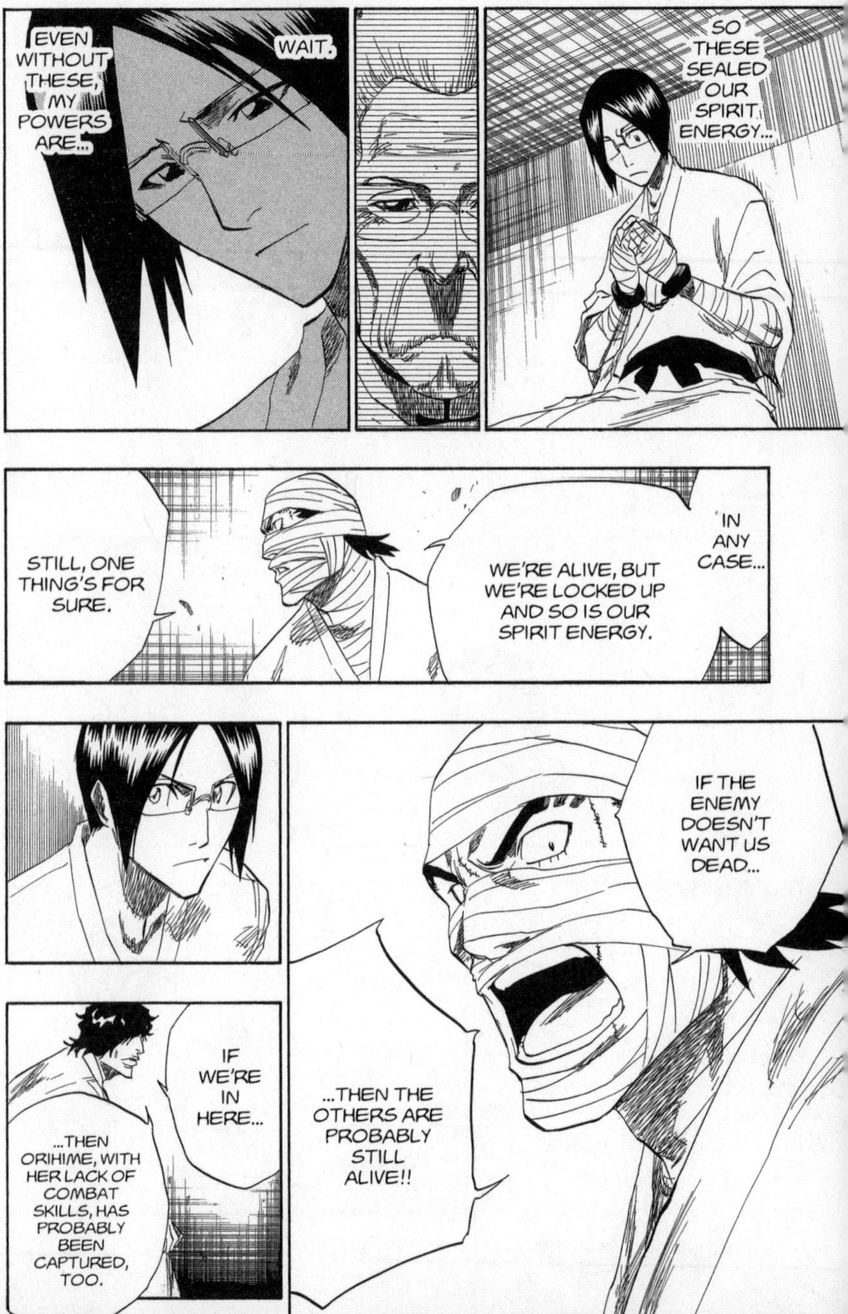
SO THESE SEALED OUR SPIRIT ENERGY...
WAIT.
EVEN WITHOUT THESE, MY POWERS ARE...
IN ANY CASE...
WE'RE ALIVE, BUT WE'RE LOCKED UP AND SO IS OUR SPIRIT ENERGY.
STILL, ONE THING'S FOR SURE.
IF THE ENEMY DOESN'T WANT US DEAD...
...THEN THE OTHERS ARE PROBABLY STILL ALIVE!!
IF WE'RE IN HERE...
...THEN ORIHIME, WITH HER LACK OF COMBAT SKILLS, HAS PROBABLY BEEN CAPTURED, TOO.

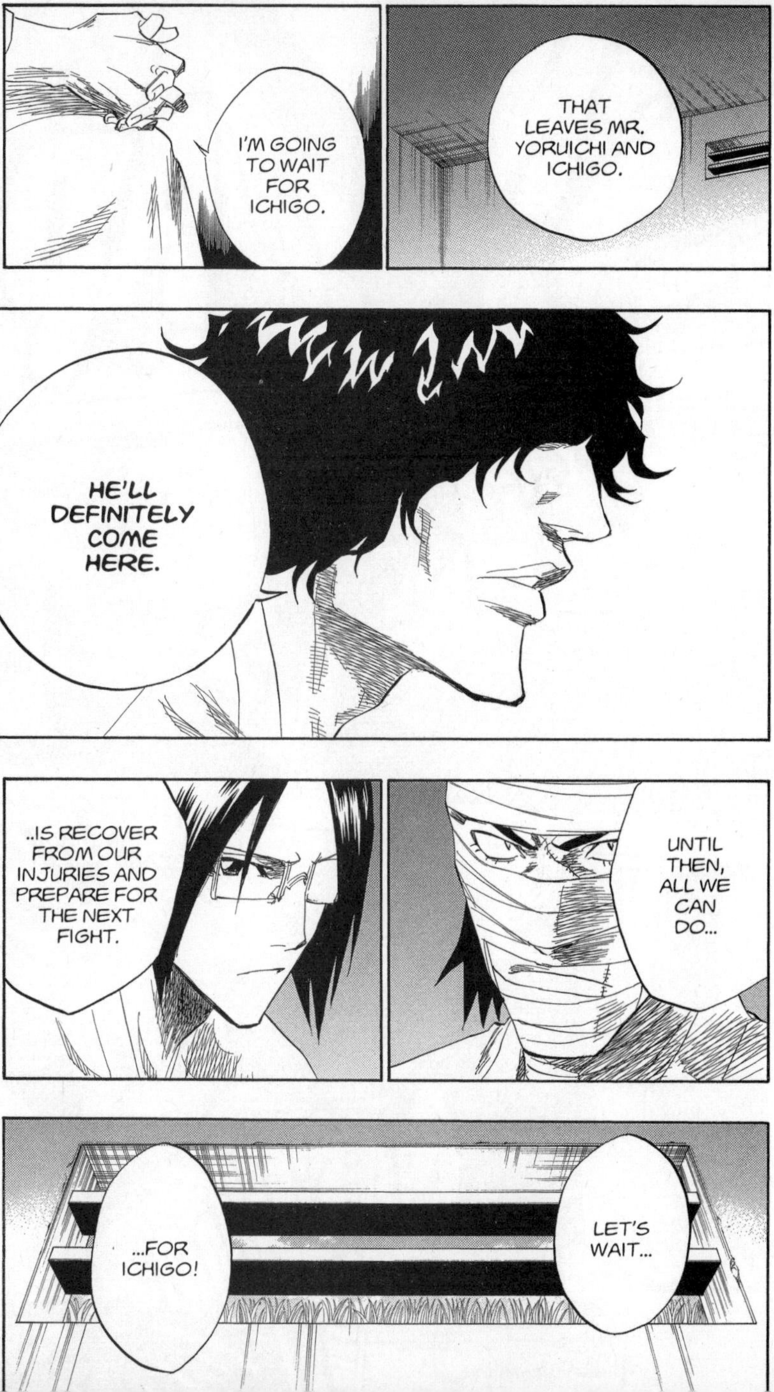
THAT LEAVES MR. YORUICHI AND ICHIGO.
I'M GOING TO WAIT FOR ICHIGO.
HE'LL DEFINITELY COME HERE.
UNTIL THEN, ALL WE CAN DO...
..IS RECOVER FROM OUR INJURIES AND PREPARE FOR THE NEXT FIGHT.
LET'S WAIT...
...FOR ICHIGO!

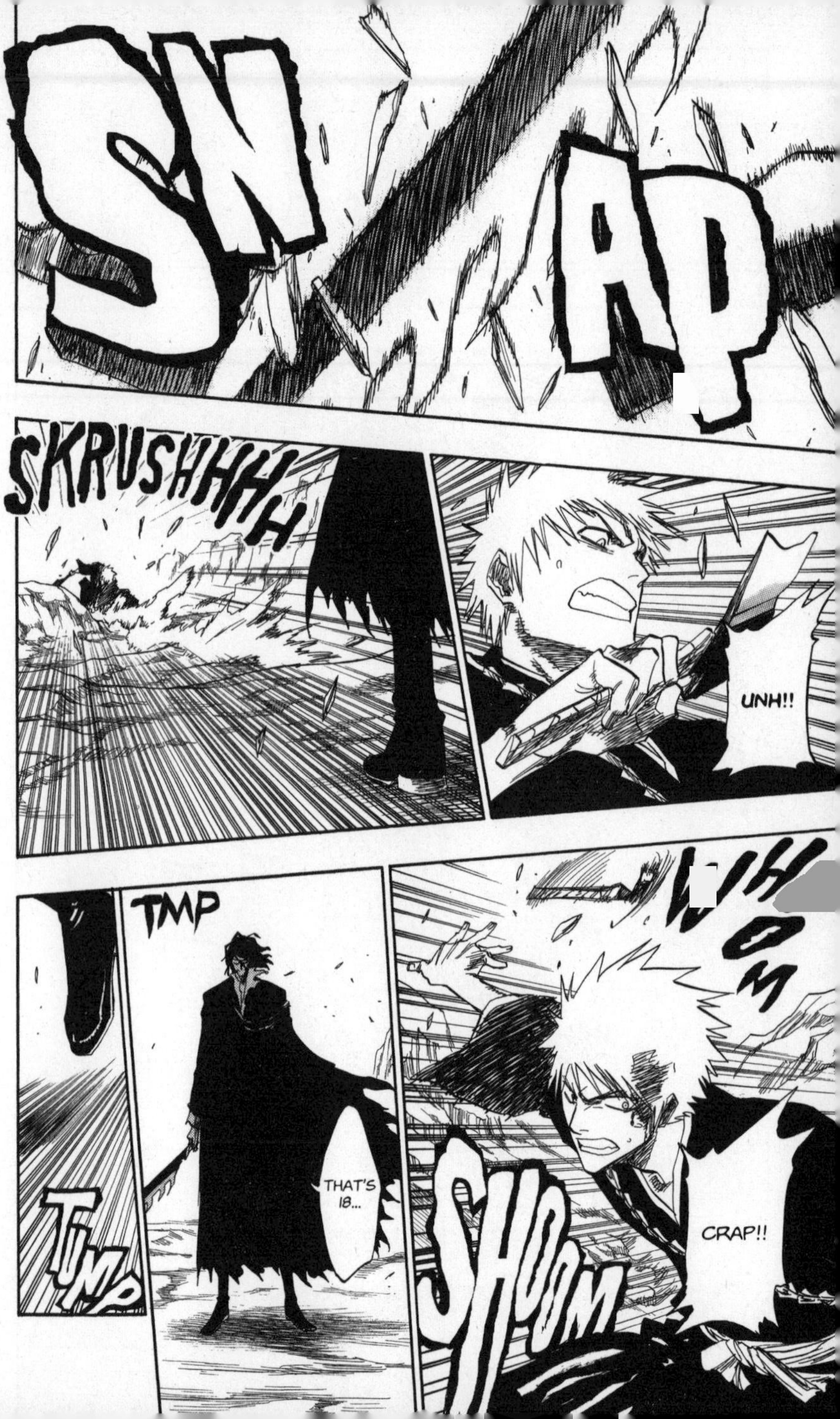
SNAP
UNH!!
SKRUSHHHH
WHOM
CRAP!!
SHOOM
TMP
THAT'S 18...
TUMP

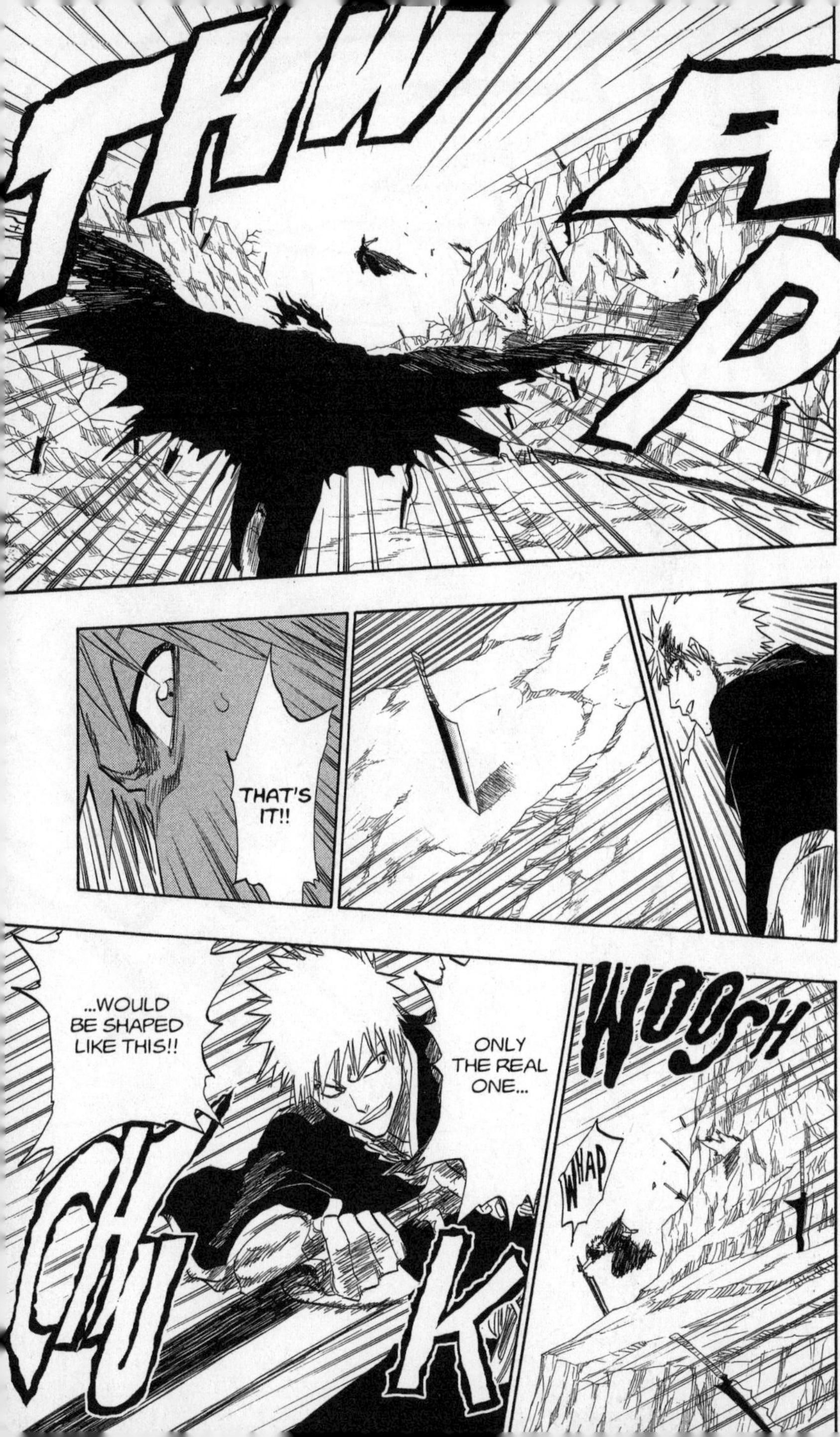
THWAP
THAT'S IT!!
WOOSH
WHAP
ONLY THE REAL ONE...
...WOULD BE SHAPED LIKE THIS!!
CHUK

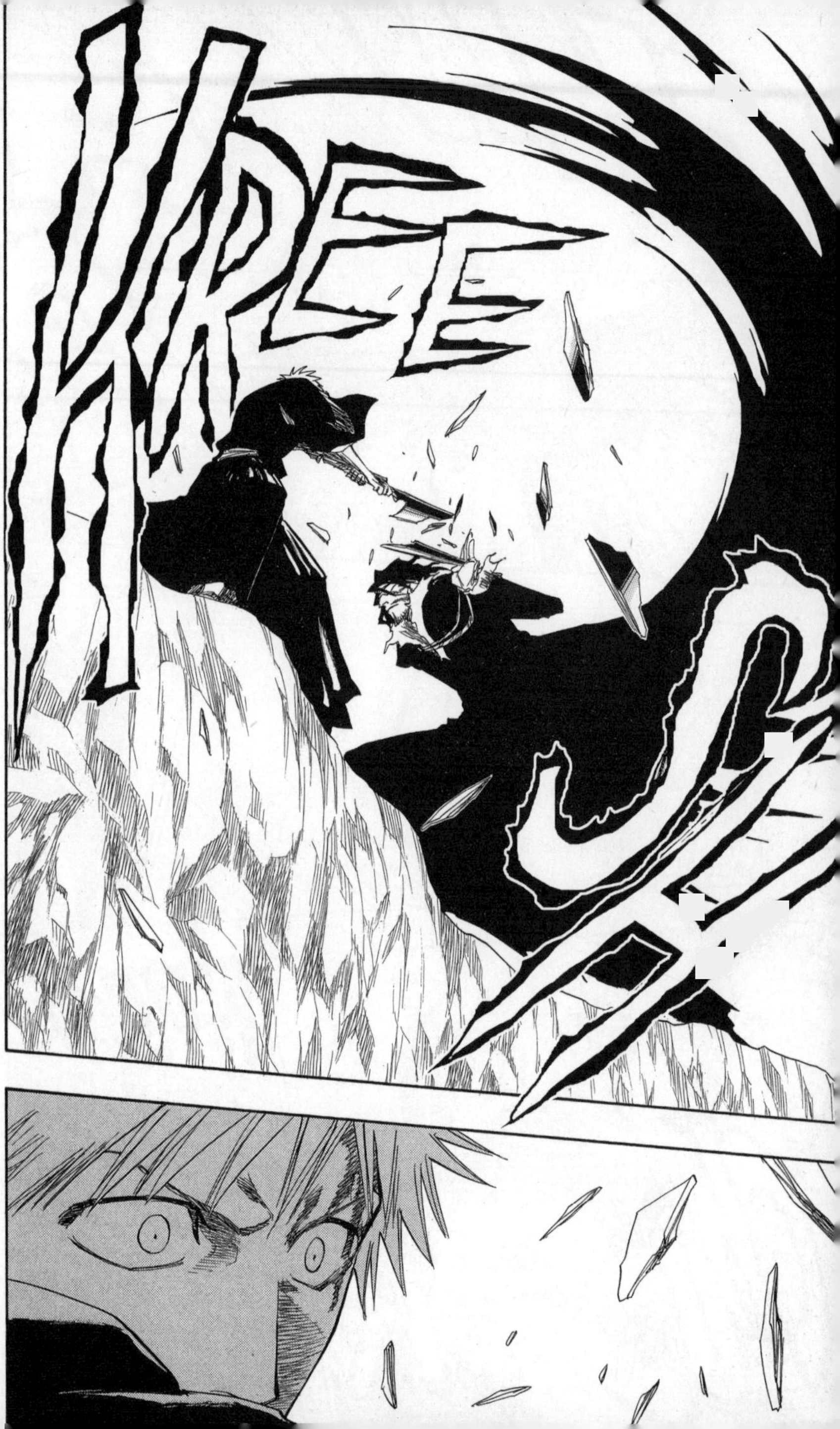

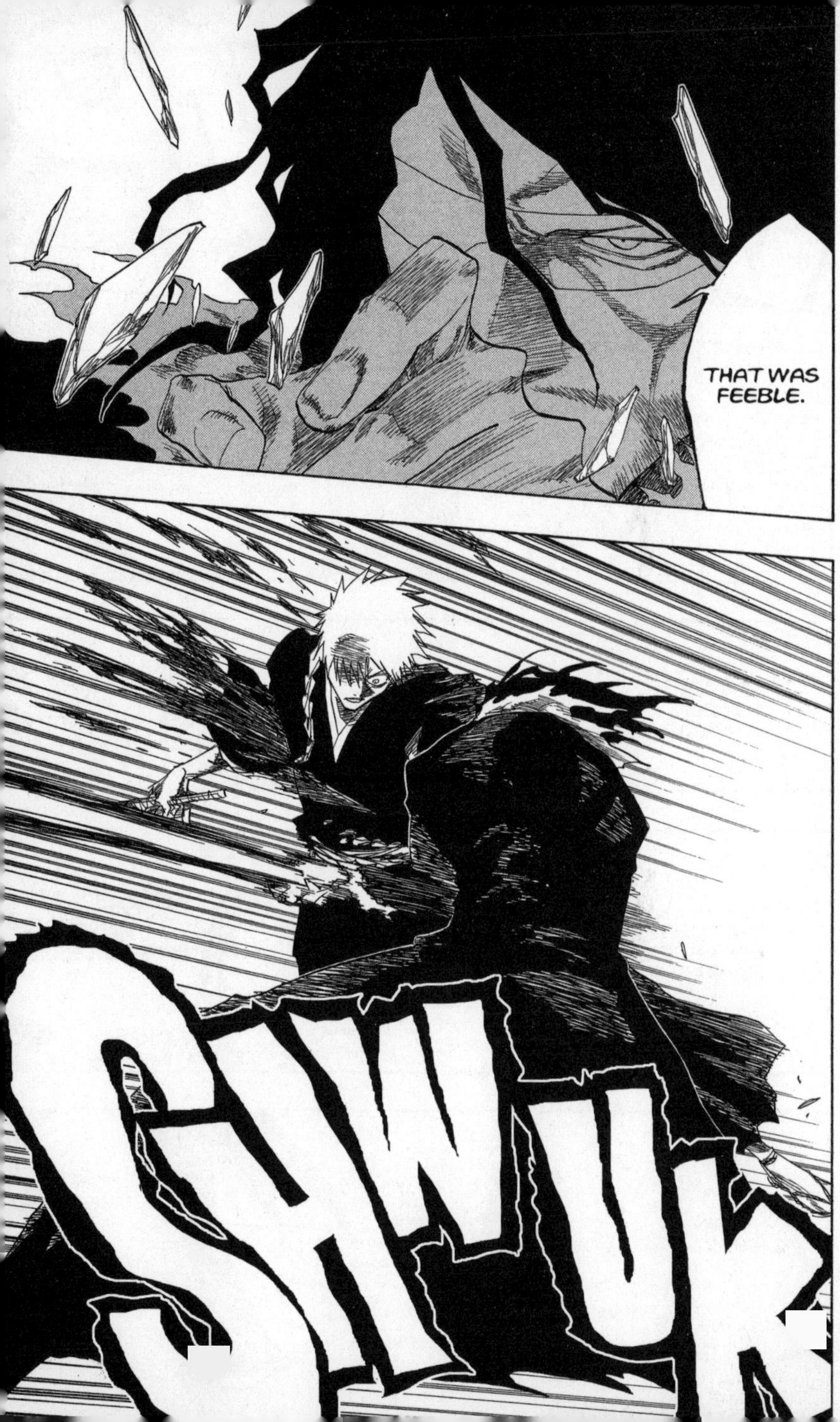
THAT WAS FEEBLE.
SHWUK

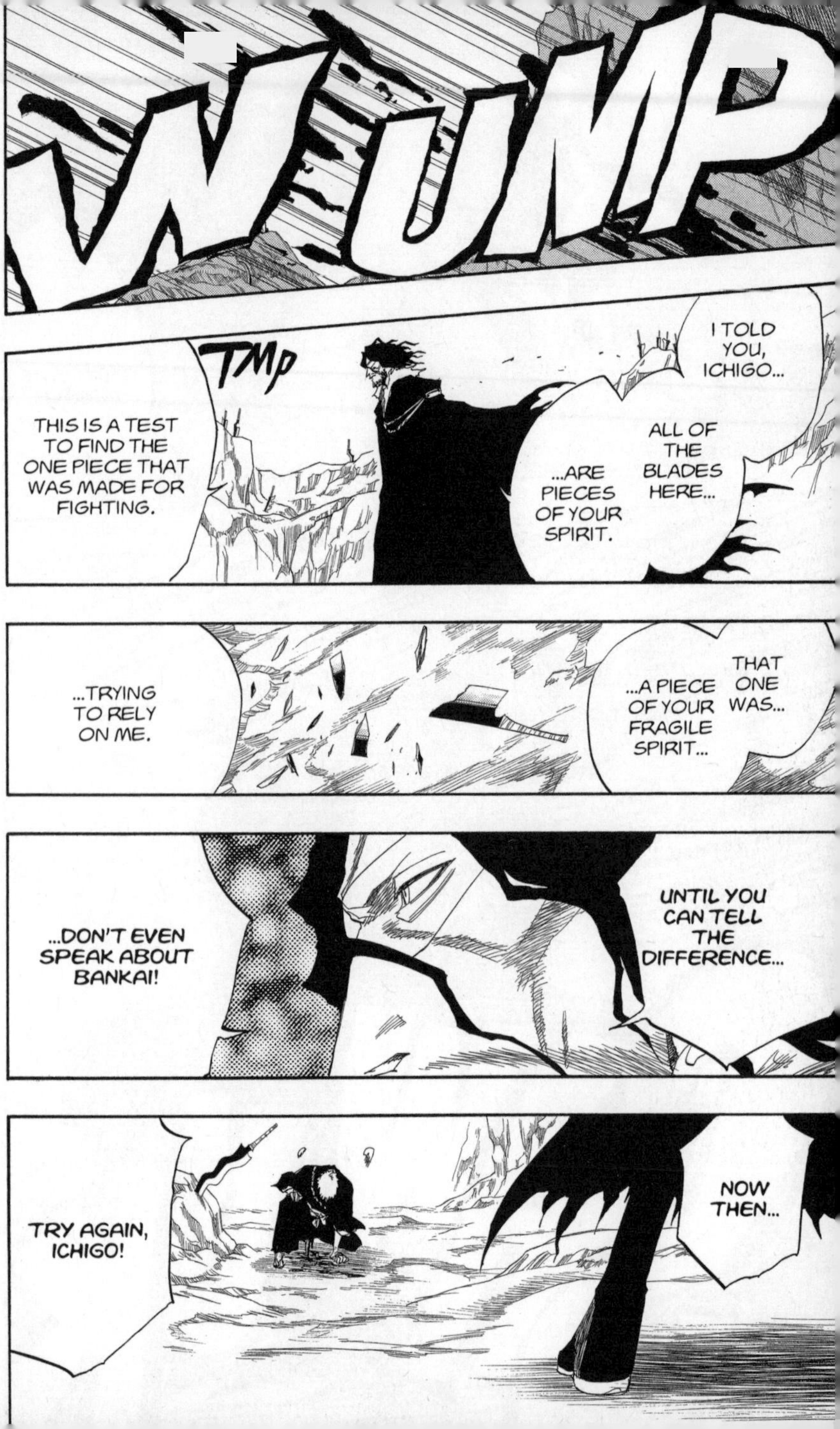
WUMP
I TOLD YOU, ICHIGO...
ALL OF THE BLADES HERE...
...ARE PIECES OF YOUR SPIRIT.
TMP
THIS IS A TEST TO FIND THE ONE PIECE THAT WAS MADE FOR FIGHTING.
THAT ONE WAS...
...A PIECE OF YOUR FRAGILE SPIRIT...
...TRYING TO RELY ON ME.
UNTIL YOU CAN TELL THE DIFFERENCE...
...DON'T EVEN SPEAK ABOUT BANKAI!
NOW THEN...
TRY AGAIN, ICHIGO!

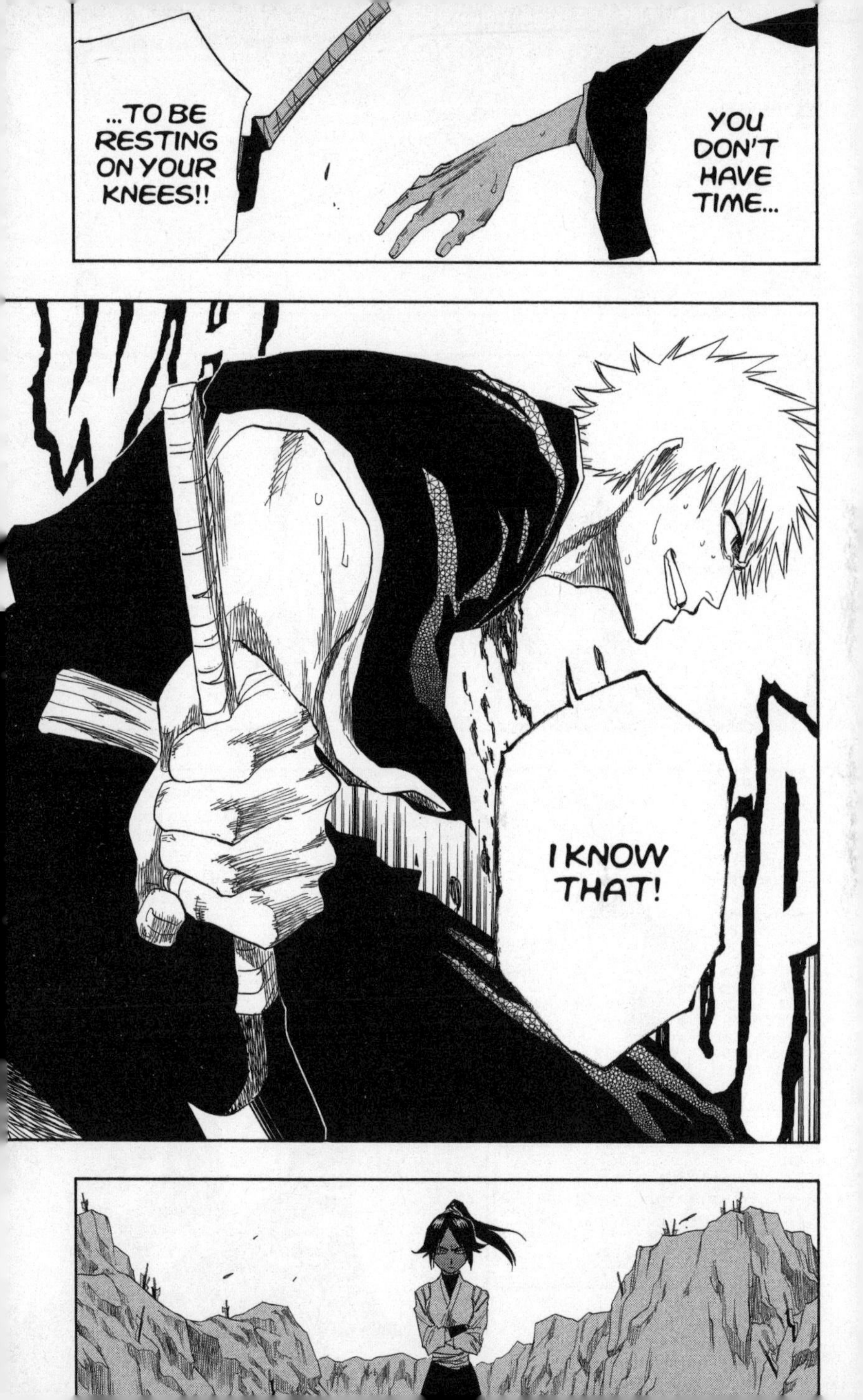
YOU DON'T HAVE TIME...
...TO BE RESTING ON YOUR KNEES!!
I KNOW THAT!

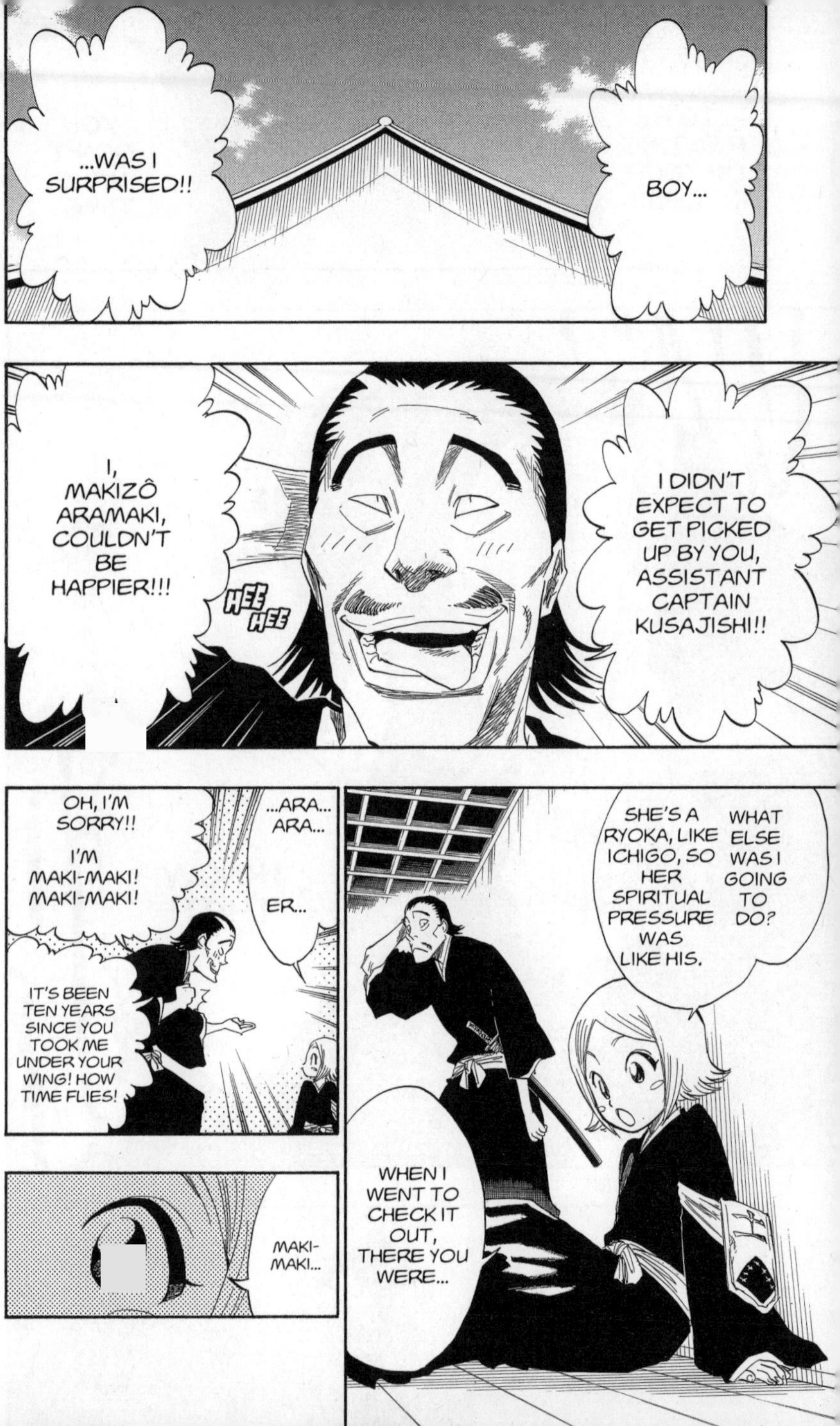
BOY...
...WAS I SURPRISED!!
I DIDN'T EXPECT TO GET PICKED UP BY YOU, ASSISTANT CAPTAIN KUSAJISHI!!
HEE HEE
I, MAKIZÔ ARAMAKI, COULDN'T BE HAPPIER!!!
WHAT ELSE WAS I GOING TO DO?
SHE'S A RYOKA, LIKE ICHIGO, SO HER SPIRITUAL PRESSURE WAS LIKE HIS.
WHEN I WENT TO CHECK IT OUT, THERE YOU WERE...
...ARA... ARA...
ER...
OH, I'M SORRY!! I'M MAKI-MAKI! MAKI-MAKI!
IT'S BEEN TEN YEARS SINCE YOU TOOK ME UNDER YOUR WING! HOW TIME FLIES!
MAKI-MAKI...

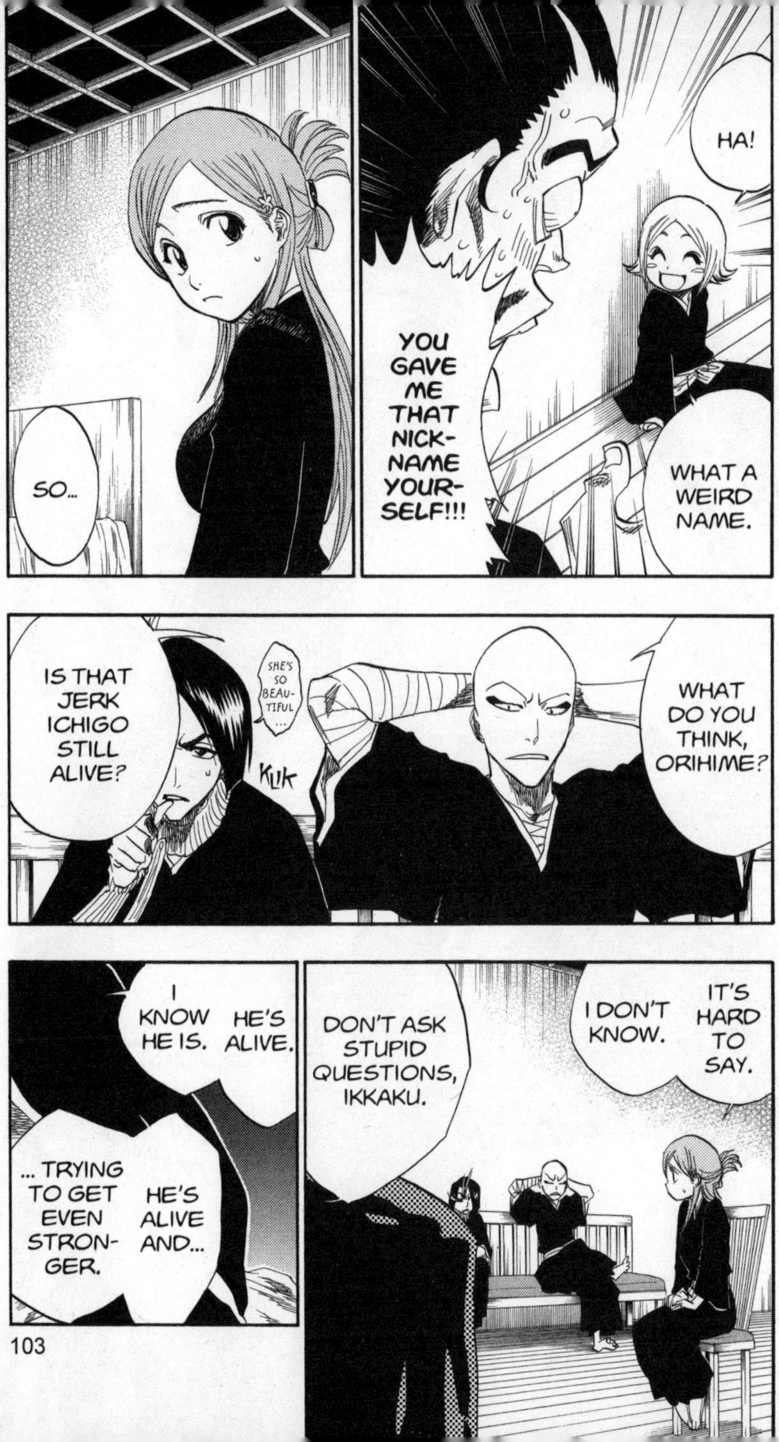
HA!
WHAT A WEIRD NAME.
YOU GAVE ME THAT NICK-NAME YOUR-SELF!!!
SO...
WHAT DO YOU THINK, ORIHIME?
SHE'S SO BEAU-TIFUL...
KLIK
IS THAT JERK ICHIGO STILL ALIVE?
IT'S HARD TO SAY.
I DON'T KNOW.
DON'T ASK STUPID QUESTIONS, IKKAKU.
HE'S ALIVE.
I KNOW HE IS.
HE'S ALIVE AND...
... TRYING TO GET EVEN STRON-GER.

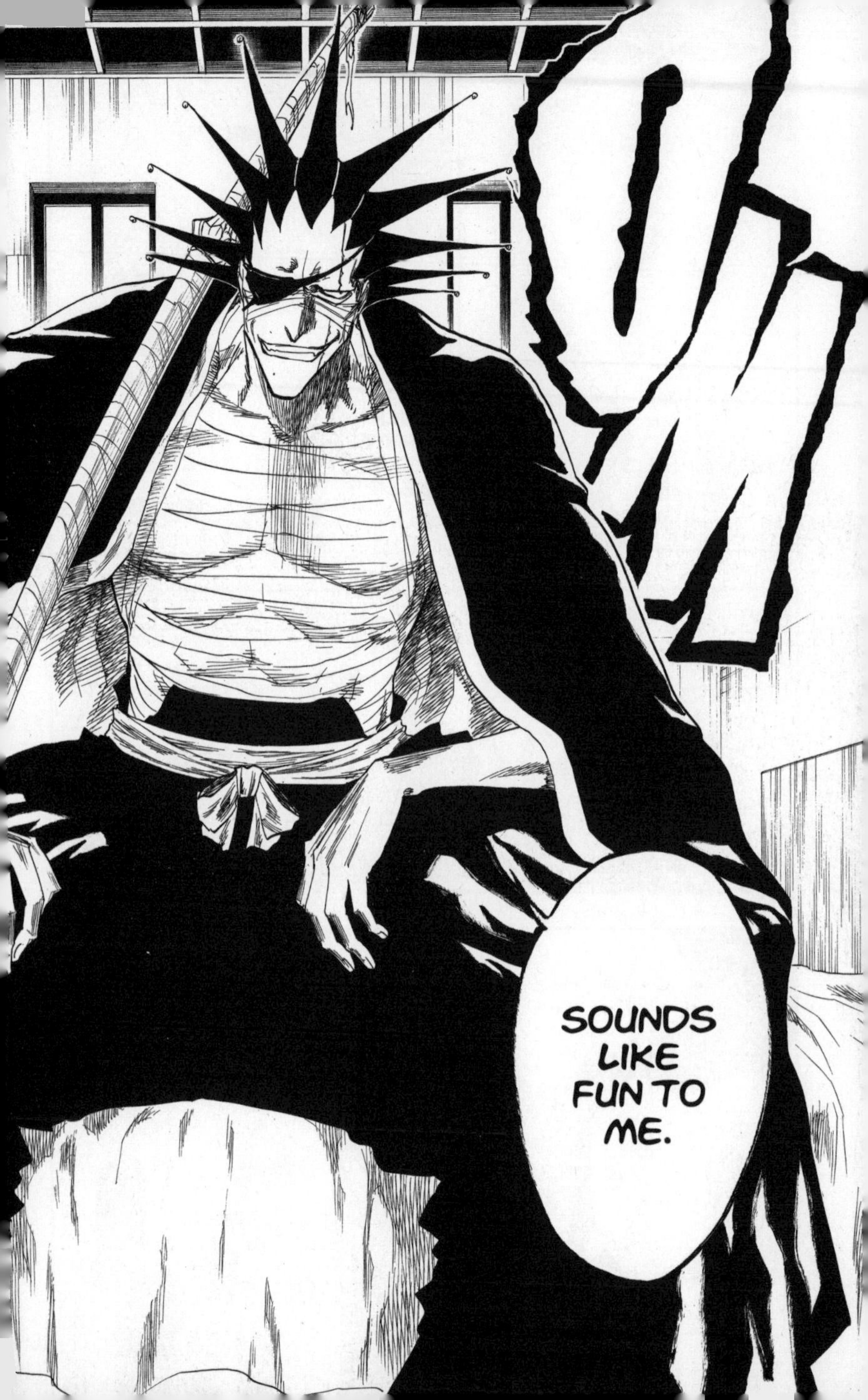
SOUNDS LIKE FUN TO ME.

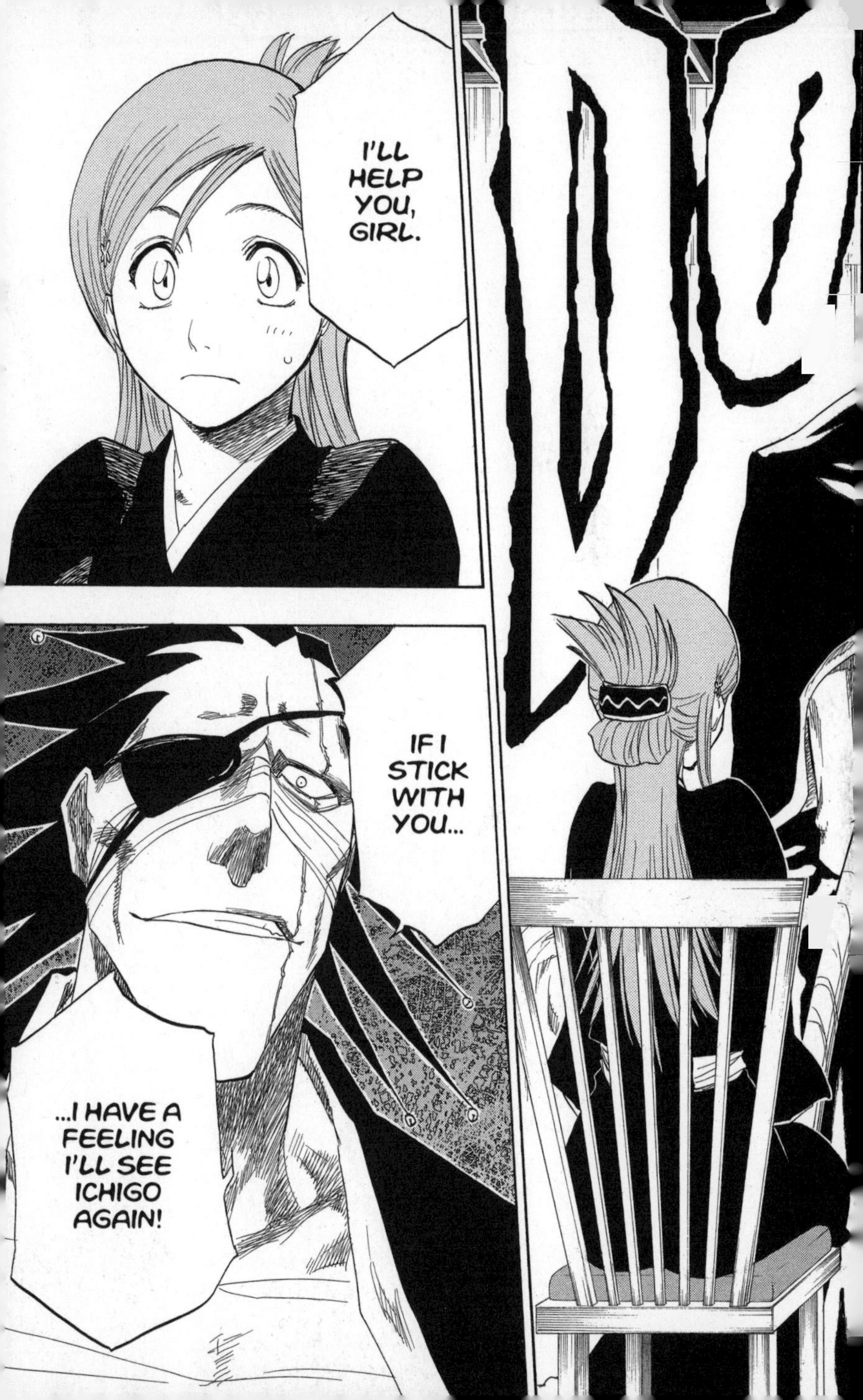
I'LL HELP YOU, GIRL.
IF I STICK WITH YOU...
...I HAVE A FEELING I'LL SEE ICHIGO AGAIN!

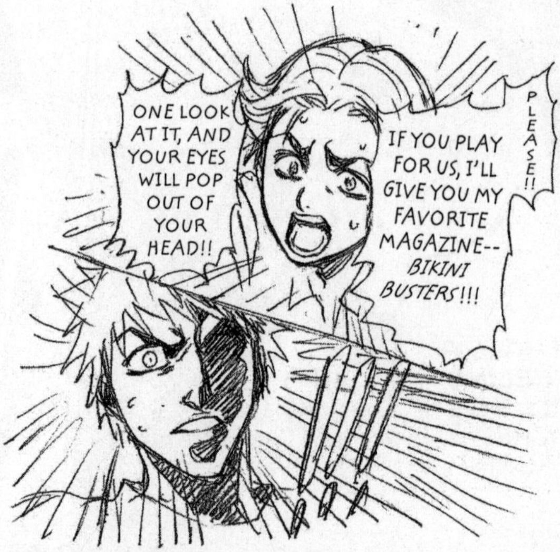
PLEASE!!
IF YOU PLAY FOR US, I'LL GIVE YOU MY FAVORITE MAGAZINE-- *BIKINI BUSTERS*!!!
ONE LOOK AT IT, AND YOUR EYES WILL POP OUT OF YOUR HEAD!!

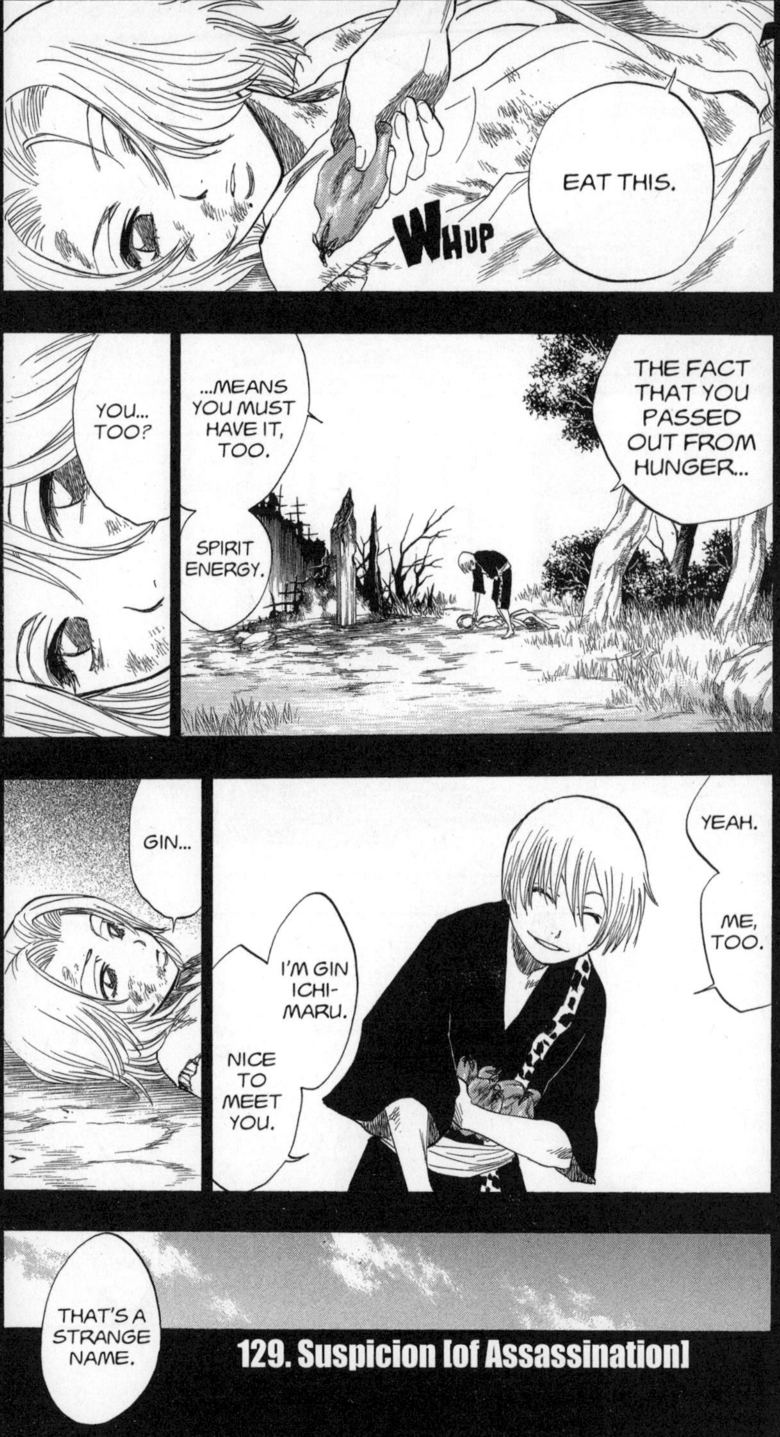
EAT THIS.
WHUP
THE FACT THAT YOU PASSED OUT FROM HUNGER...
...MEANS YOU MUST HAVE IT, TOO.
SPIRIT ENERGY.
YOU... TOO?
YEAH.
ME, TOO.
I'M GIN ICHI-MARU.
NICE TO MEET YOU.
GIN...
THAT'S A STRANGE NAME.
129. Suspicion [of Assassination]

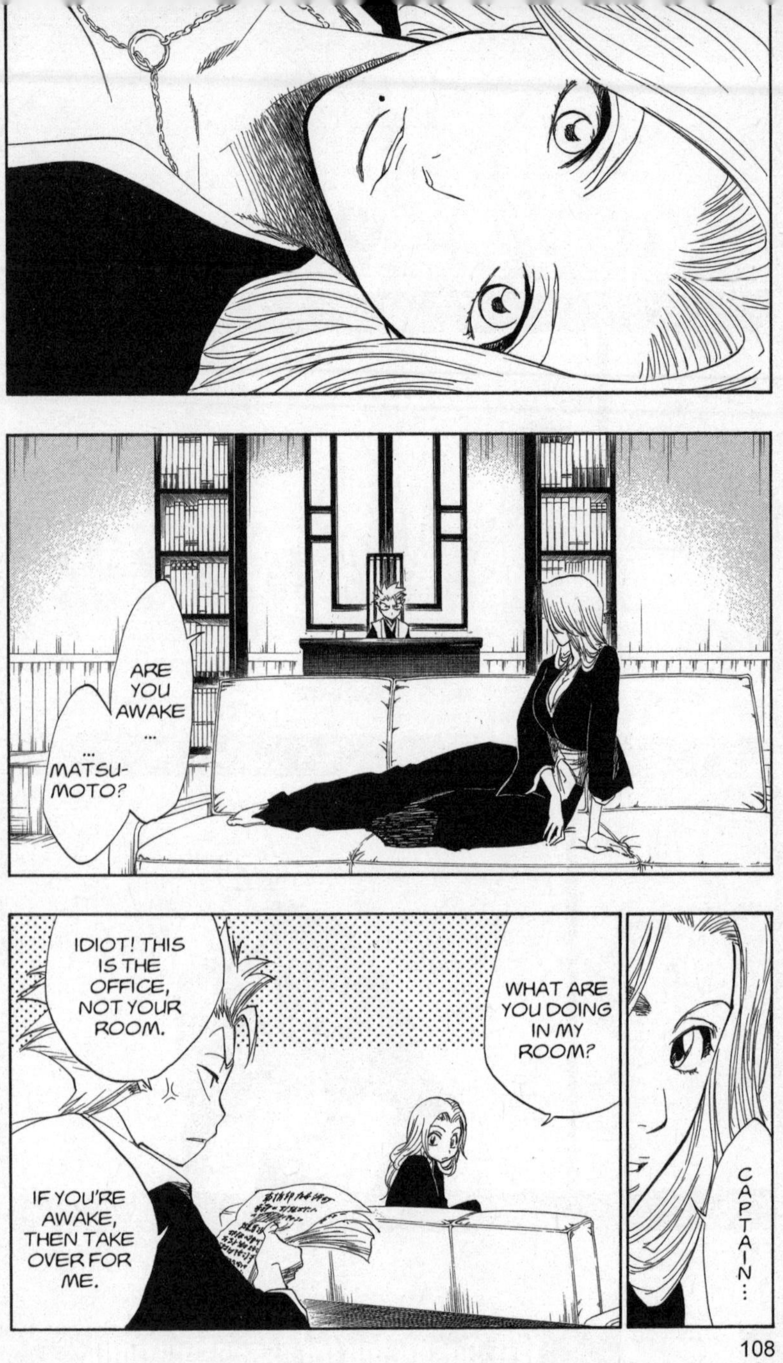
ARE YOU AWAKE ...
... MATSUMOTO?
CAPTAIN...
WHAT ARE YOU DOING IN MY ROOM?
IDIOT! THIS IS THE OFFICE, NOT YOUR ROOM.
IF YOU'RE AWAKE, THEN TAKE OVER FOR ME.

READ THIS WAY

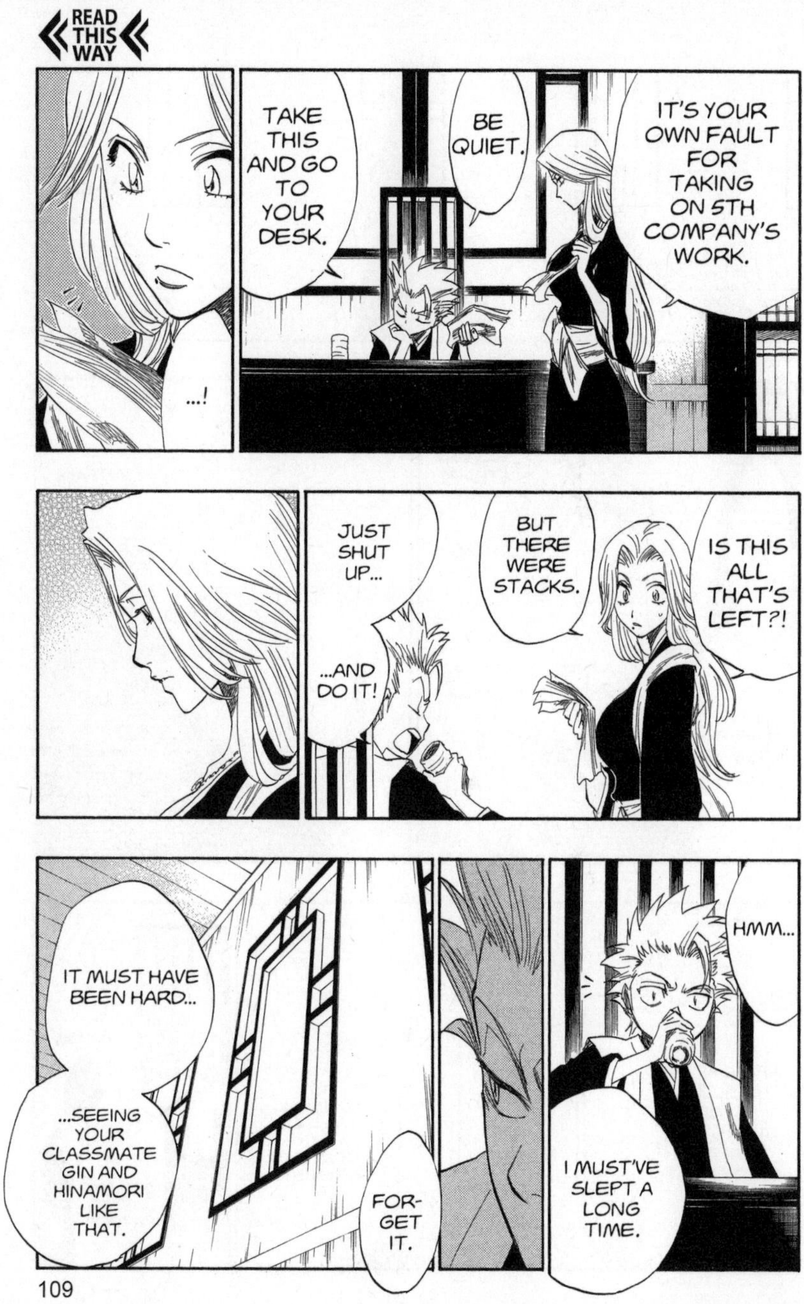

IT'S YOUR OWN FAULT FOR TAKING ON 5TH COMPANY'S WORK.
BE QUIET.
TAKE THIS AND GO TO YOUR DESK.
...!
IS THIS ALL THAT'S LEFT?!
BUT THERE WERE STACKS.
JUST SHUT UP...
...AND DO IT!
HMM...
I MUST'VE SLEPT A LONG TIME.
IT MUST HAVE BEEN HARD...
...SEEING YOUR CLASSMATE GIN AND HINAMORI LIKE THAT.
FOR-GET IT.

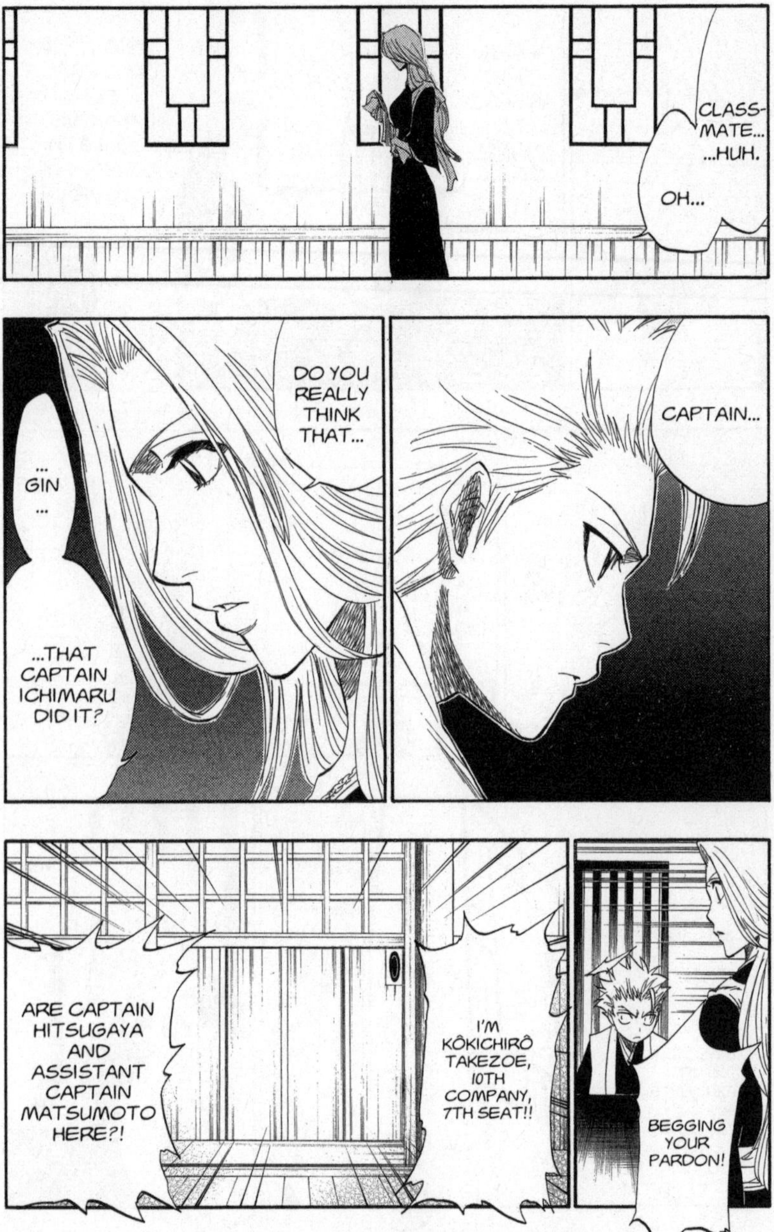

CLASS-MATE... ...HUH.
OH...
CAPTAIN...
DO YOU REALLY THINK THAT...
... GIN ...
...THAT CAPTAIN ICHIMARU DID IT?
BEGGING YOUR PARDON!
I'M KÔKICHIRÔ TAKEZOE, 10TH COMPANY, 7TH SEAT!!
ARE CAPTAIN HITSUGAYA AND ASSISTANT CAPTAIN MATSUMOTO HERE?!

READ THIS WAY

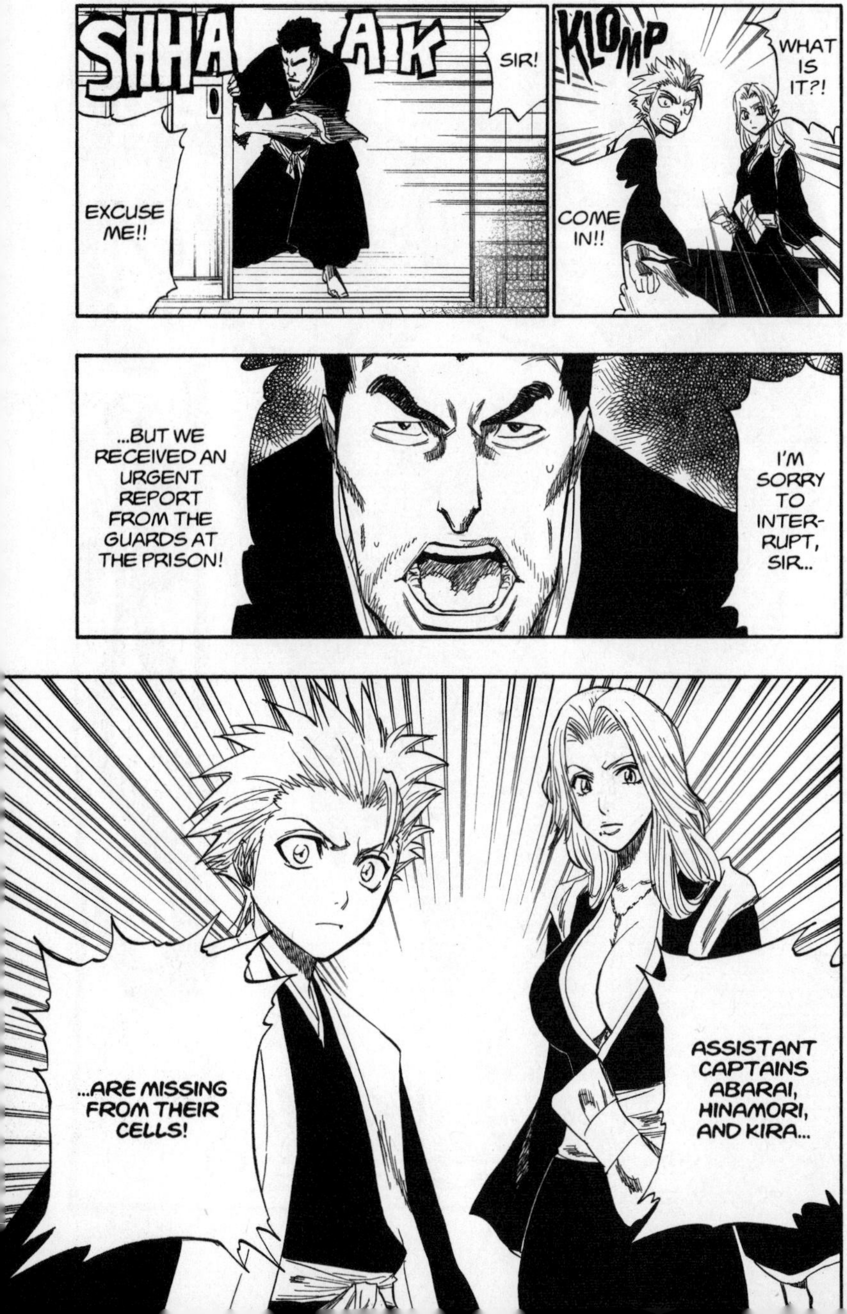
KLOMP
WHAT IS IT?!
COME IN!!
SIR!
SHHAAK
EXCUSE ME!!
I'M SORRY TO INTER-RUPT, SIR...
...BUT WE RECEIVED AN URGENT REPORT FROM THE GUARDS AT THE PRISON!
ASSISTANT CAPTAINS ABARAI, HINAMORI, AND KIRA...
...ARE MISSING FROM THEIR CELLS!

129. Suspicion [of Assassination]

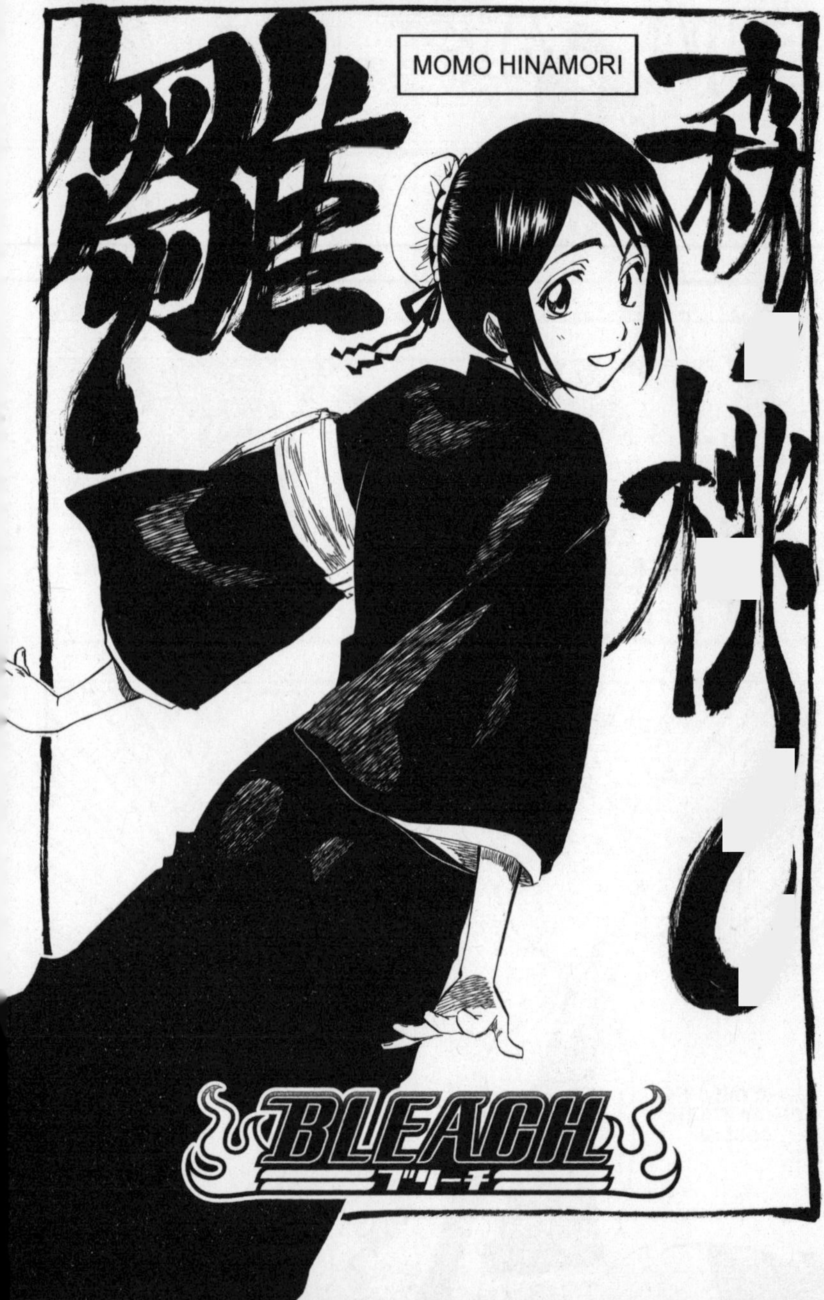
MOMO HINAMORI
雛森桃
BLEACH
ブリーチ

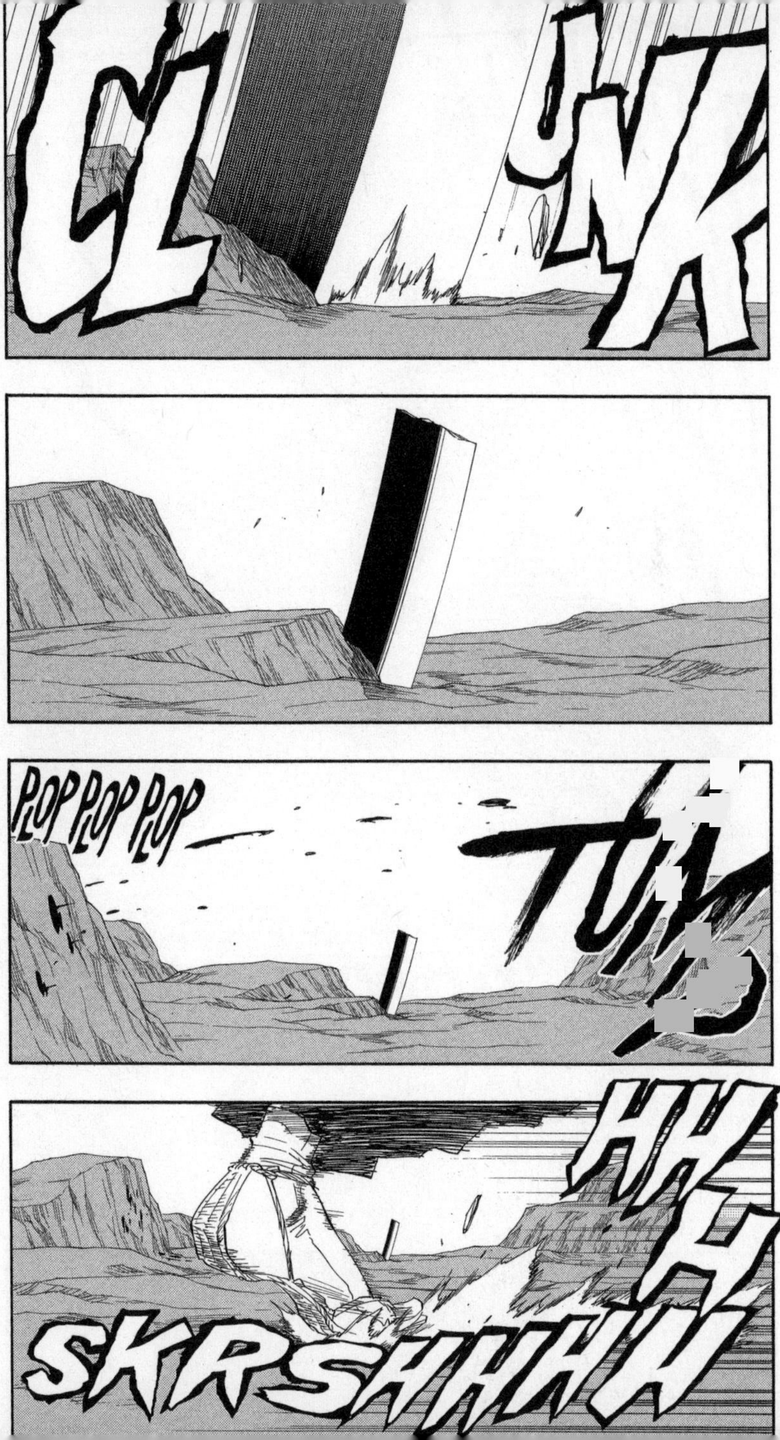
CL
UNK
TUMP
PLOP PLOP PLOP
HHH
SKRSHHHH

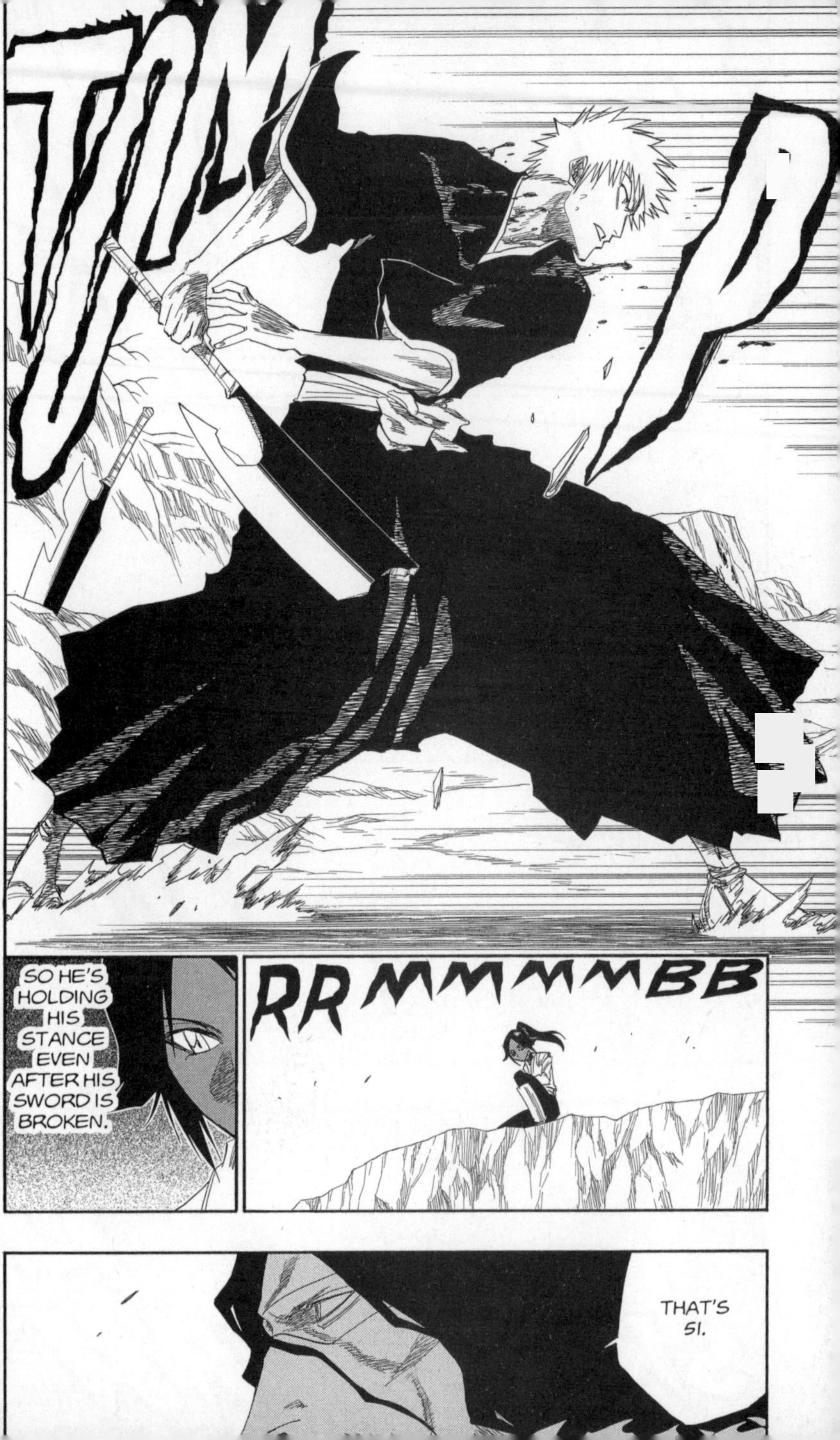
RRMMMMMBB
SO HE'S HOLDING HIS STANCE EVEN AFTER HIS SWORD IS BROKEN.
THAT'S 51.

READ THIS WAY

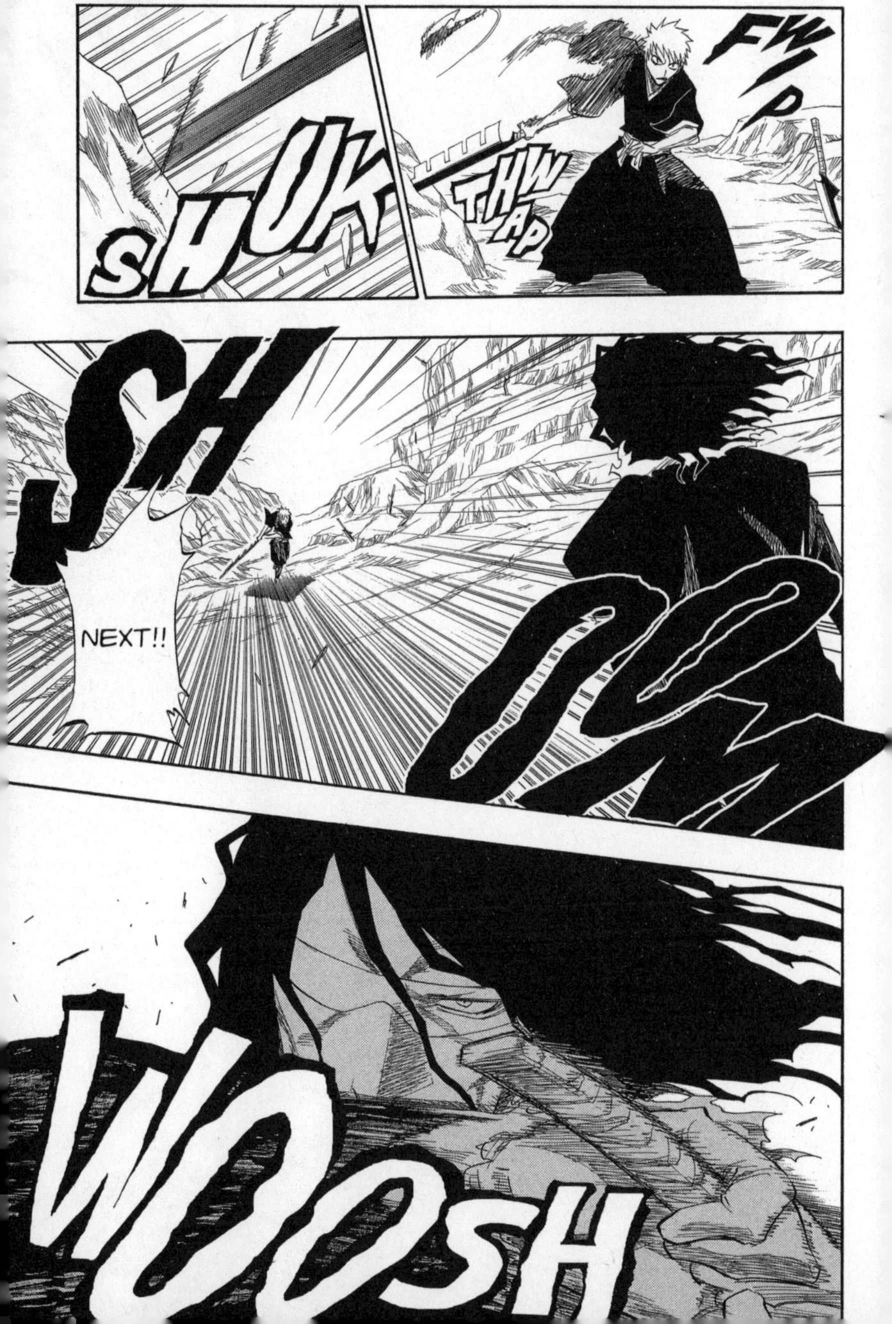
FWIP
THWAP
SHUK
SH
NEXT!!
WOOSH

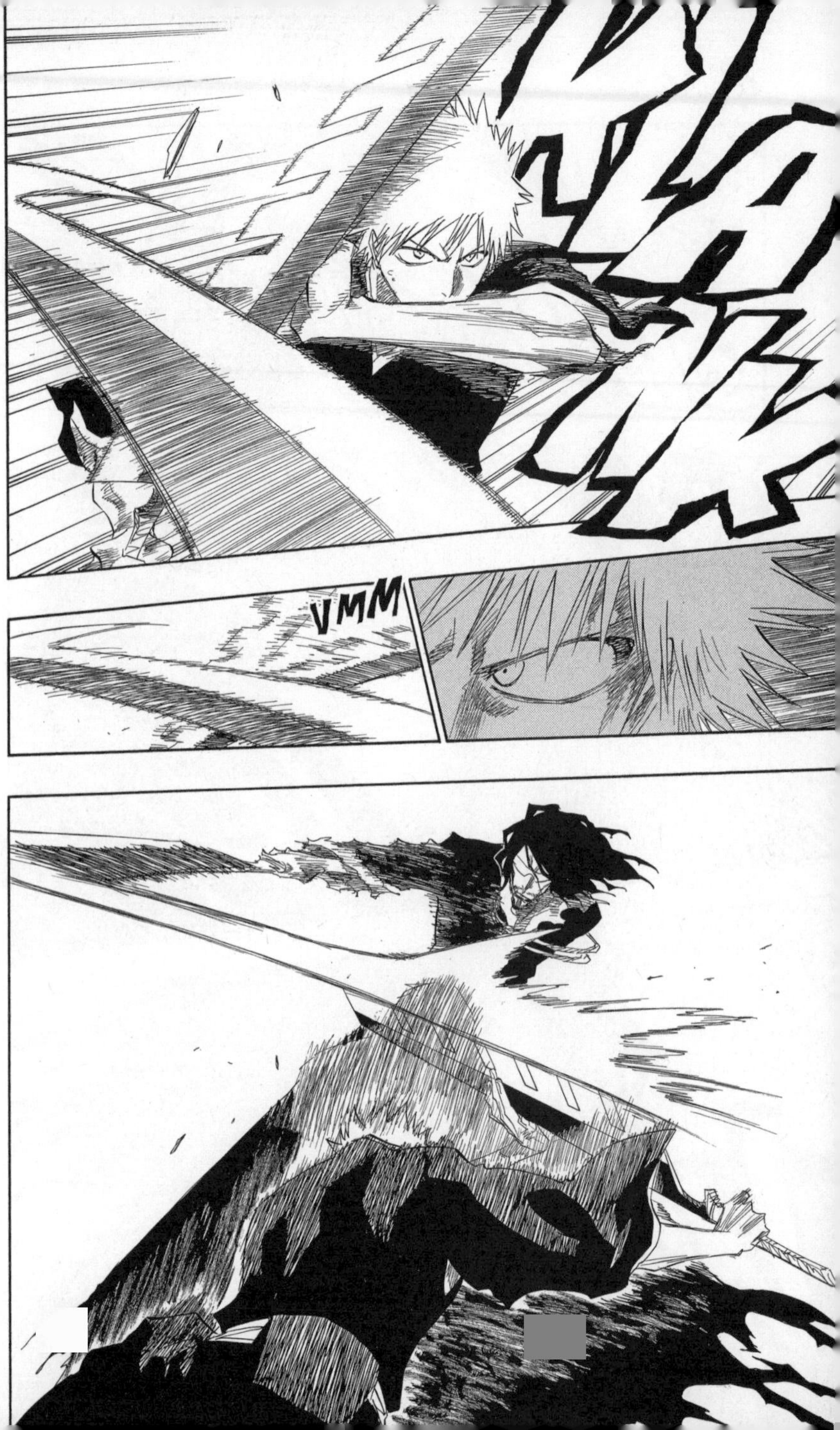
VMM

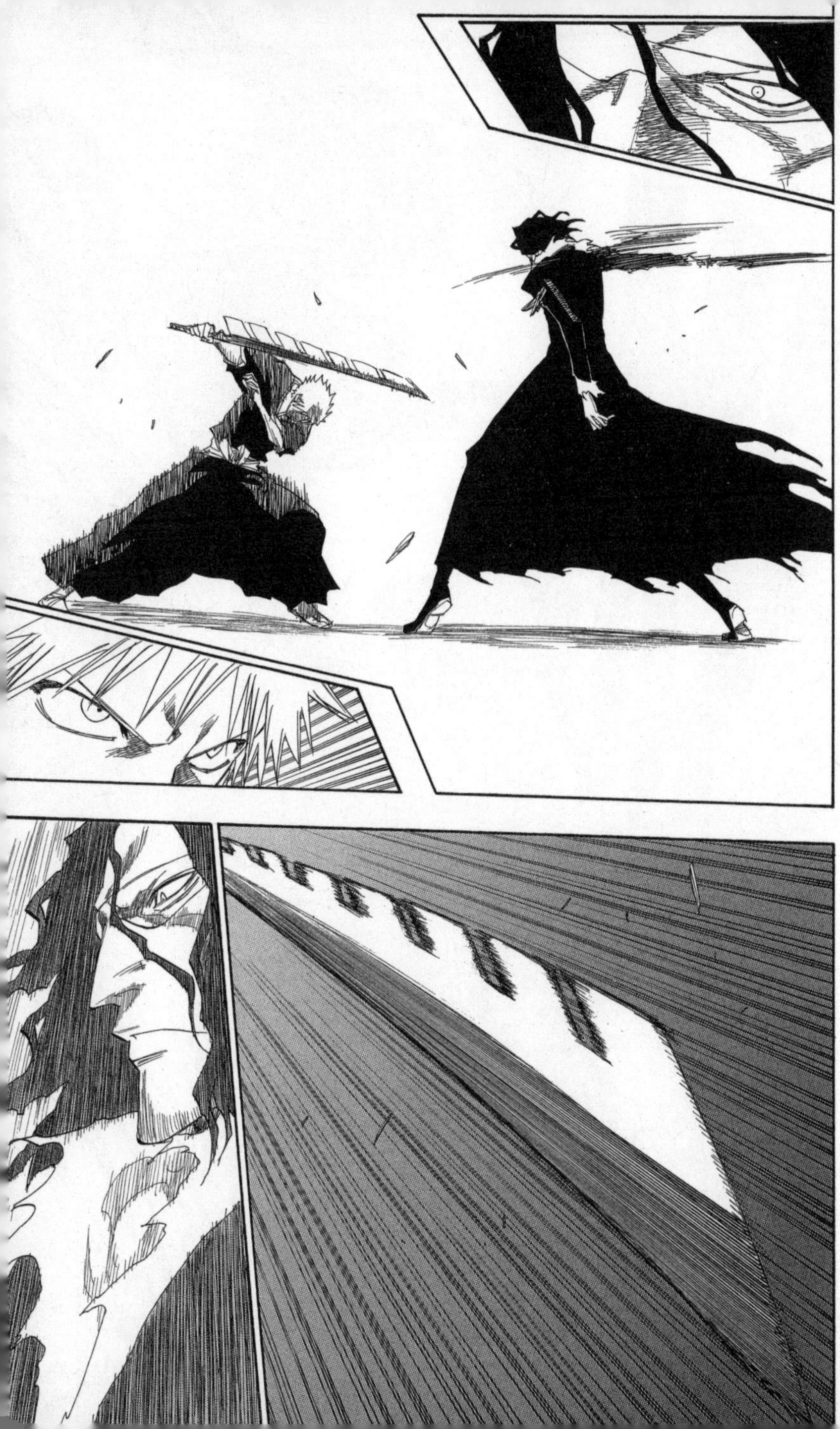

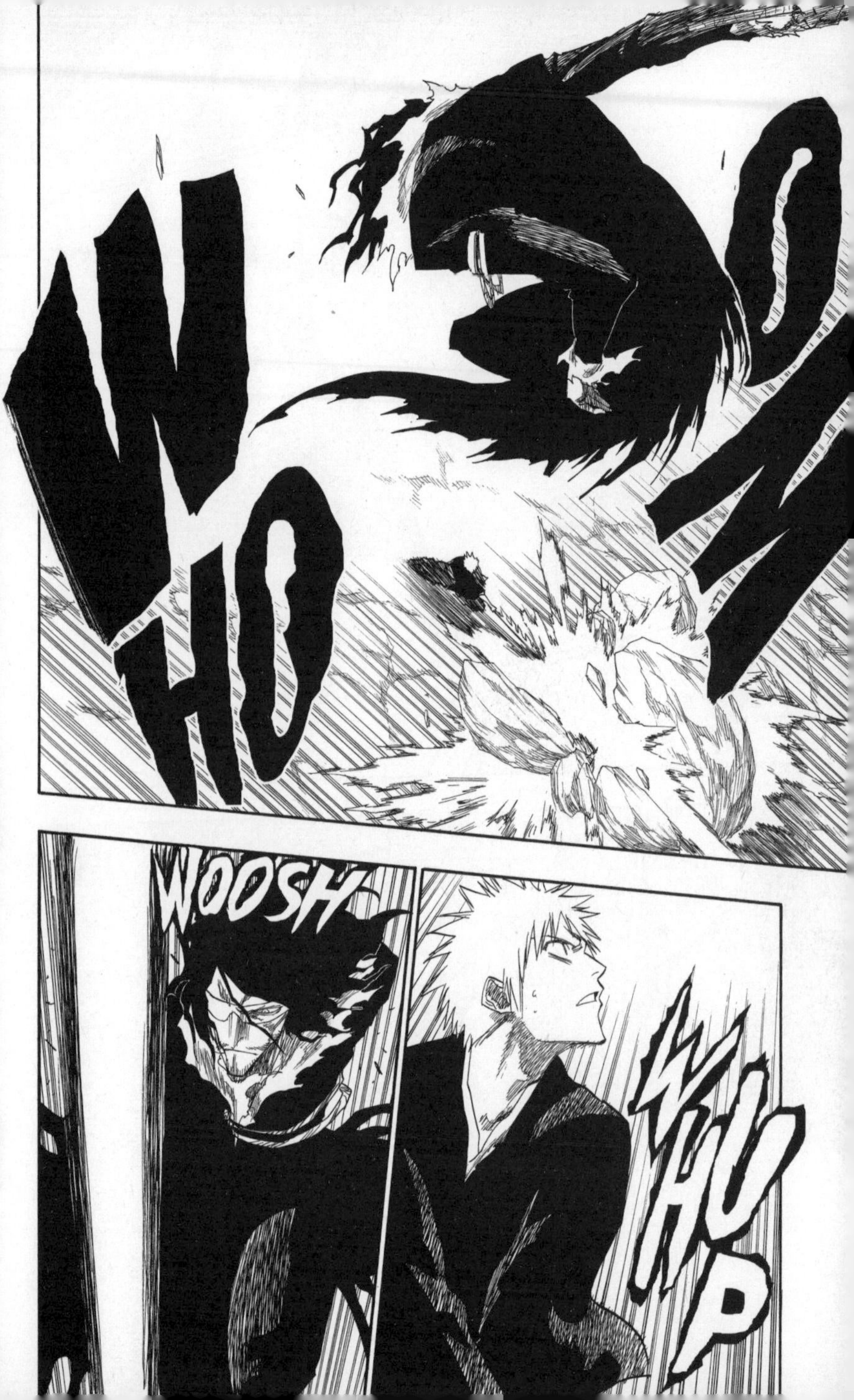
WHOOM
WHUP
WOOSH

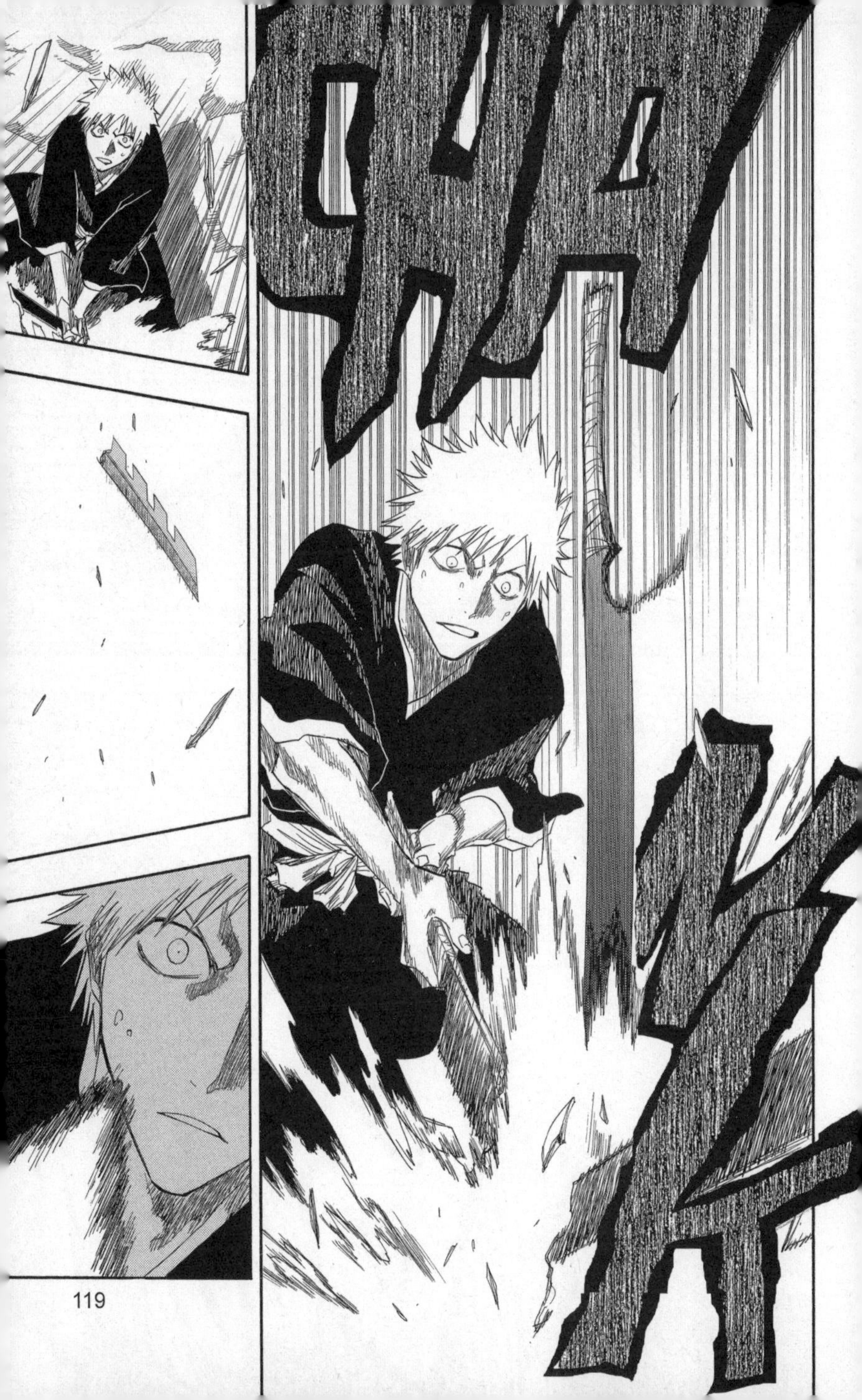

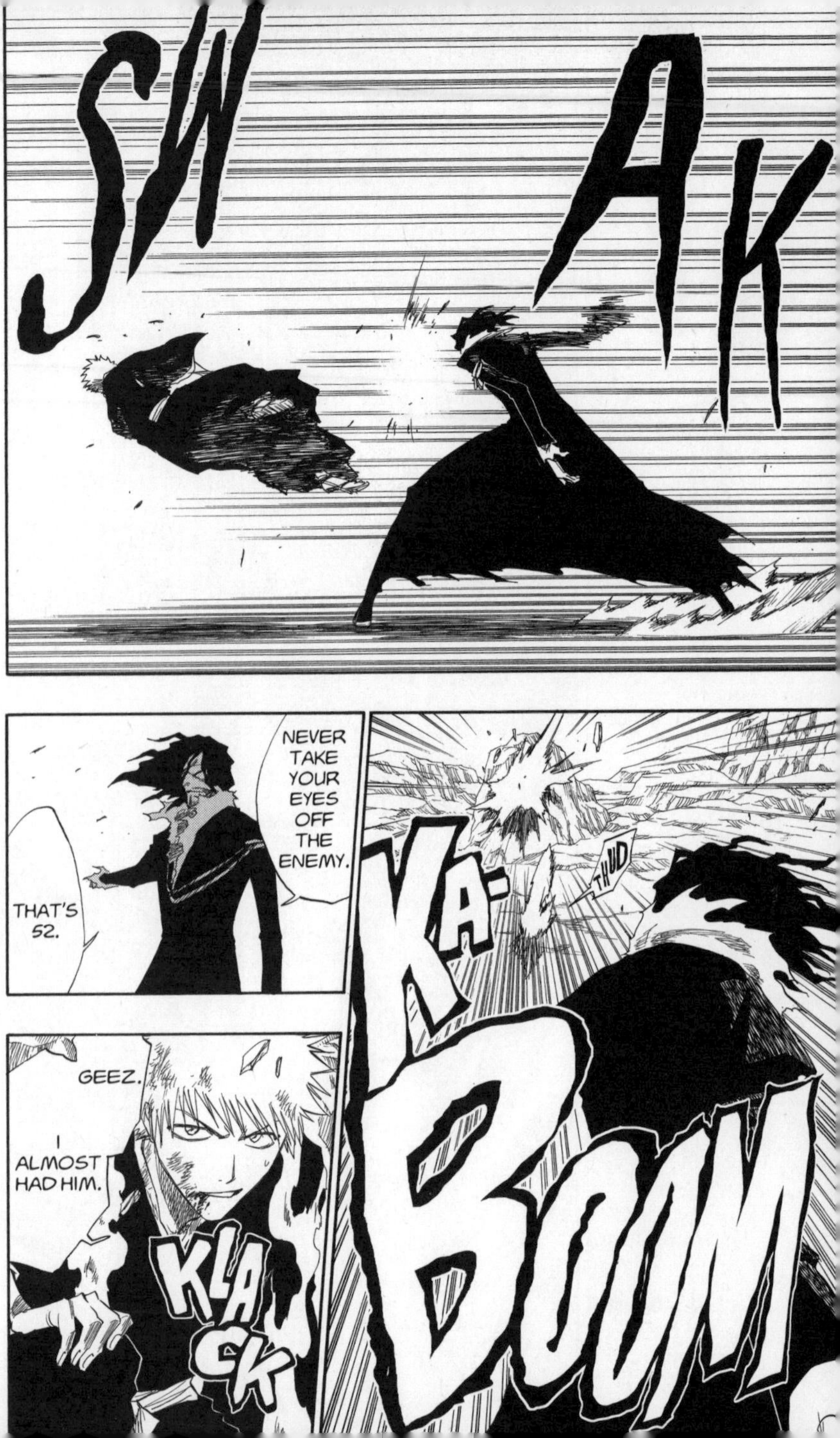
SWAK
KA-BOOM
THUD
NEVER TAKE YOUR EYES OFF THE ENEMY.
THAT'S 52.
GEEZ.
I ALMOST HAD HIM.
KLACK

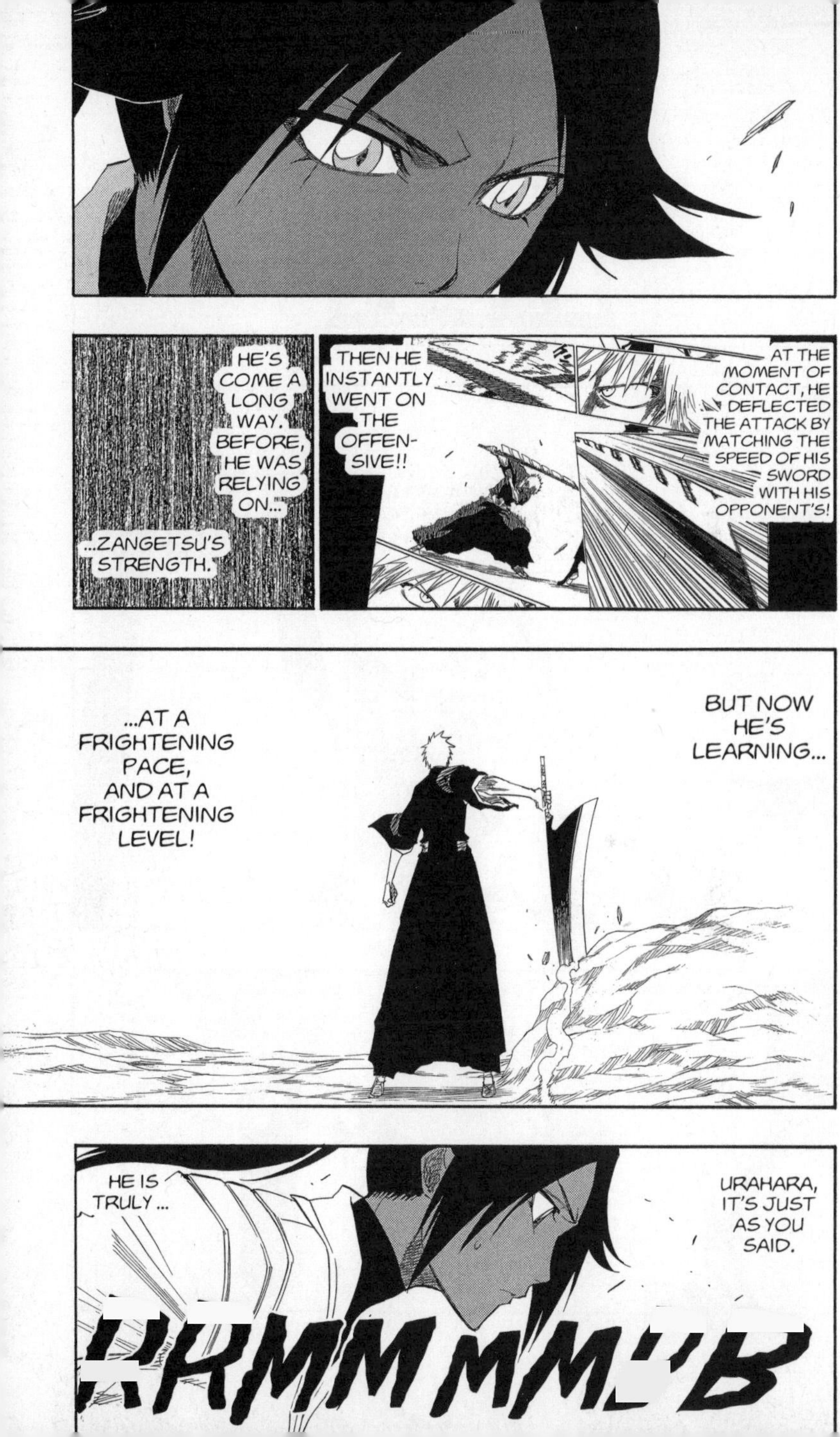
AT THE MOMENT OF CONTACT, HE DEFLECTED THE ATTACK BY MATCHING THE SPEED OF HIS SWORD WITH HIS OPPONENT'S!
THEN HE INSTANTLY WENT ON THE OFFENSIVE!!
HE'S COME A LONG WAY. BEFORE, HE WAS RELYING ON...
...ZANGETSU'S STRENGTH.
BUT NOW HE'S LEARNING...
...AT A FRIGHTENING PACE, AND AT A FRIGHTENING LEVEL!
URAHARA, IT'S JUST AS YOU SAID.
HE IS TRULY...

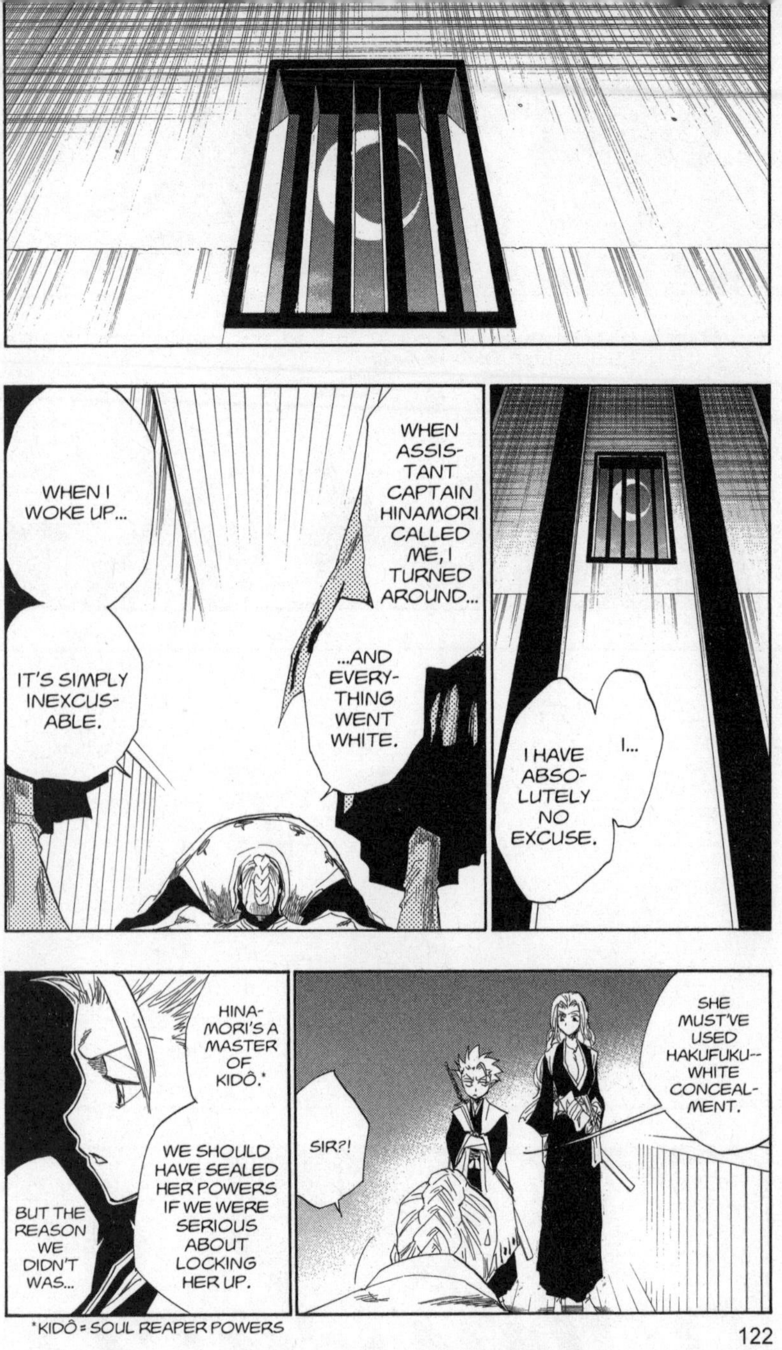
I...
I HAVE ABSOLUTELY NO EXCUSE.
WHEN ASSISTANT CAPTAIN HINAMORI CALLED ME, I TURNED AROUND...
...AND EVERYTHING WENT WHITE.
WHEN I WOKE UP...
IT'S SIMPLY INEXCUSABLE.
SHE MUST'VE USED HAKUFUKU--WHITE CONCEALMENT.
SIR?!
HINAMORI'S A MASTER OF KIDÔ.*
WE SHOULD HAVE SEALED HER POWERS IF WE WERE SERIOUS ABOUT LOCKING HER UP.
BUT THE REASON WE DIDN'T WAS...

*KIDÔ = SOUL REAPER POWERS

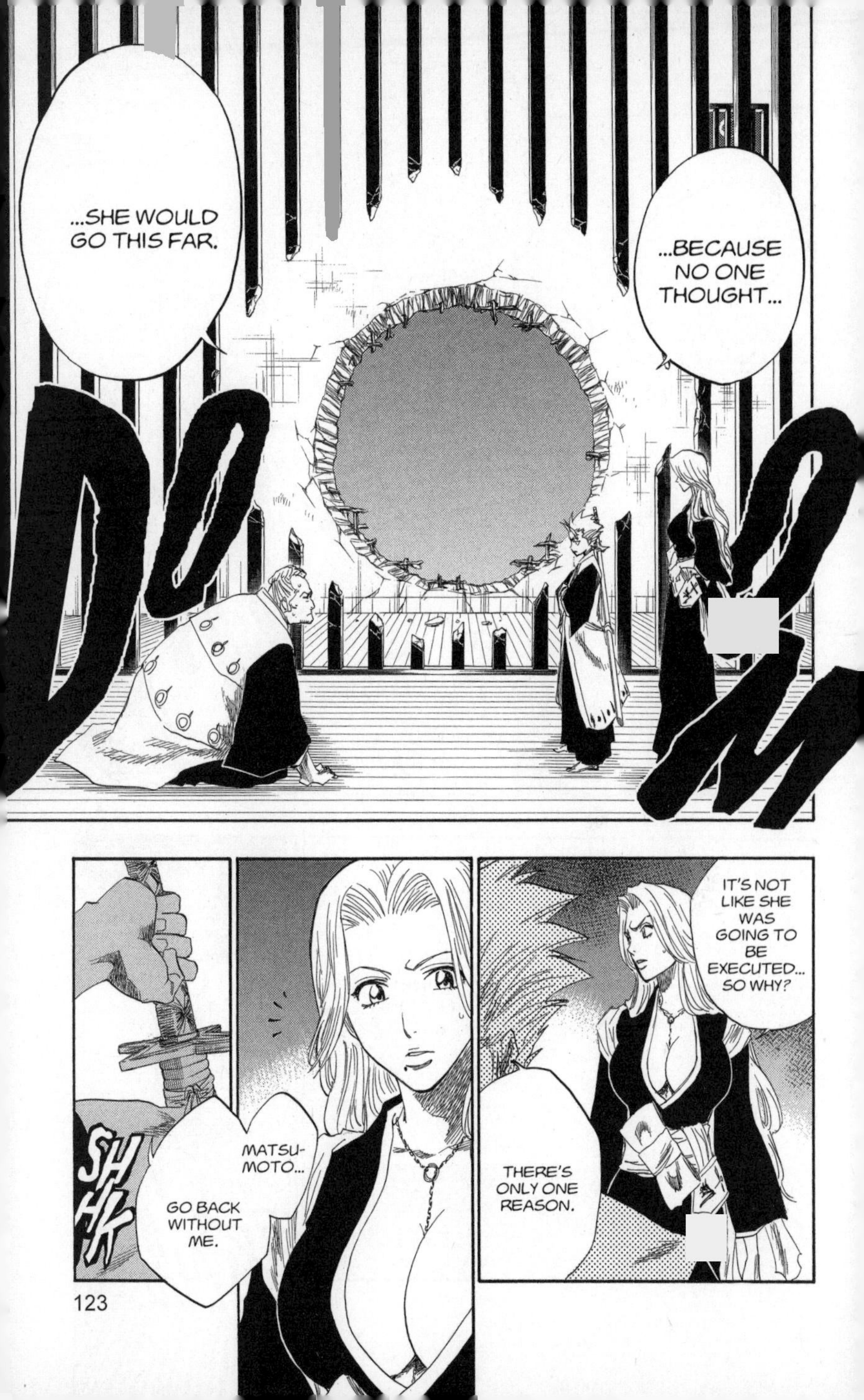
...BECAUSE NO ONE THOUGHT...
...SHE WOULD GO THIS FAR.
DOOM
IT'S NOT LIKE SHE WAS GOING TO BE EXECUTED... SO WHY?
THERE'S ONLY ONE REASON.
MATSU-MOTO...
GO BACK WITHOUT ME.
SHHK

...GOING TO RESCUE HINAMORI.

I'M...

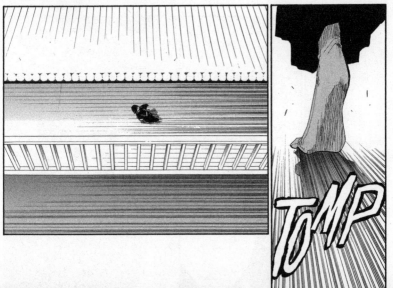

READ THIS WAY

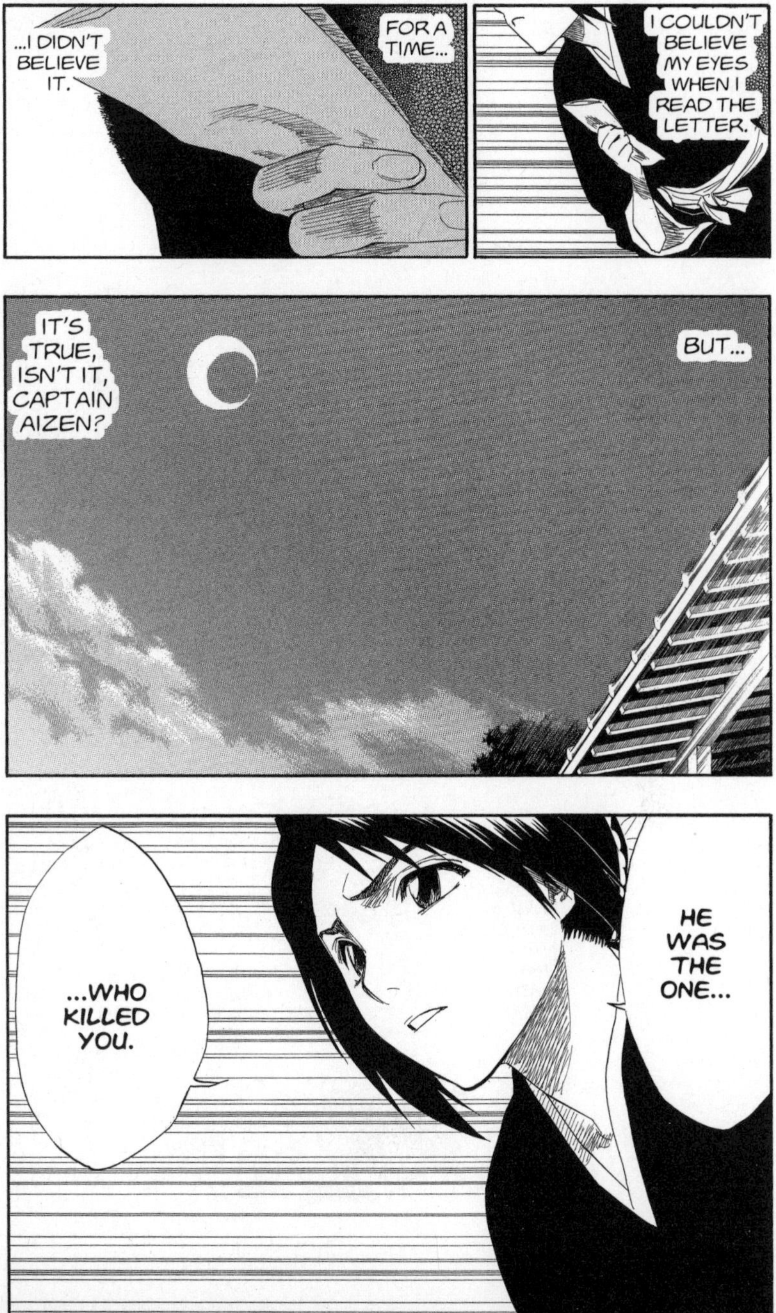
I COULDN'T BELIEVE MY EYES WHEN I READ THE LETTER.
FOR A TIME...
...I DIDN'T BELIEVE IT.
IT'S TRUE, ISN'T IT, CAPTAIN AIZEN?
BUT...
HE WAS THE ONE...
...WHO KILLED YOU.

AUGUST 11. SUNNY. THEIR FRIENDSHIP AND LOVE OF SOCCER GOT TO ME, SO I DECIDED TO HELP THEM. WE STARTED PRACTICING AT THEIR SECRET BASE-- THE LOCAL PARK.
KA-BOOM
MY TALENTS AS A STRIKER QUICKLY BLOOMED, BUT I HAD NO IDEA OF THE TRAGEDY THAT AWAITED ME!!

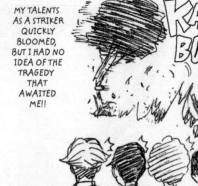

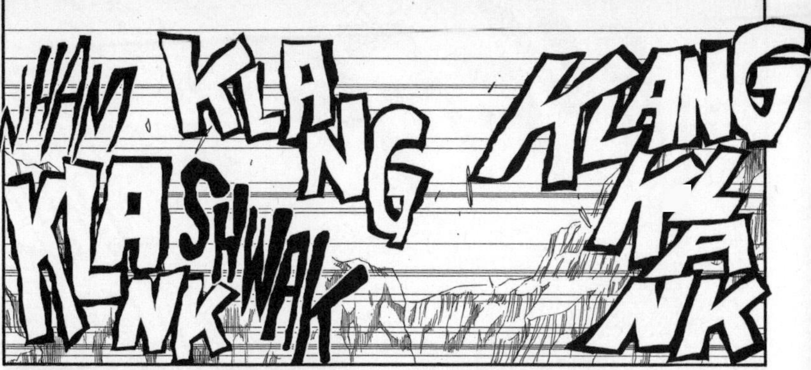
KLANG
WHAM
KLANG
KLANK
SHWAK

130. Suspicion 2 (of Tears)

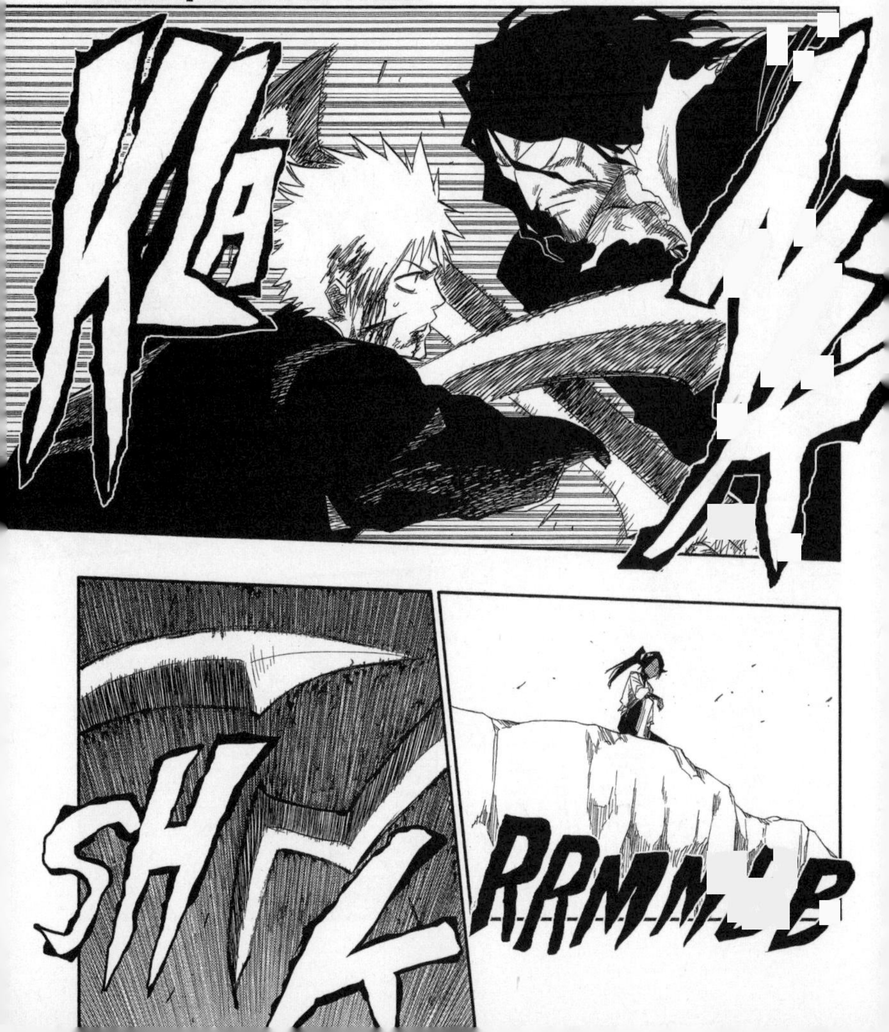

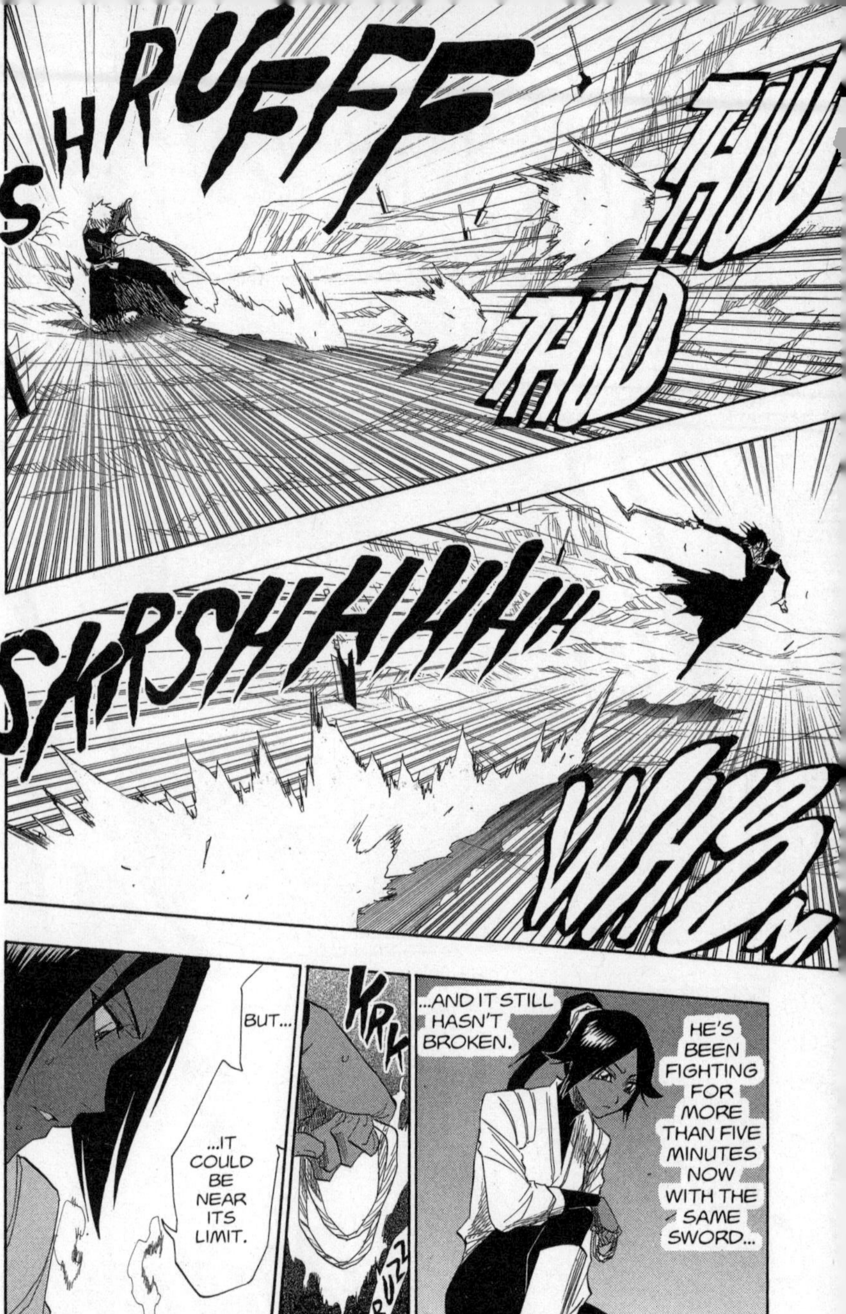
SHRUFFF
THUD
THUD
SKRSHHHHH
WHOM
HE'S BEEN FIGHTING FOR MORE THAN FIVE MINUTES NOW WITH THE SAME SWORD...
...AND IT STILL HASN'T BROKEN.
KRK
BUZZ
BUT...
...IT COULD BE NEAR ITS LIMIT.

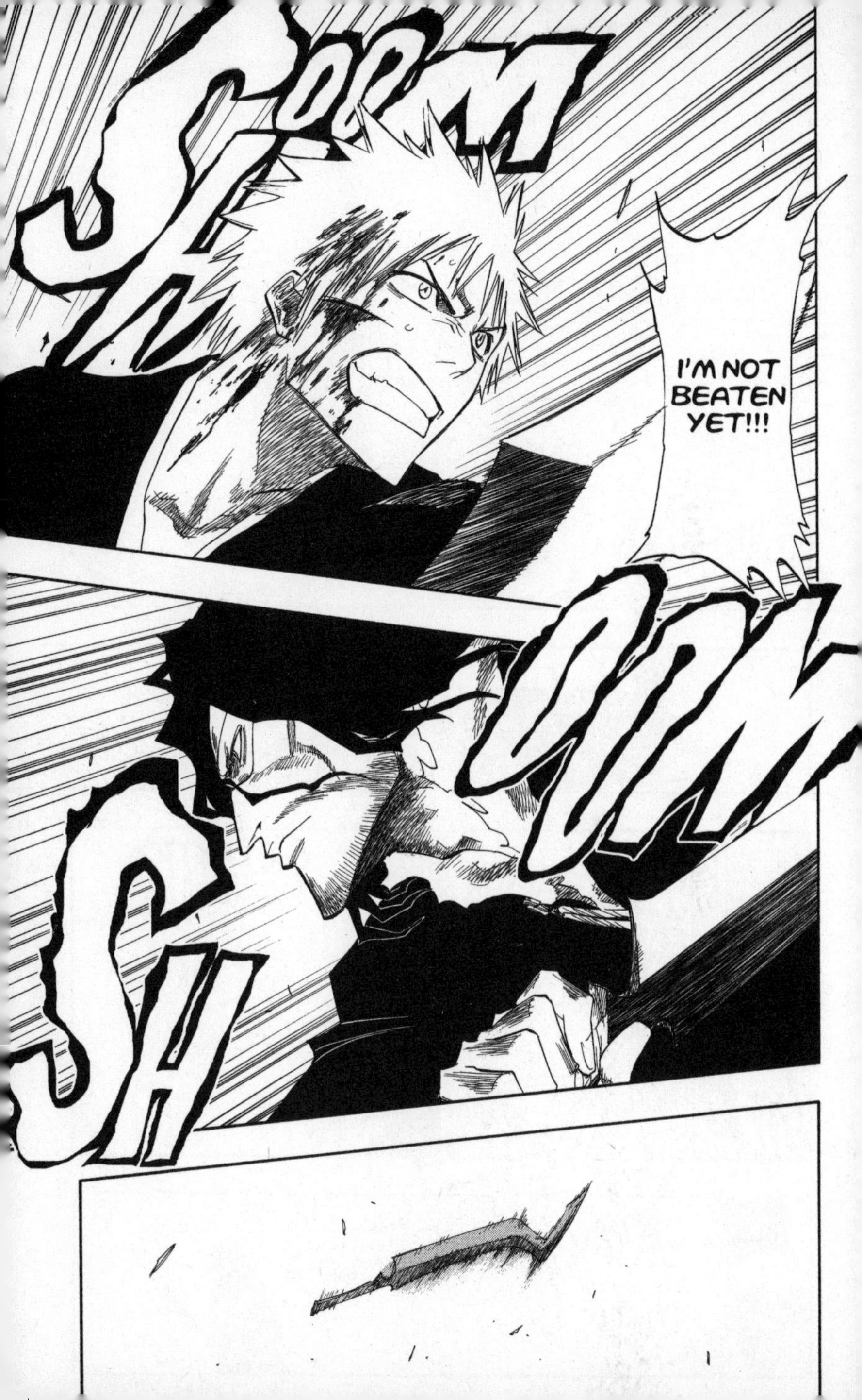
I'M NOT BEATEN YET!!!

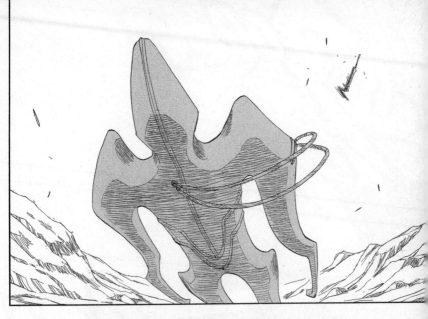

HUH?

SHUNK

THW UMP

TMP

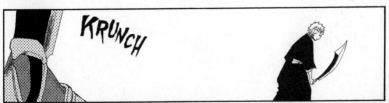

KRUNCH

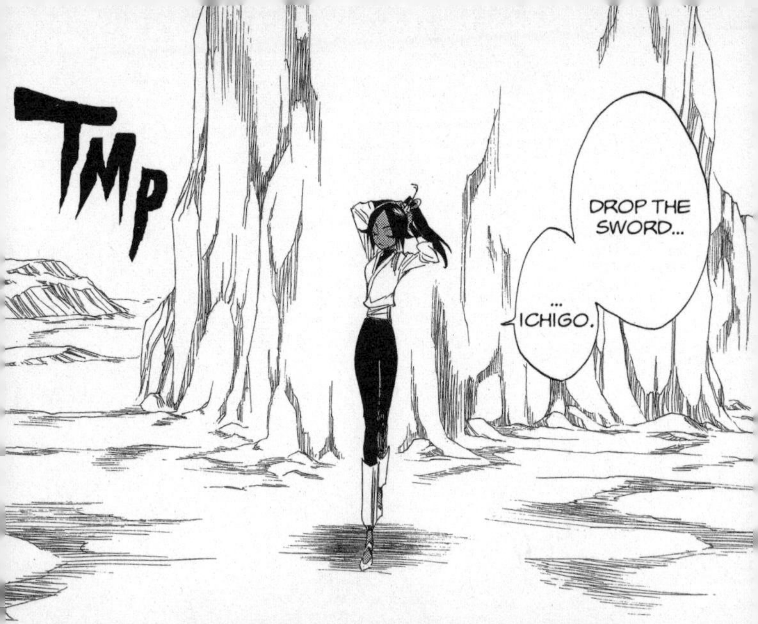
TMP
DROP THE SWORD...
...ICHIGO.

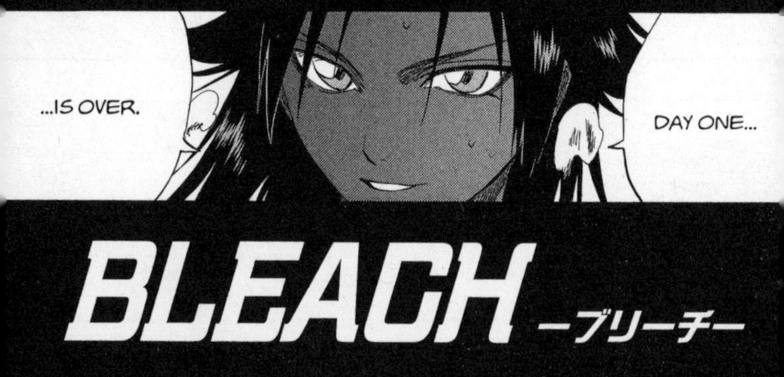
DAY ONE...
...IS OVER.

BLEACH —ブリーチ—

130. Suspicion 2 (of Tears)

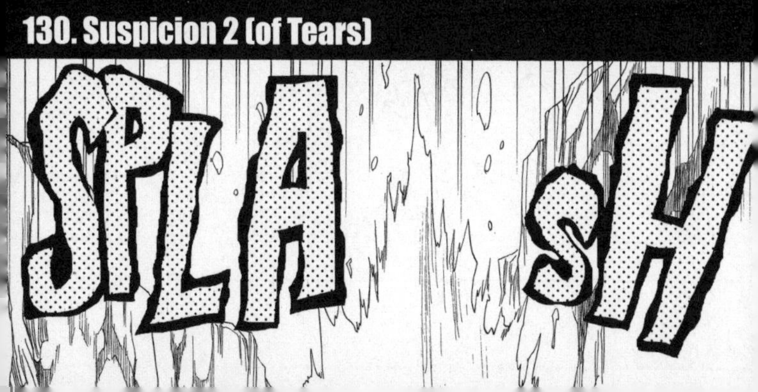
SPLASH

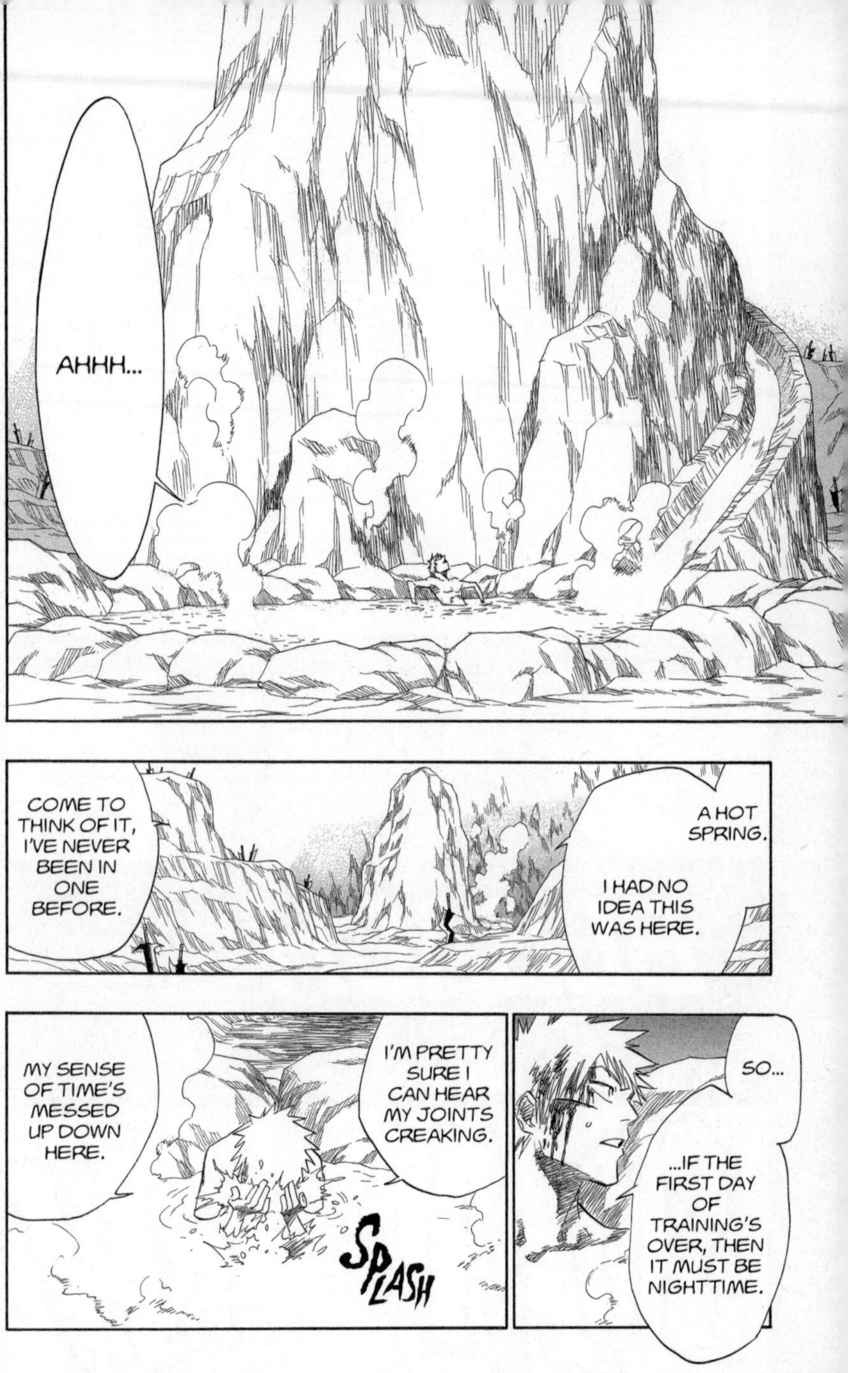
AHHH...
A HOT SPRING.
I HAD NO IDEA THIS WAS HERE.
COME TO THINK OF IT, I'VE NEVER BEEN IN ONE BEFORE.
SO...
...IF THE FIRST DAY OF TRAINING'S OVER, THEN IT MUST BE NIGHTTIME.
I'M PRETTY SURE I CAN HEAR MY JOINTS CREAKING.
MY SENSE OF TIME'S MESSED UP DOWN HERE.
SPLASH

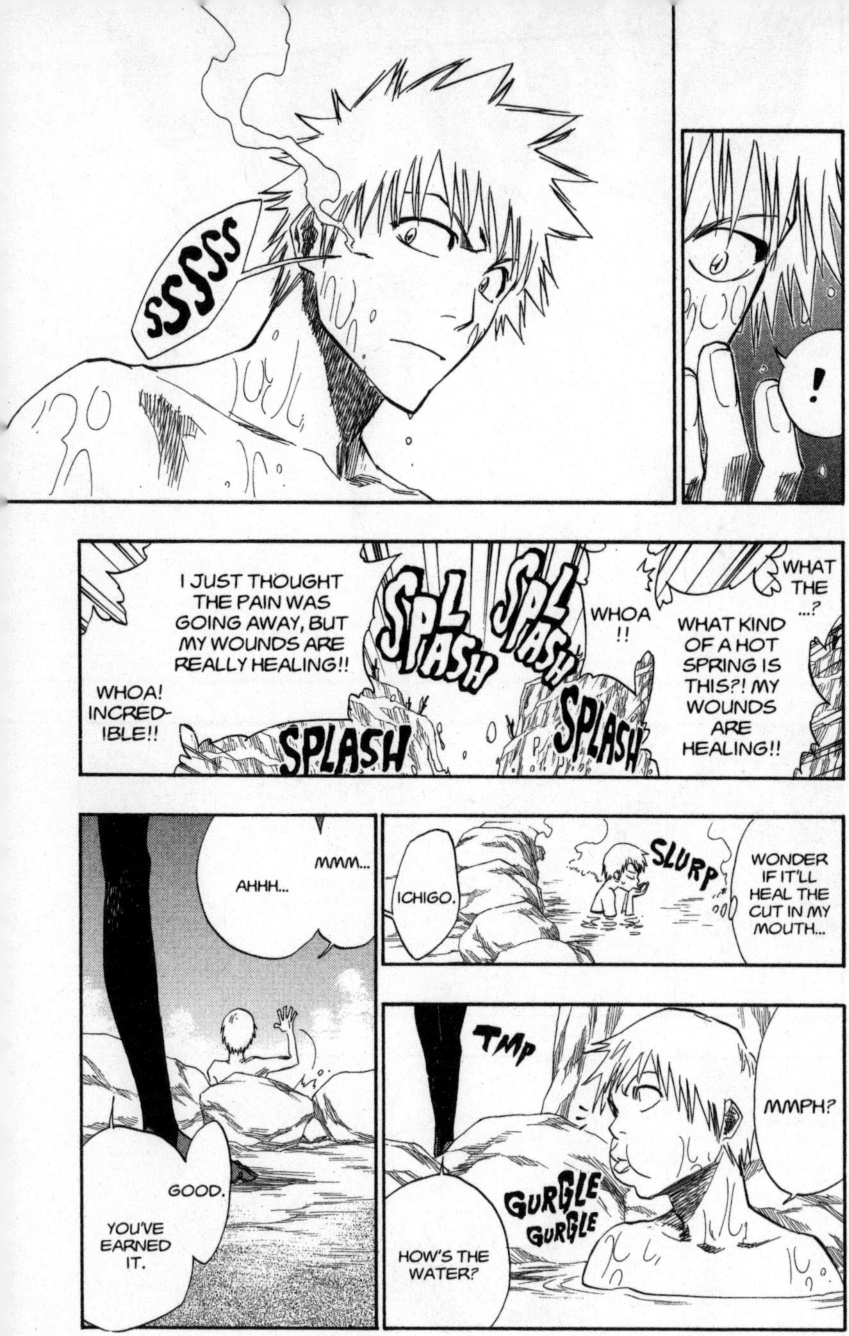
!
SSSSS
WHAT THE ...?
WHAT KIND OF A HOT SPRING IS THIS?! MY WOUNDS ARE HEALING!!
WHOA !!
SPL SPLASH
SPL SPLASH
SPLASH
SPLASH
I JUST THOUGHT THE PAIN WAS GOING AWAY, BUT MY WOUNDS ARE REALLY HEALING!!
WHOA! INCRED-IBLE!!
WONDER IF IT'LL HEAL THE CUT IN MY MOUTH...
SLURP
ICHIGO.
MMPH?
TMP
GURGLE GURGLE
HOW'S THE WATER?
MMM...
AHHH...
GOOD.
YOU'VE EARNED IT.

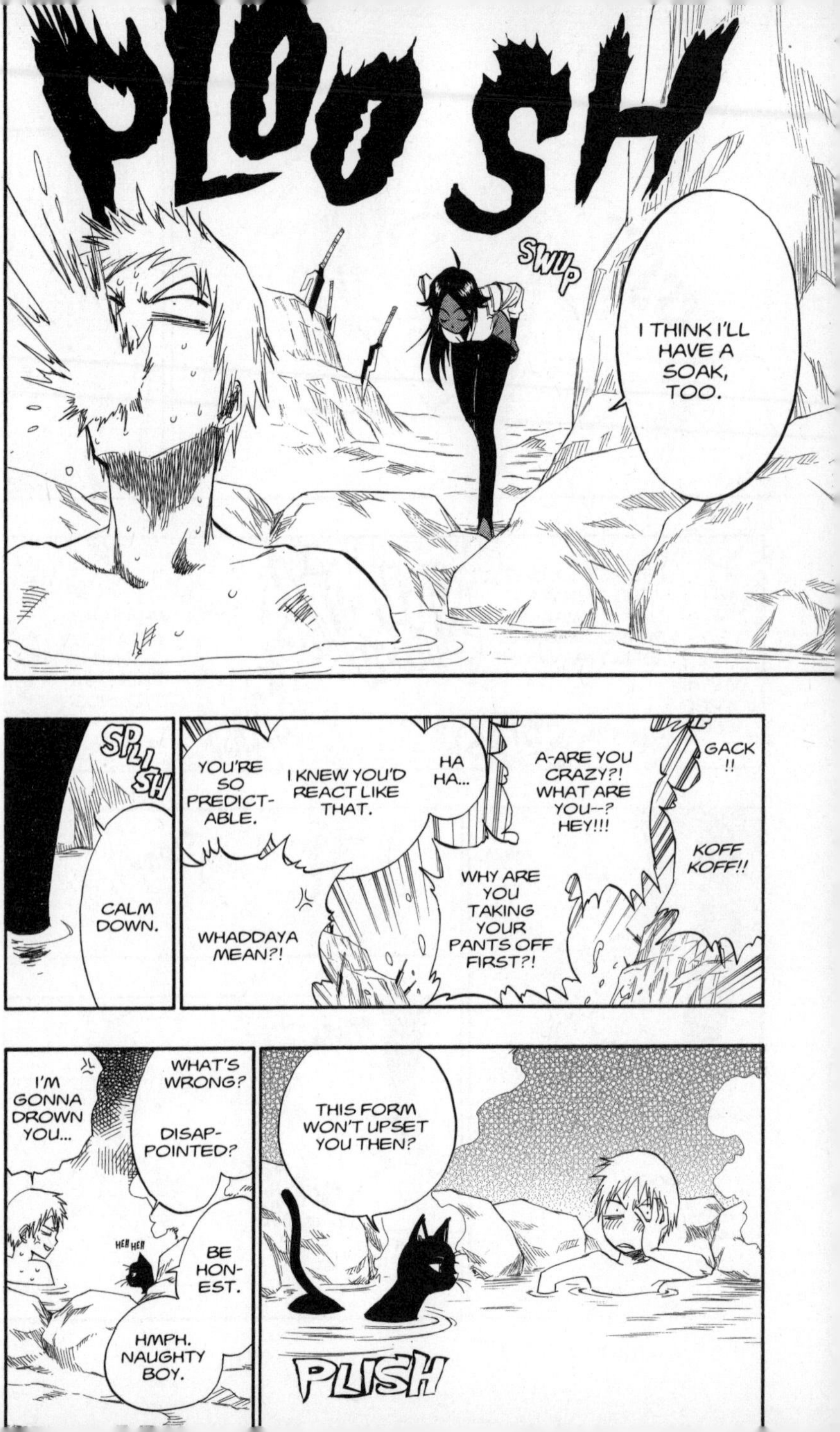
PLOOSH
SWUP
I THINK I'LL HAVE A SOAK, TOO.
GACK!!
A-ARE YOU CRAZY?! WHAT ARE YOU--? HEY!!!
KOFF KOFF!!
HA HA...
I KNEW YOU'D REACT LIKE THAT.
WHY ARE YOU TAKING YOUR PANTS OFF FIRST?!
YOU'RE SO PREDICT-ABLE.
WHADDAYA MEAN?!
SPLISH
CALM DOWN.
THIS FORM WON'T UPSET YOU THEN?
PLISH
WHAT'S WRONG?
DISAP-POINTED?
I'M GONNA DROWN YOU...
BE HON-EST.
HEH HEH
HMPH. NAUGHTY BOY.

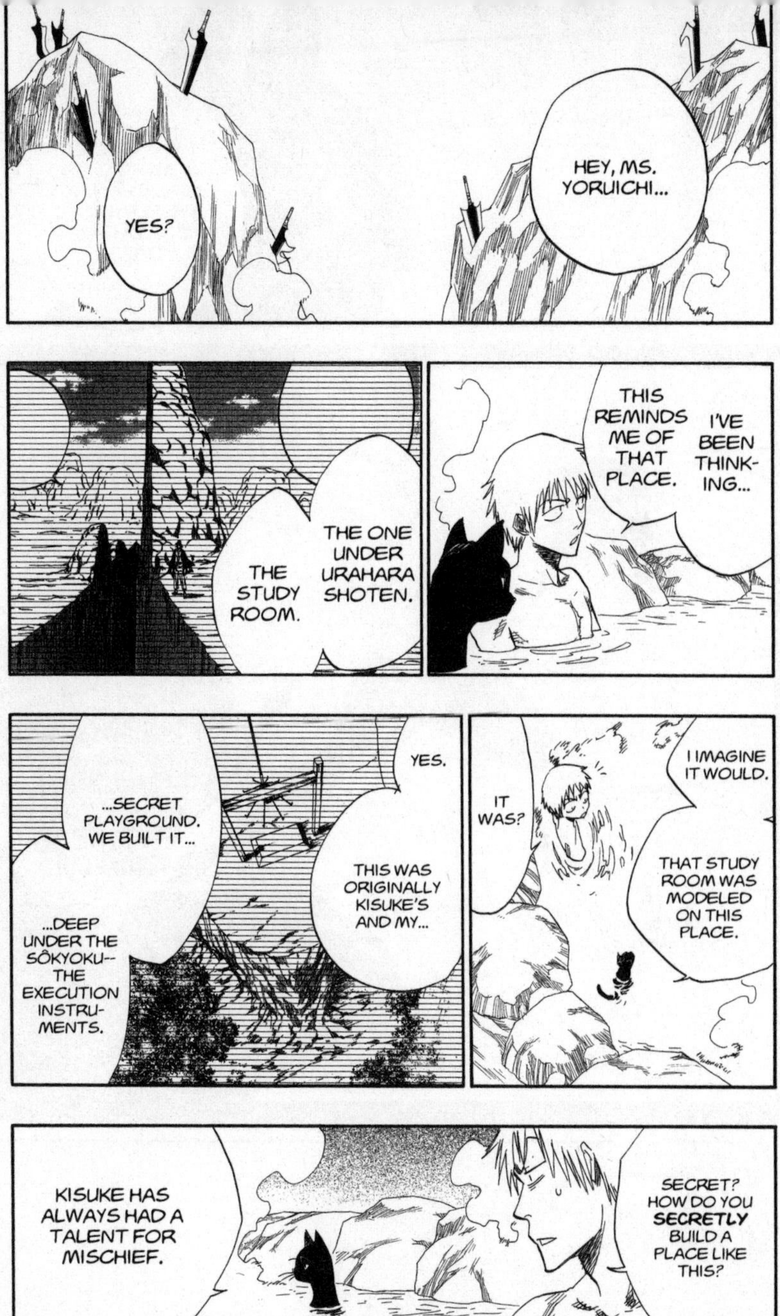
HEY, MS. YORUICHI...
YES?
I'VE BEEN THINKING...
THIS REMINDS ME OF THAT PLACE.
THE ONE UNDER URAHARA SHOTEN.
THE STUDY ROOM.
I IMAGINE IT WOULD.
THAT STUDY ROOM WAS MODELED ON THIS PLACE.
IT WAS?
YES.
THIS WAS ORIGINALLY KISUKE'S AND MY...
...SECRET PLAYGROUND. WE BUILT IT...
...DEEP UNDER THE SÔKYOKU--THE EXECUTION INSTRUMENTS.
SECRET? HOW DO YOU **SECRETLY** BUILD A PLACE LIKE THIS?
KISUKE HAS ALWAYS HAD A TALENT FOR MISCHIEF.

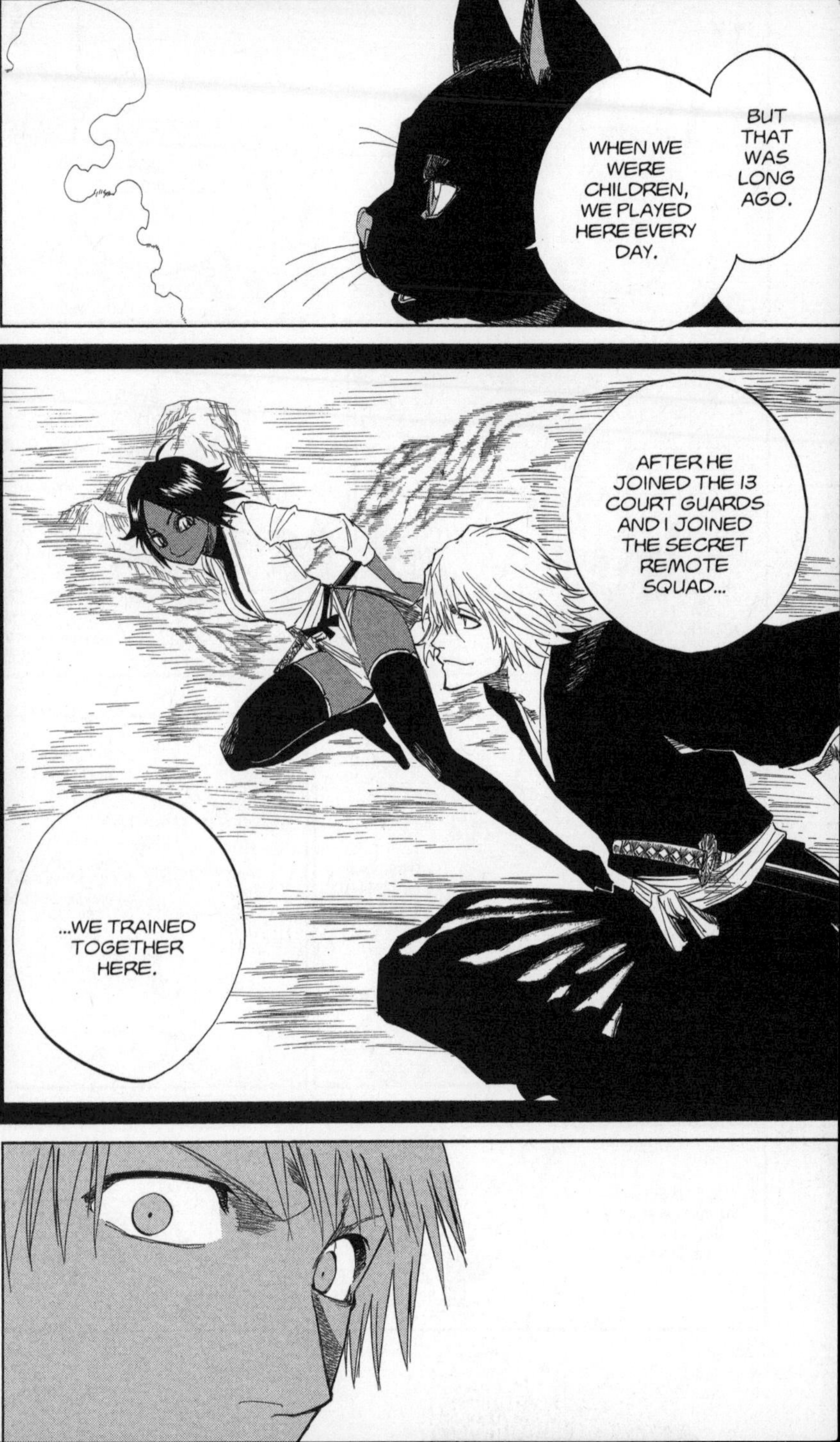
BUT THAT WAS LONG AGO.
WHEN WE WERE CHILDREN, WE PLAYED HERE EVERY DAY.
AFTER HE JOINED THE 13 COURT GUARDS AND I JOINED THE SECRET REMOTE SQUAD...
...WE TRAINED TOGETHER HERE.

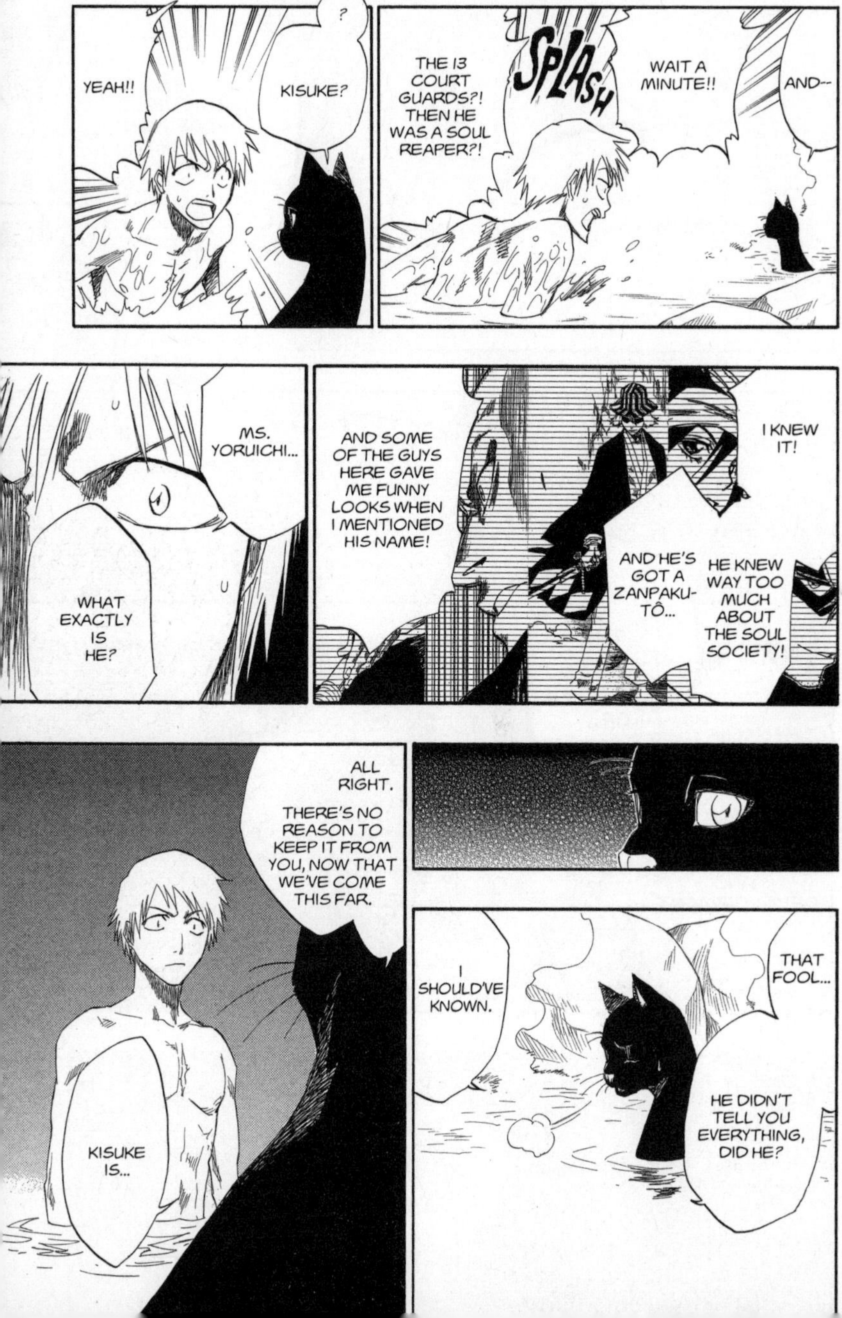
AND--
WAIT A MINUTE!!
SPLASH
THE 13 COURT GUARDS?! THEN HE WAS A SOUL REAPER?!
?
KISUKE?
YEAH!!
I KNEW IT!
HE KNEW WAY TOO MUCH ABOUT THE SOUL SOCIETY!
AND HE'S GOT A ZANPAKU-TÔ...
AND SOME OF THE GUYS HERE GAVE ME FUNNY LOOKS WHEN I MENTIONED HIS NAME!
MS. YORUICHI...
WHAT EXACTLY IS HE?
THAT FOOL...
HE DIDN'T TELL YOU EVERYTHING, DID HE?
I SHOULD'VE KNOWN.
ALL RIGHT.
THERE'S NO REASON TO KEEP IT FROM YOU, NOW THAT WE'VE COME THIS FAR.
KISUKE IS...

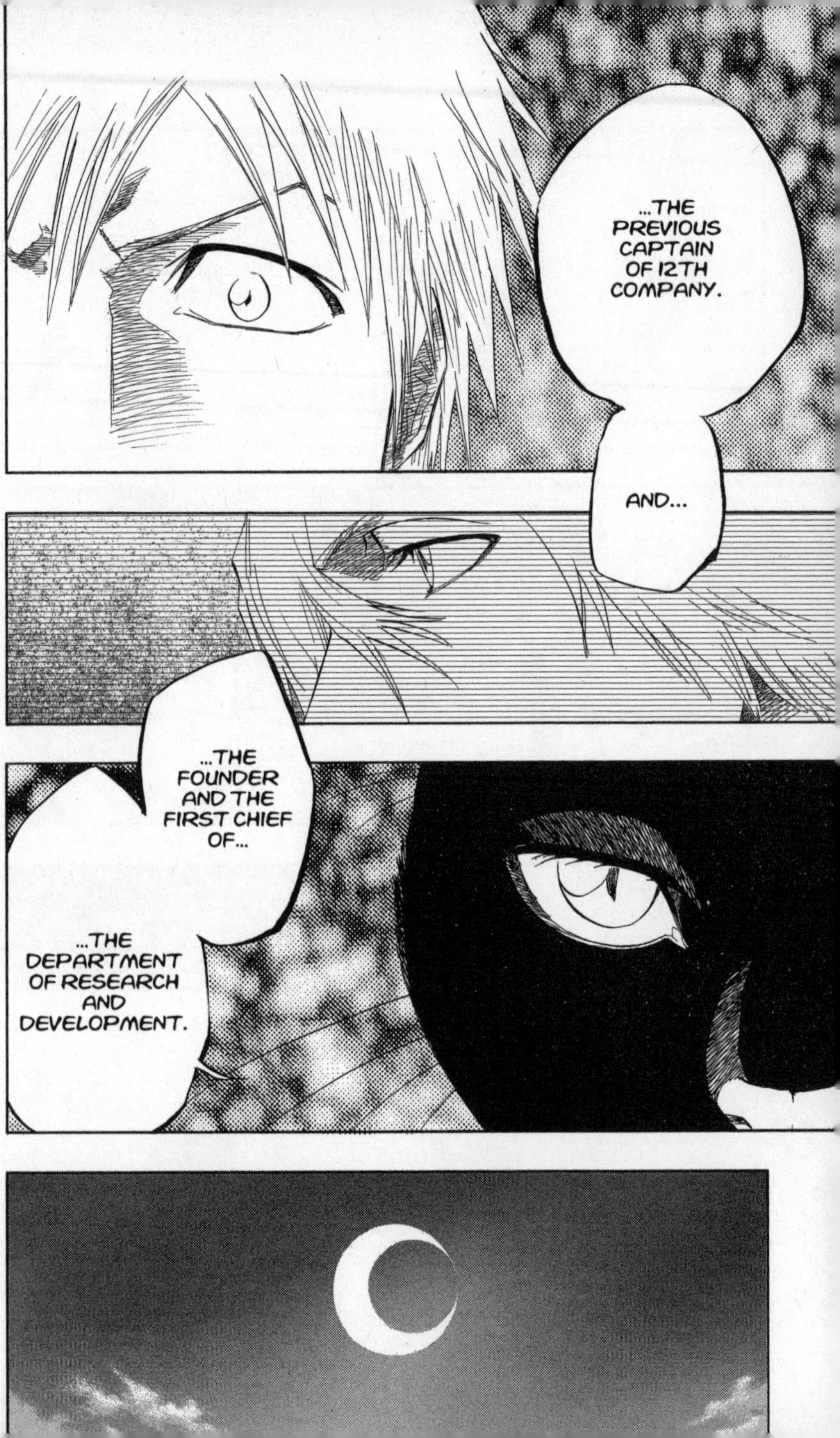
...THE PREVIOUS CAPTAIN OF 12TH COMPANY.
AND...
...THE FOUNDER AND THE FIRST CHIEF OF...
...THE DEPARTMENT OF RESEARCH AND DEVELOPMENT.

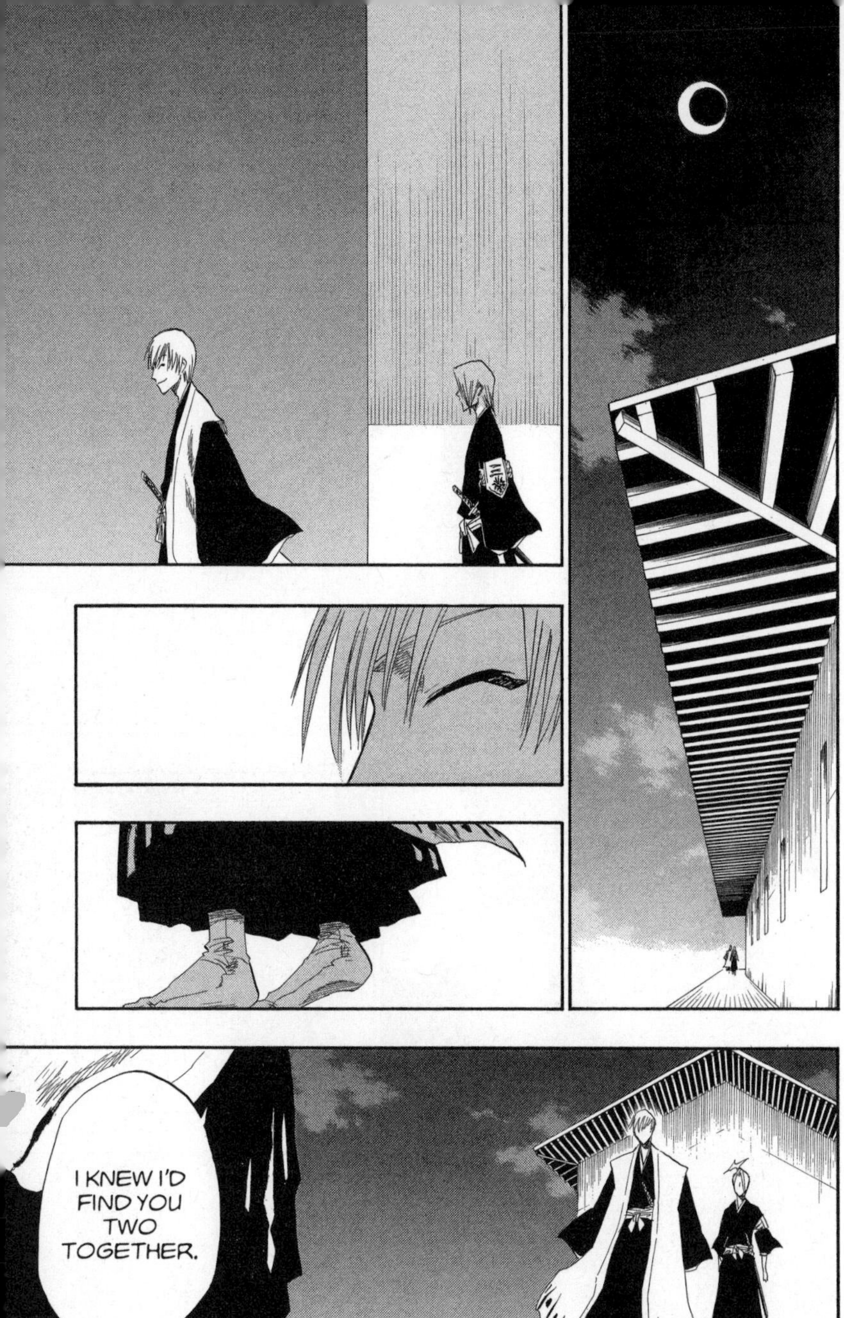
I KNEW I'D FIND YOU TWO TOGETHER.

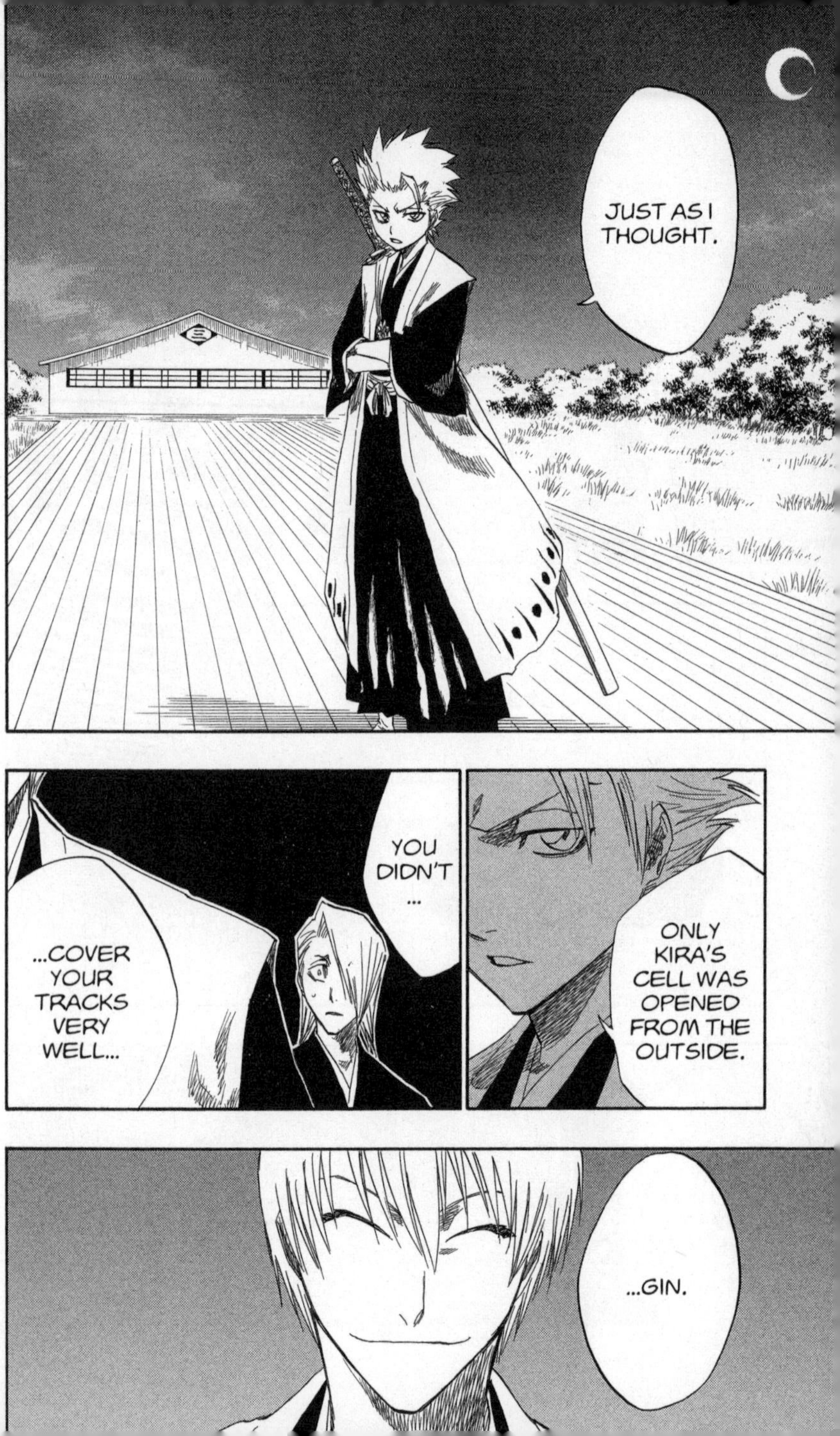
JUST AS I THOUGHT.
ONLY KIRA'S CELL WAS OPENED FROM THE OUTSIDE.
YOU DIDN'T ...
...COVER YOUR TRACKS VERY WELL...
...GIN.

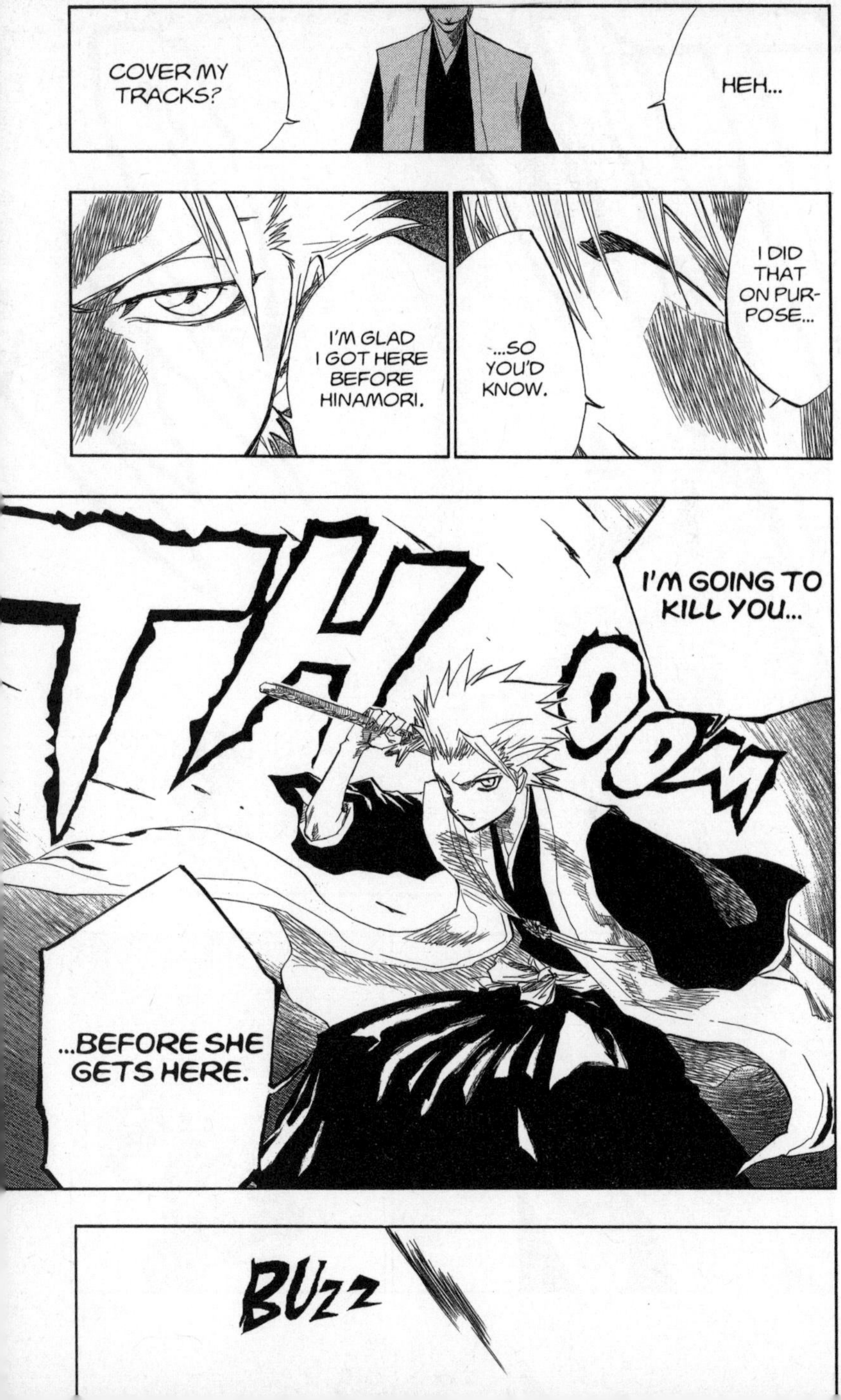
HEH...
COVER MY TRACKS?
I DID THAT ON PURPOSE...
...SO YOU'D KNOW.
I'M GLAD I GOT HERE BEFORE HINAMORI.
I'M GOING TO KILL YOU...
THOOOM
...BEFORE SHE GETS HERE.
BUZZ

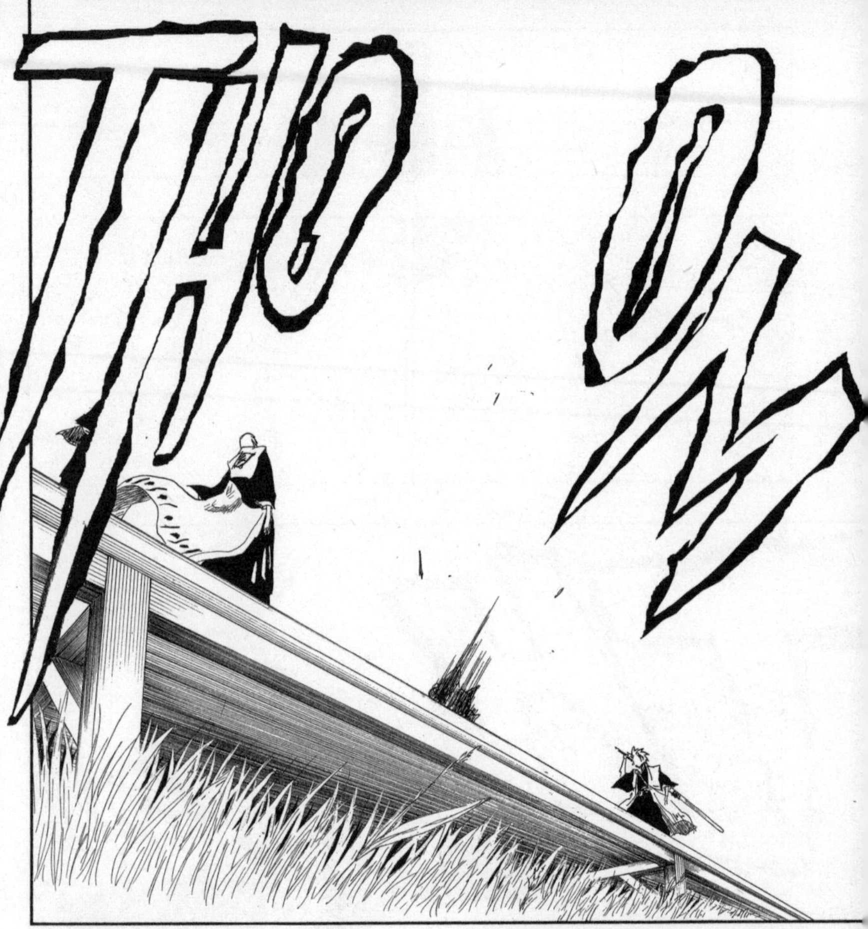
THOOM

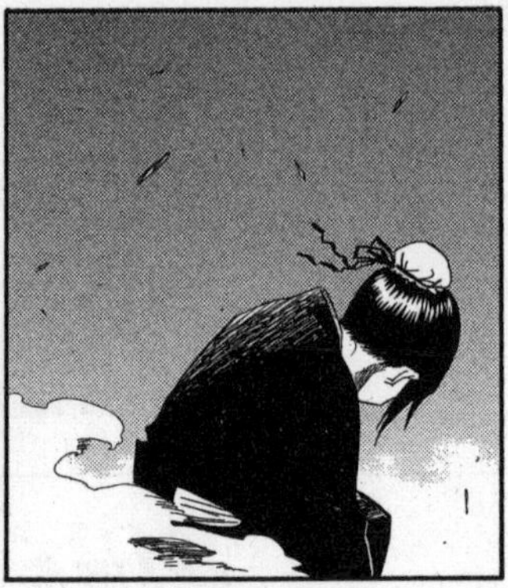

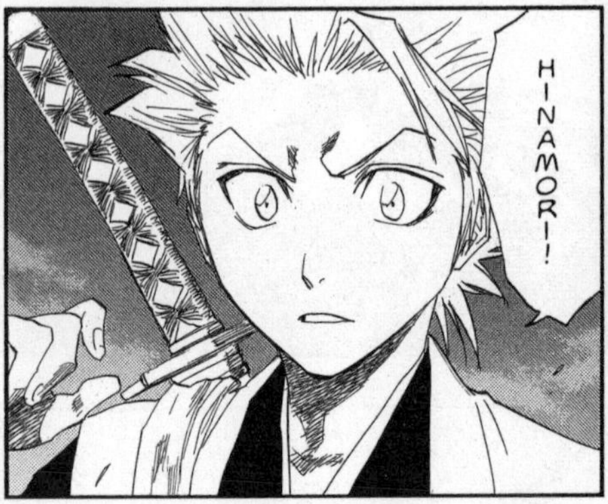
HINAMORI!

READ THIS WAY

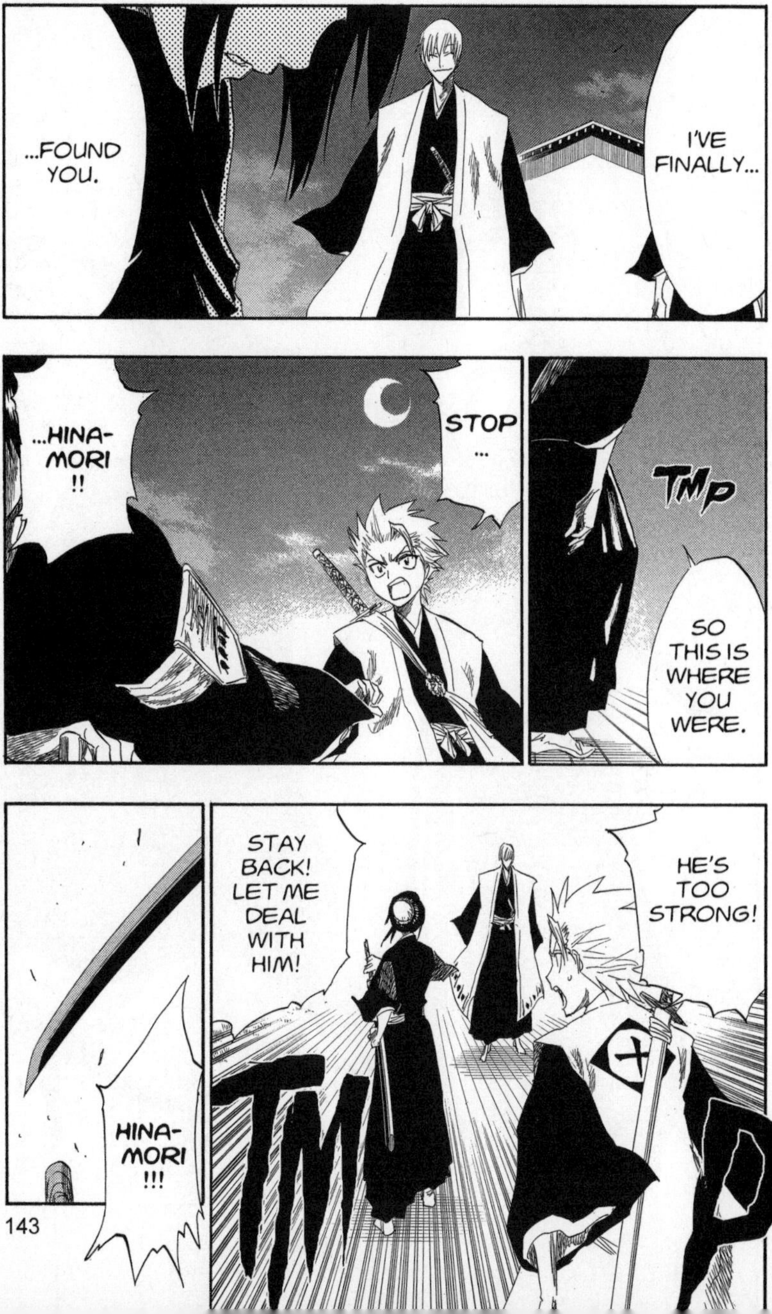

I'VE FINALLY...
...FOUND YOU.
TMP
SO THIS IS WHERE YOU WERE.
STOP...
...HINA-MORI!!
HE'S TOO STRONG!
STAY BACK! LET ME DEAL WITH HIM!
TMP
HINA-MORI!!!

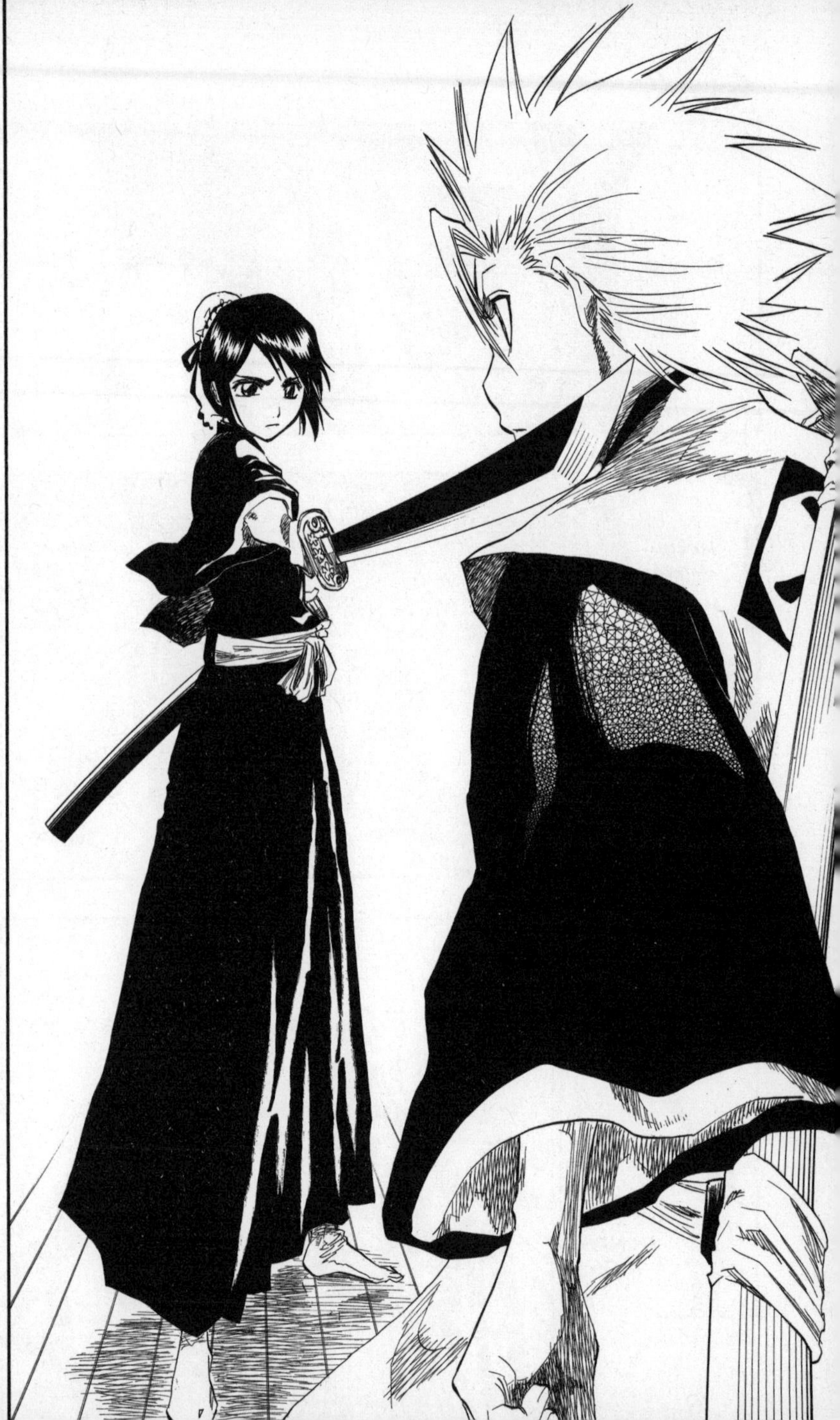

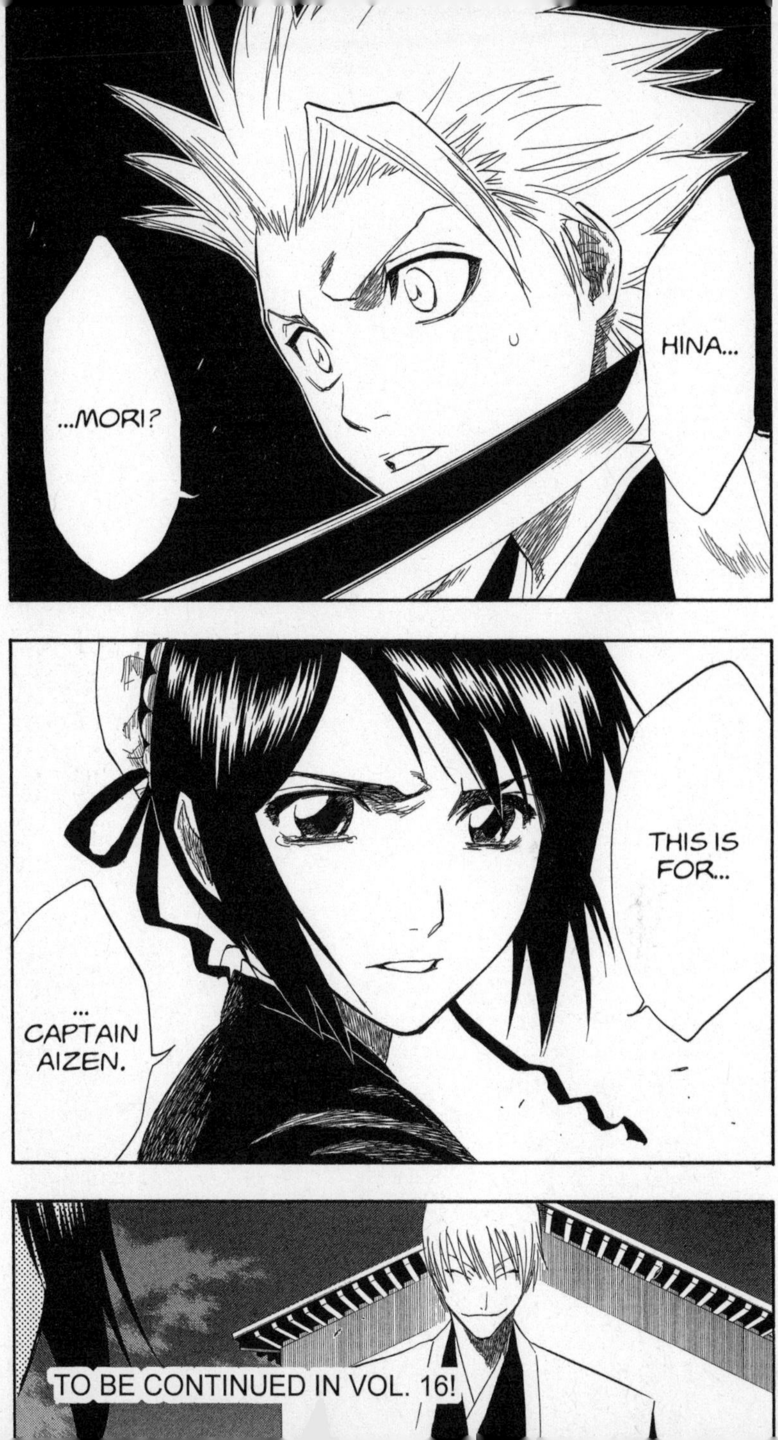
HINA...
...MORI?
THIS IS FOR...
... CAPTAIN AIZEN.
TO BE CONTINUED IN VOL. 16!

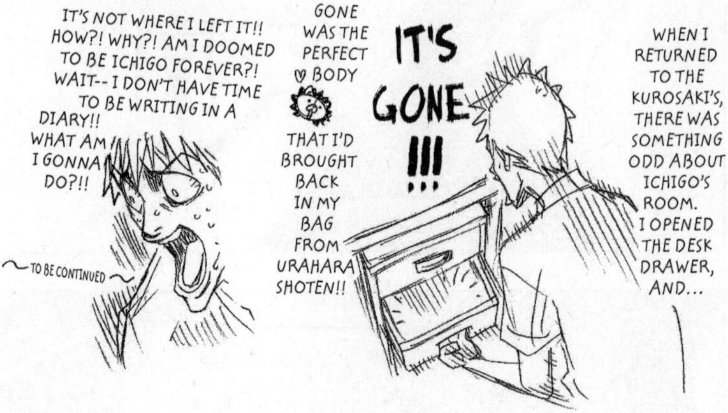
WHEN I RETURNED TO THE KUROSAKI'S, THERE WAS SOMETHING ODD ABOUT ICHIGO'S ROOM. I OPENED THE DESK DRAWER, AND...
IT'S GONE!!!
GONE WAS THE PERFECT ♡ BODY THAT I'D BROUGHT BACK IN MY BAG FROM URAHARA SHOTEN!!
IT'S NOT WHERE I LEFT IT!! HOW?! WHY?! AM I DOOMED TO BE ICHIGO FOREVER?! WAIT-- I DON'T HAVE TIME TO BE WRITING IN A DIARY!! WHAT AM I GONNA DO?!!
~TO BE CONTINUED~

BLEACH

ブリーチ

-17. PRELUDE FOR THE STRAYING STARS

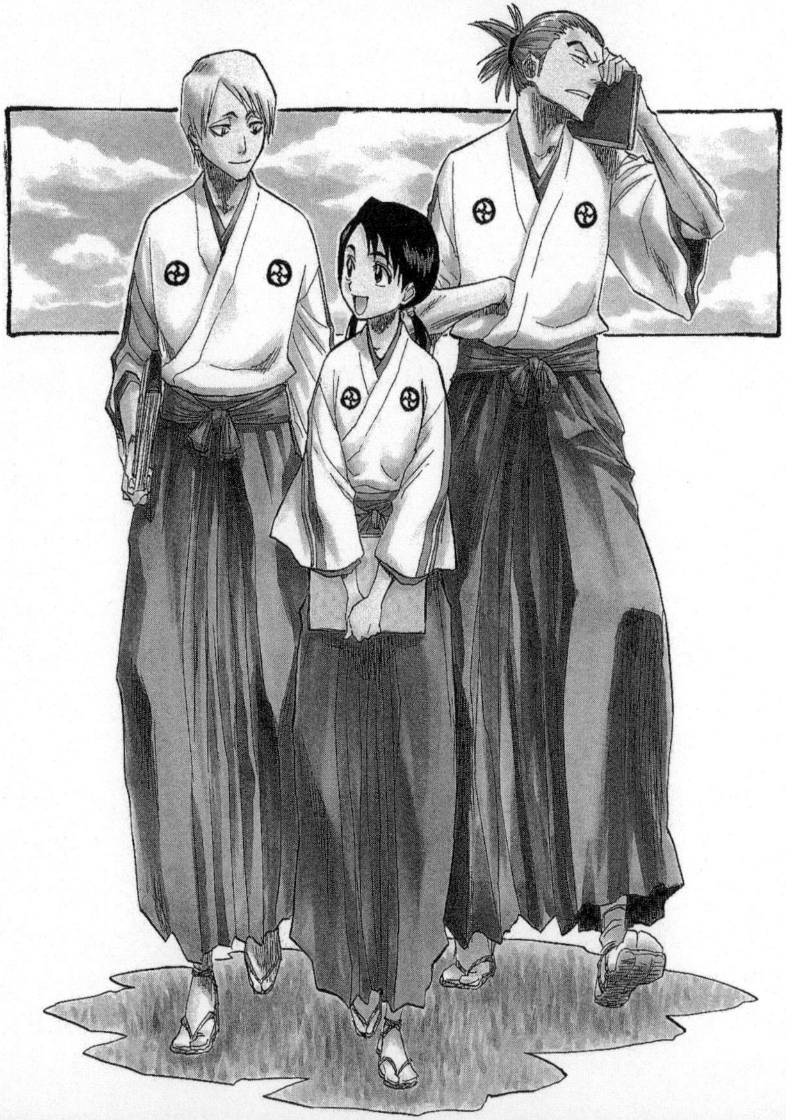

WE WILL
NOT STOP
WALKING

THOUGH
THE PATH
MAY
EVENTUALLY
FORK.

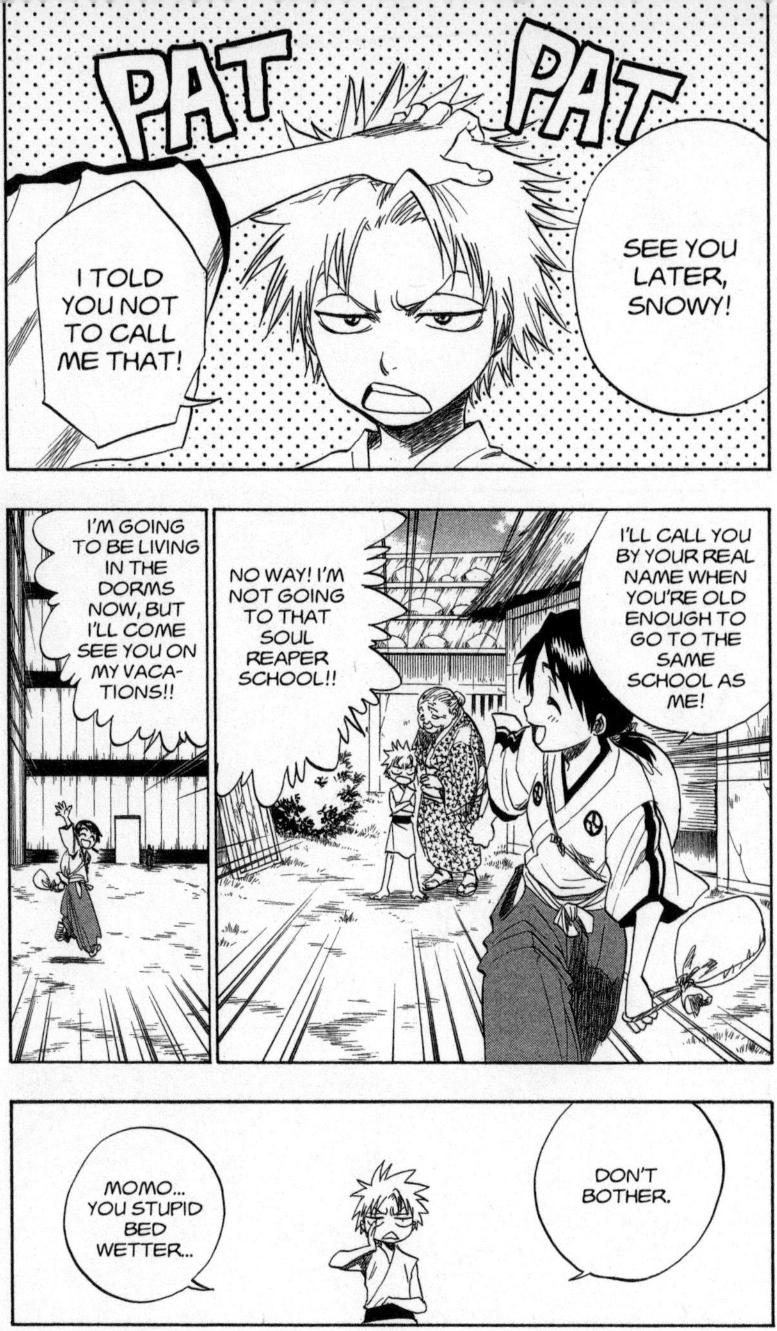
PAT
PAT
SEE YOU LATER, SNOWY!
I TOLD YOU NOT TO CALL ME THAT!
I'LL CALL YOU BY YOUR REAL NAME WHEN YOU'RE OLD ENOUGH TO GO TO THE SAME SCHOOL AS ME!
NO WAY! I'M NOT GOING TO THAT SOUL REAPER SCHOOL!!
I'M GOING TO BE LIVING IN THE DORMS NOW, BUT I'LL COME SEE YOU ON MY VACA-TIONS!!
DON'T BOTHER.
MOMO... YOU STUPID BED WETTER...

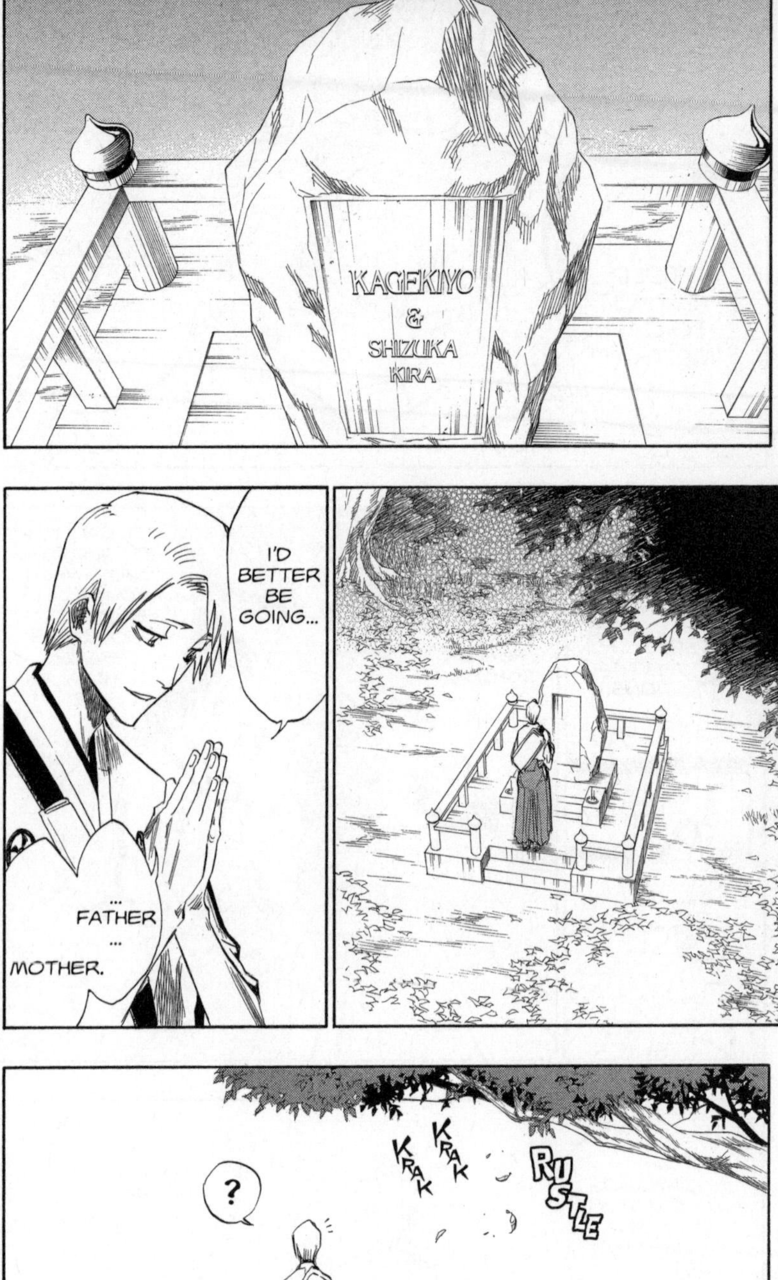
KAGEKIYO
&
SHIZUKA
KIRA
I'D BETTER BE GOING...
...FATHER ... MOTHER.
RUSTLE
KRAK
KRAK
?

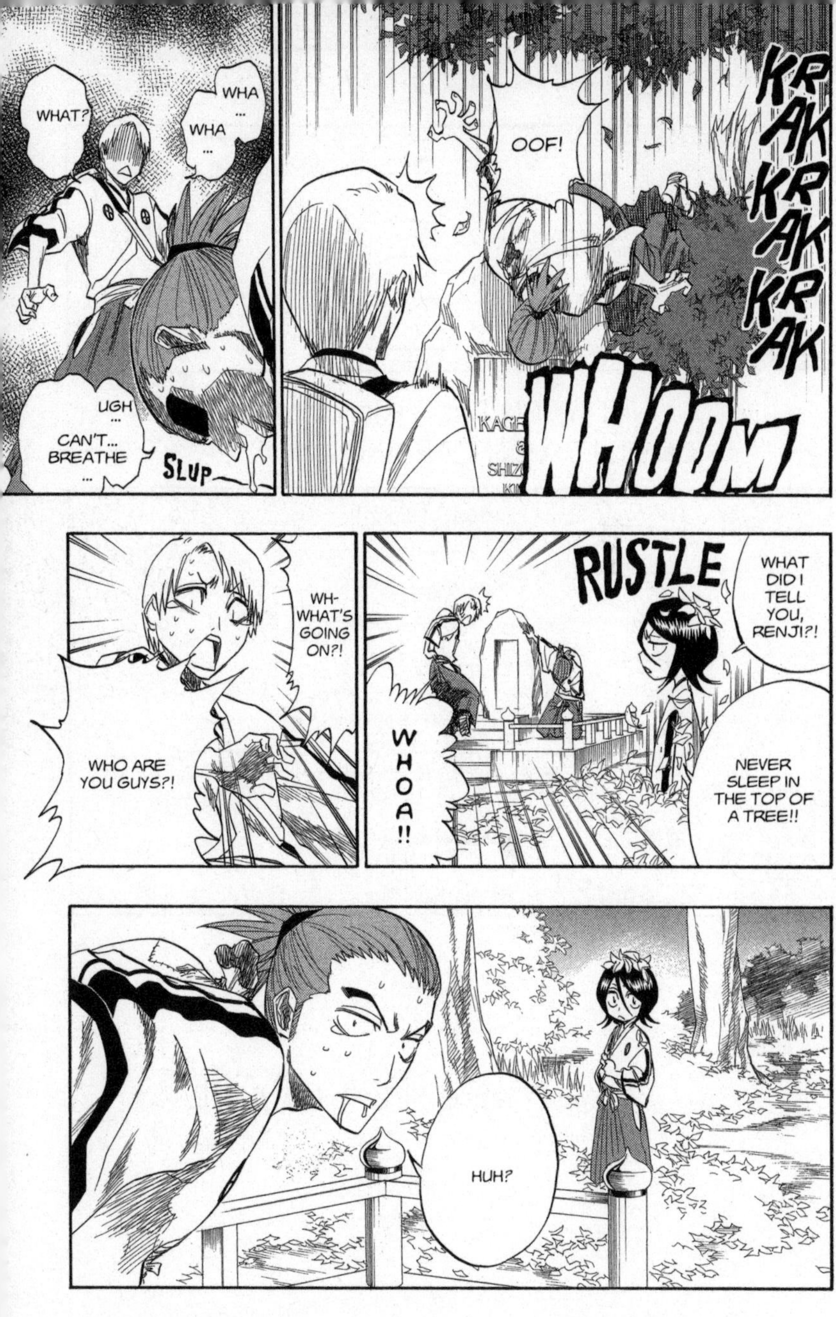
OOF!
KRAKKRAKKRAKKRAK
WHOOM
WHA ... WHA ...
WHAT?
UGH ... CAN'T... BREATHE ...
SLUP
RUSTLE
WHAT DID I TELL YOU, RENJI?!
NEVER SLEEP IN THE TOP OF A TREE!!
WHOA!!
WH- WHAT'S GOING ON?!
WHO ARE YOU GUYS?!
HUH?

IT TURNS WITHOUT STOPPING.

AND WE NEVER STOP EITHER.

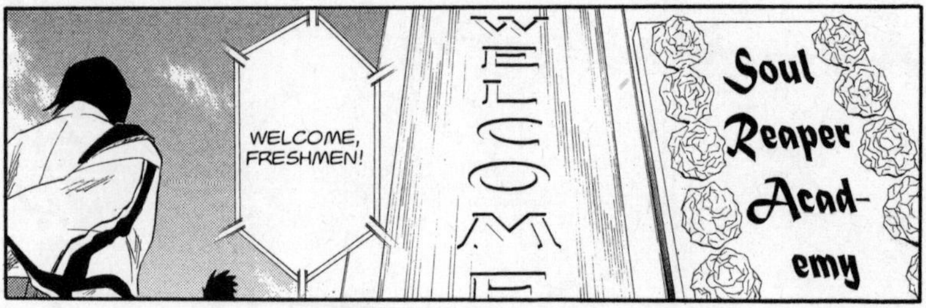
Soul Reaper Acad- emy
WELCOME
WELCOME, FRESHMEN!

BUT WHEN THE TIME COMES, WHEN WE LEARN FEAR AND LOOK BACK

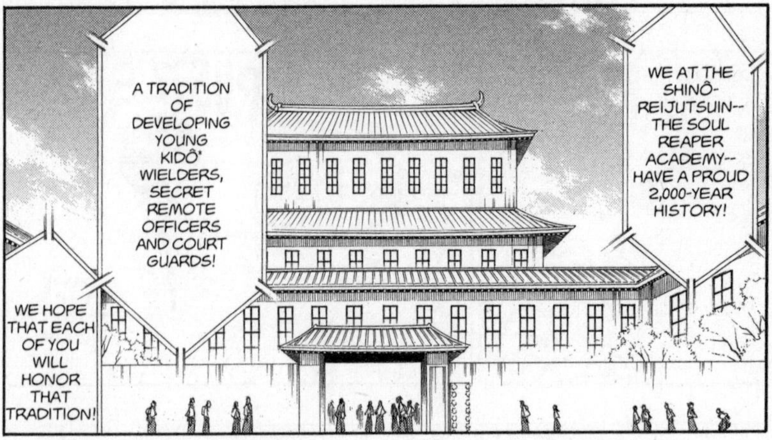
WE AT THE SHINÔ-REIJUTSUIN--THE SOUL REAPER ACADEMY--HAVE A PROUD 2,000-YEAR HISTORY!
A TRADITION OF DEVELOPING YOUNG KIDÔ* WIELDERS, SECRET REMOTE OFFICERS AND COURT GUARDS!
WE HOPE THAT EACH OF YOU WILL HONOR THAT TRADITION!

*POWERS THAT THE SOUL REAPERS HAVE

...WOULD WE CALL THAT FATE?

READ THIS WAY

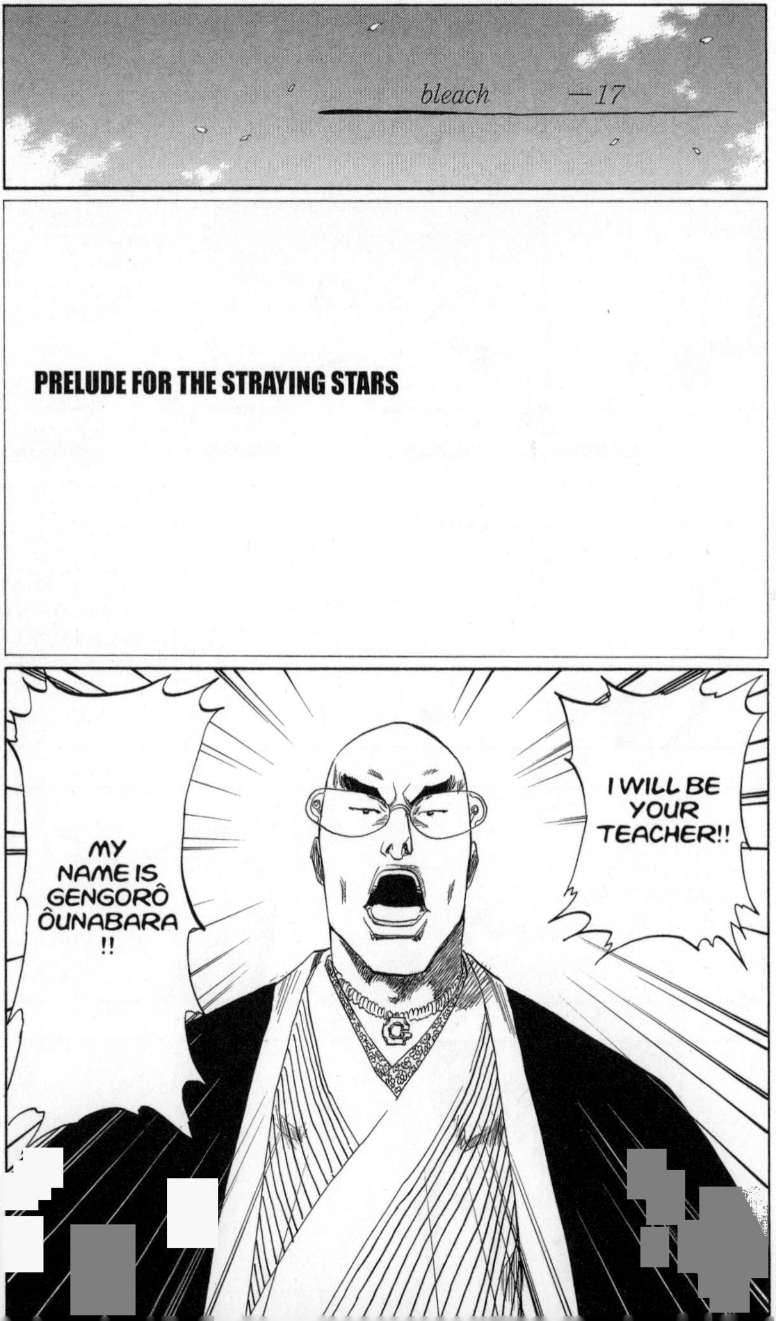
bleach —17
PRELUDE FOR THE STRAYING STARS
I WILL BE YOUR TEACHER!!
MY NAME IS GENGORÔ ÔUNABARA!!

THIS FRESH-MAN CLASS...

...CONTAINS STUDENTS WITH THE HIGHEST EXAM SCORES!

YOU ARE THE ELITE!

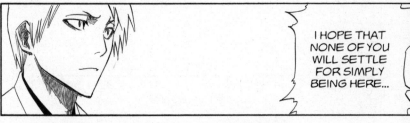

I HOPE THAT NONE OF YOU WILL SETTLE FOR SIMPLY BEING HERE...

...BUT INSTEAD WILL STRIVE TO SOMEDAY LEAD THE COMPANIES YOU JOIN!

IN ORDER FOR YOU TO DO THAT, YOU MUST...

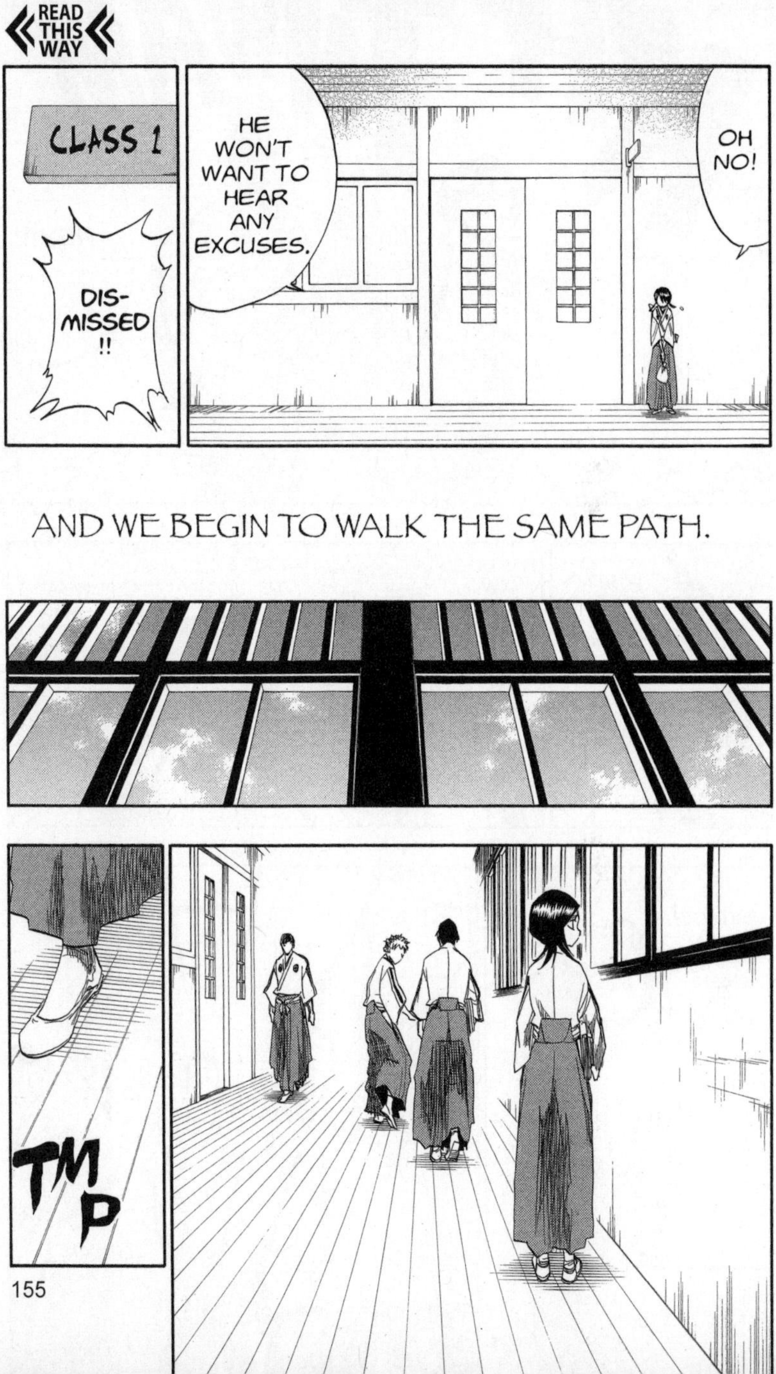
READ THIS WAY
OH NO!
HE WON'T WANT TO HEAR ANY EXCUSES.
CLASS 1
DIS-MISSED!!
AND WE BEGIN TO WALK THE SAME PATH.
TMP

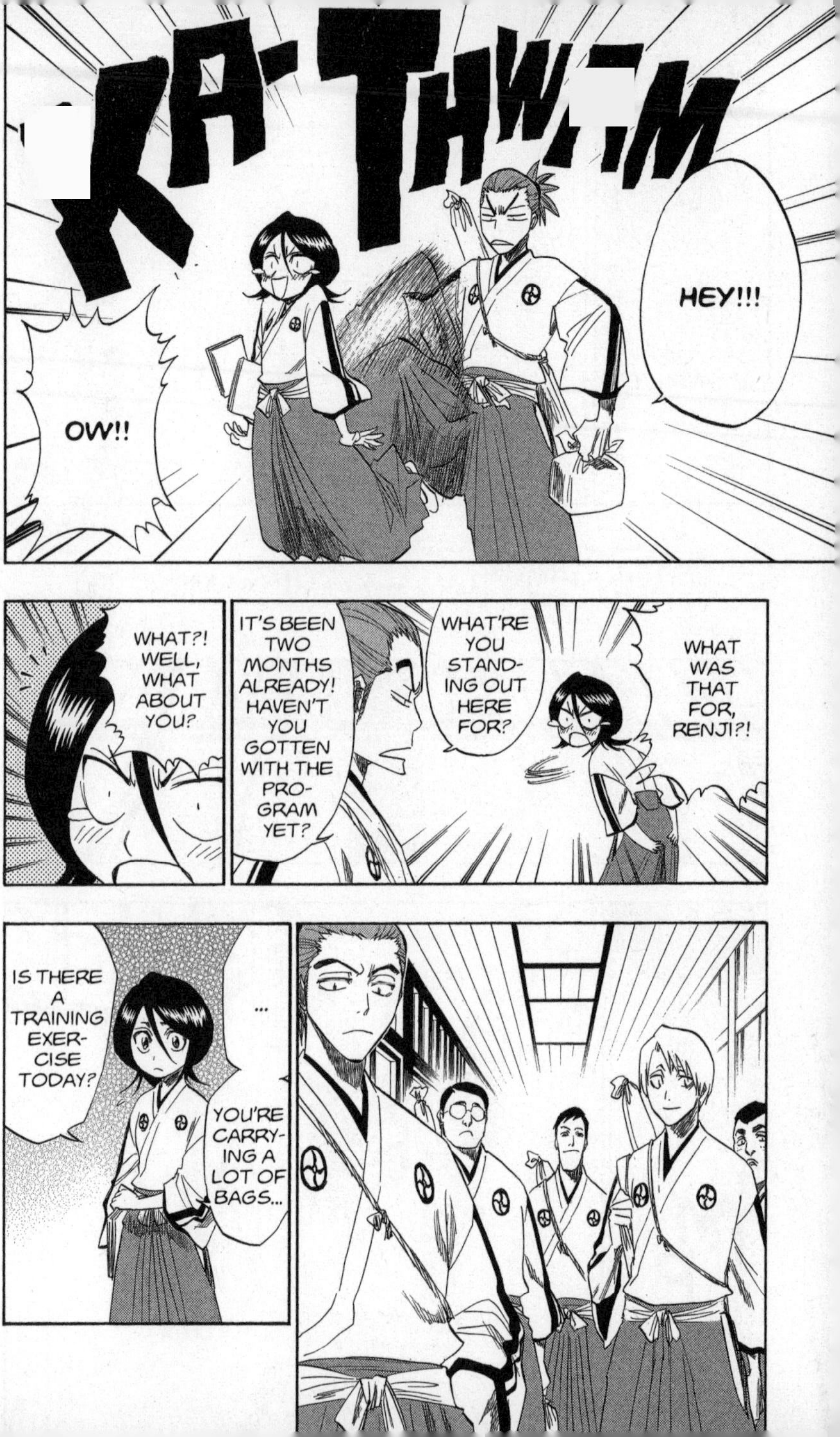
HEY!!!
OW!!
WHAT WAS THAT FOR, RENJI?!
WHAT'RE YOU STANDING OUT HERE FOR?
IT'S BEEN TWO MONTHS ALREADY! HAVEN'T YOU GOTTEN WITH THE PROGRAM YET?
WHAT?! WELL, WHAT ABOUT YOU?
...
IS THERE A TRAINING EXERCISE TODAY?
YOU'RE CARRYING A LOT OF BAGS...

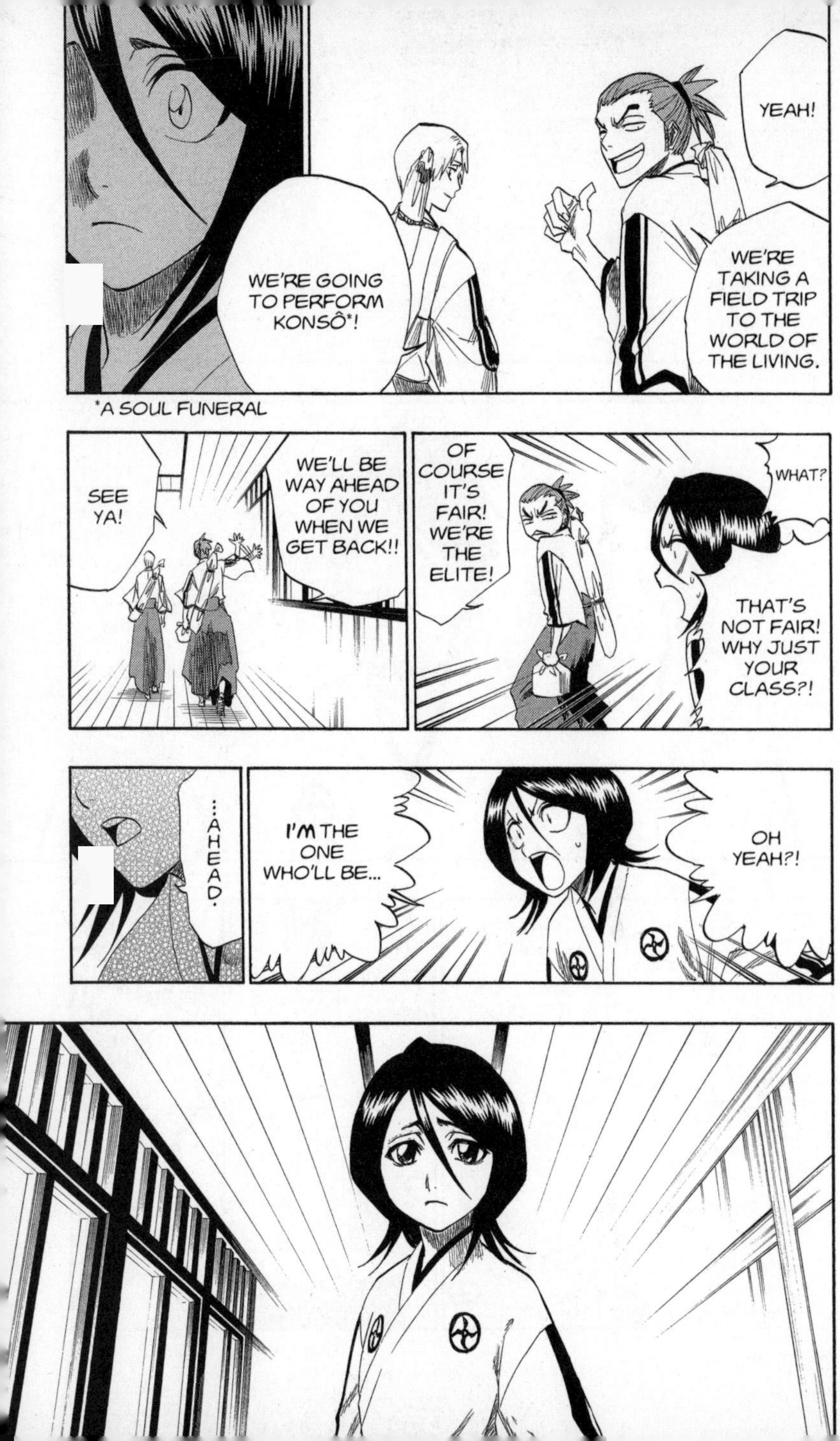
YEAH!
WE'RE TAKING A FIELD TRIP TO THE WORLD OF THE LIVING.
WE'RE GOING TO PERFORM KONSÔ*!
*A SOUL FUNERAL
WHAT?
THAT'S NOT FAIR! WHY JUST YOUR CLASS?!
OF COURSE IT'S FAIR! WE'RE THE ELITE!
WE'LL BE WAY AHEAD OF YOU WHEN WE GET BACK!!
SEE YA!
OH YEAH?!
I'M THE ONE WHO'LL BE...
...AHEAD.

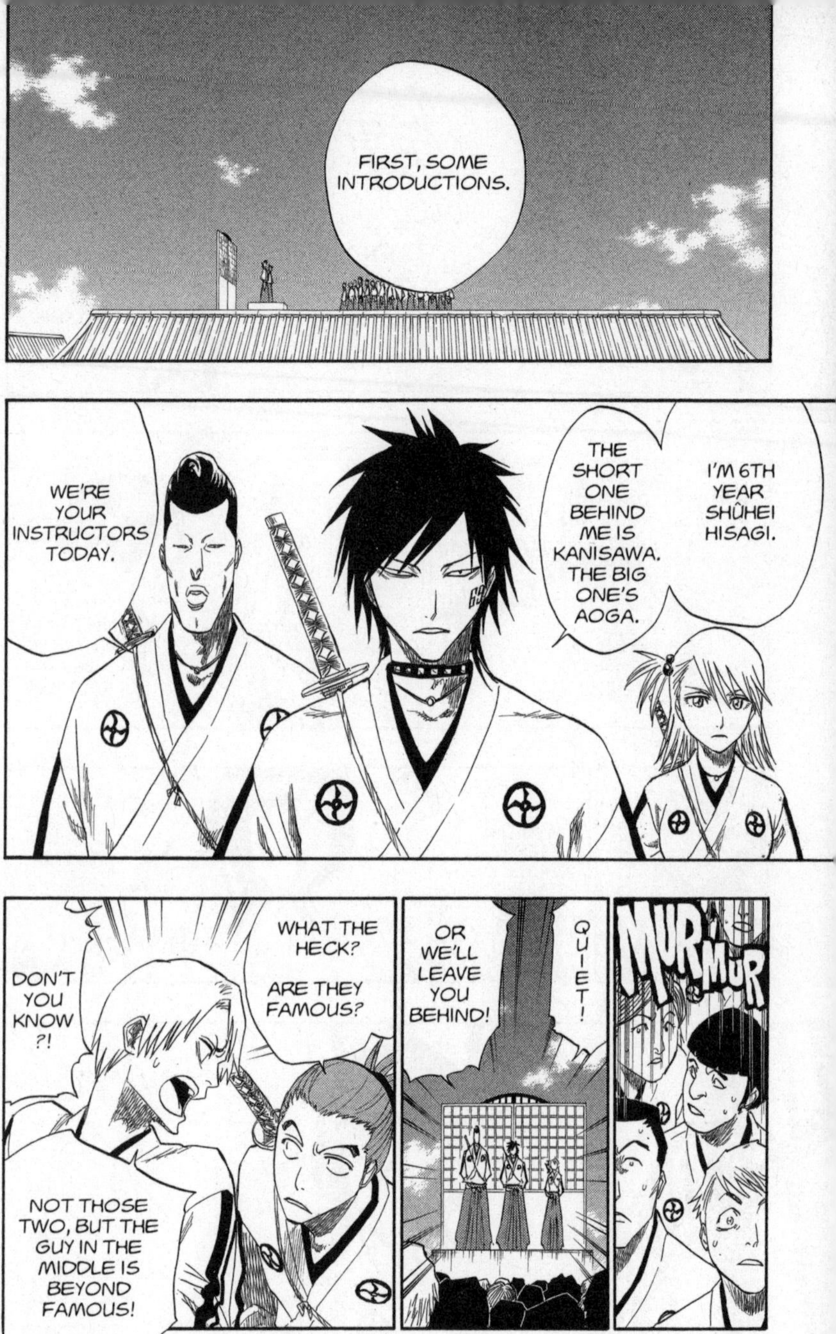
FIRST, SOME INTRODUCTIONS.
I'M 6TH YEAR SHÛHEI HISAGI.
THE SHORT ONE BEHIND ME IS KANISAWA. THE BIG ONE'S AOGA.
WE'RE YOUR INSTRUCTORS TODAY.
MURMUR MURMUR
QUIET!
OR WE'LL LEAVE YOU BEHIND!
WHAT THE HECK?
ARE THEY FAMOUS?
DON'T YOU KNOW?!
NOT THOSE TWO, BUT THE GUY IN THE MIDDLE IS BEYOND FAMOUS!

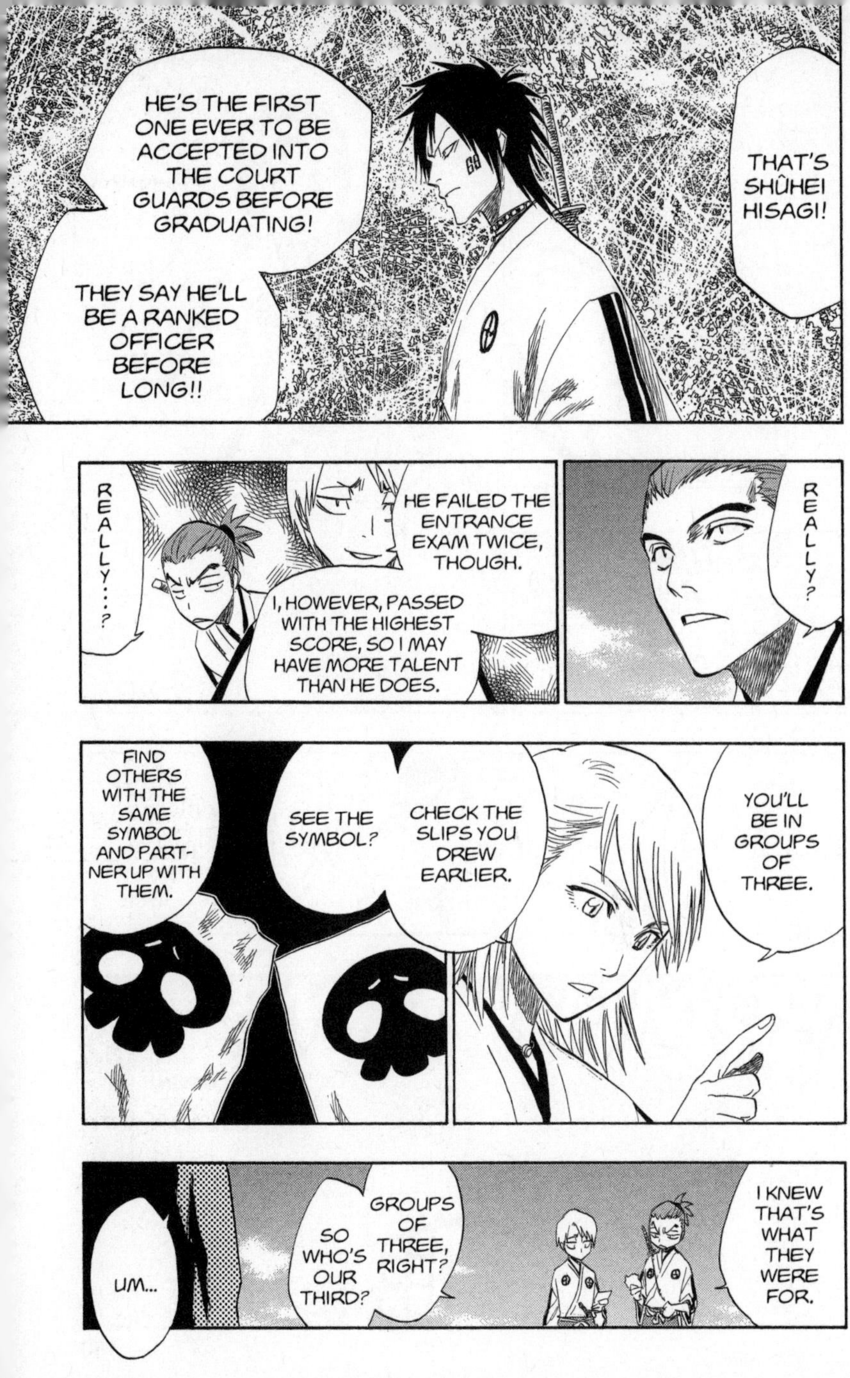
THAT'S SHÛHEI HISAGI!
HE'S THE FIRST ONE EVER TO BE ACCEPTED INTO THE COURT GUARDS BEFORE GRADUATING!
THEY SAY HE'LL BE A RANKED OFFICER BEFORE LONG!!
REALLY?
HE FAILED THE ENTRANCE EXAM TWICE, THOUGH.
I, HOWEVER, PASSED WITH THE HIGHEST SCORE, SO I MAY HAVE MORE TALENT THAN HE DOES.
REALLY...?
YOU'LL BE IN GROUPS OF THREE.
CHECK THE SLIPS YOU DREW EARLIER.
SEE THE SYMBOL?
FIND OTHERS WITH THE SAME SYMBOL AND PART-NER UP WITH THEM.
I KNEW THAT'S WHAT THEY WERE FOR.
GROUPS OF THREE, RIGHT?
SO WHO'S OUR THIRD?
UM...

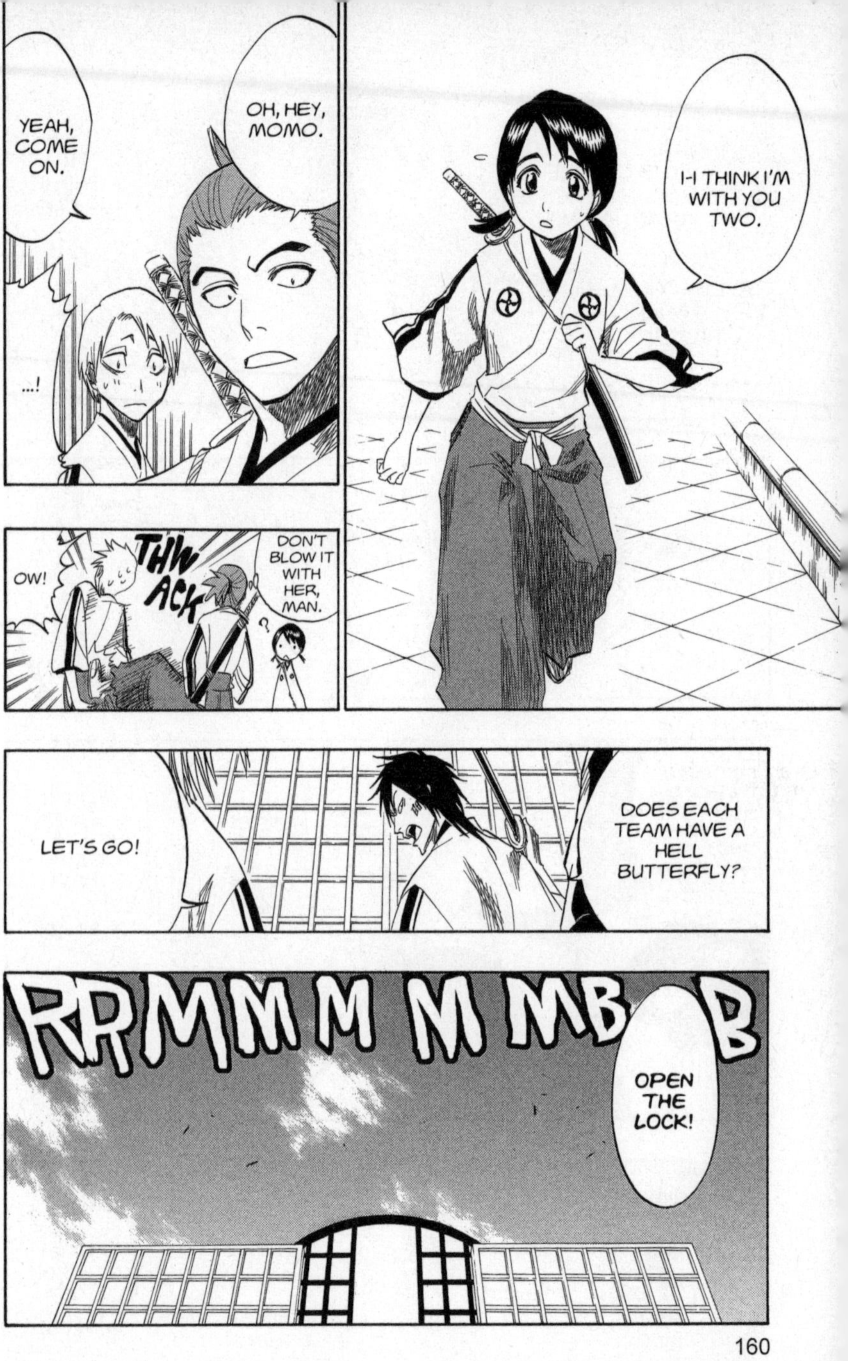
I-I THINK I'M WITH YOU TWO.
OH, HEY, MOMO.
YEAH, COME ON.
...!
DON'T BLOW IT WITH HER, MAN.
THWACK
?
OW!
DOES EACH TEAM HAVE A HELL BUTTERFLY?
LET'S GO!
RRMMM M M MB B
OPEN THE LOCK!

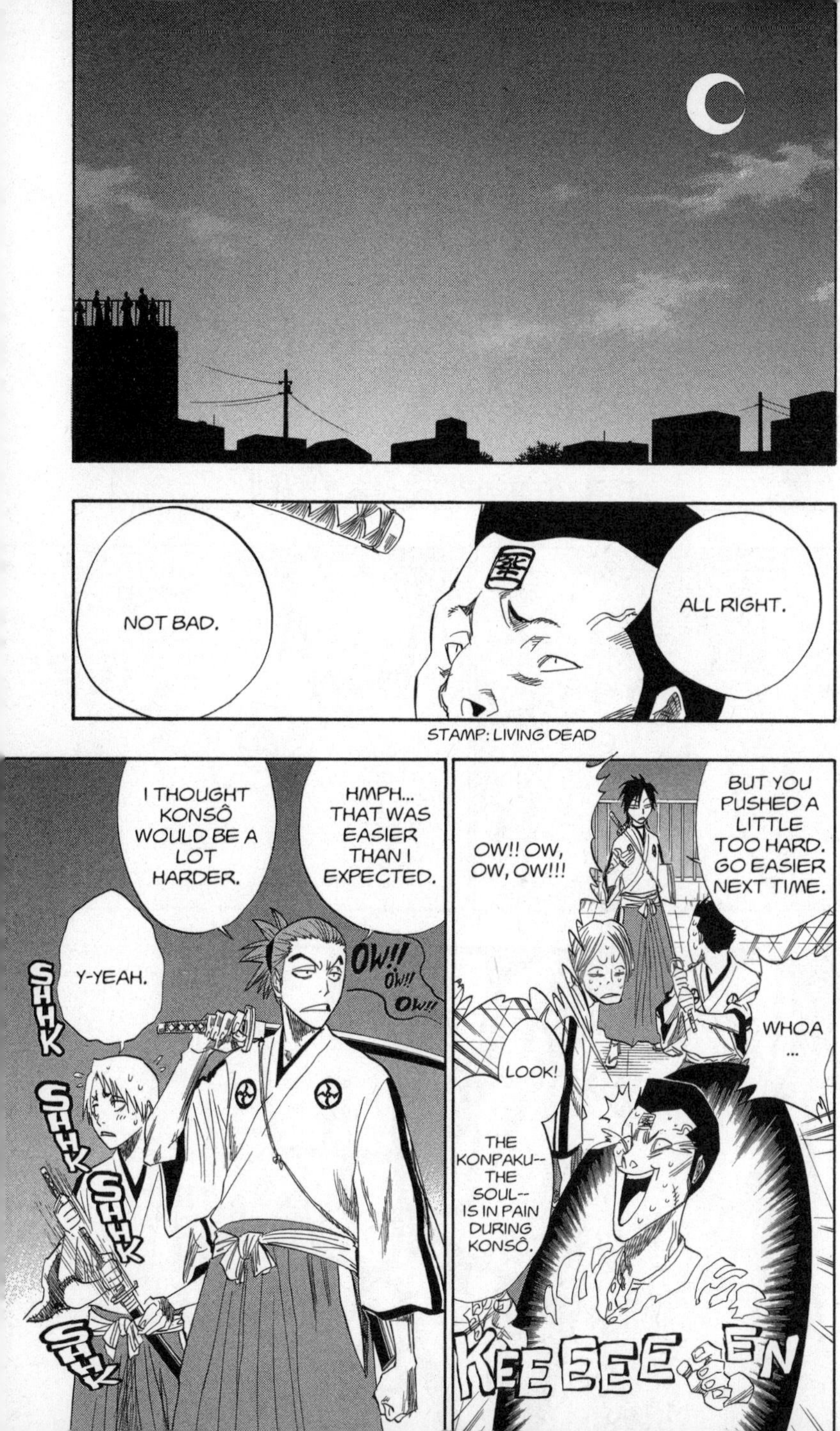
ALL RIGHT.
NOT BAD.
STAMP: LIVING DEAD
BUT YOU PUSHED A LITTLE TOO HARD. GO EASIER NEXT TIME.
OW!! OW, OW, OW!!!
WHOA ...
LOOK!
THE KONPAKU-- THE SOUL-- IS IN PAIN DURING KONSÔ.
KEEEEEE...EN
HMPH... THAT WAS EASIER THAN I EXPECTED.
I THOUGHT KONSÔ WOULD BE A LOT HARDER.
OW!! OW!! OW!!
Y-YEAH.
SHHK SHHK SHHK SHHK SHHK

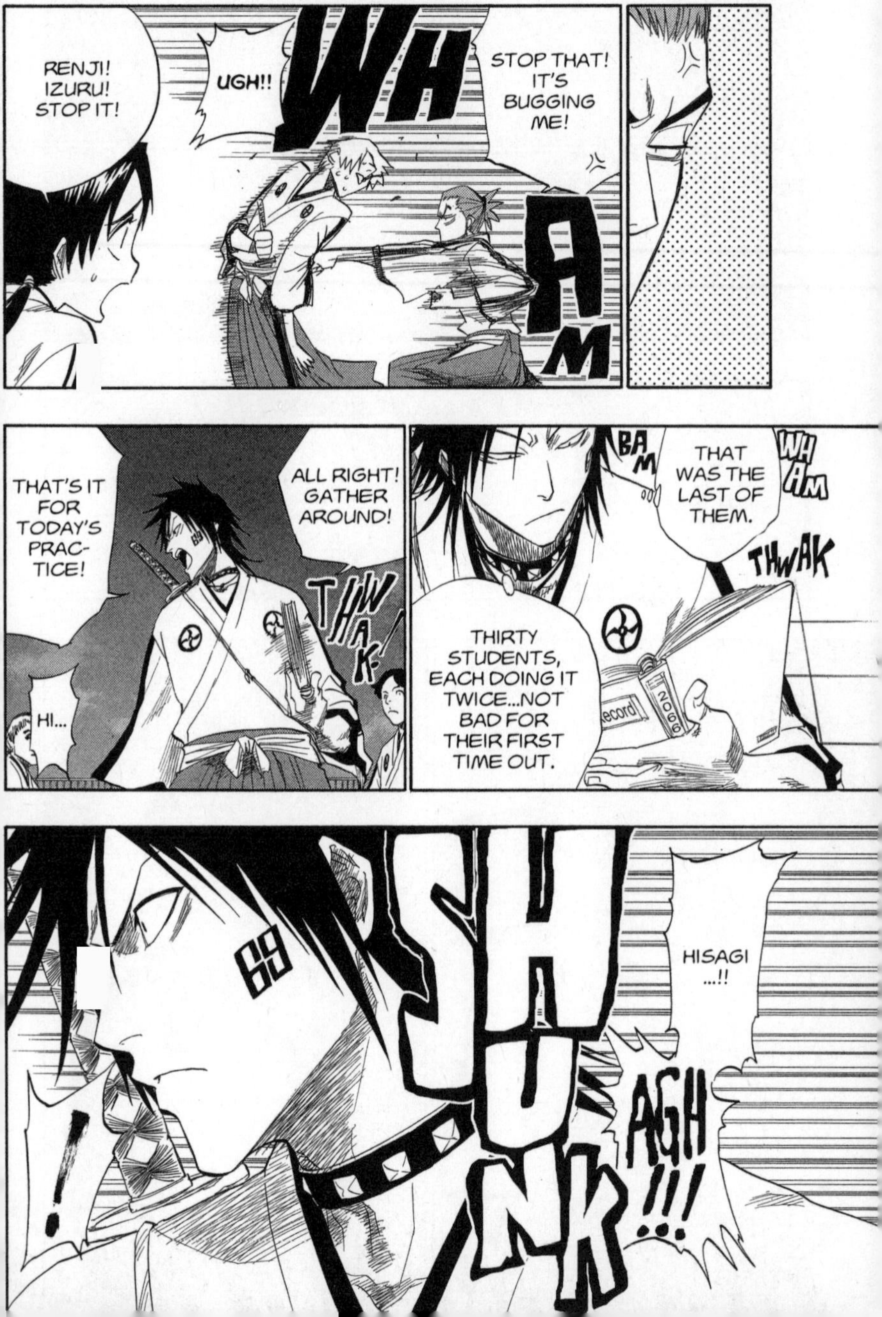
STOP THAT! IT'S BUGGING ME!
WHAM
UGH!!
RENJI! IZURU! STOP IT!
WHAM
THAT WAS THE LAST OF THEM.
BAM
THWAK
THIRTY STUDENTS, EACH DOING IT TWICE...NOT BAD FOR THEIR FIRST TIME OUT.
record
2066
ALL RIGHT! GATHER AROUND!
THAT'S IT FOR TODAY'S PRAC-TICE!
THWAK!
HI...
HISAGI ...!!
AGH!!!
SHUNK!!
!

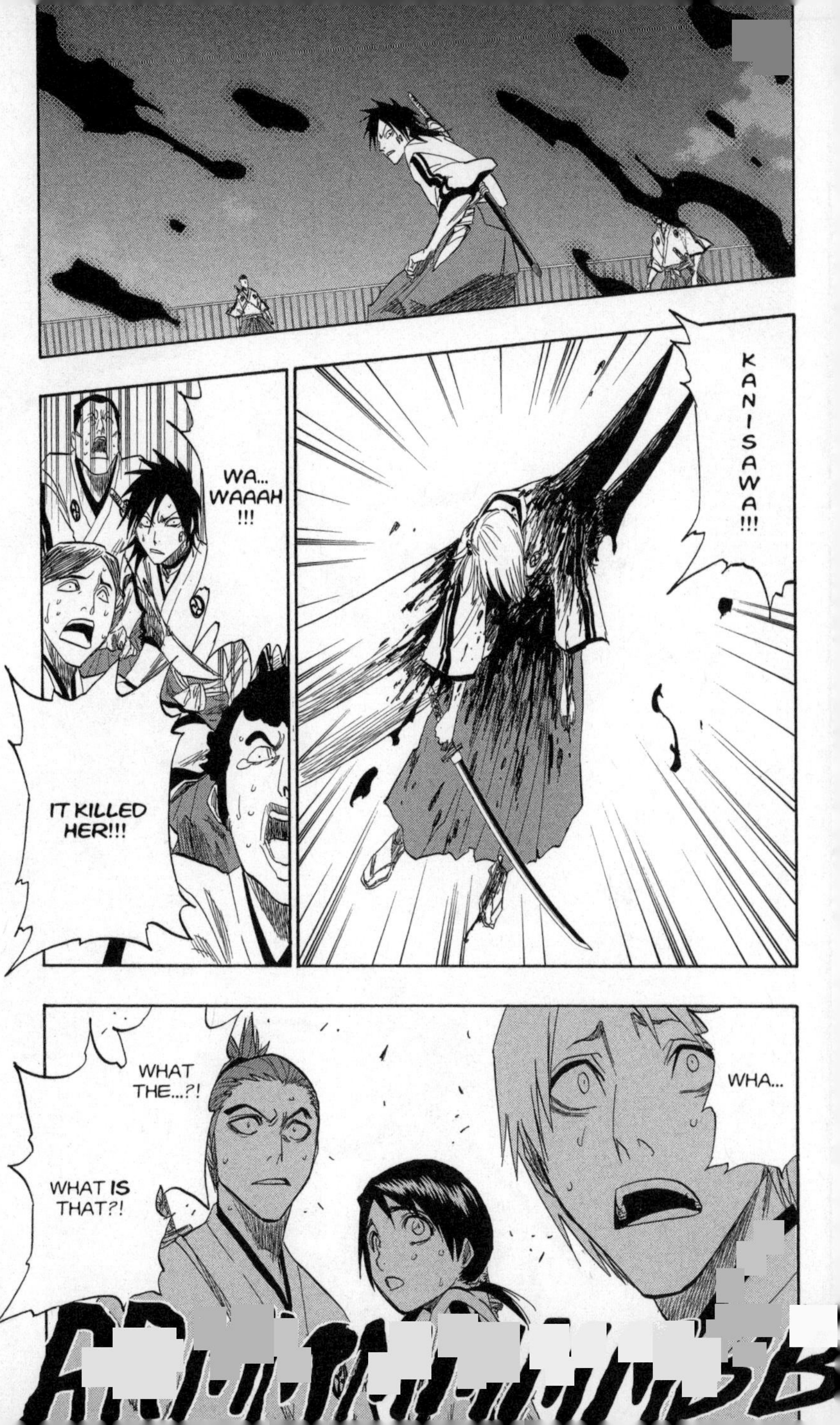
KANISAWA!!!
WA... WAAAH!!!
IT KILLED HER!!!
WHA...
WHAT THE...?!
WHAT IS THAT?!

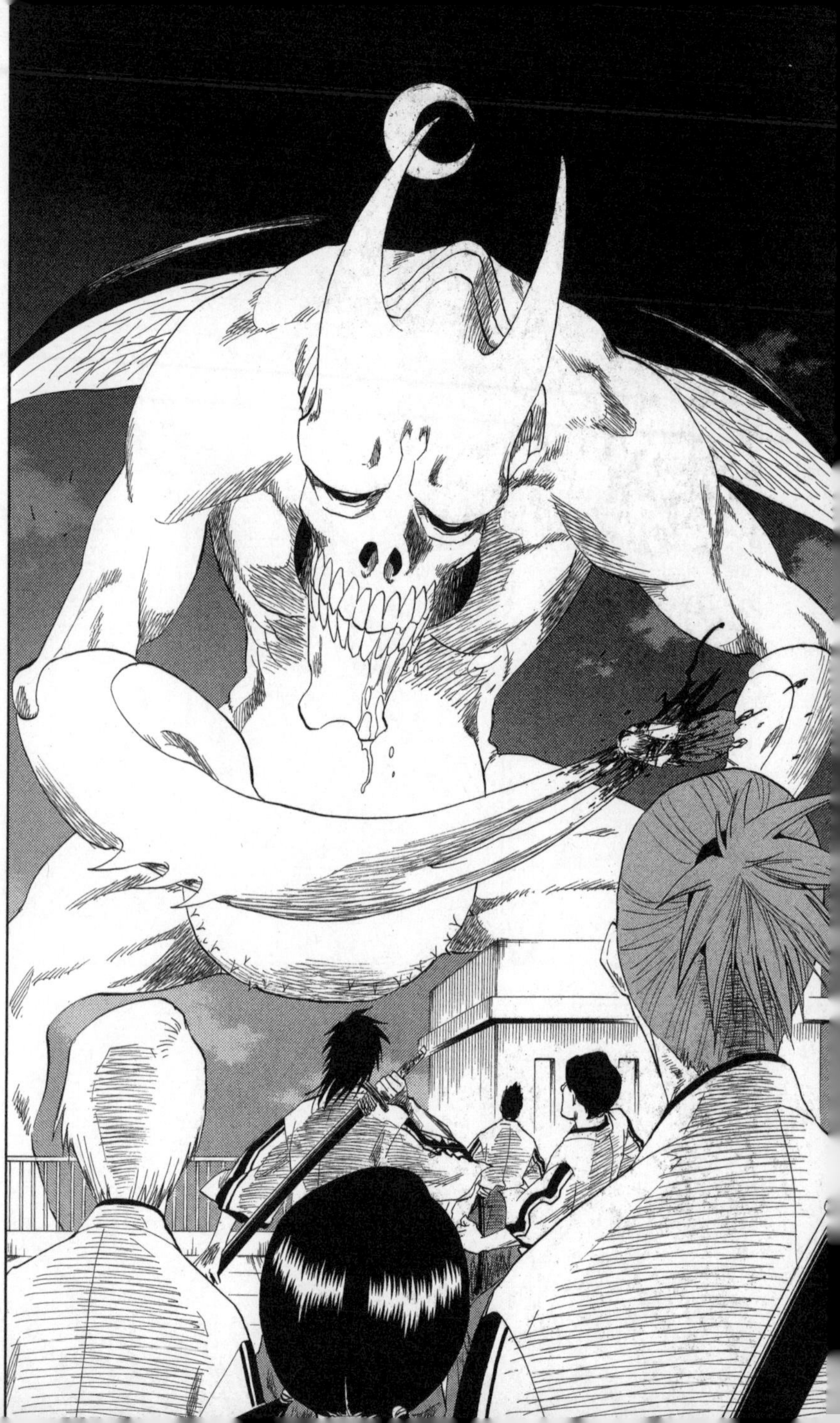

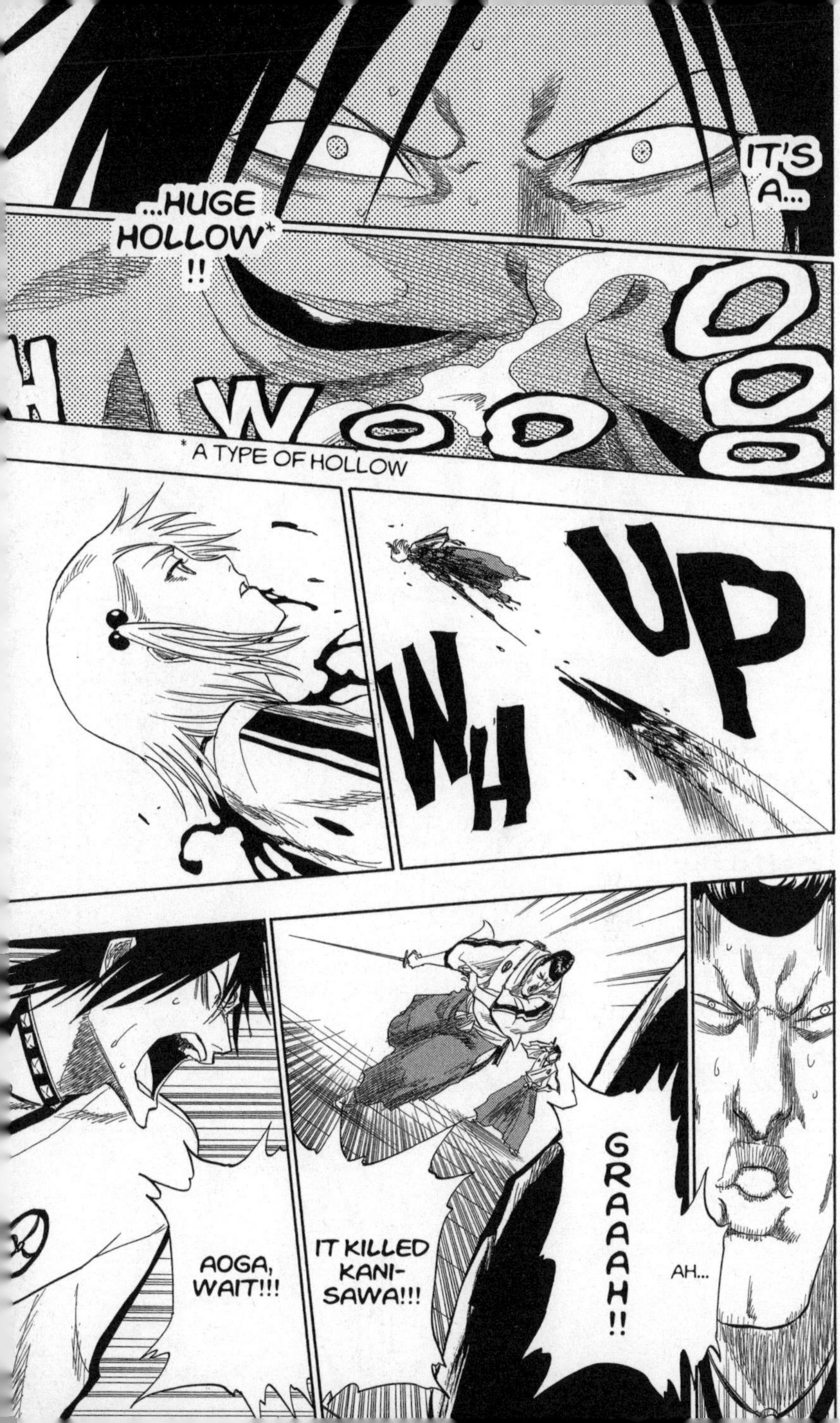

IT'S A...
...HUGE HOLLOW* !!
WOOOOOOO
* A TYPE OF HOLLOW
WHUP
AH...
GRAAAAH!!
IT KILLED KANI-SAWA!!!
AOGA, WAIT!!!

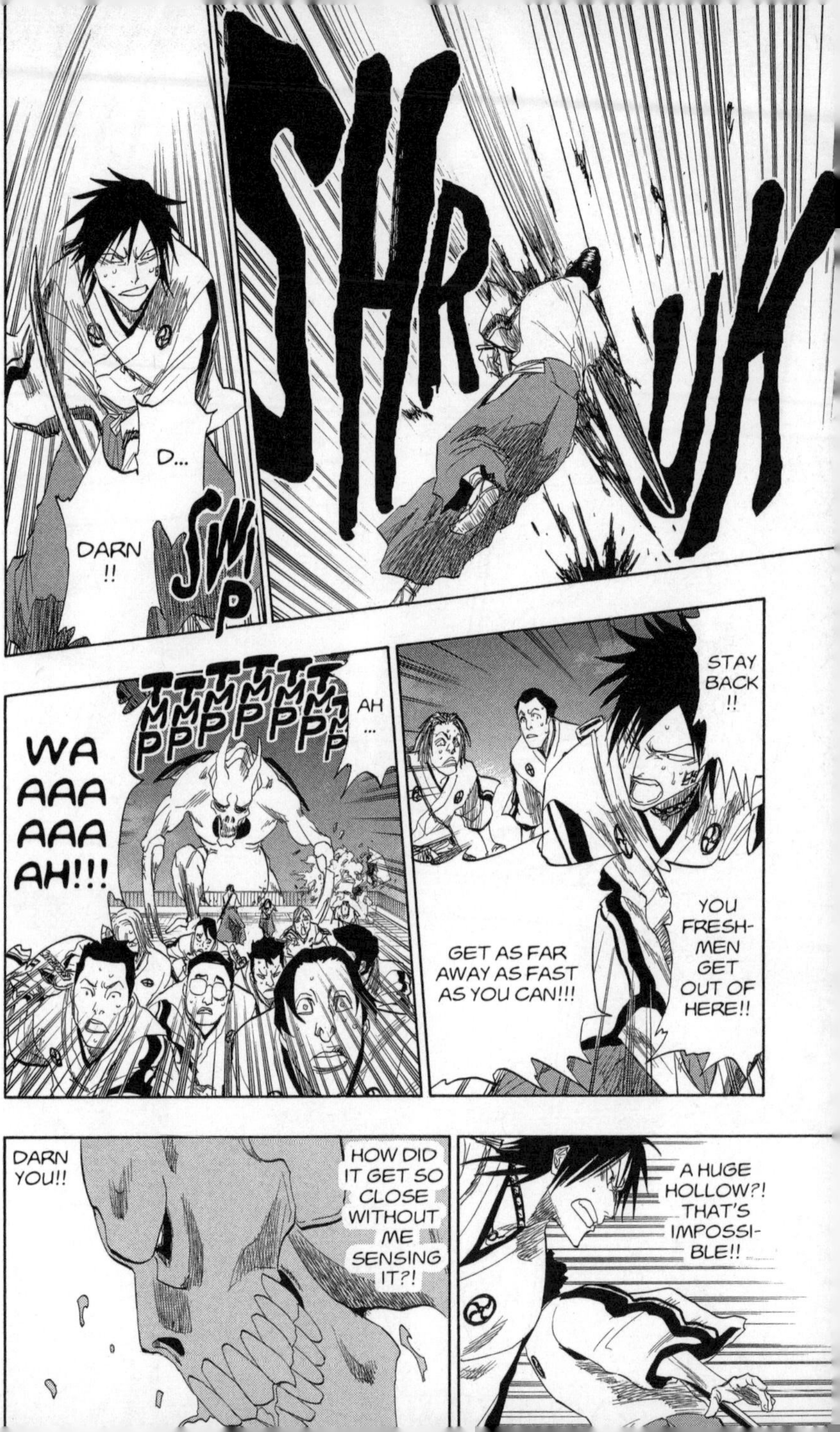
SHRUK
D...
DARN!!
SWIP
STAY BACK!!
YOU FRESHMEN GET OUT OF HERE!!
GET AS FAR AWAY AS FAST AS YOU CAN!!!
TMP TMP TMP TMP TMP TMP TMP
AH...
WAAAAAAAAAH!!!
A HUGE HOLLOW?! THAT'S IMPOSSIBLE!!
HOW DID IT GET SO CLOSE WITHOUT ME SENSING IT?!
DARN YOU!!

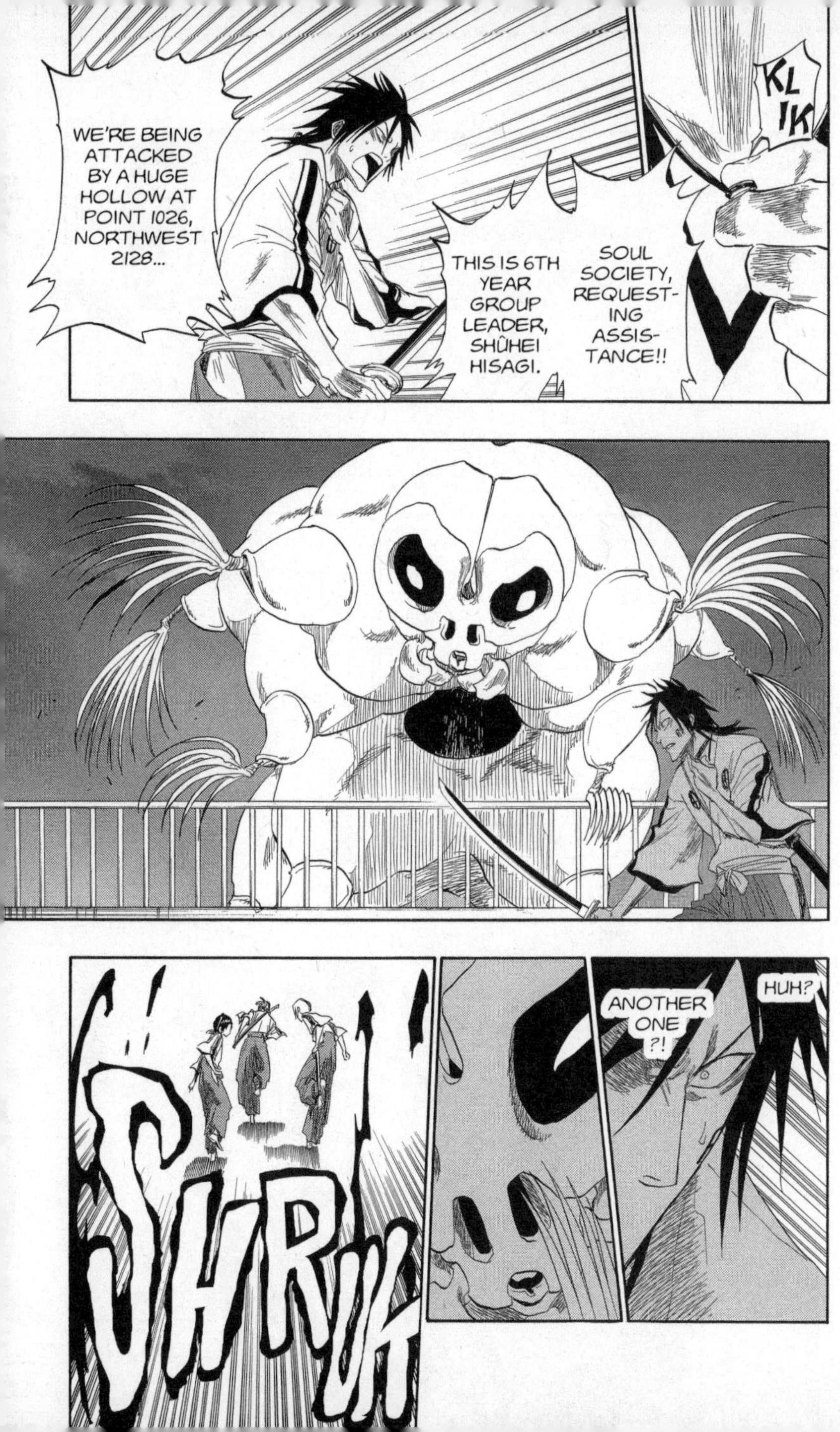
KLIK
SOUL SOCIETY, REQUESTING ASSISTANCE!!
THIS IS 6TH YEAR GROUP LEADER, SHÛHEI HISAGI.
WE'RE BEING ATTACKED BY A HUGE HOLLOW AT POINT 1026, NORTHWEST 2128...
HUH?
ANOTHER ONE ?!
SHRUK

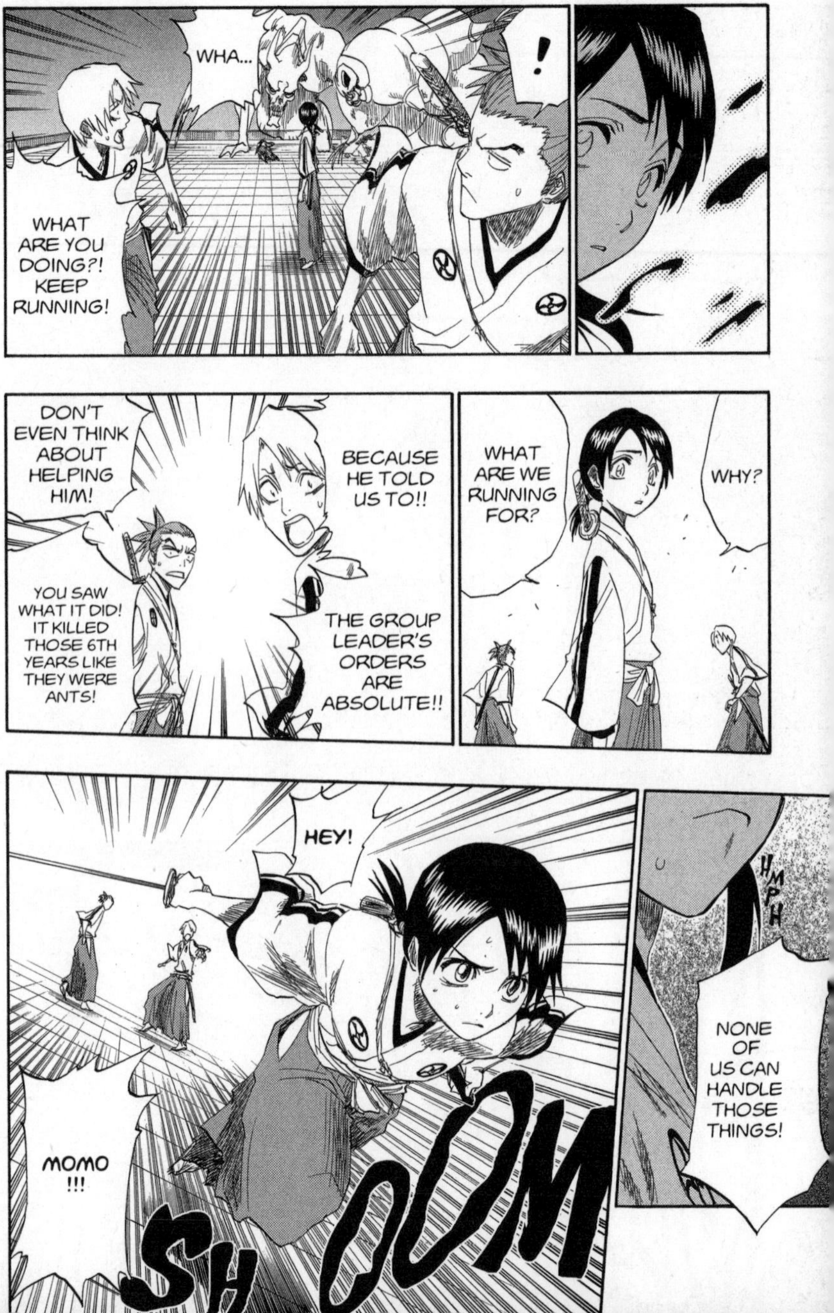
!
WHA...
WHAT ARE YOU DOING?! KEEP RUNNING!
WHY?
WHAT ARE WE RUNNING FOR?
BECAUSE HE TOLD US TO!!
THE GROUP LEADER'S ORDERS ARE ABSOLUTE!!
DON'T EVEN THINK ABOUT HELPING HIM!
YOU SAW WHAT IT DID! IT KILLED THOSE 6TH YEARS LIKE THEY WERE ANTS!
HMPH
NONE OF US CAN HANDLE THOSE THINGS!
HEY!
MOMO !!!
SHOOM

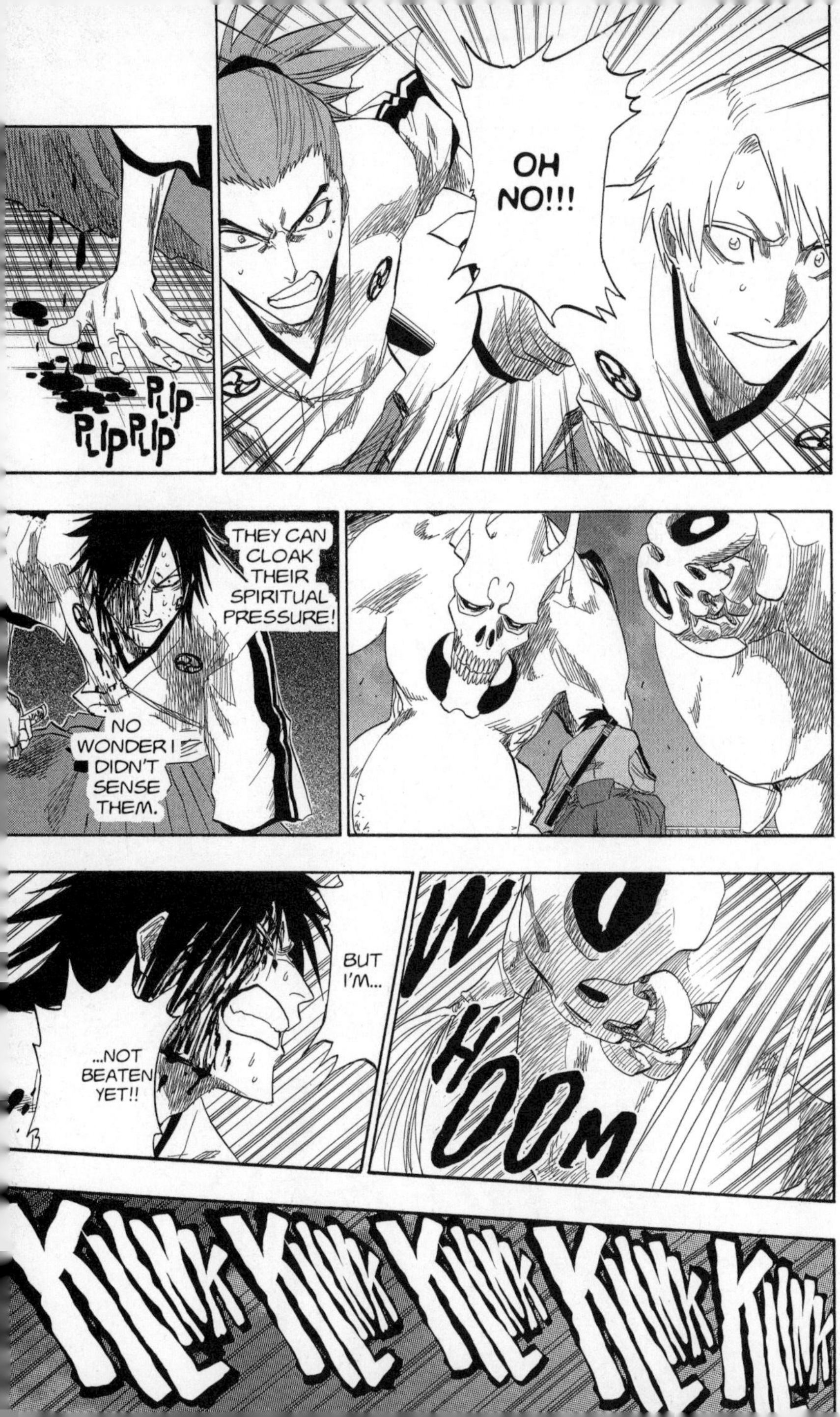
OH NO!!!
PLIP PLIP PLIP
THEY CAN CLOAK THEIR SPIRITUAL PRESSURE!
NO WONDER I DIDN'T SENSE THEM.
WHOOOM
BUT I'M...
...NOT BEATEN YET!!
KLINK KLINK KLINK KLINK KLINK

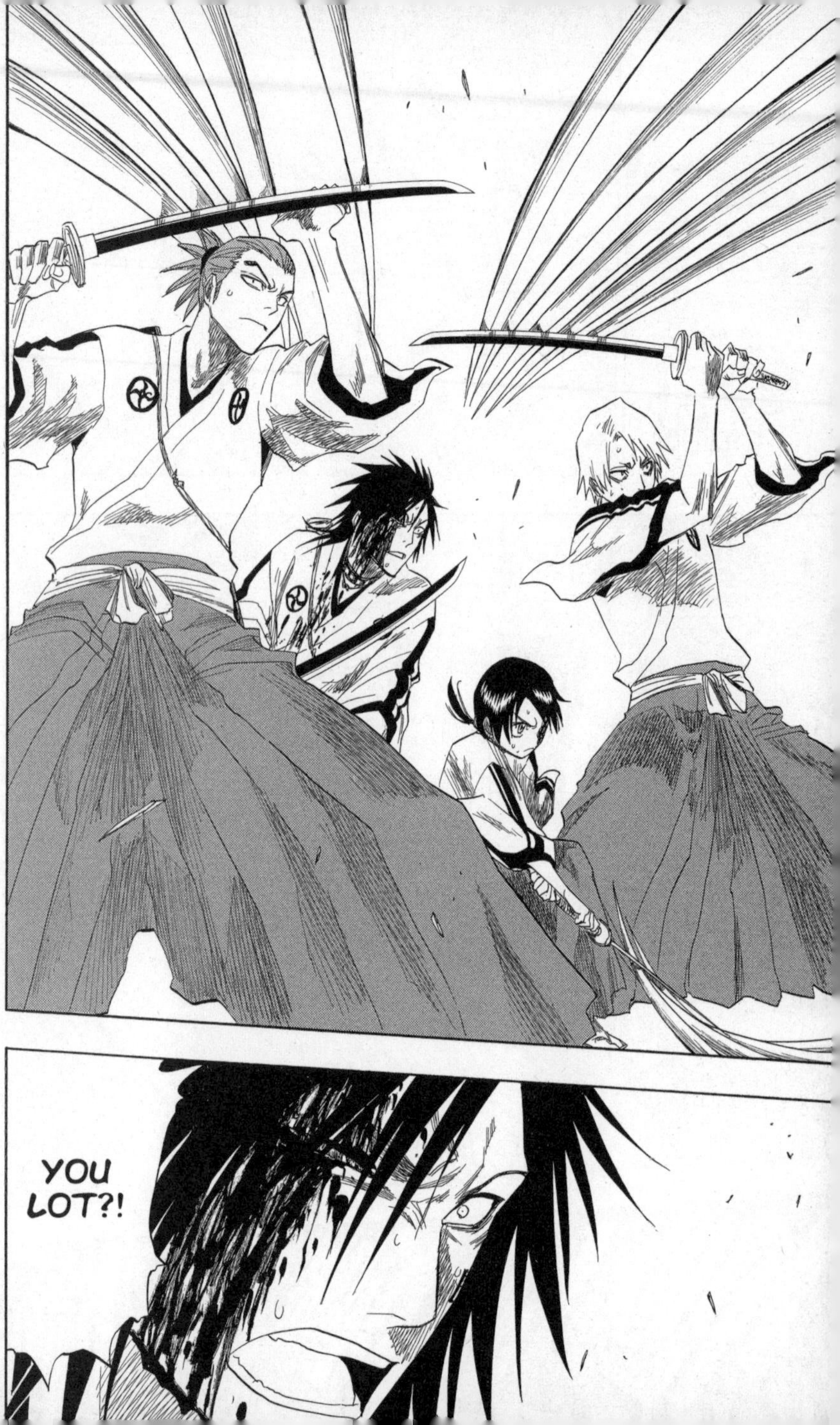
YOU LOT?!

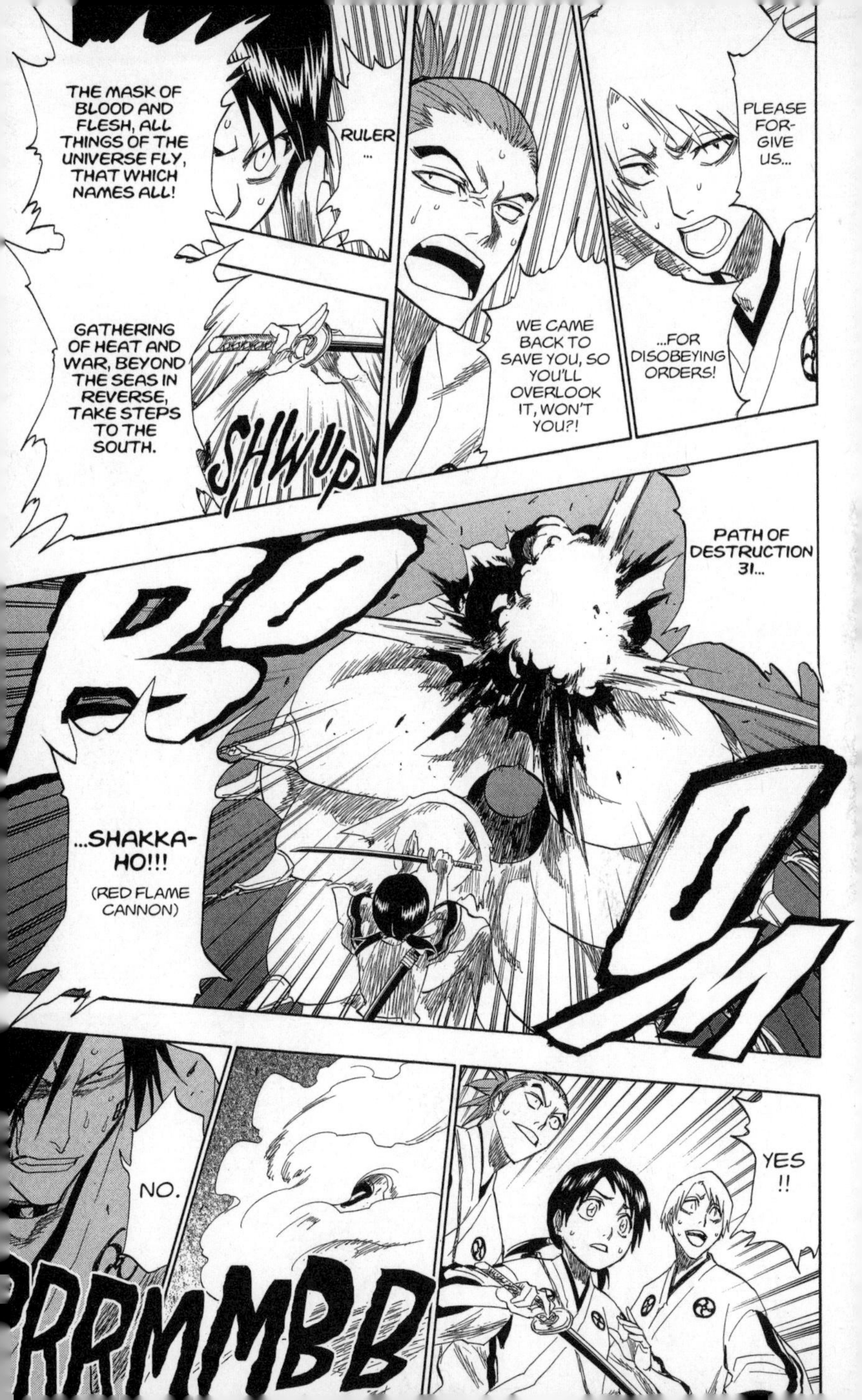
PLEASE FOR-GIVE US...
...FOR DISOBEYING ORDERS!
WE CAME BACK TO SAVE YOU, SO YOU'LL OVERLOOK IT, WON'T YOU?!
RULER ...
THE MASK OF BLOOD AND FLESH, ALL THINGS OF THE UNIVERSE FLY, THAT WHICH NAMES ALL!
GATHERING OF HEAT AND WAR, BEYOND THE SEAS IN REVERSE, TAKE STEPS TO THE SOUTH.
SHWUP
PATH OF DESTRUCTION 31...
BOOM
...SHAKKA-HO!!!
(RED FLAME CANNON)
YES !!
NO.
RRRMMBB

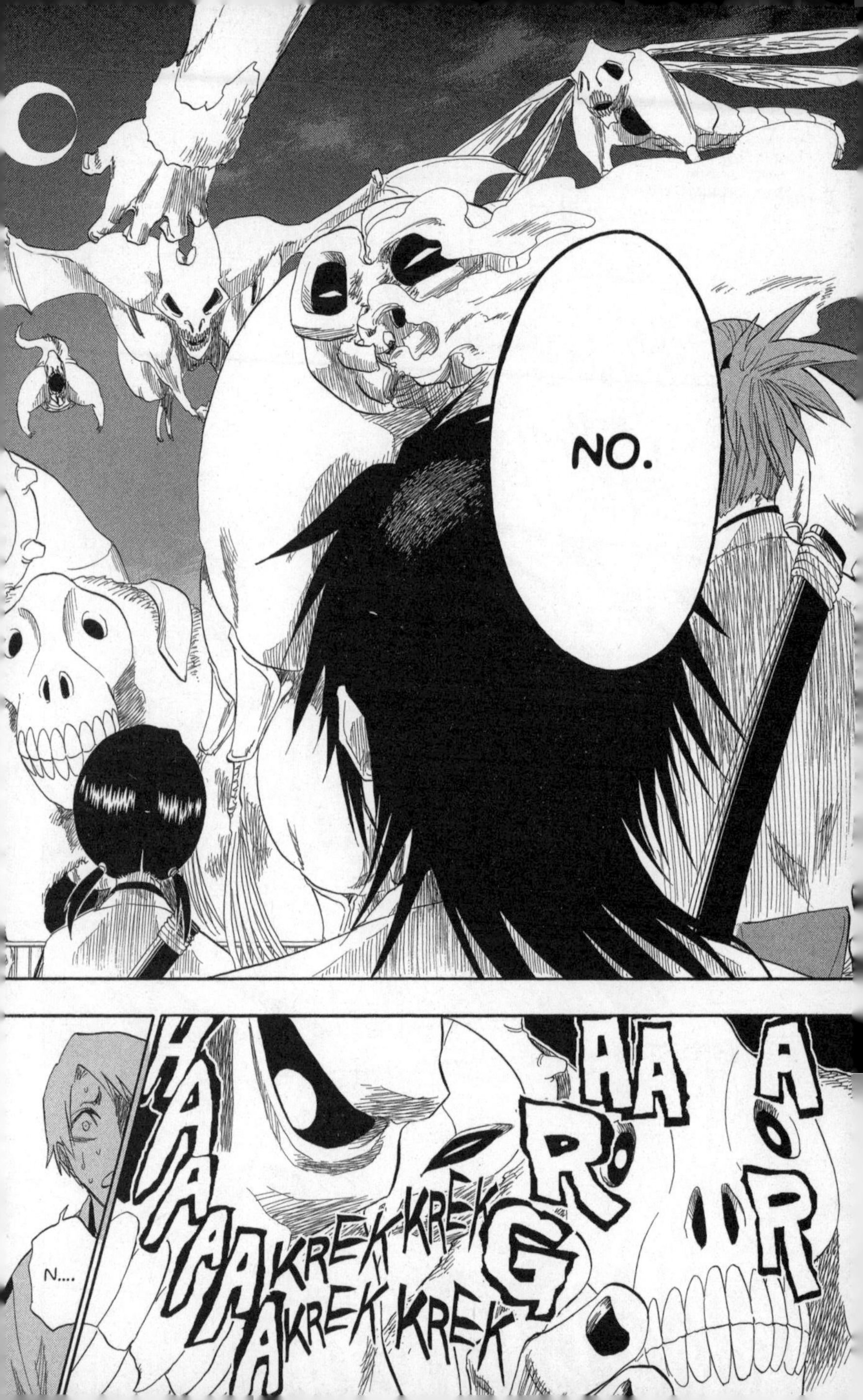
NO.
KREK KREK KREK
KREK KREK
N....

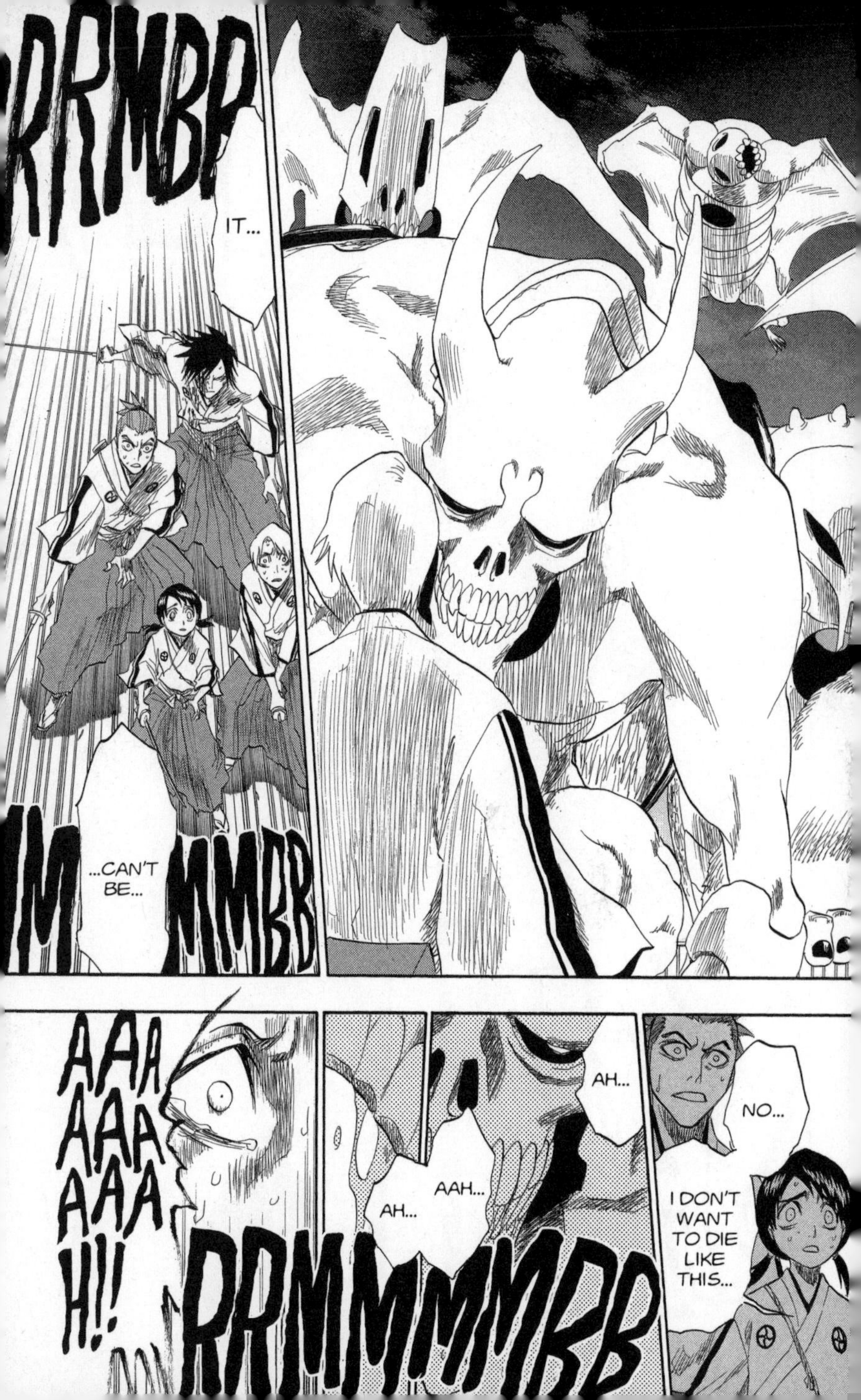
RRMBR
IT...
...CAN'T BE...
MMBB
NO...
I DON'T WANT TO DIE LIKE THIS...
AH...
AAH...
AH...
RRMMMMRB
AAAAAAAAAH!!

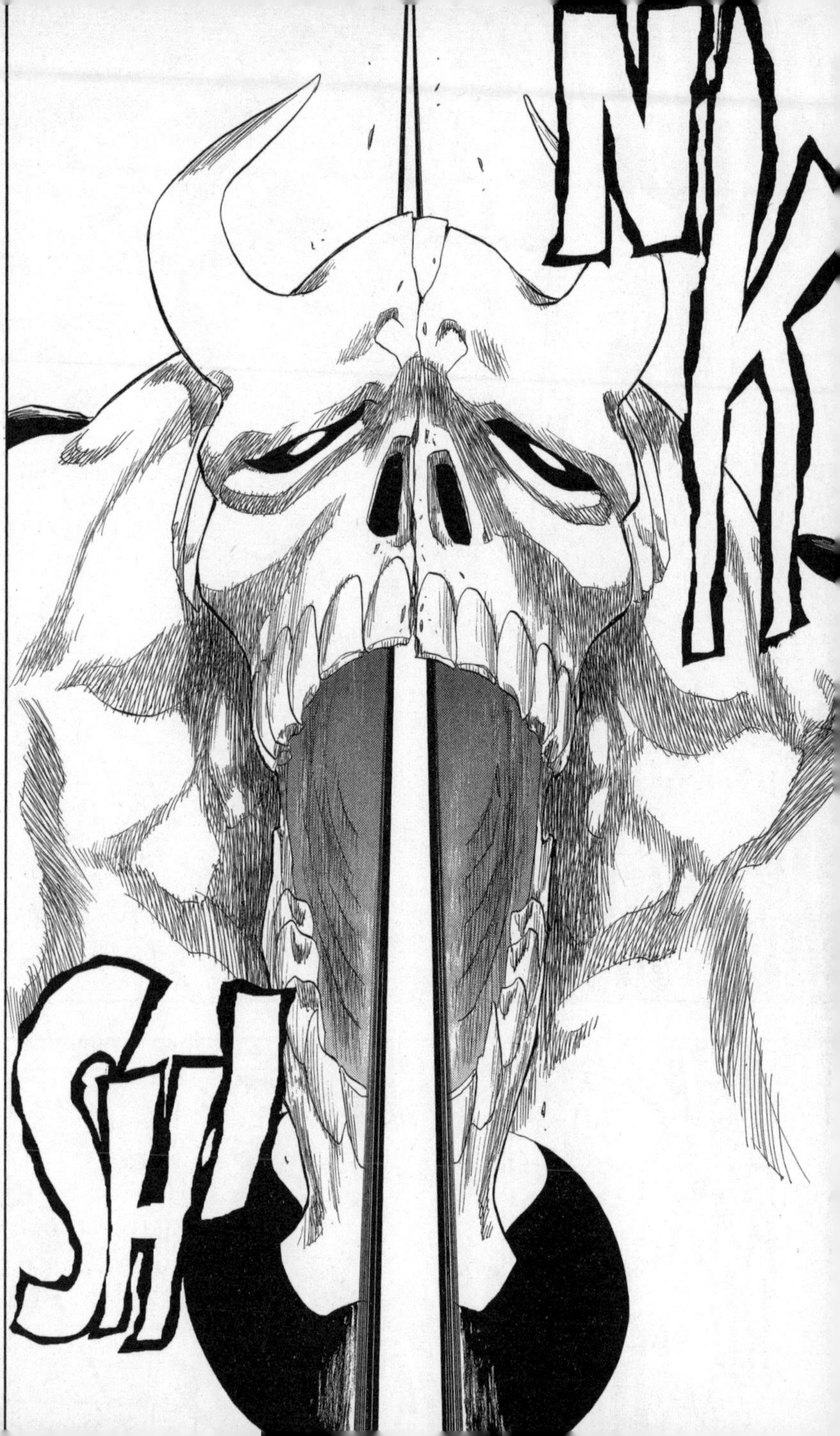

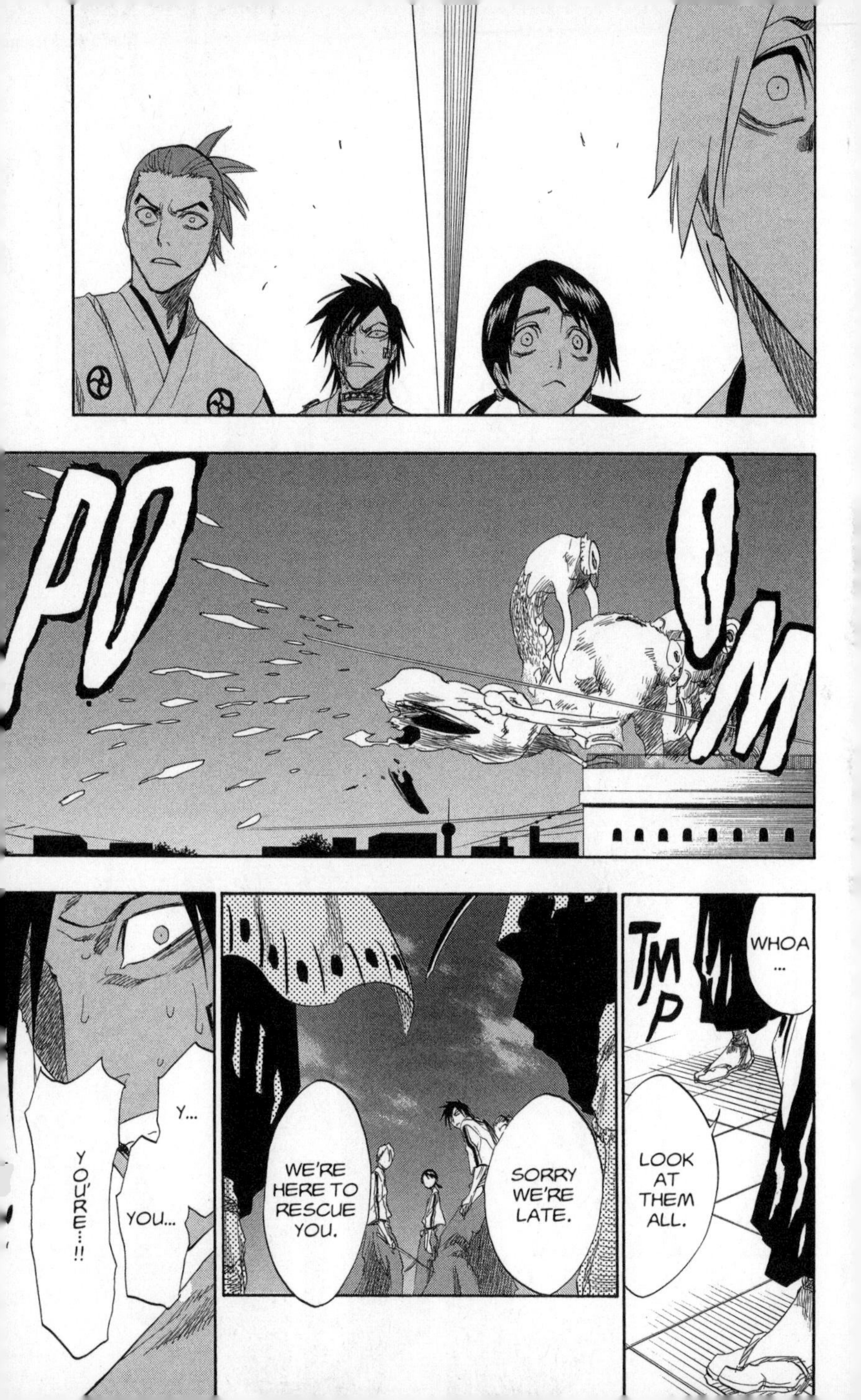
POOM
TMP
WHOA...
LOOK AT THEM ALL.
SORRY WE'RE LATE.
WE'RE HERE TO RESCUE YOU.
Y...
YOU...
YOU'RE...!!

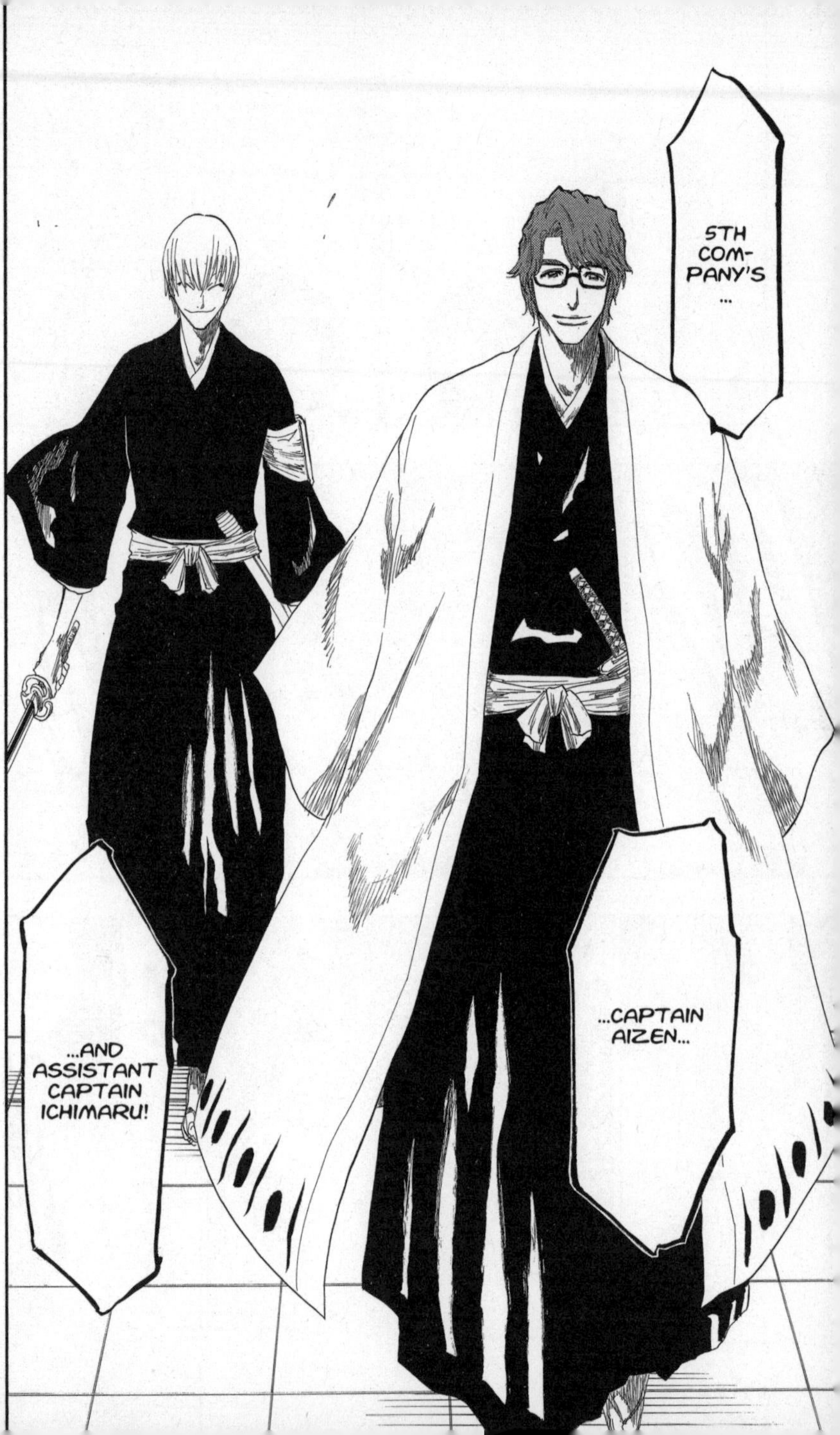
5TH COM-PANY'S ...
...CAPTAIN AIZEN...
...AND ASSISTANT CAPTAIN ICHIMARU!

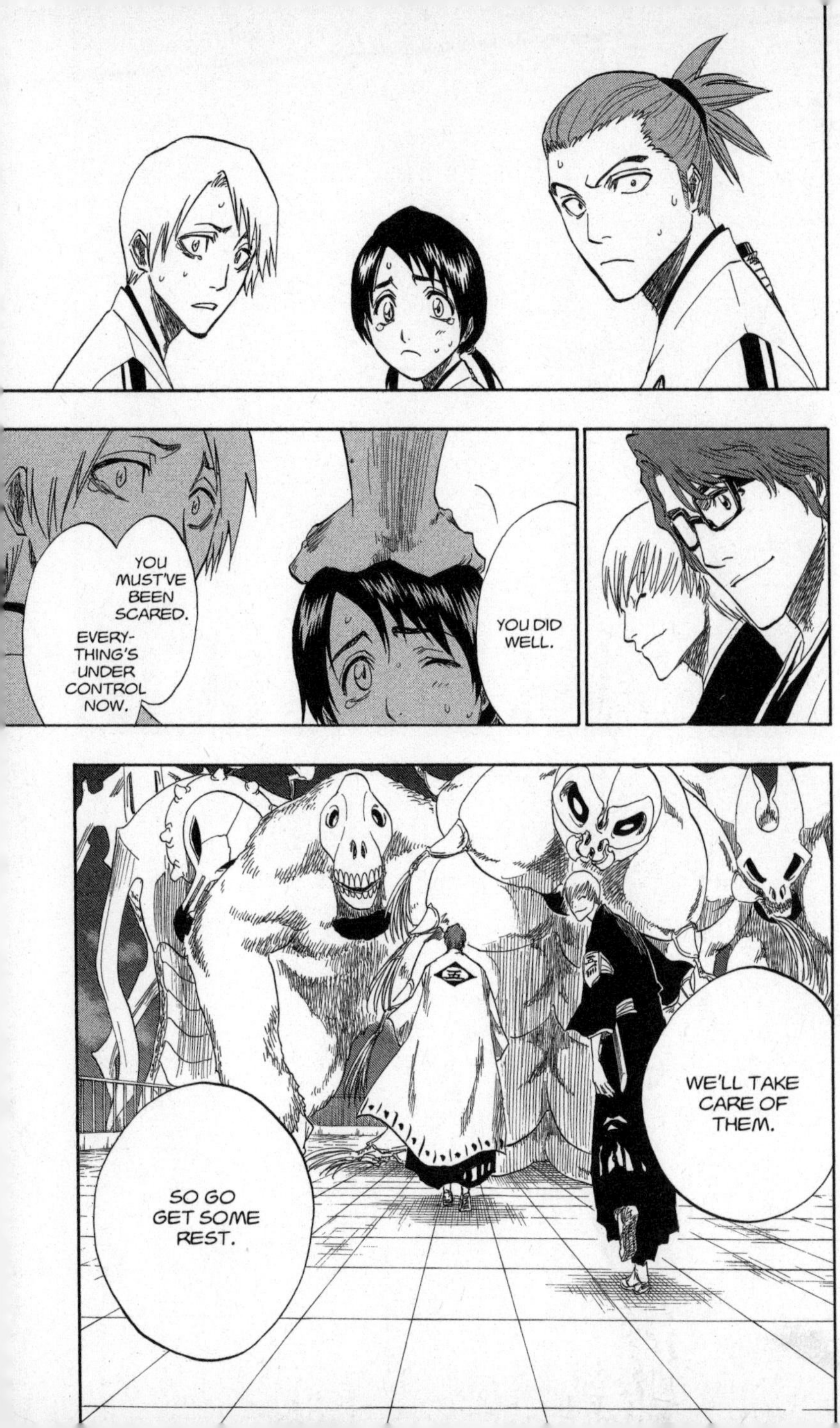
YOU DID WELL.
YOU MUST'VE BEEN SCARED.
EVERYTHING'S UNDER CONTROL NOW.
WE'LL TAKE CARE OF THEM.
SO GO GET SOME REST.

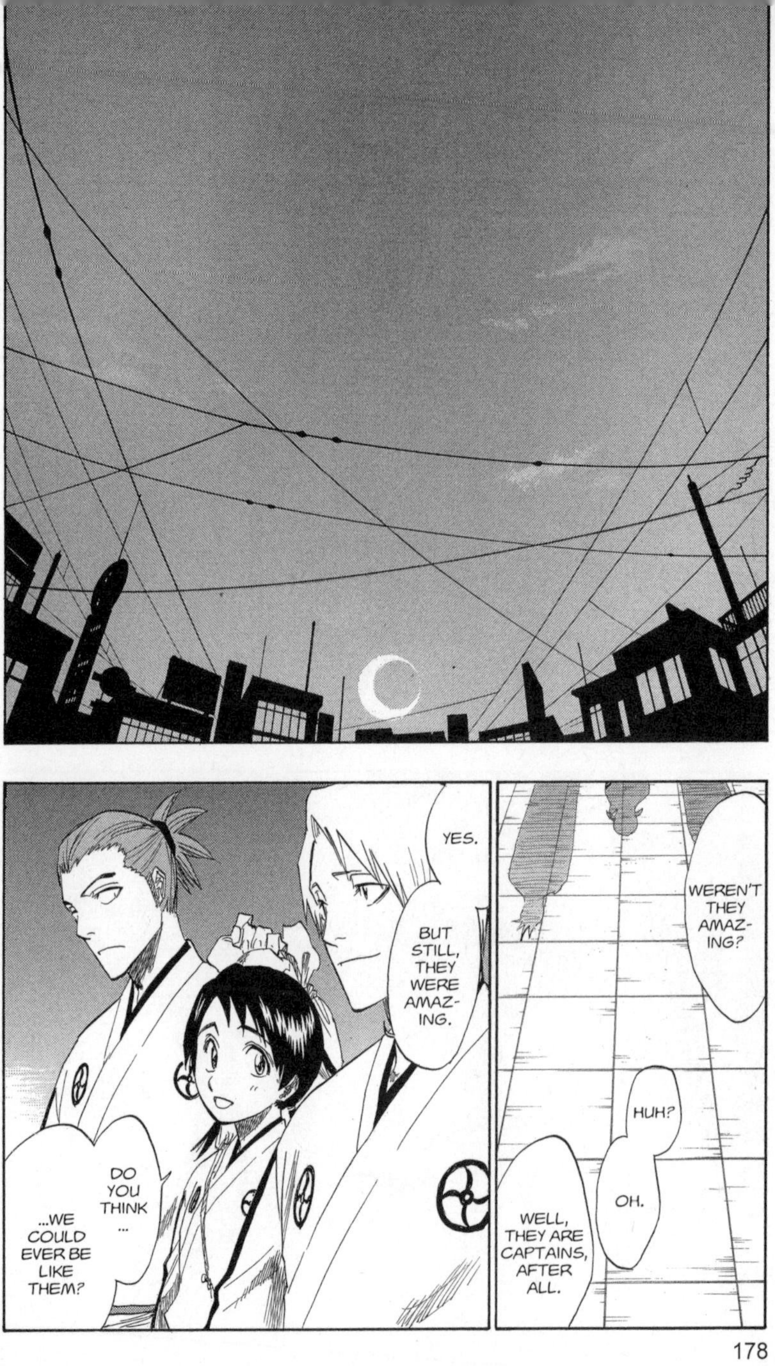
WEREN'T THEY AMAZING?
HUH?
OH.
WELL, THEY ARE CAPTAINS, AFTER ALL.
YES.
BUT STILL, THEY WERE AMAZING.
DO YOU THINK ...
...WE COULD EVER BE LIKE THEM?

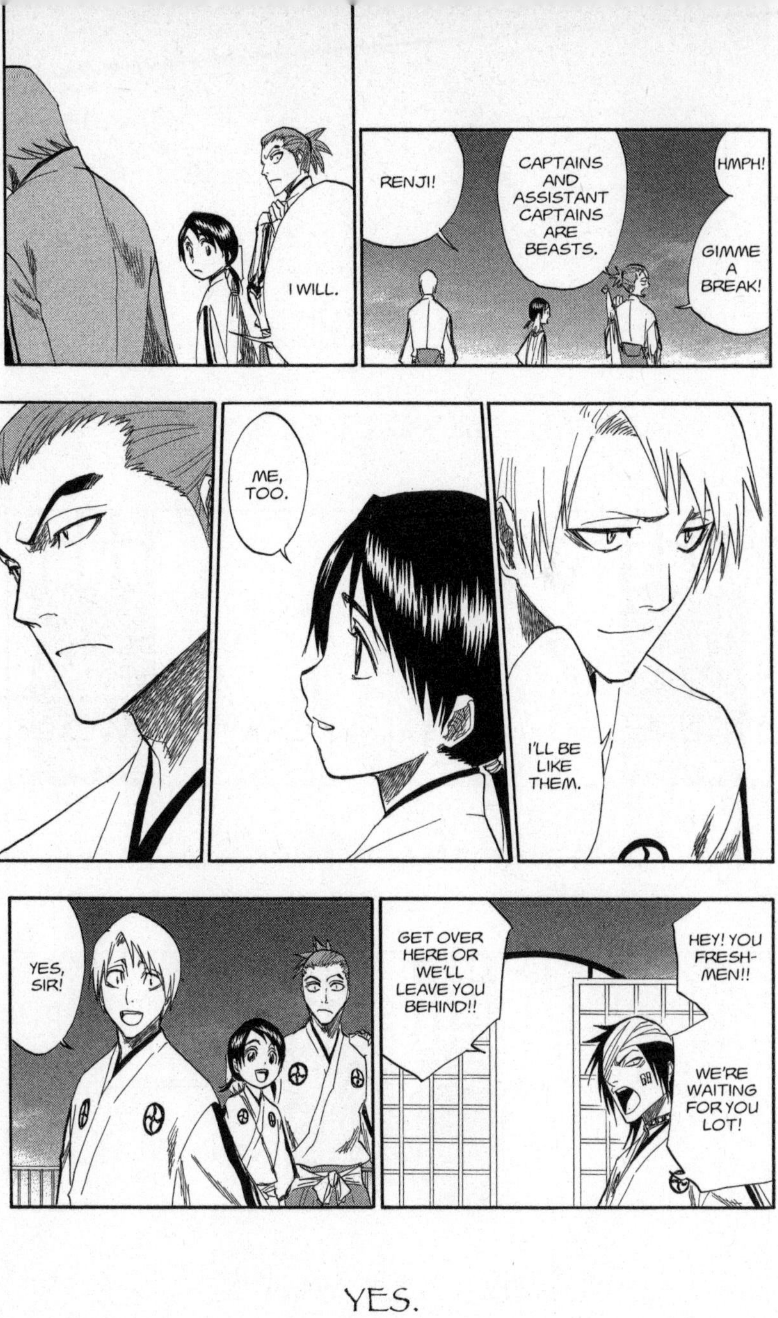
HMPH!
GIMME A BREAK!
CAPTAINS AND ASSISTANT CAPTAINS ARE BEASTS.
RENJI!
I WILL.
I'LL BE LIKE THEM.
ME, TOO.
HEY! YOU FRESH-MEN!!
WE'RE WAITING FOR YOU LOT!
GET OVER HERE OR WE'LL LEAVE YOU BEHIND!!
YES, SIR!

YES.

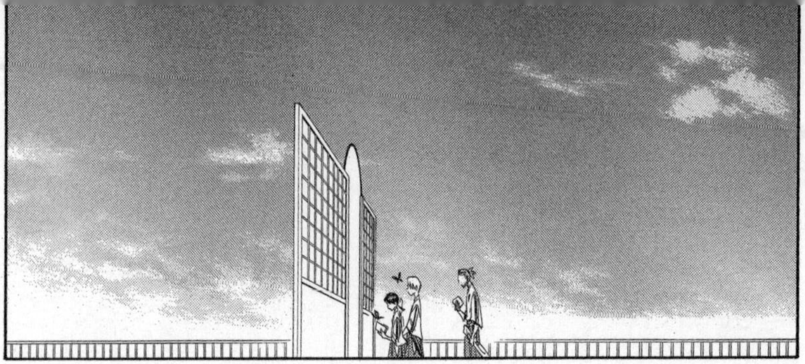

THAT IS WHY WE WON'T STOP WALKING

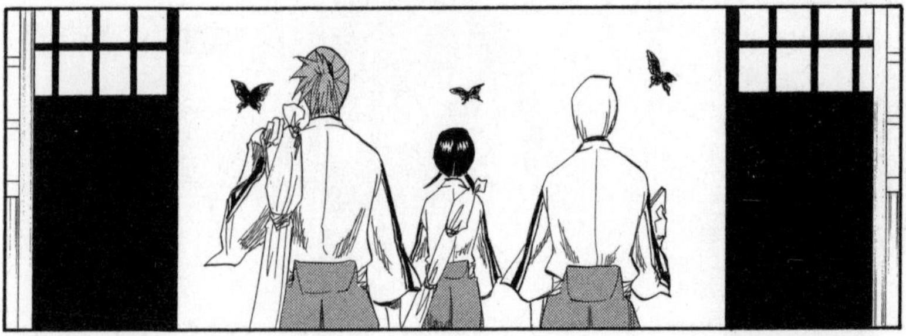

THOUGH THE ROAD MAY EVENTUALLY FORK.

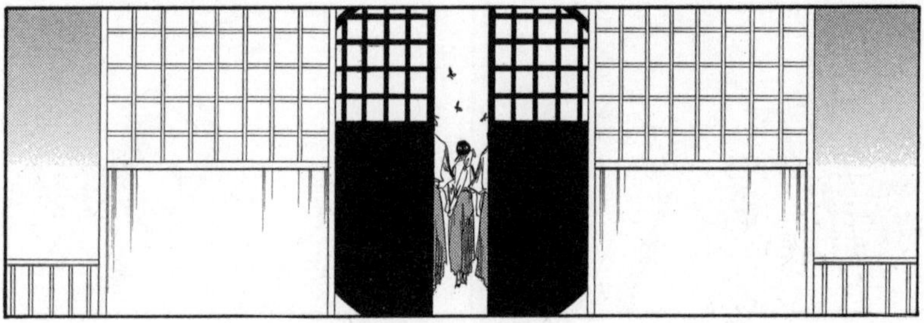

WE WON'T STOP WALKING...

EVEN THOUGH

THE ROAD MAY EVENTUALLY END.

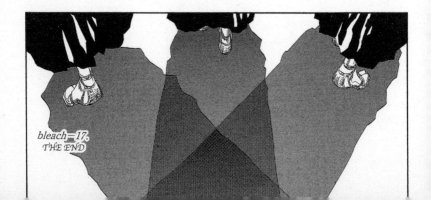

bleach=17.
THE END

CONTI
NUED
IN
BLEACH
16

Next Volume Preview

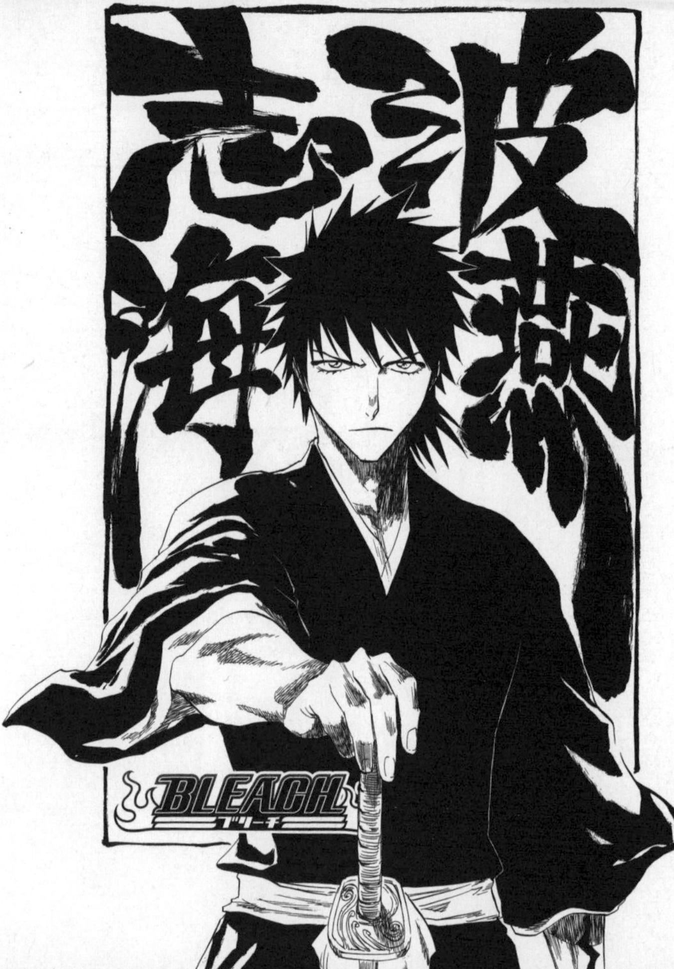
志波海燕
BLEACH
ブリーチ

While ex-Soul Reaper Rukia Kuchiki awaits her final hour, she relives a nightmare from her dark past. When she first entered the 13 Court Guard Companies, a kindly Soul Reaper named Kaien Shiba befriended her. Little did she know that she would be the one to end his life!

Available Now

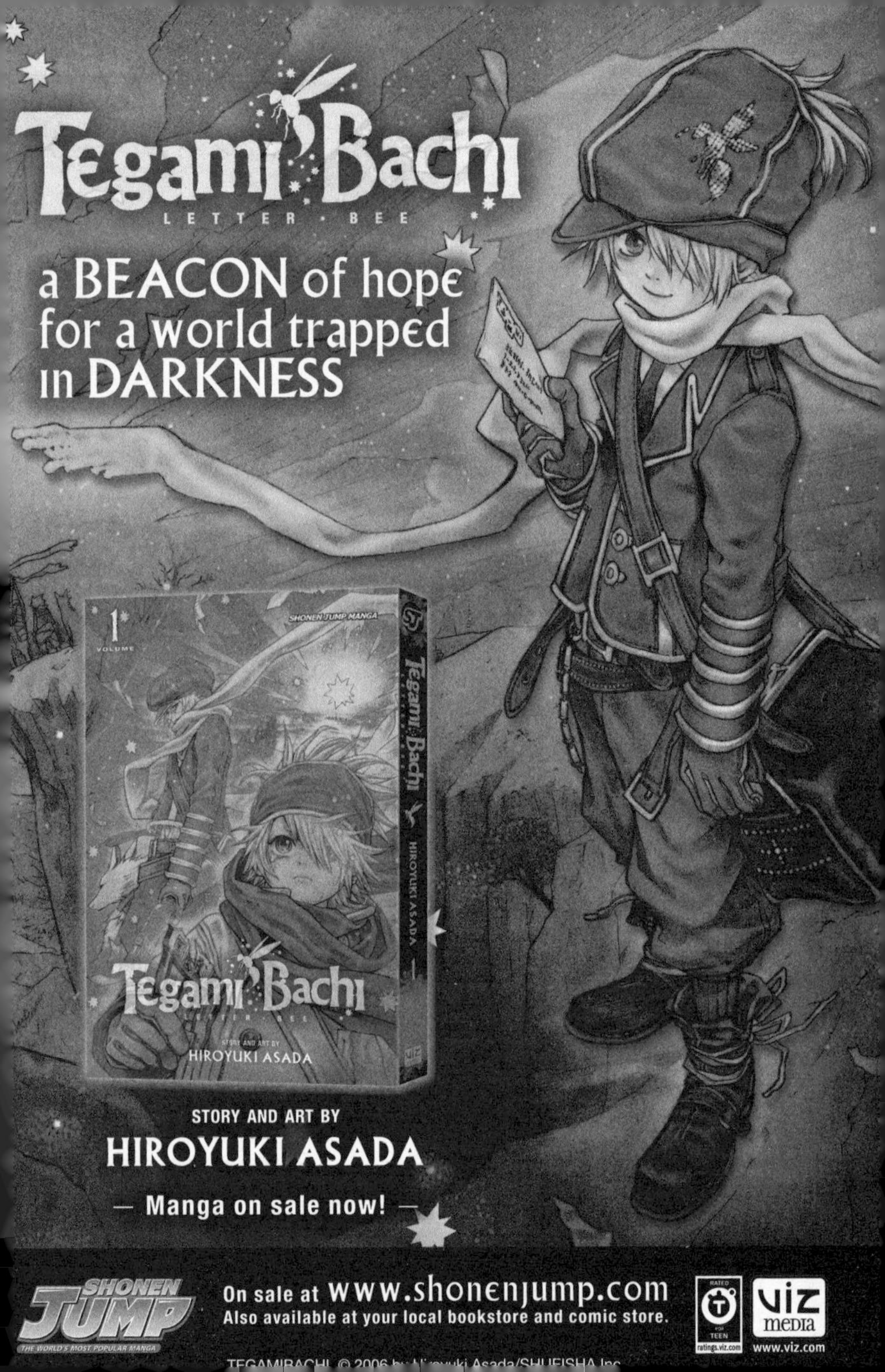
Tegami Bachi
LETTER BEE
a BEACON of hope for a world trapped in DARKNESS
SHONEN JUMP MANGA
1
VOLUME
Tegami Bachi
LETTER BEE
STORY AND ART BY
HIROYUKI ASADA
STORY AND ART BY
HIROYUKI ASADA
— Manga on sale now! —
SHONEN JUMP
THE WORLD'S MOST POPULAR MANGA
On sale at www.shonenjump.com
Also available at your local bookstore and comic store.
RATED T FOR TEEN
ratings.viz.com
VIZ media
www.viz.com
TEGAMIBACHI © 2006 by Hiroyuki Asada/SHUEISHA Inc.

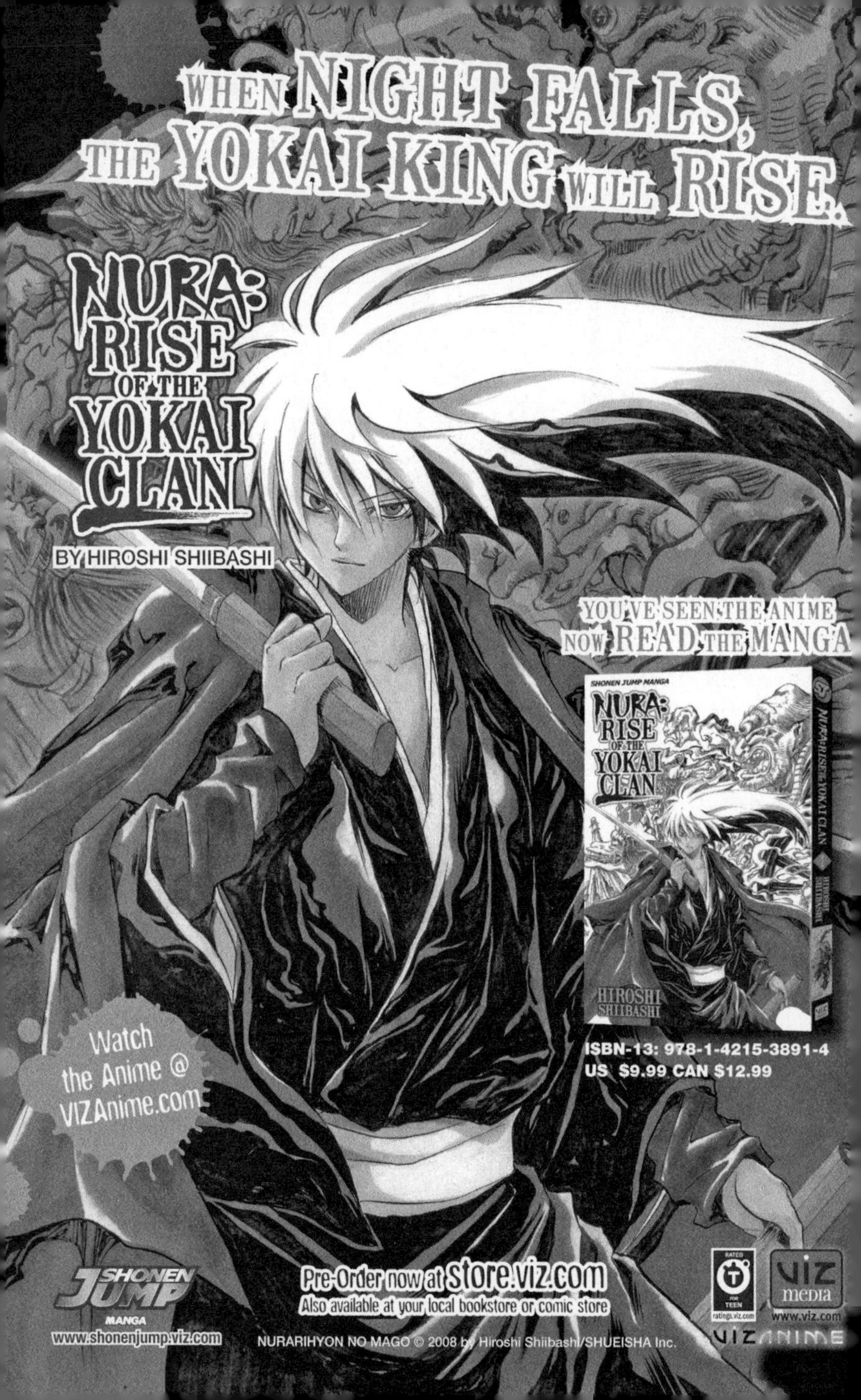
WHEN NIGHT FALLS, THE YOKAI KING WILL RISE.
NURA: RISE OF THE YOKAI CLAN
BY HIROSHI SHIIBASHI
YOU'VE SEEN THE ANIME NOW READ THE MANGA
SHONEN JUMP MANGA
NURA: RISE OF THE YOKAI CLAN
HIROSHI SHIIBASHI
ISBN-13: 978-1-4215-3891-4
US $9.99 CAN $12.99
Watch the Anime @ VIZAnime.com
SHONEN JUMP MANGA
www.shonenjump.viz.com
Pre-Order now at Store.viz.com
Also available at your local bookstore or comic store
RATED T FOR TEEN
ratings.viz.com
VIZ media
www.viz.com
VIZANIME
NURARIHYON NO MAGO © 2008 by Hiroshi Shiibashi/SHUEISHA Inc.

You're Reading the Wrong Direction!!

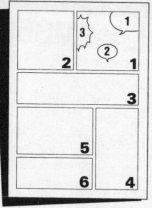

Whoops! Guess what? You're starting at the wrong end of the comic!

...It's true! In keeping with the original Japanese format, **Bleach** is meant to be read from right to left, starting in the upper-right corner.

Unlike English, which is read from left to right, Japanese is read from right to left, meaning that action, sound effects and word-balloon order are completely reversed... something which can make readers unfamiliar with Japanese feel pretty backwards themselves. For this reason, manga or Japanese comics published in the U.S. in English have sometimes been published "flopped"—that is, printed in exact reverse order, as though seen from the other side of a mirror.

By flopping pages, U.S. publishers can avoid confusing readers, but the compromise is not without its downside. For one thing, a character in a flopped manga series who once wore in the original Japanese version a T-shirt emblazoned with "M A Y" (as in "the merry month of") now wears one which reads "Y A M"! Additionally, many manga creators in Japan are themselves unhappy with the process, as some feel the mirror-imaging of their art skews their original intentions.

We are proud to bring you Tite Kubo's **Bleach** in the original unflopped format. For now, though, turn to the other side of the book and let the adventure begin...!

—Editor